Best wishes
and good hunting!

David Morris

Hunting Trophy Whitetails

Hunting Trophy Whitetails

By David Morris

Published by Venture Press
Bigfork, Montana

Dedication

To my wife, Debbie, who has patiently endured my hunting all these years. To my mother, Thelma Morris, who always had time to listen to my hunting stories when I was growing up, even though she had better things to do. To my daddy, Flynn Morris, Sr., who taught me early on not to shoot quail on the ground. And to my Lord Jesus Christ, who made it all possible.

Table Of Contents

Section V
The "How" Of Hunting Trophy Whitetails

SECTION VI
MAKING THE MOST OF THE MOMENT OF TRUTH

SECTION VI
CLOSING THOUGHTS

Acknowledgements

THE PEOPLE WHO HAVE CONTRIBUTED in one way or another over the years to making this book a reality are legion. Though I can mention only a few in this space, my heart-felt gratitude goes out to everyone who helped along the way. Here, I would like to extend a special thanks to:

My partners at Game & Fish Publications — Steve Vaughn, Chuck Larsen and Chip Gerry. Finer partners, friends and hunting companions a fellow never had.

Dick Idol, whose enthusiasm, knowledge and friendship have helped expand my own understanding and enjoyment of the whitetail.

The Game & Fish Publications staff, especially Editorial Director Ken Dunwoody, whose professionalism made it possible for me to step away from magazine duties to write this book, and *Whitetail* Editor Gordon Whittington, who is the finest editor in the business and a veritable fountain of information on the whitetail.

Tim Hogan, who designed and produced this book and stuck with me through thick and thin.

The staff, past and present, of Burnt Pine Plantation — particularly Lawrence Wood, Steve Spears, Trey Morris, Bill Young, Bob Johnston, Steve Hallman, David Blanton and Bay Webb. Their efforts have contributed much to my knowledge.

Priscilla Brown, who proofed the book, and Cindy Robinson, my longtime secretary and friend who typed most of the manuscript, and Sandy Beetler, who provided critical secretarial support.

My hunting buddies — David and Jim Goodchild, David Ott,

Amos Dewitt, Carl Frohaug, Jim Clarey, Randy Moring, George Cooper, Bob Parker, Wayne Shirey, Wayne Holt, Roberto Chiappelloni, Jack Crockford, John Creamer, Bryant Wright, Guy Shanks, Max Corder and my daughters, Jennifer, Samantha and Kristen.

Bob Zaiglin, James Kroll and Joe Kruz, three of the most knowledgeable deer biologists around, who freely shared with me what it took them years to learn.

The Boone & Crockett Club for granting permission to reprint their score sheets and to use quotes and data from their books.

Field & Stream for allowing me to use excerpts in Chapter 18 from an article I wrote for the December 1979 issue of the magazine.

Information Outfitters for permitting me to reprint their map, "Whitetail Deer Populations."

Harris Publications for granting permission to use excerpts in Chapter 16 from a 1982 article I wrote for one of their annuals.

Finally, my special friend and mentor, Charlie Elliott, who got me started in the outdoor writing field back when I thought rattling for deer meant riding down a bumpy country road in an old pickup.

Foreword

By Dick Idol

DAVID MORRIS AND I WERE DESTINED to cross paths. Little did we know at the time, but from early on, our lives were tracking a course so nearly parallel that our meeting was inevitable.

We both grew up in the South — David in Alabama and me in North Carolina. We are about the same age. (David is "slightly" younger, though I try not to let it show when we're climbing mountains.) For both of us, hunting, fishing and athletics were preoccupations during our youth. David's path took him to Auburn University; mine to North Carolina State. Not surprisingly, we both majored in wildlife biology ... and I guess you could also say in whitetail hunting and bass fishing.

Once college was over, he and I both made the decision to somehow find a career and a life in the outdoors. "Traditional" outdoor careers such as a biologist or game warden held little appeal for either of us. David started out as a professional bass guide on Lake Eufaula on the Alabama/Georgia line, and then later, he became the managing partner of a large hunting plantation in Georgia. In the meantime, I had packed my gun, boots and rifle and headed to the wilds of the Alaskan frontier. There, I became involved in guiding big game hunters, booking hunts and in taxidermy.

For the next several years, we continued with our careers, sampling various other outdoor endeavors along the way. Many might contend (especially our wives) that we mainly found ways of getting paid to hunt and fish, and that wouldn't be entirely untrue. But, somehow we did manage to earn enough to make ends meet for more than a decade.

Inexorably, destiny kept directing our paths toward a fateful meeting. More and more, our lives and our careers were drifting in the direction of the whitetail deer. Although there are more than 12 million white-tail hunters in America, it seems that the real fanatics (a group to which we both admittedly qualify) sooner or later cross trails. For us, that meeting occurred in the Spring of 1982 at one of the first "whitetail shows" in history, the Dixie Deer Classic in Raleigh, North Carolina. David and I were there as guest seminar speakers. After the show, we had the opportunity to "talk whitetails" and immediately established a lasting friendship based on our common interest in the whitetail.

At that point, David was well underway in a career as one of the owners and the editor of Game and Fish Publications of Marietta, Georgia. I was living in Montana and engaging in a variety of white-tail-oriented activities I still called my "job." As fate would have it, I was planning to put on a national whitetail show in Pennsylvania and wanted some type of whitetail literature to enhance and broaden the show concept. Since David was in the publication business, we had a lot to talk about and some interesting ideas soon began to take shape.

About a week after the Dixie Deer Classic, David and Steve Vaughn, publisher of Game and Fish Publications, flew to my home in Montana. There, the three of us engaged in a little bear hunting and a lot of dialogue about big whitetails, whitetail shows and the concept of a publication devoted entirely to whitetail hunting, specifically trophy whitetail hunting. After numerous meetings, telephone conversations and considerable planning over the next few months, *North American Whitetail* magazine was conceived and born at a time when its success was anything but certain. While the whitetail hunting phenomenon of today clearly reflects a huge market, a decade ago the hope for a suc-cessful whitetail magazine was based mostly on our collective positive gut feelings.

Now, *North American Whitetail* is an unparalleled success story and is clearly the nation's leading whitetail publication. From the beginning, David's input and efforts as the editor and later the executive publisher were largely responsible for *Whitetail's* top standing in the market. His ability to ferret out meaningful information from the reams of white-tail material available and to shape that information into enjoyable, state-of-the-art articles quickly set *North American Whitetail* apart. Part of the reason David was able to do this is because he is not just a whitetail hunter, he is indeed one of the best whitetail hunters in the country. His extensive hunting experience not only includes many of the top trophy states in the United States but also extends into Mexico and most of Canada's famous big buck provinces.

In addition to David's magazine and hunting experience, he founded Middle Georgia's Burnt Pine Plantation in the early 1970's and until recently served as the managing partner of this 13,000-acre plantation, which has historically been one of the leaders in the commercial whitetail hunting industry. Although this successful hunting operation is not high-fenced, David was able to continually upgrade the quality of the bucks and produce many fine trophies over the years.

There is virtually no other writer in America as uniquely qualified to write this book as David Morris. He has the experience in the field as a hunter, the overview understanding of the sport and its participants as the former editor of the nation's leading whitetail magazine and the track record of operating one of the country's most successful commercial whitetail hunting operations. And perhaps more importantly, David has an unquenchable thirst for knowledge, the hallmark of those who excel, and the unique ability to communicate what he knows to others.

This book is without question one of the most complete literary works ever written on whitetail hunting. All of us smitten with the longing to learn more about whitetails and whitetail hunting realize that we are on a perpetual learning curve. Certainly, no other book to date better captures and presents today's state-of-the-art information on hunting trophy whitetails.

Introduction

Dawn broke clear and cold that December morning in 1965. Gradually, the sky brightened enough for me to distinguish between the woodline some 125 yards distant and the edge of the frost-covered rye field. As I lay behind the trunk of a fallen tree, my thoughts turned to the deer tracks in the corner of the field. True, there weren't many, but the few I'd seen had been enough to lure me to this place for nine consecutive mornings. Maybe, just maybe, this would be the morning I would see my first whitetail ever!

Deer season in southeastern Alabama had opened for the first time the previous fall. Since that first opener, it was the rare day that hadn't found me after deer. High school football or basketball practice spoke for most of my afternoons, so I hunted mainly in the mornings before school. The fact that the first year had passed without my having seen a deer did little to curb my enthusiasm. It was enough just to hunt them, to carry a real deer rifle (even if it was a .222 Remington), to see tracks and to know that I could see a deer any time.

The second fall began like the first had ended. Day after day passed, but still I saw no deer. Books and magazine articles about deer and successful hunts encouraged me. I marveled when I read about hunters who actually saw deer, let alone killed one. As far as I could tell, deer were totally nocturnal. I couldn't imagine seeing a deer in the daylight. In fact, by the middle of that second season, I found it increasingly difficult to imagine seeing a deer at all.

Finally, I settled on a plan to hunt this particular rye field nestled deep in the woods on my family's farm. There were more tracks there than any other place I'd found. My strategy was simple: Hunt the field every day and sooner or later a deer would have to show up.

For the ninth straight morning, I stared across the rye field, trying to envision what it would be like to see a deer. I wondered if I would fall victim to that thing called buck fever I'd read about. Surely the many squirrels, rabbits, foxes and assorted other small game that had fallen to my rifle had prepared me. I wouldn't get buck fever, whatever it was. I was wrong.

At first, my mind refused to acknowledge what my eyes saw. My pulse pounded in my ears. My three layers of clothing rose and fell visibly with each gasping breath. I began to shiver, but not from the cold. There, some 75 yards away, stood a deer. How he had gotten there I did not know. This was what I had waited for. I had to act ... now!

A couple of deep breaths of the cold air settled my nerves a bit. Then, I realized for the first time what stood before me. No, it wasn't a trophy buck. It didn't even have antlers. It was a button buck! With the crosshairs wiggling back and forth somewhere around the front shoulder of the deer, I faced a most difficult decision. Pull the trigger or not? So many days of hunting. The temptation was great. My finger tightened on the trigger. Then, I decided. I would not shoot. There would be another time, another deer. I would wait. And, wait I did!

It was three more years before that first antlered buck finally came along. The year was 1968. My efforts to get that first buck had continued unceasingly, but success still eluded me. However, I entered that hunting season with renewed confidence. During the previous season, I had hunted new places where I had seen deer with some consistency. With this turn for the better, I believed it was only a matter of time before a buck would be mine.

At the time, I was attending Auburn University, where eventually I would graduate with a master's degree in biology. It was there that I began dating a lovely coed named Debbie, whose hometown of Jackson, Alabama, was located in the middle of the South's finest deer hunting. During previous visits to this southwestern Alabama town, I had met avid deer hunter Wayne Holt. When Wayne invited me to join him on a deer hunt during the upcoming Christmas holidays, I eagerly accepted his offer.

The Christmas season arrived at last and found me in Jackson as planned. Wayne's work prevented an early start on that first day. It was mid-afternoon before we could leave for the farm near the Alabama River where Wayne had gained permission to hunt. On that cold December afternoon, my four-year quest for a whitetail buck finally would be realized.

After arriving at the farm, we quickly mapped our strategy. On the back side of the farm was a small field known as the "Lower 40," where Wayne had planted a rye patch. My plan was to slip up to the rye field late in the afternoon in hopes of catching a buck feeding there. Hunting slowly toward my destination, I neared the food plot an hour later. Before beginning my final approach, I got the idea to climb a tree so I could see if anything was in the field. After no small amount of effort, I reached the top of the pine tree and could see into the field some 250 yards away. Several deer were there already. When my binoculars revealed a small four-point buck, I could barely keep my rather tenuous grip on the tree. From my lofty perch, I could visually follow the course of a deep-banked streambed that ran from about 50 yards on my left to the very edge of the field. That was how I would approach the field. I would wade the ankle-deep stream, and once at the edge of the field, I would ease up to the top of the 10-foot embankment. There, I should have an easy 30 to 40-yard shot.

Plans don't always work out the way they are intended, but this time they did. I crept down the streambed in total silence and out of sight. My excitement rose with each step. Finally, after 45 minutes, I reached the edge of the rye field. I began a slow, careful crawl to the top of the streambank. The sight that awaited made me forget my cold, wet feet. At least 20 deer were feeding in the rye patch! The forkhorn buck I had spotted earlier stood no more than 15 yards to my right! I eased the rifle over the lip of the embankment, steadied it against a small tree and began to squeeze the trigger of my .243 Winchester. Then, something to the left caught my eye. A buck — a big buck was walking into the rye patch! Without hesitation, I shifted positions, found his shoulder with the crosshairs and fired. Suddenly, doubt flooded my mind. Did I have the scope on him? Did I jerk the trigger? Was he hit? I had no answers … and no time for further consideration. The buck was coming straight toward me in a choppy, bouncing gait. I jumped to my feet and bolted in another cartridge. Just as I was about to fire again, he fell. At last, I had my first whitetail buck. In my eyes, no Boone & Crockett buck ever killed could have been more impressive than that 15-inch nine-pointer. In that remote little field in South Alabama, I knelt down and gave thanks to the great God who had created this magnificent animal, the whitetail deer.

Now, many years later, much has changed. Debbie is my wife of 22 years. Our marriage had nothing to do with the excellent deer hunting around her hometown, although she's still not sure of that. Well over 100 whitetail bucks have been added to my record and my memories. This has been made possible by Alabama's liberal deer limit of one buck a day, my long association with a 13,000-acre hunting plantation in Georgia and the opportunity to hunt whitetails all over the continent in my position as one of the owners and the former editor of Game & Fish Publications and *North American Whitetail* magazine. Along the way, I've learned some things about whitetails and those who hunt them, including myself. No longer do I measure success by how many bucks I kill in a year, as I did in those early years when 8 to 10 bucks often fell to my bow, muzzleloader or rifle in a single season. Like most hunters given the chance, I have gone through stages. First, my goal was to kill as many deer as possible. Next, I tried to kill deer with as many different weapons as I could. Then, gradually, I set my sights on big bucks, my standards growing higher each year. That process began for me in 1976 when I begrudgingly passed up my first antlered buck, a young six-pointer.

Conventional wisdom has it that there is a final stage beyond trophy hunting. It is reached when a person hunts for the sheer enjoyment of being in the woods and seeing game and doesn't care whether or not he shoots anything. I must confess that I have not yet fully attained that lofty position. However, I do find myself enjoying the chase more and more and gaining gratification from having given my best in pursuit of a big whitetail — whether or not I get him. Don't get me wrong. My goal, my earnest desire, is to shoot that trophy buck. After all, the kill is the final reward, the ultimate measure of success. But if I do all I can to get him and he wins, then my hunt is far from a failure.

There's something else I've noticed in my recent years of deer hunting. More than ever before, I find pleasure in hunting with others of less experience and fewer opportunities. As my personal standards for a trophy deer have risen, it has become increasingly unrealistic to expect to find a deer of the size I want to shoot on some of my more readily available hunting grounds. My solution has been to take someone with me whose personal trophy standards will allow him or her to get satisfaction from shooting the size bucks that are present. Frankly, when it's a good friend or relative who scores, it's as rewarding for me as if I had done it myself.

When all is said, the years of hunting, the countless deer I've seen and the many bucks I've taken have done nothing to diminish my enjoyment or enthusiasm for whitetail hunting. Indeed, with knowledge and experience have come even more anticipation and reward. Today, I know what it takes to be successful, and I expect success when I do my part. The same thrill I experienced when that first buck walked into view still sends adrenalin pumping through my veins when I see a trophy whitetail today. Now, the object of my hunt is not just a buck, it's that big racked survivor of many seasons — the trophy whitetail.

I write this book for those who share my enthusiasm and love for hunting trophy whitetails, and for those who will in time. They are the ones who will understand. They can trace their deer hunting roots back to a first sighting and a first buck. They can recount their own progress leading up to the time when they came to call themselves a "trophy whitetail hunter." They know what it's like to stare in awe and respect at a magnificent buck slipping through the woods and to stand over that downed trophy and say "thanks" to Someone greater than us all.

— David Morris

The Trophy Whitetail – Our Greatest Game Animal

Chapter 1

What Is
A Trophy Whitetail?

"THAT'S ONE ADVANTAGE of the cold," I thought to myself. "I can always tell which direction the wind is blowing by watching my breath."

That was small consolation, however. My feet had mercifully numbed an hour earlier, but a penetrating chill was creeping across my shivering body. I didn't know how much longer I could stay in that tree stand. I dug into the pocket of my heavy parka for my watch. It was 4:50 p.m. Prime time at last. I was determined to endure for the remaining 30 minutes left in legal shooting hours here in the central Canadian province of Saskatchewan.

The light wind had shifted and was quartering left to right across my back, taking my scent just to the north of the snow-covered clearing in front of me. There, three does fed on a large alfalfa bale. They had been there undisturbed for an hour. Now, the change in wind direction threatened to give me away or alert any buck that might approach from the dense evergreens to the north. I reached for the bottle of cover scent I had placed on a nearby board for just such an event. It was frozen

Wide, heavy and tall, this is a trophy buck by any standard. Photo by Mike Biggs.

solid by the minus 10 degree temperature. The thought crossed my mind that I might be crazy for sitting in this weather for 3½ hours. "I'll have to hope he doesn't come from the north," I resigned.

Ten long minutes later, one of the does jerked her head away from the hay bale and stared into the woods to my left. She took a couple of steps toward the source of her concern. The other two does went "on point" behind her. Something was coming. Since the rut was in full swing in this part of Canada, I suspected it was a buck. I was not disappointed. As soon as I saw him, my first inclination was to shoot. I fought back that urge as I raised my binoculars to my eyes.

Showing the characteristic caution of a mature buck, he stood signpost still for several minutes well inside the woodline. I could see he was good, but I couldn't make out how good. Finally, he started moving upwind around the edge of the clearing, staying just inside the cover. I now could see long main beams, good mass and at least two fairly tall tines on his near side. He was a potential shooter, no doubt, but I wanted to be sure exactly what he was.

An open, frozen-over streambed entered the clearing just in front of the buck. When he reached it, I would be able to see and judge him clearly at a distance of only 75 yards. I shifted slightly so I could rest my shaking elbows and steady my 8X binoculars.

The buck reached the streambed and stopped, only his head and shoulders clear of the brush. His impressive rack stood out against the white background. I saw immediately he was a 10-pointer. I guessed his spread at 20 inches inside. His beams were long, maybe 24 inches, and fairly heavy. His beaded brow tines stood five to six inches tall. Both of his first primary tines were at least 10 inches long. His second primaries topped eight. Only the last tine on each side held back a shot. They were short, one about three inches, the other two. Despite that, I figured him to be a 150-class buck on the Boone & Crockett scale. I agonized over what to do. No doubt he was a fine buck. But in this land of great bucks, I was not quite ready to settle for him with five days of hunting left. When he turned and walked down the streambed away from the clearing, his rack looked twice as large as it had seconds before, exaggerated by adrenalin and a strong dose of the "shoot-'im-before-he-gets-away" urge. Shaking, but no longer from only the cold, I managed to resist, though it was through my rifle scope rather than binoculars that I watched him disappear.

Two weeks later found me in the friendlier climes of Georgia after whitetails once again. A steady drizzle had fallen all afternoon, making conditions ideal for slipping quietly through the woods. It had been a good day. I had seen a handful of small bucks and two fairly good bucks that had quickened my pulse. Now, with less than a half-hour of shooting light left, I was tired, having maintained intense concentration and exacting control of each footfall and movement during the last three hours of still-hunting. I planned to spend the waning minutes of the day watching a long, straight stretch of a logging road that ran from one hill down across a small stream and up another hill. From my vantage point on the near hill, I could see any deer crossing within 200 yards. I

After passing up a 150-class buck in Saskatchewan, I shot this 130-class buck in Georgia a few days later. Why? Because trophy size varies by region. A 130-point buck is big for Georgia, but I had a reasonable chance of shooting something better than a 150 in Central Canada.

took up my position on a fallen log just as a dense fog settled into the streambottom before me.

A light mist combined with the failing light and gathering fog to lend an eerie effect. The woods were graveyard quiet except for the steady drip from the pines and oak trees. It was one of those surreal occasions when the imagination takes free rein. In my mind, I would have been only slightly more surprised to see a gorilla rather than a whitetail cross the logging road.

Time was running out when I saw movement 120 yards away on the opposite hill. A squirrel scurried across the logging road in unnatural haste. Many times before, this had been a tip-off to an approaching deer. Such was the case again. A dark form moved to the edge of the road. My binoculars showed it to be a big-bodied buck. His rack was partially obscured by the vegetation along the roadside. I would have to wait for him to step clear of the brush and into the road before I could judge his antlers. Since bucks have a way of hurrying across roads, sensing their vulnerability there, I traded my binoculars for the 2½X–8X scope atop my .280 Rem. I would have to judge and shoot him quickly … very quickly.

True to form, the buck walked briskly into the road, stopping momentarily upon my whistle. "Main beams to the end of his nose," I registered, my mind racing down an oft-practiced checklist. "He's heavy. Two good tines showing on this side. An eight-pointer. Spread is so-so, maybe 17. Can't tell about brows."

With that, he started across the road toward the woods. "No time to worry about brows. I'll take him on the strength of what I see," I decided. "He'll score at least 130."

The 140-grain Nosler cleared the barrel of the .280 just as the buck's head disappeared into the woods. If the scattered brush along the roadside hadn't deflected the bullet, I knew he was mine. I hurried to the place he had crossed. The buck lay 20 yards inside the wet, dark woods. He was a heavy eight-pointer scoring in the low 130's. A fine Georgia whitetail.

How do I justify passing up a 150-point buck on one hunt but shooting a 130-point buck on another? The answer to that question lies in the two ways "trophy buck" can be defined. First, a buck can be defined as a trophy based on size. Since we know that size varies greatly from place to place, we can take it a step further and say a buck can earn trophy status by being "big" relative to the other bucks taken in that particular location. This size and place-related definition is objective and straightforward. It also explains why I shot the 130-class buck, which was "big" for that part of Georgia, but didn't shoot the 150-class buck in Saskatchewan, which was good but not great for there.

The second way a buck can be defined as a trophy is based on pride of accomplishment, which may have nothing at all to do with size. No one can dispute it if a hunter considers a buck he shot to be a "prized memento of one's personal accomplishment," as one dictionary defines the word "trophy." That's a personal matter. This is why a spike can rightfully be called a "trophy" by a novice hunter tagging his very first buck.

In areas where few bucks survive their first antlered year because of heavy hunting pressure, a small 2½-year-old like this one may be rightfully considered a trophy by the hunter who takes him. In such cases, a "trophy" is defined based on an individual's pride of accomplishment rather than size. Photo by Mike Biggs.

For our purposes, however, a definition based on pride of accomplishment rather than size is much too subjective and variable. Still, understanding the factors that influence one's personal trophy standards is useful since these factors apply equally to every hunter. So, we'll start by discussing this personal definition of a trophy before looking at the size and place-related definition to be used throughout this book.

PERSONAL DEFINITION

Four factors shape an individual's personal definition of a trophy. They are the place being hunting, the experience of the hunter, the time available to hunt and the conditions under which one hunts.

Only a few places in the country are capable of producing bucks like this giant from Iowa. His shed antlers were found and scored after this photo was taken. The buck scored well over 200 points as a non-typical. Photo by Mike Biggs.

The Place

If there is a secret to killing big deer — and there is — it is hunting where there are big deer. Sounds simple, doesn't it? And, it is! The best hunter in the world will not kill big deer where there are none. Likewise, the worst hunter in the world can kill big bucks — given time — where there are lots of them. A hunter can only hope to shoot what's there, and what's there will to a great extent determine the size buck a hunter in a given place deems a trophy.

The number and size of "big" bucks vary greatly from place to place in North America. A hunter must accurately analyze the trophy buck situation where he hunts in order to set his own trophy standards for that area. In my home state of Georgia, there are bucks as big as just about anywhere, but due to high hunting pressure, these king-sized bucks are relatively few in number. Therefore, my individual chances of killing a really high-scoring buck there are slim. My Georgia standard is based on a size representing the biggest buck I have a reasonable chance to harvest there. In my part of Georgia, that means a 130-point buck. True, 150-point-plus bucks are taken there occasionally, and I may shoot a buck of that size once every six or eight years in Georgia. For me, that doesn't represent a "reasonable chance." My personal minimum standard for a trophy whitetail (with a gun) regardless of where I'm hunting is a buck in the 130-point class. In Georgia, I have a reasonable chance of shooting one of that class every year or two.

If you are hunting a place where you seldom or never see a buck of the size you consider a trophy, then either your minimum standards are too high or you are hunting in the wrong place. I frequently find this situation among hunters who occasionally travel to some faraway place where there are truly big bucks. There, they kill a good buck and take the trophy standards of that location back to their home territory. Then, they impose these unrealistic standards on a place incapable of producing deer of that caliber. The result is a frustrated hunter left with three choices. One, he can lower his standards to a realistic level for where he hunts. Two, he can hunt somewhere else where his standards can be met. Three, he can remain frustrated!

Even after a hunter establishes his personal minimum size for a trophy under any circumstances, that doesn't mean he will shoot every deer that meets his minimum. It depends on the situation and the place. For example, in Georgia I'm allowed two bucks a season. So, I start out with intentions to shoot any 130-class Georgia buck I see and like. If I'm successful, my goal goes up on the second buck. On a trip to big buck country such as South Texas, Montana or Canada, my standards are based on the trophy potential of that particular place. I try to determine the largest size buck I have a reasonable chance to take at the location I'm hunting. In places with such high trophy prospects, I would not even consider shooting a 130-class buck.

Hunting Experience

Hunting experience is an important consideration in determining one's personal definition of a "trophy." First, hunting experience determines skill level, which translates into a hunter's ability to kill one of the better bucks a place has to offer. Second, one's past hunting experience will help establish his minimum acceptable size for a trophy under any circumstances, based on the size bucks he has taken previously.

A person with little experience has to take pot luck when he goes hunting because he has few skills to call upon. He also may be happy with any buck, having taken few, if any, bucks before. In such a case, a spike well may be a "trophy" to him, even though better bucks are available where he hunts. Yet, a more experienced hunter in the same place might hold out for a 140-class buck because he has skills that put the odds for success in his favor and because he already has a sufficient number of lesser bucks to his credit.

While it is safe to assume that someone with much hunting experience has developed a higher level of skill, it cannot be assumed that someone with much hunting experience automatically has high personal trophy standards (relative to Boone & Crockett scores). The size of the bucks where he hunts will determine this. For instance, a hunter with years of hunting experience in a heavily hunted region in the East might possess the skills to kill one of the best bucks in his area every year. But if 90 percent of the bucks there are 1½ years old, the best he can hope to kill may be a small six or eight-pointer. In this case, the hunter has the experience and the skill to match trophy hunters anywhere, but his minimum trophy standard might be a small six-pointer. Whereas, a hunter in a big buck state like Kansas with the same or even less experience and skill might not even consider shooting such a small buck.

Time Available

The time available to a hunter during a hunt or a season will determine in part what he deems to be a "shootable" trophy. For instance, if I were hunting for two weeks in Alberta (where bucks reach outrageous size but where deer are relatively few), I might initially set my goal at nothing smaller than a 160. If, however, I were planning to be there only three days, I would shoot the first 145-class buck I saw since my chances of seeing more than a handful of bucks during such a short time are low.

Why 145 instead of 130, my personal trophy minimum? Because I would not trade even the outside chance for one of those Canadian super bucks for a 130, but I draw the line at a 145 "buck in the hand." What to shoot under a specific set of circumstances is a personal decision every trophy hunter has to make when the time comes.

During the course of a hunt or a season, the criteria for a shootable trophy can change as time draws short. Often, I will set a trophy standard that is to last until a certain point in the hunt. If I am unsuccessful at that point, my standards will drop due to the lack of remaining time. This may result in shooting a buck smaller than I've already passed up, but such is trophy hunting.

A word of caution is in order here. As the time begins to wind down on a hunt, the pressure builds ... and builds. This is when a hunter is most likely to make a mistake and shoot something he really doesn't want. The best way to relieve a little of the pressure is to be mentally prepared to go home without a buck. Frankly, that's not easy. It is truly amazing how a buck can grow in the mind's eye during the last day or two of a hunt or season. I liken this to the overwhelming pressure on a hunter when a marginal buck starts to leave. The old "shoot-'im-before-he-gets-away" syndrome kicks in, and the trigger finger is hard to restrain. And every time the tag is filled with a lesser "pressure" buck, it seems the hunter ends up seeing a monster soon afterwards. The pressure, by the way, doesn't just come on the last day or two. It starts at the halfway point of the hunt, or after your buddy has scored, and mounts rapidly thereafter.

The Hunting Conditions

The hunting conditions — weather, cover thickness, hunting pressure, the rut (or lack of it), etc. — go a long way in determining what size buck a hunter can reasonably expect to shoot in a given location. Even where there are bucks far exceeding one's personal minimum standards, the conditions a hunter encounters will determine to a large extent how big a deer he can realistically hope to take. A hunter must evaluate the conditions, weigh his odds and set realistic trophy standards for the circumstances.

Hunting conditions have much the same effect as time. It's all a matter of evaluating the odds. More time means better odds, and better hunting conditions mean better odds. Neither time nor conditions affect the size or number of bucks on the place being hunted — only the odds of taking one of the better ones.

I've had hunting conditions work for me, resulting in a higher goal, and against me, forcing a lower standard. On a Texas hunt a few years

My old hunting pal, Steve Spears, poses with a 22-inch 12-pointer I shot in South Texas after a "norther" blew in and put the bucks on the move.

ago, favorable weather allowed me to move my trophy criteria up after a slow start. The first couple of days were warm and overcast. Bucks were few and far between. After sizing up my chances, I set as my minimum goal a 145-class buck. Fortunately, he didn't show up the next day. That night a "norther" blew into South Texas, and dawn brought 40 degree temperatures and drizzle. Bucks were running everywhere. I readjusted my goal upward to a "solid-150" buck. Two days later, I achieved my revised goal by shooting a 22-inch 12-pointer with a seven-inch drop tine.

On my second trip to Manitoba, Canada, in 1984, hunting conditions forced a change in my minimum trophy goal — this time downward. Seven of us trekked to this frigid land to hunt its giant bucks.

A successful trip there the year before had given us reason to think a 160-class buck was a real possibility. But, three days into the hunt, not only had we not shot any 160-class bucks, we weren't seeing deer of any kind. Some blamed the extreme cold. (The mercury didn't see the high side of zero the entire week.) Others believed the severe winter the year before had decimated the local deer herd. From what we had seen — or not seen — a die-off seemed a plausible explanation. Add severe cold and knee-deep snow, and the situation seemed hopeless.

When I pulled my white snowsuit over my clothes on the fourth morning, I decided a 140-class buck was now a shooter. As I plowed through a clearcut late that afternoon, a buck stood up in a brushtop 200 yards away, looking as cold and miserable as I was in the minus 15 degree weather. Through my binoculars, he appeared to be an eight-pointer about 20 inches wide with good mass. I was shaking too much to be sure, but his antlers had the dimensions to better 140. When a cold wind cut through my seven layers of clothes, my decision was made. I sat down and tried to steady my 7mm Rem. Mag. The 140-grain bullet flew true. The buck was a fine nine-pointer and scored 144. My decision was a good one. Only one other buck was killed that week, and hardly anything else was seen.

OUR DEFINITION

So, we can see that the personal definition of a trophy varies with each hunter, depending on where he hunts, his experience, the time available to hunt and the hunting conditions. But, a definition based more on pride of accomplishment than on size is too subjective for our purposes. A more objective, size-related definition is needed, and it should take into account the size differences in "big" bucks across the continent. Surely, for most hunters, the words "trophy whitetail" conjure up an image of a mature, big-racked buck, one that is among the biggest found in an area. From this collective perspective, we get the definition of a trophy buck that will be used throughout this book. **A trophy whitetail is a mature buck, at least 3½ years old, with antlers large enough to rank him among the best bucks consistently harvested in a given area.** This definition establishes two essential requirements for a trophy buck anywhere in the country.

First, a trophy whitetail must be "mature," meaning he must have

Under this book's definition, a trophy whitetail must be at least 3½ years old and large enough to be among the best bucks consistently harvested in a given area. This fine 10-pointer qualifies just about everywhere. Photo by Mike Blair.

had time to grow an impressive rack and hone his survival instincts. This takes a minimum of 3½ years. A 2½-year-old buck can have a fairly impressive rack, but he will not yet behave like a mature buck. On the other hand, a 3½-year-old, though not as big or as keen as he will be when he's older, has come far enough in his education to offer hunters a real challenge and can carry very impressive antlers, even Boone & Crockett record size. (Note: A deer's age in the fall is given in "½-year" terms since deer are typically born in the late spring and early summer.)

Secondly, in addition to being at least 3½ years old, a trophy buck must have a rack large enough to place him among the best bucks consistently taken in a given area. This obviously has different implications in different places. For instance, in heavily hunted areas of the East, relatively few bucks survive to age 3½; therefore, any 3½ harvested would be among the best bucks taken in the area and would rightly be considered a trophy. In the big ranch country of South Texas, there are a great many mature bucks. There, 3½ or 4½-year-old bucks would seldom rank "trophy" status since it would be unlikely for deer of that age to be among the best bucks consistently taken in the area. In the worst case extreme where hardly any bucks reach 3½ years old, trophy hunting under this book's definition is virtually an impossible endeavor. In such cases, a hunter must fall back on his personal definition of a trophy.

As we have defined a trophy, we see there is some room for both individual interpretation (based on the same four factors discussed previously) and place-to-place size differences. An arbitrary, fixed size standard for a trophy whitetail that would be applicable everywhere in the country would be impractical and unfair. The size of South Carolina bucks cannot be compared to that of Texas deer. Nor can a trophy buck in Pennsylvania be fairly compared to one in Saskatchewan. It is neither fair nor realistic to fix a trophy standard that would say to a Florida hunter that his 5½-year-old, 120-point buck, which may be the biggest killed in his part of the state, is not a trophy. Yet, it is equally unrealistic to try to convince Iowa hunters that a buck of that size is a trophy. But, any hunter can rest assured that if he shoots a mature buck, one 3½ years old or older, large enough to rank among the best bucks consistently taken in that region he has indeed taken a trophy whitetail — one of the greatest game animals on earth!

Chapter 2

The Making Of A Trophy

MY PATH FIRST CROSSED Dick Idol's in March 1982 at the Dixie Deer Classic in Raleigh, North Carolina. Dick, who even then was on the road to fame as a trophy whitetail hunter, and I were both attending the deer gathering as guest speakers. Right away I was impressed with Dick's knowledge of whitetails. One night after the Classic had closed its doors, Dick and I, together with some friends, journeyed to a local restaurant for dinner and to continue our discussions on deer. During the course of the conversation, Dick asked about my hunting plans for the year. I briefly mentioned my upcoming deer trips. Then, I told him I had booked a spring grizzly hunt to Alaska and a fall hunt in British Columbia for moose, elk and bear. Dick's response surprised me.

"That's good. You'll like hunting those far off places and exotic animals ... for awhile," he said. "I went through all that. I hunted Alaska, Africa and all those places several times. Really enjoyed it. But in the end, I came back to whitetails. You will, too. Hunting the other animals a couple of times will be enough, but you'll never get enough of hunting trophy whitetails."

I have never forgotten what Dick said that night. I was already

Few other animals can match a trophy whitetail's senses, wariness and intelligence. One on one, the trophy whitetail is unquestionably one of the most challenging animals in the world to hunt. Photo by Mike Biggs.

a die-hard whitetail hunter. But now, after having had the opportunity to hunt big game in Alaska, the Yukon, most Canadian provinces, several Western states, Mexico, Spain and Africa, I can look back on Dick's words and better understand what he was saying.

While I have never grown tired of the adventure and excitement of hunting distant lands and exotic animals, I always return to the trophy whitetail. With nearly all the other species I've pursued, hunting them successfully one or two times has been enough. After that, the animals became secondary to the place and the experience. Not so with whitetails. I never tire of hunting them. The animal itself remains the focus of the hunt, not the place or the experience. It took hunting all those other species to realize I already had the best in the trophy whitetail.

One on one, the trophy whitetail is unquestionably one of the most challenging animals in the world to hunt. Anything more difficult would have to get its edge from remoteness, difficult terrain, harsh climate, scarcity, aggressiveness or its nocturnal nature. Few other animals can match a trophy whitetail's senses, wariness and intelligence. The only other animal I've ever hunted offering the same type one-on-one challenge as the whitetail is the beautiful and elusive African kudu, both the lesser and the greater.

What goes into the making of a trophy whitetail? Biologists tell us three factors determine the size a whitetail buck will attain. They are age, nutrition and genetics. The size potential of a whitetail is determined by genetics. Attaining that size potential at any given age is dependent upon quality nutrition. Whether or not a buck ever realizes his ultimate size potential is dependent on both age and nutrition. Of course, injury, disease and stress from extreme weather or parasites can affect the growth of a deer. However, we'll focus only on age, nutrition and genetics, the primary factors influencing antler size.

AGE

Under this book's definition of a trophy whitetail — at least 3½ years old and among the best bucks consistently taken in the area — age is the most important factor in the making of a trophy whitetail. Even a buck benefiting from superior genetics and high-quality nutrition will not meet this definition of a trophy unless he's at least 3½ years old. Why? One of the main reasons a trophy whitetail is so prized is the degree of difficulty he offers those hunting him. Sure, the antler size is very important to hunters, but what sets the trophy whitetail apart from other game animals is his wariness, intelligence and ability to challenge the hunter. Many other animals have more impressive headgear, such as mule deer, caribou, elk and moose, but they do not offer the one-on-one challenge of the trophy whitetail. This great characteristic of the whitetail only comes with maturity, and maturity comes only with age, at least 3½ years of it for our purposes. There's no shortcut. It takes 3½ years to get 3½ years' worth of experience — and honed survival skills. An exceptionally large 2½-year-old may have the antlers, but he will not have the savvy of a 3½-year-old buck.

An examination of a buck's aging process, or educational process, will help explain the necessity of time in the making of a trophy whitetail. It has been said that there is so much difference between a trophy buck and other whitetails that they might as well be different species. I

A 1½-year-old buck like this one is fairly easy to get in rifle sights. Most of the bucks killed in the United States are 1½'s. Photo by Bill Kinney.

agree. The rate at which a hunted whitetail buck learns is remarkable. Time and experience lead to a complete change in behavior and habits. He is a totally different animal at 3½ years old than what he was at 1½ years old. By the time he reaches 5½ or 6½, generally considered peak antler years for a whitetail, he is so well educated that it's a simple matter for him to elude 95 percent of the hunters after him. If you want to hunt trophy whitetails — the biggest, oldest and smartest of the species — you must think "trophy whitetails," not just deer, not even just bucks!

For nearly 20 years, I have been involved with a large hunting plantation in Middle Georgia. During that time, plantation guests have harvested close to 1,500 bucks on the property. The plantation's biologists keep meticulous records on deer sighted and harvested by the guests. In addition, the biologists conduct off-season deer censuses. Among other things, they record the total number of deer seen and the number of bucks spotted. The bucks are then carefully classified into one of three age groups: 1½-year-olds, 2½-year-olds or 3½-year-olds and older. Through the years, vast amounts of consistent data have been collected that allow certain conclusions to be

A 2½-year-old still doesn't have the savvy of a mature buck, but he has wised up considerably. All indications are that a 2½ is twice as hard to kill as a 1½-year-old. Photo by Mike Blair.

drawn about the vulnerability of each age class. This is done by comparing the ages of the bucks sighted or killed by hunters during the season to the known age structure of the buck population as determined by the trained biologists. The results clearly show the increasing difficulty of killing a buck with each passing year.

A 1½-year-old buck is fairly easy to get in rifle sights. He's a lot like a teenage boy who is on his own in the world for the first time and has just discovered girls. The yearling buck wanders around big-eyed, driven by the rutting urge but not sure what to do about it. He frequents the doe hangouts. Just hunt deer and you'll find yearling bucks. They travel around rather aimlessly in the fall and usually end up where the crowd is. My guess is that over 70 percent of all the bucks killed in North America each year are 1½-year-olds. They differ little from does in vulnerability, except they are even more naive once a hunter makes contact with them.

When a buck reaches 2½ years old, he has wised up considerably but still has a long way to go. He has learned a lot from the experiences of his first year. The naive, almost air-headed attitude of his adolescent first season has been tempered now with a touch of maturity and the knowledge that danger might be nearby. The 2½ responds strongly to the lure of the rut and tends to stay near the doe concentrations. Hunters after "just bucks" will bump into their share of 2½-year-olds, assuming a significant number of bucks survive their first antlered season. Yet, they are warier and less likely to expose themselves than a yearling. In fact, the plantation's records make the argument that a 2½-year-old buck in

The buck on the left is a 3½-year-old, and the one on the right is a very good 2½. Note the differences in antler and neck size and in how blocky their faces are. But, these things aren't where the greatest difference lies ... a 3½ is three times harder to kill than a 2½ and six times harder to kill than a 1½! Photo by Mike Biggs.

a hunted population is twice as hard to kill as that same buck at 1½ years old. But, what a difference a year makes!

By the time a buck reaches 3½ years old, our minimum age for trophy status, he has pretty well caught on to the basics but still has room to improve on the fine points. With two seasons as a legal target behind him and the added maturity that time and experience afford, he has learned that the dangers are real. He has become deliberate in his travels and actions, and he spends less and less time around the doe concentrations during daylight hours. His daytime travel is less frequent and more restricted to thicker cover. Still, he's vulnerable, mainly when his new-found caution is compromised by the rutting urge, but he definitely is not easy. From the plantation's records, it appears that by the time a buck reaches 3½ years old, he is three times harder to kill than he was at 2½ and six times harder to kill than he was at 1½! Couple this increased degree of difficulty with the fact that 3½'s will be far fewer in number

Talk about "hawgs"! This old buck must weigh close to 300 pounds. He is undoubtedly 5½ years old or older. By the time a buck reaches this age, he usually has hunters patterned better than they ever will him. This buck represents the ultimate challenge for whitetail hunters. Photo by Bill Kinney.

than 1½'s or 2½'s in hunted populations, and it becomes clear why 3½-year-olds are prized trophies in many deer populations around the country.

If a buck makes it to 4½ years old, chances are good he won't fall to a hunter's bullet. A buck this age or older is now in the advanced program of trophy whitetail studies. Survival is his first priority. The urge to breed is about his only weakness, but even during the rut, rarely will he throw all caution to the wind. Chances are that he moves very little during the day, then mostly in thick cover. If pressured, he is likely to become totally nocturnal. Normal deer hunting tactics and longtime permanent deer stands are not much of a threat to him. A buck 4½ years old or older has hunters patterned far better than they him. It is this deer that offers the ultimate challenge for whitetail hunters. To have a chance to outwit this buck, the hunter must call all his skills and patience to bear … and have a good dose of luck on his side as well. When a buck tops 4½ years old in a hunted population, the odds of killing this deer are so long for the average hunter that it would be discouraging to calculate them. Each passing year only adds to the buck's survival instincts.

It is worth noting that the "maturing" or educational process of bucks described above can be slowed in lightly hunted populations with a high percentage of older bucks. There are a couple of reasons for this. First, while bucks subjected to heavy pressure must adapt quickly or become venison, bucks in places with light pressure can carry on their normal routines. They are not forced to hug thick cover or become nocturnal in order to survive; therefore, even older bucks can be somewhat naive and vulnerable to normal hunting tactics. Secondly, where there are many older bucks, it takes bucks longer to reach a position of social dominance. This delay slows the maturing process. For instance, a 3½-year-old buck may be dominant in a heavily hunted population with few older bucks. This buck would exhibit the characteristic caution and behavior of a mature whitetail. However, in a lightly hunted herd with many older bucks, a 3½-year-old is unlikely to be dominant. In this case, he would behave more like a younger or "adolescent" buck rather than like an older, dominant whitetail.

This situation is perfectly illustrated on a large South Texas ranch I am privileged to hunt each year. The ranch is very lightly hunted, except for doe cropping, and has a deer population with a high percentage of 5½-year-old and older bucks. The 3½-year-old bucks are almost naive, behaving more like a cross between a 1½ and a 2½ on more heavily hunted land. Even the 4½-year-olds haven't got it all figured out yet on this ranch. The wisdom and caution characteristic of 3½'s in hunted populations doesn't show up in bucks on this ranch until they are 5½ and 6½ years old. Why? Hunting pressure has not forced them to adopt a more secretive, cautious and nocturnal lifestyle in order to survive.

Many populations of deer simply do not include old trophy bucks, at least in any significant number. This is because most bucks are killed while still young, 1½ or 2½ years old. They simply never have a chance to get old and smart. It would be difficult to hunt a population of old bucks to extinction. But, it is quite easy for a large number of nonselective hunters to kill off nearly all the young bucks each year, leaving very few, if any, to carry over to the older age classes. In some areas in the East, biologists estimate that over 90 percent of the total buck population is harvested each year. Want to guess what your odds of killing a trophy buck there would be? Yet, even in the face of that kind of hunting pressure, if a buck can reach 3½ years old, he is able to look after himself!

NUTRITION

Nutrition is the second factor affecting a buck's ability to realize his size potential. For game managers, quality nutrition is an important focus of their management efforts. They try to assure good nutrition by maintaining the herd within the limits of the available food supply and by providing more quality food through habitat improvement and/or plantings or direct feeding. On the state or national level, the only practical way for game managers to influence nutritional quality to any substantial degree is by controlling the deer population. This is done by regulating the harvest through season length, bag limits and either-sex days or permits.

For the private land manager, the situation is different. He can concentrate his efforts on a manageable-sized tract of land. This not only allows him to control deer density but also to improve the natural food supply through habitat manipulation, such as prescribed burning, selective timber harvest, brush control, etc. Additionally, the manager can plant food plots or directly feed small grains, corn or even high-nutrition pellets, as well as make mineral blocks and such available.

Apart from overcrowding and habitat damage, the quality of nutrition from natural forage is dependent upon the fertility of the soil. This is a simple concept. Plants transfer the nutrients from the soil to themselves. Deer eat the plants or the mast they produce and transfer those nutrients to their bodies and antlers. If the nutrients are not in the soils to begin with, they will not end up in the deer. It is no accident that the biggest bucks consistently come from areas with the most fertile soils. For instance, the productive Midwest is the bread-basket of the nation and home to some of the largest bucks in the United States. The central Canadian prairie provinces are unsurpassed farm country and the land of giant whitetails. The floodplains of the Mississippi River and its tributaries are incredibly fertile and harbor heavy-bodied, big-racked whitetails. The fabled whitetail country of South Texas looks bleak and unproductive to the unknowing, but veg-

Food plots and agricultural crops not only concentrate deer for harvest, but recent research has proven that nutritious year-round plantings can greatly increase both the size and number of deer the land can support. Photo by Bill Kinney.

etation in this semiarid land draws from rich soils and is among the most nutritious anywhere. By contrast, the deep sandy soils of the Southern coastal plain, especially Florida, are leached out and infertile. This is reflected in the size of the bucks found there. The lower Appalachian Mountains have seen most of their productive top soil relocated to distant valleys and riverbottoms. The racks of the bucks there bear out this low soil fertility.

Today, researchers and private businesses are focusing much attention on ways to improve nutrition for deer. Improved grains and clovers are available for deer plantings, some specially adapted to different parts of the country. New information has emerged regarding the effectiveness of direct feeding. Pellets and other forms of highly nutritious feeds have been developed to guarantee proper nutrition for bucks. Yet, wildlife plantings and especially direct supplements are limited in application to the most intensively managed private and public land.

GENETICS

As we've said, genetics determine the size potential of a buck, but realizing his ultimate potential depends on nutrition and age. The importance of genetics in determining trophy potential cannot be overstated. Genes make living things what they are. The difference between the size of an elk and a whitetail lies in the genes. They can be fed exactly the same nutrition and be exactly the same age, and the elk will always be bigger. Why? Genetics. All other things being equal, genetics will determine the size a whitetail buck will attain.

The history of record-book bucks in Georgia illustrates the impact of genetics on trophy potential very well. An examination of the Boone & Crockett Club's records through the 1988 entry period reveals that Georgia stands head and shoulders above her neighboring states for record bucks. Georgia boasts 37 record bucks through this period, North Carolina three, South Carolina one, Alabama eight, Tennessee 13 and Florida none. In addition to rack size, Georgia bucks occasionally reach outlandish body size. Several have field-dressed over 300 pounds, including the state's heaviest buck that field-dressed 355 pounds! And, the South is a region known for small-bodied deer! Why have Georgia deer historically grown so large?

Among the factors affecting size, age can quickly be eliminated as the reason Georgia stands out for big bucks in comparison to her neighbors. There is no reason to believe that Georgia deer live longer more often than deer in the surrounding states. To the contrary, Georgia has higher hunting pressure than any of her neighbors thanks to a high human population and the presence of Atlanta in the heart of Georgia's best deer country. Surely, surrounding states have as many bucks reaching the older age classes as does Georgia. The answer can't lie in age.

What about nutrition? Do Georgia deer have higher quality food available to them? If the answer is yes, then at least one of two conditions must be in effect. One, Georgia must have more fertile soils than the other states. Two, if the soils are not more fertile, the habitat must be in better shape.

As for Georgia having more fertile soils, this is only true in the case of Florida, which does have sandy, sterile soils in many places. Although Georgia certainly has some good soils, few places in Georgia can compare to the rich bottomlands of Alabama's Tombigbee and Alabama rivers or to the fertile "Blackbelt" region of Alabama or to the incredibly productive floodplains of the Mississippi River in Tennessee. And, South Carolina and North Carolina have the same soil types as Georgia and have productive river swamps comparable to anything in Georgia. More fertile soils in Georgia is not the answer.

This 230-pound 15-pointer was killed on Middle Georgia's Burnt Pine Plantation. The buck exemplifies the impact genetics can have. After the native deer herd was nearly wiped out in Georgia, whitetails from Wisconsin and other big buck states were restocked. As a result, this Deep South state now has the genetics to produce very big bucks, as its record for Boone & Crockett bucks attests.

Does Georgia have better habitat? Again, the answer is no, but since Georgia produced many of its biggest bucks years ago when habitat was in prime condition, it is a subject worth exploring. Like some of the other Southern states, Georgia's deer were nearly wiped out during the early 1900's as all the land that could be farmed was "put under the plow." The economy was agriculturally based, and a high percentage of the population lived in rural areas. Intensive farming and land clearing together with high rural populations left little room for the whitetail. Then, a change began in the 1930's and '40's. The farm economy took a turn for the worse, and industrialization began in the cities. An exodus from the rural countryside began. The farms were abandoned, and the farmed-out openland began to grow up in secondary growth. Government agencies also began reforestation programs.

By mid-century, vast areas of prime deer habitat had sprung up throughout Georgia. The only problem was that there were no deer present to populate the habitat. This is when the state game department and private concerns began stocking deer into this spreading deer habitat. Deer found their new home to their liking. Their numbers grew thanks to high-quality food and low hunting pressure. Bucks often reached old ages and carried big racks. Many of Georgia's best bucks were taken during this time of expanding deer herds and prime habitat.

Later years would see the habitat quality decline as the deer herd grew beyond the capacity of the land to support it. Body and antler size decreased as the quality of the nutrition in the food sources suffered from overbrowsing. Yet, Georgia's neighboring states all followed this same overall pattern. So, nutrition isn't the factor that explains why Georgia bucks reach such large size in comparison to the bucks from surrounding states.

That leaves genetics as the remaining factor. But, why would the genetic potential of deer in Georgia differ from that of deer in adjoining states? The answer lies in the restocking programs and the sources of the stocked deer.

When the time came to restock in Georgia, deer were virtually extinct in the state except for a few pockets in isolated river swamps and on coastal islands. The state needed a source of deer to stock into the swelling habitat. Some were obtained from Georgia's meager remaining native population. For the most part, however, game biologists had to go out of state to find a source for restocking. Georgia turned to Wisconsin and Texas as two main suppliers of deer for restocking. These two states, both well known for trophy bucks, provided the genetic potential for Georgia's bucks to reach record size. Didn't other states do the same? Not exactly.

A review of the stocking records in neighboring states shows that they depended on native Southern deer for restocking to a far greater degree than did Georgia. Why? Because these states had populations of native deer to serve as a cheaper, more convenient source. At the time, no concern was given to where a deer came from or to genetics. A deer

The impact of genetics cannot be overstated. Genes make living things what they are. Abnormal points like those of this non-typical buck most often stem from genetics, although hormones or injury can play a role. Photo by Mike Biggs.

was a deer. Empty habitat needed to be stocked. Though nearly all neighboring states did stock some Northern and Texas deer, they never did so in the numbers Georgia stocked them. Additionally, neighboring states stocked out-of-state deer in areas where native deer either already existed or previously had been stocked in considerable numbers. The result was an immediate dilution of the gene pool. By contrast, many areas of Georgia started out with almost pure populations of Wisconsin or Texas deer. The evidence is strong that this genetic difference alone accounts for Georgia's standout history for record bucks in comparison to that of her neighboring states. This argument is supported by the fact that the great majority of Georgia's Boone & Crockett bucks have come from counties stocked directly with either Wisconsin or Texas deer.

During a fishing trip several years ago to south-central Florida, a place where palmettos and stunted pines struggle to make a living in deep, sandy soils, I came across another clear example of the impact of genetics on deer size. Upon walking into a local fish camp, I saw several deer heads hanging on the wall. Three or four of them were typical of that area's deer, small-bodied with racks that would fit inside a baseball cap. But, in the middle of these little bucks was a big-bodied eight-pointer with an 18-inch spread, probably scoring about 135.

"Did you kill that deer?" I asked, pointing to the big buck.

"Yeah," answered the fish camp operator.

"Where?" I asked, expecting to hear Texas, Georgia, Alabama or the like.

Instead, he answered, "Right down the road on a big ranch."

It didn't seem possible that a South Florida buck would be that big. I pursued the questioning. "That's a mighty big buck for this area."

"Yeah, but that deer was stocked from Wisconsin as a fawn seven years before I killed it," he replied. "They brought some in trying to have bigger deer."

Wisconsin deer stories are a dime-a-dozen, so I pressed. "Is that right? Do you know that for a fact?"

"Come here," he said, walking toward the deer. "Let me show you something."

I walked over to the deer, and he pointed up to a tattoo in its ear. "They put that number in his ear when they turned him loose. He was one of the original deer they brought down in a cattle trailer from some place in Wisconsin," he explained.

Even in Florida's sandy scrubland, the superior genetics came through on that buck despite the obvious poor nutrition. Since that dramatic example, I have personally seen many more cases of indisputable genetic impact on deer size. Certainly, game biologists today recognize the importance of genetics. Universities, state agencies and private concerns are conducting a great deal of research to better understand genetics in deer and how to put this knowledge to work. Much has been written recently about efforts to produce super bucks through the selective breeding of superior animals and through artificial insemination. This work has produced some impressive results — literally!

The controversy over whether or not a spike is genetically inferior and incapable of growing into a trophy buck has been raging for many years. New evidence proves that genetics are only a part of the story on spikes. The time of year they are born, the condition of their mother and the quality of the nutrition available to them are also factors contributing to the size of the first set of antlers. Long-term studies on penned deer have proven beyond any question that a yearling spike can grow into a trophy buck given time and nutrition. Yet, some spikes are undoubtedly genetically inferior. We now know, however, not all of them are.

One last point regarding genetics should be made. Generally, genetic differences are most obvious from one major region to another. These regional variations pretty much correspond to the differences in whitetail subspecies and varieties as recognized by the taxonomists. I say "pretty much" because the purity of the subspecies and varieties has been diluted in many cases by restocking and the expansion of a subspecies or variety into new territory, perhaps left vacant from past overexploitation. This gene pool mixing accounts in part for the rather dramatic genetic anomalies sometimes seen on very localized levels. This is the case throughout Georgia, where genetic differences in deer color, size or even antler traits can exist on a very localized basis. But, this does not account for all such differences. Sometimes unique genetic characteristics originate within a local deer herd and are passed on to the following generations. For instance, I know of one particular creek drainage in Montana where, unlike the surrounding areas, non-typicals show up with unnatural frequency. No deer have ever been stocked in this area. If the reason for this tendency toward non-typicals could be traced, it might be found to have originated with a dominant non-typical at some point in the past.

Section II

Measuring, Scoring And Judging Trophy Whitetails

Chapter 3

Measuring And Scoring

MAN HAS BEEN FASCINATED with antlers since before the first spearhead was struck from flint. Through the ages, the bigger or more unique the rack, the greater man's fascination and interest. Today is no different.

Antlers are truly one of the wonders of nature. Not only are they all different, but their growth takes place over an incredibly short period of time. By April, antler growth begins as blood vessels under the skin deposit bone salts on the buck's pedicels. As the antlers grow, they are covered by a membrane appropriately called "velvet," which looks and feels just like velvet cloth. Fed by a nutrient-rich supply of blood, the tender antlers grow at the amazing rate of a half-inch a day, making antlers one of the fastest growing forms of living tissue. Within four months, they are fully developed. Then, the velvet dries and is shed. Yes, even the largest Boone & Crockett buck grows those huge antlers in just four months! In fact, the six-foot-wide, 75-pound antlers of the mighty Alaskan moose, the largest member of the deer family, are grown in only four months!

Despite common belief, all bucks, even the biggest ones, lose their antlers every year, usually from mid-January to March. They start growing a new set in the spring. About the only exception to the annual antler-shedding process is the velvet-covered "stag" buck, which due to an injury and/or a hormonal imbalance fails to shed his

The antlers of even the largest bucks like this record-class non-typical are grown in just four months! Photo by Curt Helmick.

velvet and keeps growing antler mass, often in bizarre configurations.

Since antlers are of such interest, it is only logical for hunters to seek a way to measure and compare them. Looking back, I can see that my own need to describe the size of a buck increased with experience.

When I first started deer hunting, the only test a deer had to meet to be a shooter was to have antlers. The size didn't matter. Gradually, I began to categorize bucks into "little," "nice," "big" and "monster." Next, I realized that little usually meant 1½-year-olds. Nice meant the best 1½'s and most 2½'s. Big translated into exceptional 2½'s and nearly all 3½'s and older. Monster still meant monster.

Equating size to age was my first attempt to quantify size in a way that could be communicated with some consistency to others. In time, this method of sizing bucks became inadequate. The width of spread, number of points, etc., also proved lacking. The need to accurately and precisely describe the size of a buck's antlers became apparent, and the Boone & Crockett Club's system of measuring and scoring offered the solution. Though there are several other systems around today, I still believe the Boone & Crockett (B&C) system is the best way to size a set of antlers. I am not alone in this belief since it is the most widely recognized measuring and scoring system for North American big game, including whitetails.

THE BOONE & CROCKETT CLUB

The Boone & Crockett Club dates back 100 years to Theodore Roosevelt, one of its founders. It is a time-honored and respected organization. Every six years or so since 1950, the Club has published a book entitled *Records of North American Big Game*. This publication, known simply as "The Book" among trophy hunters, has become the accepted listing of the all-time best bucks.

In 1950, a special committee of the Boone & Crockett Club developed the current whitetail measuring and scoring system. According to a 1987 special whitetail book published by Boone & Crockett, *Records of North American Whitetail Deer*, the committee's goal was to develop "a fair system of trophy evaluation that would recognize symmetry, be based upon measurements the average hunter could understand and make and that would result in a final score that would allow for natural ranking of trophies." The system developed by that committee is essentially unchanged today.

Boone & Crockett recognizes two categories for whitetails — typical and non-typical. The "Introduction" in *Records of North American Whitetail Deer* explains the difference: "The non-typical category differs for

The B&C measuring and scoring system is the most widely accepted way to size a set of deer antlers. Boone & Crockett recognizes two categories for whitetails — typical and non-typical. The buck on the left is the current world record typical. It was taken in 1914 by James Jordan in Burnett County, Wisconsin. The buck on the right is the world record non-typical. This buck was found dead of unknown causes in St. Louis County, Missouri, in 1981. (As a point of interest, a typical whitetail was shot in Alberta in November 1991 that has been officially scored at 207⅞, exceeding the world record typical score of 206⅛. However, until the B&C Judges Panel scores the buck in 1995, it cannot be recognized as the record, assuming the panel score exceeds 206⅛. Incredibly, the buck's gross typical score is 235⅝!) Photos courtesy of **North American Whitetail.**

the typical in the recording of the abnormal points (points beyond the usual pattern for a typical whitetail). In the typical category, they are subtracted as a penalty from the final score, while in the non-typical category they are added into the final score. This is the reason for the minimum entry score being higher for the non-typical category."

In 1950, the first whitetail scoring lists included both typical and non-typical categories, as is the case today. The minimum entry score for a typical whitetail was 140, a non-typical was 160. Over time, these minimum scores for the all-time record book moved ever higher. Today, a score of 170 is needed to put a typical in the book. A non-typical must score 195 to be listed among the elite.

Typical Score Sheet

OFFICIAL SCORING SYSTEM FOR NORTH AMERICAN BIG GAME TROPHIES

Records of North American Big Game	BOONE AND CROCKETT CLUB	P.O. Box 547 Dumfries, VA 22026

Minimum Score:	Awards	All-time	TYPICAL	Kind of Deer _____
whitetail	160	170	WHITETAIL AND COUES' DEER	
Coues'	100	110		

DETAIL OF POINT MEASUREMENT

Abnormal Points	
Right Antler	Left Antler

E. Total of Lengths of Abnormal Points

SEE OTHER SIDE FOR INSTRUCTIONS		Column 1	Column 2	Column 3	Column 4
		Spread Credit	Right Antler	Left Antler	Difference
A. No. Points on Right Antler	No. Points on Left Antler				
B. Tip to Tip Spread	C. Greatest Spread				
D. Inside Spread of Main Beams	(Credit May Equal But Not Exceed Longer Antler)				
F. Length of Main Beam					
G-1. Length of First Point, If Present					
G-2. Length of Second Point					
G-3. Length of Third Point					
G-4. Length of Fourth Point, If Present					
G-5. Length of Fifth Point, If Present					
G-6. Length of Sixth Point, If Present					
G-7. Length of Seventh Point, If Present					
H-1. Circumference at Smallest Place Between Burr and First Point					
H-2. Circumference at Smallest Place Between First and Second Points					
H-3. Circumference at Smallest Place Between Second and Third Points					
H-4. Circumference at Smallest Place Between Third and Fourth Points					
TOTALS					

Enter Total of Columns 1, 2, and 3		Exact Locality Where Killed:	
Subtract Column 4		Date Killed:	By Whom Killed:
Subtotal		Present Owner:	
Subtract (E) Total of Lengths of Abn. Points		Guide Name and Address:	
FINAL SCORE		Remarks:	

THE SYSTEM

First, a distinction needs to be made between measuring and scoring. For our purposes, measuring is the procedure used to take antler dimensions, i.e., what is measured and how. Scoring, on the other hand, is how the measurements are compiled to reach a final score. Like most experts around the country, I believe the B&C measuring system is the

Typical Measuring Instructions

I certify that I have measured the above trophy on _____ 19 _____

at (address) _____ City _____ State _____
and that these measurements and data are, to the best of my knowledge and belief, made in accordance with the
Instructions given.

Witness: _____ Signature: _____

B&C OFFICIAL MEASURER

I.D. Number

INSTRUCTIONS FOR MEASURING TYPICAL WHITETAIL AND COUES' DEER

All measurements must be made with a 1/4-inch flexible steel tape to the nearest one-eighth of an inch. Wherever
it is necessary to change direction of measurement, mark a control point and swing tape at this point. (Note: a
flexible steel cable can be used to measure points and main beams only.) Enter fractional figures in eighths,
without reduction. Official measurements cannot be taken until antlers have dried for at least 60 days after the
animal was killed.

A. Number of Points on Each Antler: to be counted a point, the projection must be at least one inch long, with
the length exceeding width at one inch or more of length. All points are measured from tip of point to nearest
edge of beam as illustrated. Beam tip is counted as a point but not measured as a point.

B. Tip to Tip Spread is measured between tips of main beams.

C. Greatest Spread is measured between perpendiculars at a right angle to the center line of the skull at widest
part, whether across main beams or points.

D. Inside Spread of Main Beams is measured at a right angle to the center line of the skull at widest point
between main beams. Enter this measurement again as the Spread Credit if it is less than or equal to the length
of longer antler; if longer, enter longer antler length for Spread Credit.

E. Total of Lengths of all Abnormal Points: Abnormal Points are those non-typical in location (such as points
originating from a point or from bottom or sides of main beam) or extra points beyond the normal pattern of
points. Measure in usual manner and enter in appropriate blanks.

F. Length of Main Beam is measured from lowest outside edge of burr over outer curve to the most distant point of
what is, or appears to be, the main beam. The point of beginning is that point on the burr where the center line
along the outer curve of the beam intersects the burr, then following generally the line of the illustration.

G. 1-2-3-4-5-6-7 Length of Normal Points: Normal points project from the top of the main beam. They are
measured from nearest edge of main beam over outer curve to tip. Lay the tape along the outer curve of the beam
so that the top edge of the tape coincides with the top edge of the beam on both sides of the point to determine
the baseline for point measurements. Record point lengths in appropriate blanks.

H. 1-2-3-4 Circumferences are taken as detailed for each measurement. If brow point is missing, take H-1 and
H-2 at smallest place between burr and G-2. If G-4 is missing, take H-4 halfway between G-3 and tip of main
beam.

* * * * * * * * * * * * * * * * *

FAIR CHASE STATEMENT FOR ALL HUNTER TAKEN TROPHIES

To make use of the following methods shall be deemed as UNFAIR CHASE and unsportsmanlike, and any trophy obtained
by use of such means is disqualified from entry.

    I. Spotting or herding game from the air, followed by landing in its vicinity for pursuit;

    II. Herding or pursuing game with motor-powered vehicles;

    III. Use of electronic communications for attracting, locating or observing game, or guiding the
hunter to such game;

    IV. Hunting game confined by artificial barriers, including escape proof fencing, or hunting game
transplanted solely for the purpose of commercial shooting.

* * * * * * * * * * * * * * * * *

I certify that the trophy scored on this chart was not taken in UNFAIR CHASE as defined above by the Boone and
Crockett Club. I further certify that it was taken in full compliance with local game laws of the state,
province, or territory.

Date: _____ Signature of Hunter: _____

(Have signature notarized by a Notary Public)

best available and leaves little room for improvement. However, many
feel, including myself, that the scoring places too much emphasis on
symmetry and on "clean" typical conformation and not enough emphasis on the actual size of the rack. As a result, the final B&C score is
reached (speaking only of typicals for the moment) after deducting the
symmetry differences in each side-to-side measurement and after deduct-

Non-typical Score Sheet

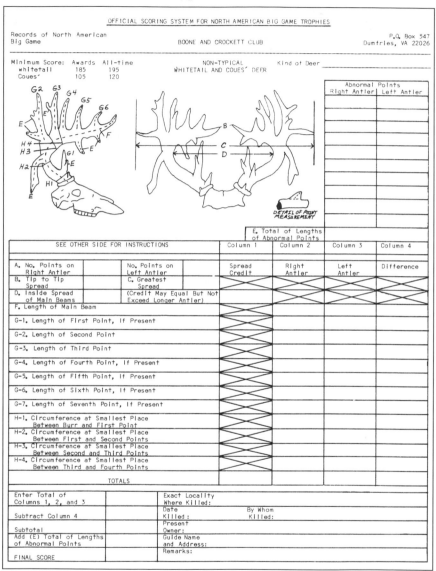

OFFICIAL SCORING SYSTEM FOR NORTH AMERICAN BIG GAME TROPHIES

Records of North American
Big Game

BOONE AND CROCKETT CLUB

P.O. Box 547
Dumfries, VA 22026

Minimum Score:	Awards	All-time	NON-TYPICAL	Kind of Deer _____
whitetail	185	195	WHITETAIL AND COUES' DEER	
Coues'	105	120		

Abnormal Points

	Right Antler	Left Antler

E. Total of Lengths
of Abnormal Points

SEE OTHER SIDE FOR INSTRUCTIONS		Column 1	Column 2	Column 3	Column 4
A. No. Points on Right Antler	No. Points on Left Antler	Spread Credit	Right Antler	Left Antler	Difference
B. Tip to Tip Spread	C. Greatest Spread				
D. Inside Spread of Main Beams	(Credit May Equal But Not Exceed Longer Antler)				
F. Length of Main Beam					
G-1. Length of First Point, If Present					
G-2. Length of Second Point					
G-3. Length of Third Point					
G-4. Length of Fourth Point, If Present					
G-5. Length of Fifth Point, If Present					
G-6. Length of Sixth Point, If Present					
G-7. Length of Seventh Point, If Present					
H-1. Circumference at Smallest Place Between Burr and First Point					
H-2. Circumference at Smallest Place Between First and Second Points					
H-3. Circumference at Smallest Place Between Second and Third Points					
H-4. Circumference at Smallest Place Between Third and Fourth Points					
TOTALS					

Enter Total of Columns 1, 2, and 3		Exact Locality Where Killed:	
Subtract Column 4		Date Killed:	By Whom Killed:
Subtotal		Present Owner:	
Add (E) Total of Lengths of Abnormal Points		Guide Name and Address:	
FINAL SCORE		Remarks:	

ing for all abnormal points. Thus, the final B&C score represents a subjective "trophy evaluation" rather than the true size of the antlers. Obviously, the reason Boone & Crockett elected to score this way was on the belief that the more symmetrical and "cleaner" a typical rack is, the more desirable it is as a trophy; therefore, any symmetry differences or extra points should be penalized and deducted from the score. This

Non-typical Measuring Instructions

I certify that I have measured the above trophy on _____ 19 _____

at (address) _____ City _____ State _____
and that these measurements and data are, to the best of my knowledge and belief, made in accordance with the
instructions given.

Witness: _____ Signature: _____

B&C OFFICIAL MEASURER

I.D. Number

INSTRUCTIONS FOR MEASURING NON-TYPICAL WHITETAIL AND COUES' DEER

All measurements must be made with a 1/4-inch flexible steel tape to the nearest one-eighth of an inch. Wherever
it is necessary to change direction of measurement, mark a control point and swing tape at this point. (Note: a
flexible steel cable can be used to measure points and main beams only.) Enter fractional figures in eighths,
without reduction. Official measurements cannot be taken until antlers have dried for at least 60 days after the
animal was killed.

A. Number of Points on Each Antler: to be counted a point, the projection must be at least one inch long, with
the length exceeding width at one inch or more of length. All points are measured from tip of point to nearest
edge of beam as illustrated. Beam tip is counted as a point but not measured as a point.

B. Tip to Tip Spread is measured between tips of main beams.

C. Greatest Spread is measured between perpendiculars at a right angle to the center line of the skull at widest
part, whether across main beams or points.

D. Inside Spread of Main Beams is measured at a right angle to the center line of the skull at widest point
between main beams. Enter this measurement again as the Spread Credit if it is less than or equal to the length
of longer antler; if longer, enter longer antler length for Spread Credit.

E. Total of Lengths of all Abnormal Points: Abnormal Points are those non-typical in location (such as points
originating from a point or from bottom or sides of main beam) or extra points beyond the normal pattern of
points. Measure in usual manner and enter in appropriate blanks.

F. Length of Main Beam is measured from lowest outside edge of burr over outer curve to the most distant point of
what is, or appears to be, the main beam. The point of beginning is that point on the burr where the center line
along the outer curve of the beam intersects the burr, then following generally the line of the illustration.

G. 1-2-3-4-5-6-7 Length of Normal Points: Normal points project from the top of the main beam. They are
measured from nearest edge of main beam over outer curve to tip. Lay the tape along the outer curve of the beam
so that the top edge of the tape coincides with the top edge of the beam on both sides of the point to determine
the baseline for point measurement. Record point lengths in appropriate blanks.

H. 1-2-3-4 Circumferences are taken as detailed for each measurement. If brow point is missing, take H-1 and
H-2 at smallest place between burr and G-2. If G-4 is missing, take H-4 halfway between G-3 and tip of main
beam.

* * * * * * * * * * * * * * * *

FAIR CHASE STATEMENT FOR ALL HUNTER-TAKEN TROPHIES

To make use of the following methods shall be deemed as UNFAIR CHASE and unsportsmanlike, and any trophy obtained
by use of such means is disqualified from entry.

    I. Spotting or herding game from the air, followed by landing in its vicinity for pursuit;

    II. Herding or pursuing game with motor-powered vehicles;

    III. Use of electronic communications for attracting, locating or observing game, or guiding the
hunter to such game;

    IV. Hunting game confined by artificial barriers, including escape-proof fencing; or hunting game
transplanted solely for the purpose of commercial shooting.

* * * * * * * * * * * * * * * *

I certify that the trophy scored on this chart was not taken in UNFAIR CHASE as defined above by the Boone and
Crockett Club. I further certify that it was taken in full compliance with local game laws of the state,
province, or territory.

Date: _____ Signature of Hunter: _____

(Have signature notarized by a Notary Public)

is a very subjective decision. Beauty is indeed in the eyes of the beholder.
Size is not!

An examination of the mechanics of B&C measuring and scoring
is needed in order to understand the basics of how the system works.
Four types of measurements are taken in determining the score: the
inside spread of the main beams, the length of both main beams, the

length of all typical and abnormal tines and the circumference of each main beam in four places. All measurements are taken in inches to the nearest one-eighth inch. The measuring procedure for both typicals and non-typicals is the same. When scoring, however, the total length of abnormal points is subtracted to reach the final typical score but added to achieve the final non-typical score.

Measuring

Boone & Crockett measuring begins with the recording of information that helps in the description of the antlers but is not used in reaching the score. This supplemental information includes the number of scorable points on each antler, inclusive of antler tips. Although inadequate when considered alone, the number of points is the most widespread way of describing a buck among hunters. Also included is the relatively meaningless spread from main beam tip to main beam tip. The last of the supplemental data to be recorded is the greatest outside spread of the antlers. This is more commonly used by hunters to describe antler width than is inside spread. There is logic in this preference for outside spread since it measures the actual extremities of the antlers themselves, which is what forms the impression of width. Inside spread measures only the "air" between the beams. However, for scoring purposes, inside spread is a better and more consistent measurement because of the possibility that outward protruding abnormal points could artificially inflate the spread measurement and bias the final score.

The greatest inside spread of the main beams is the first measurement taken that is used in scoring. This is a singular measurement that contributes directly to the final score. The inside spread credit cannot exceed the length of the longest main beam.

Next, the total length of all abnormal points is recorded. An abnormal point is described as any point originating from another point or from the side or bottom of the main beam rather than from the top. Also, any point outside the "typical" pattern for whitetail antler conformation, especially one not paired with a corresponding point on the other antler, is considered abnormal. For a point to be counted, it must be at least one inch long.

The length of both main beams is then measured from the outside of the burr along the outer curve of the beam to the tip. The difference in the length of the two beams is then determined for later deduction when calculating the final or net score.

Each typical tine is now measured and the difference in length between each pairing is figured for later deduction. If a typical tine does not have a corresponding point on the other antler — for instance a broken brow tine or the unpaired point on a typical nine-point rack — the single point is measured but becomes a full deduction later. As a result, it is as though it never existed when the final or net score is tallied. Tine length is measured along the outside edge of the tine from the tip to the base at the place on the main beam representing the continuation of the beam as though the point were not there.

The last measurements are the four circumferences taken on each beam. The first is at the smallest place between the burr and the first typical point, usually the brow tine. The second is measured at the small-est place between the first and second tine and so on. With antlers having five or more typical points on a side (counting the beam tip), the same procedure is repeated until all four measurements are taken. On a rack with only four typical points on a side, the last circumference measure-ment is taken halfway between the last point and the tip of the main beam. The difference between each corresponding circumference is deter-mined for later deduction.

Scoring

After all the measurements have been taken, the score is then calculated. In both typicals and non-typicals, the beam length, typical tine lengths and circumferences for each antler are totaled and the totals are then added to the inside spread measurement. The sum total is the "gross typical" score. No deductions for asymmetry have been made, and abnormal points have not been considered yet. As for non-typicals, when the total inches of abnormal points are added to the gross typical score, the resulting total is the "gross non-typical" score. Although gross scores have no official status in B&C scoring, they more accurately reflect size than do the official "final" scores.

Once the gross typical score has been determined, the differences in each paired measurement are then totaled and subtracted from the gross typical score. This leads to the point where typical and non-typical scoring diverges. After symmetry differences have been deducted from the gross typical score, the total length of abnormal points is deducted from a typical's score but is added to a non-typical's score. The resulting figure is the "net" or final B&C score.

EVALUATING THE SYSTEM

As stated previously, B&C's measuring system is considered the best around, but its scoring methodology is the source of considerable debate among trophy whitetail hunters. The reasons for the contention are stiff symmetry requirements and deductions for abnormal points on typical scores.

The Symmetry Question

In typical racks, I can understand some logic in rewarding symmetry, or conversely, in penalizing for the lack of symmetry. Boone & Crockett does this by determining the difference between each paired measurement and totaling these differences for a direct deduction in reaching the final score. For example, say the first primary tine (from antler base to beam tip, tines are identified as the brow tine (G-1), first primary (G-2), second primary (G-3), etc.) is 12 inches long on a buck's right antler and 10 inches on the left. The B&C system adds the total of the two tine lengths (22 inches) into the score but then subtracts the difference (two), resulting in a net credit of 20 inches, or twice the smallest measurement. By doing this on each and every paired measurement, the typical net score is reached by doubling the weakest of each paired measurement then totaling. Many feel that requiring each individual paired measurement to be exactly symmetrical is too demanding. I agree. A less critical option that still rewards symmetry would be to total all the typical measurements for each side (not including abnormal points) and deduct the difference in these two totals. This would require symmetry in total typical measurements between each antler but not between each individual paired measurement. Of course, an argument can also be mounted that no asymmetry deductions should be made at all. Just let the gross typical score reflect the size of the antlers.

While on the subject of symmetry, Boone & Crockett's requirement that the abnormal point total for non-typical racks be added to the net typical score (reached after deducting for asymmetry) rather than the gross score appears a bit counterproductive. If it is an effort to protect

The B&C scoring system requires that each paired measurement be exactly symmetrical on typical racks. Many hunters feel this is too demanding and that it results in net scores that don't accurately reflect size. This big nine-pointer is a good example. He doesn't match up well from side to side. Although he grosses in the mid 140's, his net score is just over 130. Photo by Bill Kinney.

symmetry, and it must be, it seems rather futile. Abnormal points are very often present in a helter-skelter and asymmetrical fashion, which most likely will offset any aesthetic sensitivities protected by deducting for symmetry differences in the base typical score.

The Issue of Abnormal Points

Although the symmetry question in scoring is a personal call, direct deductions for abnormal (non-typical) points on a typical rack clearly seem too severe. First of all, nearly all trophy hunters view the presence of abnormal points, i.e., forks, "sticker" points, drop tines, etc., as a plus rather than a negative. And, most truly big bucks, even basic typicals and especially the heavy-antlered bucks in the northern United States and Canada, have some non-typical points. This is the norm rather than the exception. Abnormal points usually come with age and antler mass, and hunters welcome them as giving a buck "character." Even when non-typical points are perfectly matched, they are still deducted on a typical buck in B&C scoring. I would prefer seeing them ignored in typical scoring rather than deducted, even if doing so means the minimum score to qualify for the record book is raised. If enough abnormal points are present on a rack, the antlers can be scored as a non-typical by simply adding in the abnormal point total.

The Problem

Because of the emphasis on symmetry and the penalty for extra points in typicals, not only can the final B&C score fail to reflect the true size of a buck, it is very possible for a smaller buck to score higher than a much larger, more impressive buck. For example, suppose a buck has a gross typical score of 190 but has symmetry differences of 12 points and 10 inches of non-typical points in the form of a couple of sticker points and a drop tine. After deducting the 22 points, his net typical B&C score would be 168, two points short of the record-book minimum. (Relatively speaking, he falls even further short of the records as a non-typical with a net non-typical score of 188.) Let's say a second buck has a 172 gross typical score with only two points of symmetry deductions and no extra points. His net typical score of 170 is higher than the first buck's and places him in the B&C records. Compare him to the first buck with a gross typical score of 190 and a total of 200 inches of antlers atop his head but with a net typical B&C score of only 168. Which deer is larger? Which deer is the better trophy? Which deer would you shoot if the two were standing side by side? The only reason anyone would shoot the smaller buck, all things being equal, is because he makes the record book, while the much larger one doesn't. Is this a problem with the first

This symmetrical 10-pointer from South Texas is built to score well on the B&C system. His gross typical score is close to 150, and his net score is about two inches below gross. Photo by Mike Biggs.

deer or a problem with the way he is scored?

My intention here is not to knock the Boone & Crockett Club but rather to evaluate its measuring and scoring system from the trophy hunter's point of view. It is important for those who use this system to understand it. Through years of professional and dedicated work, the Boone & Crockett Club has earned the right to be recognized as the official measuring, scoring and record-keeping organization for North American big game, including whitetails. Yet, the B&C system does include subjective criteria regarding what is and is not desirable in a trophy whitetail. Because of this subjective criteria, the B&C net scores do not always rank deer by antler size and often do not accurately reflect the true size. This is not necessarily a matter of right or wrong. It's more a matter of preference. When the B&C "trophy evaluation" system was conceived in 1950, it was decided that symmetry and no abnormal points on typicals were more important than actual antler size. The B&C scoring system reflects that decision.

Gross Scores Reflect Size

If a deer is near or over record-book size, I obviously have a keen interest in the net score and whether the buck qualifies for the lofty status of having made "The Book." Otherwise, I am more interested in a score that accurately reflects the size of the antlers. Only by actually seeing a rack can I make my own subjective decision about its aesthetic appeal. Even then, it will just be my opinion. In the meantime, give me the facts about size. The B&C gross scores do this very well. The gross typical score reveals the true size of the buck's "basic

This great Georgia buck falls through the cracks of the B&C scoring system. He's too typical to score well as a non-typical and too non-typical to score well as a typical. His basic 12-point typical frame scores 172, enough to make the B&C record book. However, he has two drop tines, one nine inches long and the other four inches long. Since Boone & Crockett deducts all abnormal points from the net typical score, he only nets 159 as a typical. His non-typical score is 185, well short of the 195 needed to make the records. Yet, he is bigger than many bucks that do qualify for the records. His drop tines are the problem!

typical frame" — no deductions for asymmetry, no arbitrary penalties for extra points. The gross non-typical score is an even more accurate reflection of absolute size. It tells precisely how many total inches of scorable antlers the buck actually grew!

It would be most interesting to see a listing of the top gross typicals and non-typicals. That information is recorded on score sheets and is probably available to Boone & Crockett. Such a listing would reveal what bucks are truly the largest ever taken in their respective classes. I doubt if the top non-typicals would change very much, but I believe the top typicals would be rearranged significantly. Perhaps Boone & Crockett will someday provide such a listing as an ancillary table.

Now, a closing comment on describing a buck beyond just his score. When one hunter talks to another about a trophy buck, not only is the score of interest, but so is a description of the buck's appearance. A pretty good job of painting a picture of a buck can be accomplished by coupling the gross score with the outside spread, the number of points and perhaps a mention of any notable features, i.e., exceptional mass, interesting abnormal points, extraordinary beam or tine length, etc. In the case of non-typicals, facts about the basic typical frame (specifically, the number of typical points and the gross typical score) help reveal what a buck is actually like. Of course, a description can get too complicated. That's why I generally try to keep it simple. Something like "he's a 22-inch 10-pointer grossing 165" says plenty!

Chapter 4

Judging Bucks
In The Field

I WANTED TO SHOOT HIM. I knew I should shoot him. He was one of those bucks so big you shoot him on sight. No judging necessary ... normally. But, this was an unusual situation. I had a full week of hunting left on this Canadian foray, and I already had a 158-point typical in the bag. Two bucks were legal. But with rumors, and the sign to support them, of a couple of 180-class bucks in the area, I was reluctant to settle for anything less than a record. The rut was in full swing. I was seeing plenty of bucks. And, I had time. Yet when I looked at the buck standing before me, I couldn't believe I hadn't already shot him.

"I don't think he'll make the book," I thought to myself as I traded my 7mm Rem. Mag. for 10X Leitz binoculars. "But, he'll be close ... real close."

He was broadside at 75 yards. I still hadn't seen him straight on, but what was on his near beam almost got him shot. His left antler was heavy and dark. The three massive tines arising from his beam told me he had a total of five points on that side, counting the main beam tip and the brow tine.

"A 10-pointer!" I shouted in my mind. I forced back the urge to

This buck, which has 22 assorted points, is so big that there's no need to worry about field-judging or field-scoring. Just shoot! Photo by Curt Helmick.

shoot as I turned my attention to the other antler. "Nooo! Only two tines up. A four-pointer on that side. He's a big nine. He'll score as a basic eight. He'll still be close. Need to field-score him."

A quick check told me his first two primary tines matched up on both sides. "What about brows?" I thought, racing down my mental checklist.

The right brow tine had a five-inch sticker point coming off the base, a direct deduction. Aside from this, his basic eight-point frame was symmetrical. All I had to do was score one side of his basic eight frame, then double it and add spread. That would give me a rough net score, after deducting the five-inch sticker point off the brow tine. The extra typical point was a wash. I'd ignore it.

I began my calculations. "Main beam, 25. At least 18 inches in circumferences. That's 43 so far. A six-inch brow gives 49. Twelve on the back tine and 10 on the second. Total, 71. Double that is 142. Spread? Haven't seen it yet. I'll give him 20. At least 162. Probably better. Knock off five for the odd point. He'll net over 155 as an eight-pointer. Gross is around 170."

Just as I concluded my figuring, the buck turned to face me for the first time. I knew instantly my calculations were off. He wasn't 20 inches inside; he was 22. His beams, which were impressive from the side, turned inward, almost touching in the middle. They were at least two inches longer than I had estimated. Still not record book but big enough!

"The heck with it! I'm shooting!" I relented with immense relief.

I dropped my binoculars and grabbed my rifle. Unfortunately, my allotted time was up with this buck. The doe he had followed into the small clearing unexpectedly bolted. The buck was right on her tail. I had just enough time to get off a hurried shot as the buck disappeared into the brush 90 yards away. A string of hair in the snow was all I had to show for my encounter.

In all my years of hunting trophy whitetails, I look on that two-minute incident as the worst I have ever blown it. I had him cold but let him get away. He would have been one of my most impressive bucks ever. All the talk of B&C bucks had caused me to lose sight of reality. You shoot that kind of buck when he comes along … if he comes along. Forget judging him. You know instantly he's a shooter. I did, but over-judging cost me a great trophy.

There is another side to the judging coin, however. A trophy hunter can shoot before he knows enough about the buck. That happened to me on my last Montana whitetail. I was hunting with Chuck Larsen, my friend and business partner, on a great ranch along the Missouri River in eastern Montana. We were four days into the week-long hunt. I had averaged seeing at least 20 bucks a day and had passed up several 135 to 145-class bucks, including a couple that were regular visitors to a nearby alfalfa field. I was sure that almost any afternoon I could get one of these bucks, specifically a 20-inch nine-pointer in the 145 class. I set out to improve upon him.

On our fourth morning, I had chosen to hunt a portable tree-stand along a series of major trails leading from a large, heavily used sugar beet field to a thick stand of cedars where the deer bedded. About 9 a.m., I saw a buck moving quickly through a stand of poplar trees about 125 yards to my right. From the side, he appeared to be a good buck. There was no time to put the glasses on him so I cranked my scope to 8X and judged him through it. His left beam, the one nearest me, was fairly heavy. His tines had ample length. I was pretty sure he had five points on the side closest to me. He had the makings of a respectable buck. This impression was fostered by a huge body. I had no idea about his other side or about his width, and there was no time for further investigation. The buck was obviously late for his nap and would disappear in seconds. The moment of decision had arrived. Shoot now or forget it.

What I could see was promising, perhaps better than anything I had seen. It is possible that my judgment was clouded by the minus 20 degree temperature, but I decided to chance it. His head was already in the cedars when the 7mm Rem. Mag. split the silence of that cold Montana morning.

After stumbling through two feet of snow, I reached the buck. The fact that no beam stood above the snow, or even above his visible ear, gave me my first clue all was not well. I reached into the snow and lifted his rack. Just as I had thought, his left side had good mass and five typical points. A matched set of forked brow tines even added character to his rack. But, his right side sported only four points, making him a basic nine-pointer. That, however, was not the worst of it. He was only 13½

Judging too fast can lead to a mistake. That's what happened when I made a hasty decision to shoot this Montana buck based on a look from only one side. He turned out to be just 13½ inches wide ... outside! Photo by Chuck Larsen.

inches wide ... outside! If there's anything I don't like, it's a "pinchy-horned" buck. I was now the owner of the definitive pinchy-horn!

In my defense, he did gross 134 on the strength of long tines and good mass. Today, the antlers of that buck are my tried-and-true "rattling horns." But, he was a mistake that cost me a near-sure bet at a 20-inch, 145-point buck. This was a case of having to judge too quickly.

Those two stories represent the range of circumstances hunters can encounter when trying to judge whitetails in the field. Actually, the opportunity given to judge the second buck is far more representative of the norm than the first. Seldom is there time to actually calculate a "field-score" as I did on the Canadian buck. Most of the time, a trophy hunter has but a few seconds to judge and shoot. In fact, all too often he only has time to judge or to shoot, but not time to do both. Because of the time problem, trophy hunters have a far greater need to learn how to "field-judge" than to "field-score." Let's define the two.

To field-score, the hunter actually tries to determine specific dimensions, as I did in Canada, in order to calculate a score. This takes time, a lot of practice, a good look at the buck (preferably from several angles) and considerable presence of mind in an unnerving situation. Field-scoring is the ultimate refinement of field-judging, and knowing how to field-score is very helpful in becoming a better field-judge. Yet, actual field-scoring has limited application for most trophy hunters and hunting situations.

To field-judge, the hunter must quickly decide if the buck meets his trophy standards based on an overall "impression" of size and, if given time, a few key indicators. If given no more than an instant, the hunter must make a snap-judgement whether to shoot or not. That's risky business since an impression is often formed from incomplete information, as was the case when I shot the narrow Montana buck. However, give a good field-judge a few seconds to flesh out his impression, and he can eliminate most of the guesswork about a buck's size. In fact, given a good enough look, some experienced trophy hunters can closely estimate the score of a buck within seconds of seeing him ... without going through the calculations necessary in actual field-scoring. That takes experience and comes from having seen, studied and measured a bunch of bucks. But, there are some principles that will help improve anyone's field-judging skills. We'll start at the beginning.

FIELD-JUDGING

A trophy buck must be at least 3½ years old according to this book's definition. Given that, let's briefly look at how to identify 1½ and 2½-year-old bucks, the two age classes that don't meet minimum trophy standards.

The Non-Qualifiers

A yearling or 1½-year-old is the easiest antlered buck to recognize in the field. With his small body and slender appearance, he looks somewhat like a doe with antlers. He has a straight belly profile. Though his neck can swell a little during the rut, it normally is rather slim. His face, with its big eyes and delicate features, bears the look of youth. A yearling's antlers may be anything from barely visible spikes to a small eight-point rack. A 1½ can even have 9 or 10 points on rare occasions. His spread will seldom exceed 10 to 12 inches, and his rack sits between

This is a remarkable buck. Although he is large enough to be considered a trophy in many regions, the buck is only 2½ years old! He represents one of the exceptions that exist in any generality about whitetails. Photo by Curt Helmick.

his ears like a baseball cap. The small, tight rack and slender, doe-like features of a 1½-year-old are sure tip-offs of his age.

A 2½-year-old is harder to identify in the field than a 1½ since he has characteristics of both the yearling and an older buck. The body of a 2½ will have started to show some bulk, but 2½'s are not yet as deep-chested or big-necked as they will be later. A 2½ has a more blockish face than a yearling's, but the big-eyed look of adolescence is still there. The antlers of a 2½ can be fairly good, but they lack mass and seldom exceed 14 to 15 inches in width. Eight points are common, and 9 to 10 points are sometimes seen in good habitat. Abnormal points are rare in 2½'s.

A 2½ can best be summed up as a nice buck that promises of things to come but clearly is not yet there.

Before going on, some qualification is necessary. While general statements can be made about the age/size relationship in deer, there are many and notable exceptions, both from region to region and within a given deer herd. For instance, great regional differences exist between a 2½-year-old buck in Central Wisconsin and a buck of the same age in Hill Country Texas. The naturally large-bodied Wisconsin deer of that age may weigh 190 pounds and carry a 125-point rack. The much smaller Texas Hill Country buck may weigh 110 pounds and have an 85-point rack. To describe the size characteristics of an age class in one region does not necessarily describe that same age class for all regions.

Significant variations in the age/size relationship also occur within the same deer population. A 3½-year-old South Texas buck killed by Richard Jackson of Tallahassee, Florida, and aged by well-known Texas biologist Murphy Ray illustrates the point well. Although the "average"

3½ from that part of the world probably scores from 115 to 120, Richard's 24-inch 12-pointer violated the norm with a gross typical score of 163 and a net of 158! In Georgia, 2½'s average less than 100 gross B&C points. Yet, I have personally scored a 2½-year-old 11-pointer at 142 typical. On top of that, many of Georgia's B&C bucks have been 3½'s … in a state where the average 3½ won't score 120! In Mississippi, the state record non-typical killed in 1988 scored 225 and was 3½ years old! Talk about defying the norm!

What Are You After?

In field-judging, the first thing a hunter must do is decide what he is after. Our definition of a trophy not only requires that a buck be at least 3½, but he must also be among the best bucks consistently taken in that given area. The last part leaves some room for individual interpretation. Each hunter has to set his own personal minimum trophy standard. As discussed in Chapter 1, the size potential of the place he is hunting, his own hunting skills, the time available and the conditions under which he is hunting all must be considered. A clear trophy goal should be the result.

Perhaps any buck 3½ years old or older is the only realistic goal in your area. Maybe your goal is a 120-class buck. Or, a 130-class. A 140-class. A 150 may even be practical where you hunt. Remember, establishing the goal before you go hunting is critical. When the buck is standing before you is no time to decide on trophy standards. An adrenalin overload can lead to a bad decision without the discipline that comes from a clear, objective goal determined in advance. (Note: The term "class" means the buck's gross B&C score is plus or minus three or so points of the designated score.)

A Clear Mental Image

Now that a trophy goal has been established, the hunter must form a clear image in his mind of what such a buck looks like where he hunts. This is key to field-judging. Experience enters the picture here. Hunters with more experience have a clearer mental image of what they are looking for and can recognize a buck meeting their criteria far quicker and with a greater degree of accuracy than someone of less experience. Hunting a certain size buck without knowing what he looks like would

It is important to decide what your personal trophy minimum is before you go hunting, not when the buck is standing before you. If you're after a 130-class buck, this deer is what you are looking for. Photo By Bill Kinney.

be similar to ordering a meal from a French menu when you can't read French. You may have an idea what you want, but if you can't recognize it, you're likely to get anything!

Over the years, I have come to rely on a rather simple procedure to help me recognize the buck I'm after. Basically, it involves burning into my mind an image of what the "stereotype" buck of that size would look like. The concept is a bit like studying a photo of a stranger before you have to pick him out of a crowd at a busy airport. Instead of a photo, I use actual dimensions to quantify the size and to draw a more precise mental "picture" of the representative trophy I seek. This technique also helps better understand measuring and scoring and directly improves field-judging and field-scoring skills. Examples will best illustrate the procedure.

In Georgia, my trophy minimum is a 130-class buck. I have a clear image of what the stereotype 130-point Georgia buck looks like. He is a well-shaped, 19-inch (outside) eight-pointer with average mass, solid brow tines and good length on all four primary tines. That "image" translates into these actual measurements: 21-inch main beams, 17-inch inside spread, 14 inches of mass per beam, four-inch brow tines and nine-inch primaries. Such is a 130-class buck. When I see a buck in the field fitting these dimensions, I know him immediately. It's like recognizing an acquaintance walking down the street. If he's weaker or stronger than "average" in a certain dimension, I can easily recognize that. A quick judgment can determine whether or not a weakness is sufficiently offset by a strength. If, for instance, his tines appear short, maybe seven to eight inches long, does exceptional mass or a wide spread offset the lack of tine length? If not, he's not a shooter.

I recently hunted a Texas ranch where my trophy minimum was a 155-class buck. There, the stereotype for this size deer is a 10-pointer with a 21-inch outside spread, nice "sweep" to the antlers, average mass, solid brow tines and good tine length, especially on the third primaries. His actual dimensions would call for a 19-inch inside spread, 24-inch main beams, 16 inches of circumferences per side, four-inch brows, 9 and 10-inch first and second primaries and five-inch third primaries. The buck I shot on that trip scored 158⅞. He was a 10-pointer with a 19½-inch inside spread (21½ inches outside), 24-inch main beams, 16½ inches of mass per side, five-inch brows, eight and nine-inch first and second primaries and seven-inch thirds. They don't always conform to the stereotype this closely.

Nothing replaces experience in forming a clear image of the buck you want or in recognizing him in the field. But, field experience takes time and can be a slow go in many places. One of the best alternatives to accelerate the process is to study mounted bucks from the area you are hunting. Really look them over. Take detailed measurements and compare the antlers to the deer's head and ears. If a game reserve or park is available nearby where you can see live bucks, all the better. Game department check stations are excellent places to study bucks of all sizes. Photos in books and magazines will help, but they can be deceptive. The point is to know what you're hunting and what it looks like. Practice does make better — albeit not perfect.

Alas, there is a variable in the equation that can change the "appear-

Body size is a major variable in judging whitetail antlers. I was fooled by this buck while hunting the King Ranch in South Texas. Instead of being a 150-class buck as I thought, the deer turned out to score 142. I hadn't counted on a live weight of only 134 pounds! Photo by Amos Dewitt.

ance" of antler size. That variable is body size. It's not hard to understand. A 130-point rack on a 140-pound Florida buck looks entirely different than a rack of the same size on a 230-pound Maine buck. In addition, the antler shape and dimensions of bucks of the same score will differ from place to place around the country. You must know what your trophy minimum looks like on the deer where you are hunting.

This problem was brought home to me very clearly a few years ago. After hunting Georgia for three weeks, I traveled to Saskatchewan, Canada, looking for something in the mid 150's or better. Two days into the hunt I passed up a 10-pointer I thought would score in the upper 140's. Fortunately, I had another chance at him four days later and realized he was better than I had first thought. He ended up scoring just under 160. I had not taken into account a body size pushing 300 pounds. A month later found me on the King Ranch in coastal South Texas. My sights were set on a 150. The first afternoon out with my guide, Amos Dewitt,

I came across a buck that put my heart into overdrive. He looked like a solid 150, even after factoring in the knowledge these deer were smaller bodied than bucks in either Canada or Georgia. When I walked over to where he fell, I actually thought I had found a different buck from the one I had shot. I could not believe the ground shrinkage! My 150-point-plus buck turned out to be a 134-pound (live weight), 142-point buck! If a Canadian buck appeared as large as that Texas buck did, he would easily make the record books. Body size must be taken into account. For the traveling hunter, that's not always easy.

Confirming the Size

Most opportunities at trophy bucks allow no more than a fleeting moment to match a preconceived mental image to an impression of size. From that, a shot must be made or forgotten. There are, however, times when a hunter has a few seconds, maybe even a minute or longer to analyze a buck. When such an opportunity arises, there are some criteria that can be used to further pin down the size of the critical dimensions.

If given time, one of the first things I check is the number of points. The first impression often reveals much about spread, mass and tine length. But, the number of points is sometimes uncertain until studied through the magnification of a scope or binoculars, which are essential in field-judging and field-scoring. Of greatest interest is how many primary points arise from the main beam. If there are two primaries on each beam, I know he's an eight-pointer, assuming brow tines are present. If three primaries are standing, he's a 10-pointer. Just that information alone can be enough to sway the decision to shoot or not. Once I verify primaries, brows are next. Are they both present? If so, what size? The presence of any abnormal tines only heightens my interest in the buck.

The angle from which the antlers are viewed will determine what tines can be seen. From straight on, the brows are most visible. Whether or not all the primaries are visible from the front view depends on the shape of the rack. Often, the primaries line up from this view and are difficult to count, making it necessary for the buck to turn for all the primaries to be visible. A side view will allow the nearside beam and its primaries to be seen, but caution is in order. An offside tine sometimes can be mistaken for an additional point. Be sure.

Often, it is very difficult to count points when a deer is looking straight at you. Here's a classic example. From the front, this buck looks very mediocre, but when the side view reveals all his points, it's another story. This 15-point buck grosses in the 160's! Photos by Mike Biggs.

A quartering view may allow a look at all tines. Each rack is different.

Next, I try to determine tine length. The first impression of good tine length sometimes comes from the longest tines. Others may be significantly shorter. A quick check will tell if any are unduly short or broken. On a 10-pointer, I pay special attention to the length of the third primaries. When all else checks out, this tine is where the score can run up on a buck. Third primaries over five or so inches constitute a solid 10-pointer. Brow tines can also greatly affect the score. In Texas, brow tines tend to be short and thin and many bucks break off one or both during the rut. Just one broken brow tine on a buck with, say, a remaining five-inch brow reduces his net typical score by 10 points. Longer than usual brows can elevate a marginal buck into a shooter class.

I have found that tines can be categorized into length groupings based on the appearance of their length. On antlers in the 135 class or better, primary tines of less than seven inches "appear" short. Primaries from seven to nine inches appear appropriate or average. Tines topping nine or 10 inches appear long. For brows, anything less than 2½ inches seems short. From 2½ to 4½ inches appears appropriate. Over 4½ inches

*Tine length adds up in a hurry. This buck will score about 140 on the
strength of six-inch brow tines and 13 or 14-inch first primaries. Although
good width makes a buck look larger, spread is not a major factor in scoring.
Photo by Mike Biggs.*

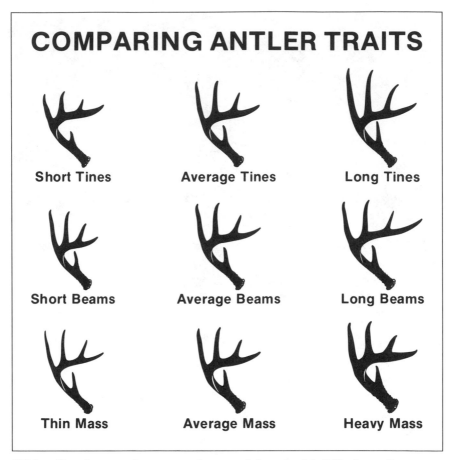

COMPARING ANTLER TRAITS

Short Tines   **Average Tines**   **Long Tines**

Short Beams   **Average Beams**   **Long Beams**

Thin Mass   **Average Mass**   **Heavy Mass**

Whitetail antlers come in so many shapes and sizes that it's difficult to tell someone exactly how to judge them in the field. Experience is invaluable in determining relative tine length, beam length and mass. However, this chart gives the hunter a general idea of the judgments involved.

gives the appearance of being long. It is worth noting that the inward curve or the forward slant of tines can cause them to look shorter than they are. Conversely, straight tines can appear longer than they'll measure.

The Luxury Details

If a hunter gets this far in judging a buck, the chances are good that he'll know enough to make a decision. Sufficient spread, mass and main beam information probably would have been gleaned from the first impression or from the tine evaluation that followed. But if time and

Mass is an obvious characteristic, and this buck obviously has it! This record-class whitetail has over 20 inches of circumferences per side. Photo by Curt Helmick.

circumstances allow, considering these other aspects of a rack can be helpful in your final decision.

Mass is an obvious characteristic. If a rack is thin, it looks so. If it is heavy, that will be one of the first things noticed. Average mass appears appropriate for the rack. For an eight-pointer in the 130 class, I use a total circumference measurement of 14 inches per side to represent average mass. Anything less than 13 inches is thin. Mass topping 15 or 16 inches per side is heavy. For a 150-class 10-pointer, 16 is average, less than 15 is thin and over 17 or 18 is heavy. The massive northern bucks can have circumference totals well into the 20's on each side. An eight-pointer with the same relative mass as a 10-pointer will measure about an inch less in his circumferences per side since an eight-pointer's fourth measurement (taken halfway between the last tine and the tip of the main beam) comes from farther out the beam. With four mass measurements per side, exceptional weight really can add up in the score. Since I don't like spindly antlers, mass is very important to me.

Main beam length is one of the more difficult features to accurately determine. The shape of the antlers can affect the appearance of beam length. The height of the beams above the head, the distance they come back before arcing forward, the distance they extend toward the nose and how far they turn in toward the middle are all factors to be considered. No one indicator can be used to determine beam length. Some say if the beam extends to or past the nose, it's long. Often that's true, but one buck of mine has antlers an inch past his nose with a beam length of only 23 inches. The beams of a similar scoring buck on the wall next to him turn inward four inches short of his nose, but they measure 26 inches.

While no one indicator accurately reflects beam length, I have found that the overall impression of beam length usually is fairly accurate. Short beams look short when studied in relation to the overall rack. Long beams have a way of being evident. Average beams appear appropriate. For 130-class bucks, 20 to 21-inch main beams are about average. Bucks in the 140 range could be expected to have 22 to 23-inch beams. The beams of 150-class bucks will probably average close to 24 inches. The super bucks can have 25 to 30-inch beams. If the main beam doesn't look disproportionately short or long, I assume it is average length for the size buck I'm judging.

Spread is best judged when the buck is facing directly toward you with his ears forward. If you know the spread of a buck's ears, figuring antler width is fairly easy. Small-bodied deer have ear spreads of about 16 inches. Medium-sized deer, those in the 160 to 200-pound range, have ears with about a 17-inch spread. The ears of the biggest bucks span 18 inches. Either the inside or outside spread can be estimated when a buck is accommodating enough to face you with his ears forward. The outside

If you like spread, here it is in spades! This super-wide buck has a spread of about 25 inches inside and 27 inches outside. However, his tines are relatively short. The nine-pointer will score around 140. Photo by Mike Biggs.

spread of a big buck is usually 1½ to 2 inches greater than inside spread. Little or nothing can be determined about spread when the antlers are viewed from the side. A quartering angle will reveal general width. A rear view will show full width. But remember, the spread always appears wider from the rear, maybe by as much as two or three inches! Like other dimensions, I like to lump spreads into groupings. To me, inside spreads of 15 inches or less are narrow. Fifteen to 19 inches inside is average. Over 19 is wide. Spread, being only one measurement, counts relatively little in the overall score unless it leans to one extreme or the other. But after spindly horned bucks, my strongest bias is against very narrow spreads.

Do You Like Him?

The only other consideration in field-judging is whether or not you like the deer. There are a few bucks that meet all the size requirements but are just plain ugly. I passed up one such buck repeatedly over a week's hunt in Montana. He was an upper 140's 10-pointer with a 13-inch drop tine off the base of his right beam. Sounds good doesn't he? However, he was exceptionally ugly. His rack stuck straight up with almost no curve to his beams. From the front he looked like a huge spike with stickers. The drop tine came down over his face like the shovel of a caribou. His 10 points were fully visible only from the side. Another big buck easily making the size requirements escaped my bullet in Manitoba, Canada, because one main beam was six to eight inches higher than the other. His antlers were warp-sided. Certainly, size is the major consideration, but you still have to like a buck.

It is possible to come across a buck that doesn't quite make the size grade but is still a desirable trophy. Abnormal points like drop tines, forks or several sticker points could do it. Extreme spread or mass may strike a hunter's fancy. I ran into an impressive but slightly undersized buck on a hunt a while back that I couldn't resist. Though I was looking for something over 150, when a 21-inch, heavy eight-pointer came along with a big fork in his left first primary, I shot him. With a gross score of 147, he had the frame of a 150-class 10-pointer. He was just missing the third primaries.

That does bring up an interesting point: Eight-pointers of the same score as 10-pointers are almost always more impressive. Why? The absence of the two third primary tines means that they have to make those inches up in mass, spread, tine length or beam length, i.e., their basic frame. It is this basic frame of height, width and mass that gives the impression of size.

As I said earlier in this chapter, the best and most experienced field-judges actually can estimate the score of a buck within seconds of seeing him. No figuring or calculating is necessary, at least not consciously. From long years of experience, they know instinctively what a buck of that size will score. The only "hard" information they must have is the number of points and their general length. They gain sufficient information about width, mass and beam length from overall impression. Even the best can be fooled sometimes, but experience brings surprising accuracy and consistency.

Size is not the only consideration. You also have to like a buck. This old guy doesn't score real high, probably 140 or so, but he sure has appeal. Note the unshed velvet still on his antlers. Photo by Bill Kinney.

FIELD-SCORING

For most trophy hunters and hunting situations, actual field-scoring is somewhat academic. First of all, seldom is the time and opportunity sufficient. Secondly, few hunters require that a potential shooter be sized to a specific score before deciding whether or not to shoot. Thirdly, most hunters lack the experience necessary to accurately estimate dimensions under the stress and trying conditions of the field.

I knew the instant this buck came into view that he was a great trophy. The only question was how quickly I could shoot him. He grossed nearly 180, but abnormal points caused him to fall just shy of the record book.

When

For the serious trophy hunter, however, there are certain situations where field-scoring can be helpful in deciding upon a potential trophy. One such time is when the hunter is likely to have a choice between several potential shooters. A misjudgment here could mean the loss of a near-sure chance at a buck that would meet the hunter's trophy standards. Field-scoring also can be good insurance against a mistake when a marginal buck walks into view. Often, the difference between a shooter and a non-shooter is only an inch or two here and there. Field-scoring can help objectively quantify these important subtleties during what is normally an adrenalin-charged time. This could prevent a hunter from learning firsthand about that thing called "ground shrinkage."

If there are marginal or potential bucks, then there must also be bucks that are obviously too small to consider and some clearly so large as to require no further consideration. There are. Lucky indeed is the hunter who sees a buck so large that he knows immediately a great trophy is before him. A buck like this is easy to recognize. Don't let any more time pass than is required. Every second wasted represents missed opportunity that may later be looked back on with regret. These exceptional bucks have an uncanny way of escaping encounters with hunters unscathed. Take the first good shot you have at them. That's a lesson I learned the hard way.

How

In field-scoring, the basic principle is to score one side of the rack, double it and add inside spread to reach a rough total score. On symmetrical typical racks, this results in an accurate total score. On typicals with an unmatched typical tine, such as a nine-pointer, I ignore the unmatched tine to reach a rough net score. I then add the unmatched typical point to the net score to reach a gross score. The same procedure is used to field-score bucks with non-typical points. Just add in the abnormal tines after reaching the total for the basic typical frame.

The first step in field-scoring is to estimate the length of the main beam. Does it look shorter or longer than average? Next, I estimate the total of all circumference measurements for one beam. I don't worry about the individual measurements. That would be too cumbersome in the field. I know what the average mass in inches is for a buck of a given size. From that standard, I add or subtract inches based on the mass of the buck before me. After estimating the main beam length and the total of the mass measurements for one antler, I add them together.

Tine length is now added to the score. For the moment, only the paired typical tines are considered. If the lengths of the individual paired tines are significantly different, I use the rough average of the two. The brow tine is added in first, followed by the first primary, then the second, etc. When the lengths for all paired tines on one antler are added to the total for beam length and mass, the typical score for one side is reached. This total is now doubled. Then, the inside spread is added. The result-

Let's field-score the clean 10-pointer pictured here from two angles. He's a northern deer so he'll weigh upwards of 200 pounds. To field-score, estimate the measurements for one side, double them and add inside spread. Here we go. Main beam length, 24 inches. Main beam circumferences, 17 inches to a side. That's 41 inches so far. Brow tine, three inches. First primary, 11 inches. Total of 55. Second primary, nine inches. 64. Third primary, five inches. A total of 69 inches per side. Double that is 138. Add an inside spread of 21 inches. The final score is 159. The net and gross scores of this very symmetrical buck won't differ by more than two or three points. Photos by Curt Helmick.

ing total is the rough net typical score. The gross score is reached by adding in the unmatched typical points and abnormal points.

An example will show how the procedure works and the circumstances under which it may be used. Let's assume you're hunting for a 130-class buck on a deer club in western Kentucky. A buck steps into the edge of a cut cornfield about 75 yards from your deer stand. He begins to feed. The wind is in your favor. You see though your binoculars that he's a good eight-pointer, but you're not sure he'll score better than 130. You decide to field-score him. It might go like this:

"Beam length looks average. Give him 21 inches. Mass is slightly above average. Probably 15. Total is 36. Very good brows. At least six inches. Total, 42. First primary is 11 inches on right, but two inches shorter on left. Give him 10. That's 52. Second primary is eight. Sixty.

Double that is 120. Inside spread is 16. Total is 136!" The next sound you hear is the safety sliding forward on your gun.

The procedure is actually very simple and straightforward. With experience, field-scoring can be completed in 30 or so seconds, or certainly less than a minute. Always be conservative in your estimates. Excitement exaggerates the size.

In summary, the speed and accuracy of field-judging depends on how clear a mental image the hunter has of the buck he's after and how complete his impression is of the buck he's judging. If time allows, a quick check of the number of points and their length can firm up a decision. In places where many chances at potential shooters are possible or when a marginal buck shows himself, field-scoring can be helpful in pinning down the size and preventing a mistake. If, however, a buck comes along that is so big, so awesome that you know instantly he's something special, forget all of the above and shoot that buck immediately!

Section III

The "Where" Of Hunting Trophy Whitetails

Chapter 5

Sizing Up
The Trophy Prospects
Where You Hunt

THE ROUTINE WAS A FAMILIAR ONE. Slipping silently, sometimes crouching, even crawling along the well-traveled game trail through the thick brush, my every move was slow and calculated. My eyes searched unceasingly for a telltale patch of hide, a horizontal line among the tangled stems or perhaps a hint of movement to give away my quarry. Big tracks and fresh droppings along the trail encouraged me in my pursuit. I had done this countless times before, but this hunt was different.

After nearly an hour of measuring each footfall and straining and twisting to avoid limbs in the thicket, a welcome opening lay ahead. Just short of the edge, I stopped and studied the small clearing. Nothing. I slowly moved into the open and enjoyed the relief of temporary freedom from the confines and pitfalls of the thick brush. My eyes scanned the surroundings as I mentally mapped the route of my continuing hunt. I would skirt the edge of the clearing, using the scattered brush along the fringe to conceal my movement. I had to be careful now. This was no place for a mistake. Somehow, I knew the trophy I had come for was near.

Hunting pressure will largely determine which of these bucks you are likely to kill. If you hunt a heavily pressured area, a buck like the 1½-year-old on the right may be the best you can find. If the place you hunt receives little pressure, you have a chance of running into something like the 12-pointer on the left. Photo by Mike Biggs.

With painful deliberateness, I began moving along the edge, watching the brushy hill just beyond the clearing. Then, a faint sound stopped me. The .300 Win. Mag. slipped from my shoulder. A limb cracked at the foot of the hill. A couple of quick steps forward gave me a clear view of the hillside. Those two unguarded steps brought an immediate response. Something big crashed up the hill. My eyes fixed on a small area of low, scattered brush. When he crossed there, I would have my shot ... if he was what I was after. The instant he came into view, I knew it was him. A 180-grain bullet slammed into his rib cage. He staggered but continued up the hill. His shoulder absorbed the fatal impact of the second bullet, and he fell heavily to the ground.

That fateful afternoon had been played out exactly like so many whitetail hunts before — the careful stalk in thick cover, the reading of sign and the tension of challenging an animal with far better senses than

Everytime a buck is killed, there's a void left where that buck once was. If too many bucks are harvested from a herd, in time there simply won't be any older, trophy bucks left. And, the best hunter in the world can't kill something that's not there!

my own. There had been that inexplicable feeling that he was near, followed by the exhilaration of finally seeing and shooting that prized trophy. Yes, I had been there many times before — in Georgia, Alabama, Texas, Oklahoma, Montana, Canada, Mexico and other such locations. But, this time was different. I was not in North America; I was in Tanzania, Africa. And, the trophy I walked up to that warm July afternoon in 1983 was not a whitetail; it was that magnificent African antelope, the greater kudu!

Hunting greater kudu is almost exactly like hunting trophy whitetails. The kudu lives in the same type habitat, has the same superior senses and is just as wary and elusive as the whitetail. The same skills and tactics are called for. All time and effort I had put into whitetail hunting over the years had made me a pretty darn good kudu hunter. Why, then, had I not killed a kudu before that day in 1983? The reason is simple: I had never before hunted where greater kudu live! Obvious isn't it? Yet, countless would-be trophy whitetail hunters around the country go through the motions of hunting trophy bucks year after year and never kill one for the very same reason I had never shot a kudu. They are hunting where no trophy whitetails exist ... or so few that their chances of success are practically nil!

You see, nobody, but nobody can kill something that isn't there! It's not a question of skill or tactics. Those things only become factors in success when the game you seek is present. This is as true for trophy whitetails as it is for kudu. The most skillful whitetail hunter in the world using the most deadly tactics in existence will not kill a trophy buck where none exist. Yet, even the fabled "little old lady in tennis shoes" could kill one while driving down the road in her car in a place where such bucks live. The only absolute prerequisite for killing a trophy whitetail is being where there are trophy whitetails! That being the case, let's explore the major factors determining the presence, and huntability, of trophy bucks.

HUNTING PRESSURE

Hunting pressure has to be at the top of the list of factors influencing trophy prospects. It directly impacts the buck age structure, the buck/doe ratio and the huntability of the bucks, that is, the predictability of their daily and seasonal patterns and their daylight movement. A close look at these three elements will reveal their importance in your trophy hunting success.

Buck Age Structure

The greatest impact of hunting pressure is seen in the buck age structure, which is simply the distribution of bucks throughout the various age classes. High hunting pressure means fewer mature (3½ years old or older) bucks in a population and lower trophy prospects. Light hunting pressure assures the presence of mature bucks, greatly enhancing the trophy outlook. Age is, after all, the most limiting factor in trophy production across the country, and hunting pressure more than anything else will determine the age of the bucks in a population.

Not only is the number of mature bucks determined by the buck age structure, but it also affects both the average size and top-end size. Under our definition, a trophy must be at least 3½ years old, but a buck

There are 1½, 2½ and 3½ -year-old bucks here. This promises of a favorable buck age structure and good trophy hunting. The lack of age in the buck segment of a deer population is the most common problem in trophy hunting. Photo by Bill Kinney.

is not as big at 3½ as he will be at, say, 5½ or 6½. If bucks are distributed throughout all the "mature" age classes (3½ to 9½), they will average older and bigger than the bucks in a population consisting primarily of 3½'s in the mature age classes. Plus, the top-end size will be greater because of the increased presence of peak-size 5½, 6½ and 7½-year-old bucks. It's simply a matter of more bucks getting to the age necessary to achieve their genetic potential under existing nutritional conditions.

How can the buck age structure be gauged? One of the best indicators of the buck age structure is the percentage of 1½-year-old bucks in the buck harvest, assuming it is nonselective. The higher the percentage of 1½'s harvested, the greater the percentage of the total buck population killed each year and the fewer the number of 3½'s or older. Information on 1½'s in the buck kill usually can be obtained from local game departments. What will it tell you? The following chart developed from years of data gathered by the Georgia Game & Fish Division will help quantify the relationship between the 1½'s killed and both the percent 3½'s present and the percentage of the total buck population killed each year.

Yearling Bucks and Age Structure		
(The following table shows the relationship of the percentage of 1½-year-old bucks in the buck harvest to the percentage of mature bucks present and to the percentage of the total buck population harvested annually.)		
% 1½-Year-Old Bucks In The Buck Harvest	% Bucks 3½ Years Old & Older In The Population	% Of Total Buck Population Harvested
<40%	>30%	<25%
50%	20%	40%
60%	15%	55%
70%	10%	65%
>80%	< 5%	>75%

These numbers are only rough averages, but they dramatically show the negative impact of increased hunting pressure on the number of mature bucks and on your odds for success. In some heavily hunted populations, 95 percent of the antlered bucks are killed each season. A very lightly hunted place may see less than 15 percent of its buck population taken each year. Obviously, there would be a big difference in the trophy prospects of two such places. Most trophy hunting takes place in situations falling somewhere between these two extremes.

As a point of interest, even disregarding hunting pressure, bucks generally experience a higher mortality rate than does. This stems primarily from stress associated with the rut. Biologists know it as post-rut mortality. It is especially prevalent in populations with a strong contingency of mature bucks and a distinct, competitive rut. During the rut, active bucks eat very little and can lose up to 30 percent of their body weight, leaving them in a weakened state to face the rigors of oncoming winter or the threat of predators. The highest post-rut mortality seems to be among the mature, active breeders. The severity of the mortality varies by place and by year, but well-known deer specialist Dr.

James Kroll of Nacogdoches, Texas, says post-rut mortality can take 20 percent or more of the active breeders each year!

I have firsthand knowledge of a couple of interesting examples of predator-related post-rut mortality. One takes place in South Texas. Bob Zaiglin, head of the wildlife program for Harrison Ranches, tells me that coyotes there single out rut-stressed bucks during the winter as their targets. In an effort to escape the pursuing coyotes, the weakened bucks seek refuge in the water of the ranch's many tanks (ponds), which are commonly very low that time of year. The bucks mire up in the mud around the remaining water. The much lighter coyotes don't break through the crusted mud surface like the heavier deer, and they are unhindered in their attack. Even the largest bucks are easy prey under these circumstances. A barn full of big racks retrieved from low-water tanks is mute testimony to the effectiveness of the coyotes' tactics.

An old trapper in Canada told me of similar selectivity in his neck of the woods for mature bucks by both wolves and coyotes during and after the rut. He offered two possible reasons for this. One, the bucks are weakened or possibly even injured from the rut. Two, the bigger bucks, knowing they have some defense in their antlers, are more likely to turn and fight when chased than are does, fawns and even young bucks. His theories are plausible, and from what I've seen, the evidence will support them.

Buck/Doe Ratio

The second way hunting pressure impacts a deer herd is in the ratio of "adult" (1½ years old and older) bucks to adult does, known simply as the buck/doe ratio. Generally speaking, the buck/doe ratio is "lower" in lightly hunted populations and "higher" in heavily hunted herds, especially those with disproportionate pressure on bucks. Fawns are not included in the buck/doe ratio; therefore, the ratio between antlered and antlerless deer will reflect an even greater spread, sometimes nearly twice as much since a healthy herd can average close to a fawn per adult doe in the fall. As a result, a buck/doe ratio of, say, 1:3 could mean an antlered/antlerless ratio of around 1:6. Antlerless sightings could give the wrong impression of the buck/doe ratio without taking this into account.

The buck/doe ratio is simply a means of expressing the makeup of

A bunch of does and fawns and a couple of young bucks — if this represents the makeup of the deer herd, it doesn't bode well for the trophy hunter. High buck/doe ratios and an absence of older bucks are usually the result of heavy hunting pressure. Photo by Bill Kinney.

the adult deer herd. It can be easily translated into percentages. For instance, a buck/doe ratio of 1:1 means 50 percent are bucks and 50 percent are does; a 1:2 translates into 33 percent bucks and 67 percent does; a 1:3 results in 25 versus 75 percent and so on. With this understanding, it is easy to see that the buck/doe ratio has a direct bearing on the number of bucks in the population. Assuming a piece of property is capable of carrying only so many deer without sacrificing size and ultimately reproduction, then it is obviously to the trophy hunter's advantage to have as many bucks represented in that population as possible. The lower the buck/doe ratio, the greater the percentage and the higher the total number of bucks present. And, logic dictates that more bucks in a herd lead to a greater likelihood that mature bucks are present, yielding better odds for success. As for does, it is only necessary to have enough to replenish the loses each year, assuming the herd is at carrying capacity. A buck/doe ratio unnecessarily weighted toward does means space is occupied by does that could be filled by bucks.

Another big benefit associated with a low buck/doe ratio comes during the rut. Normally, the lower the buck/doe ratio, the more competitive the rut, especially in populations with an abundance of older bucks and hunting pressure low enough not to unduly suppress natural deer movement. This competition works to the hunter's advantage. More of the ritual activities associated with the rut, which are more important to the trophy hunter than the breeding per se, are played out in daylight hours as the bucks vie for dominance ... and for does. Bucks lay down more sign — rubs and scrapes — and this sign can be hunted with a level of predictability. Bucks can be seen with some frequency trailing and chasing does. Much of their time during this period is spent preoccupied with the rut instead of survival. That spells opportunity for the hunter.

By contrast, a high buck/doe ratio, usually associated with heavy hunting pressure and a poor buck age structure, brings with it an indistinct, spread-out rut. Most of the breeding and rutting activity will take place at night. Daylight movement is spotty and unpredictable. Visible evidence of the rut often appears rather halfhearted and disjointed. Scrapes, when they can be found, are used infrequently and are undependable. All in all, this situation makes for tough hunting.

While it's true that a low buck/doe ratio usually accompanies light pressure and a high ratio normally goes with heavy pressure, there are a couple of notable exceptions to this generality. First, even in the case of light hunting pressure, a high buck/doe ratio can exist where low reproduction combines with a minimal doe harvest and a continuous, even though light, buck harvest. I once saw a situation like this on a large closely controlled tract of land in southwestern Alabama. After years of total doe protection and only light buck pressure, the herd became so severely overcrowded that reproduction declined dramatically. The buck/doe ratio had been slowly worsening for a long time, but the drop in reproduction, which replenishes the herd at roughly a 1:1 buck/doe ratio, really accelerated the process. This decline, coupled with the light buck harvest and the usual post-rut mortality (along with some neighbors' help with wandering bucks), resulted in a badly imbalanced buck/doe ratio pushing 1:8 after a few seasons. The reluctant landowner finally made a major effort to shoot does. A ratio of 1:2 was restored after several years by eliminating does and stimulating reproduction.

The other exception worth discussing takes place when a low

buck/doe ratio is maintained in the face of high hunting pressure. Two conditions are necessary for this to occur — one, a balanced harvest of both bucks and does and, two, high reproduction. Middle Georgia is an example of such a situation. That part of Georgia has a 49-day gun season. Does are legal from 15 to 25 of these days. The Georgia limit allows up to five deer, of which no more than two can be bucks. All can be does. Hunting pressure in this area is moderate to high. A relatively high percentage of the total deer herd is harvested each year, probably 30 percent or more. Does represent a substantial part of the harvest. The result is a fairly low buck/doe ratio, seldom over 1:2, and a dynamic population consisting of relatively young deer. Some mature bucks are present, mostly 3½'s, but they are hard to come by unless the land is managed or protected.

Is there ever a situation where an imbalanced buck/doe ratio is desirable? Yes, if the objective is to produce numbers of deer in the face of high hunting pressure. In such a case, a disproportionately high number of does is both desirable and inevitable. On some of the large public land tracts in Pennsylvania, the hunting pressure is so great that nearly all the antlered bucks are killed every year. The season is held after the rut to assure the does are bred. Game managers in that state basically try to shape a harvest that allows as many does and fawns to be carried through the winter as the habitat will support. The number of antlered bucks surviving a season is negligible. The fawns carried over from the year before become that fall's antlered bucks. Obviously, the buck/doe ratio is skewed toward does, but such a situation provides the maximum number of deer for the region's many hunters. There is, however, not much promise there for the trophy hunter.

The situation described above sounds as though it would lead to the worst possible buck/doe ratio, but that is not necessarily true. The fact is that the buck/doe ratio of the population entering the fall is seldom in excess of 1:5. Yet, as seen in the earlier Alabama case, populations with low reproduction and disproportionate buck pressure eventually can become even more heavily weighted in favor of does. Reproduction is the main key. In the Pennsylvania scenario, let's assume that all the antlered bucks are killed each fall and that 0.8 fawns per remaining doe are carried over every year. This means that for every 100 does surviving the winter 80 fawns also survive. Roughly 50 percent of the fawns

When mature bucks are pressured, they will become nocturnal, or at best move only during first and last light. Photo by Mike Biggs.

are bucks. Therefore, 40 yearling does and 40 yearling bucks would enter next fall's population, assuming no natural mortality for simplicity. The resulting fall population will consist of 40 bucks and 140 does, which is a 1:3.5 buck/doe ratio at the beginning of season despite a total buck harvest the previous year. This is made possible by a high reproductive rate and the 1:1 buck/doe ratio among fawns. (Actually, slightly more buck fawns are born than doe fawns.)

Buck Huntability

The last aspect of hunting pressure to be explored is its effect on buck huntability as related to behavior. Hunting pressure both suppresses and alters deer activity. The more pressure, the less daylight movement and the less predictability in deer patterns. As we saw in the discussion of buck/doe ratios, even the rut is suppressed by high pressure. Feeding patterns are affected to an even greater degree. The extent to which deer react to human pressure is hard to fully appreciate. Normal deer movement patterns can be easily disrupted, and the deer can become almost totally nocturnal, especially mature bucks. Fortunately, even in an area with overall high hunting pressure, a hunter might be able to find remote and inaccessible places that have escaped the blunt of high pressure. We'll talk more about these "sanctuaries" later.

Hunting Pressure Summary

Now that we've looked at the factors impacted by hunting pressure, let's look at some examples of various levels of pressure — light, moderate and high — and their general characteristics. As a trophy hunter, it is imperative that you recognize the signs. Remember, the level of hunting pressure is determined both by its intensity and duration. For instance, the impact of pressure on an area may be virtually the same whether 10 people hunt every day for six weeks or 60 people hunt every day for one week. The only difference may be in buck huntability. Natural deer movement would probably be better in the first case.

A lightly hunted area would be characterized by a high percentage of 3½'s and older (30 percent or more) in the antlered buck population. A number of bucks 5½ and older would be present. Forty percent or less of a nonselective harvest would be 1½-year-olds. Less than 25 percent of all the bucks would be taken by hunters each year. The buck/doe ratio would be in the neighborhood of 1:1.5. Deer would move freely during daylight hours on somewhat predictable patterns. A distinct, competitive rut would be accompanied by an abundance of buck sign and rutting activity.

An area with moderate hunting pressure might have 10 to 30 percent of its bucks at 3½ years old or better. There would be a few 5½'s and 6½'s present at the lower end of the moderate pressure range, but the number would decrease rapidly as pressure increased. From 40 to 70

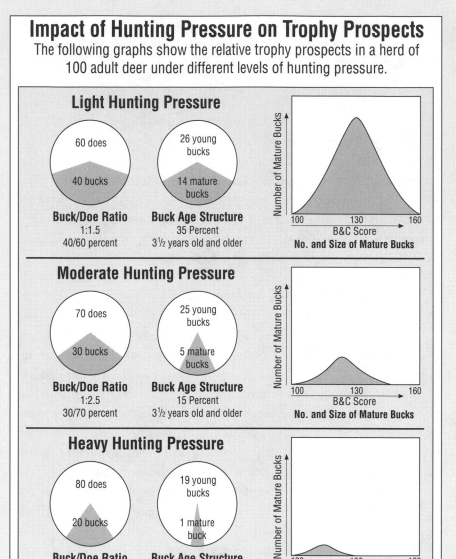

Impact of Hunting Pressure on Trophy Prospects

The following graphs show the relative trophy prospects in a herd of 100 adult deer under different levels of hunting pressure.

Light Hunting Pressure

60 does
40 bucks

26 young bucks
14 mature bucks

Buck/Doe Ratio
1:1.5
40/60 percent

Buck Age Structure
35 Percent
3½ years old and older

Number of Mature Bucks

100   130   160
B&C Score
No. and Size of Mature Bucks

Moderate Hunting Pressure

70 does
30 bucks

25 young bucks
5 mature bucks

Buck/Doe Ratio
1:2.5
30/70 percent

Buck Age Structure
15 Percent
3½ years old and older

Number of Mature Bucks

100   130   160
B&C Score
No. and Size of Mature Bucks

Heavy Hunting Pressure

80 does
20 bucks

19 young bucks
1 mature buck

Buck/Doe Ratio
1:4
20/80 percent

Buck Age Structure
5 Percent
3½ years old and older

Number of Mature Bucks

100   130   160
B&C Score
No. and Size of Mature Bucks

BUCK/DOE RATIO

The benefits of the low buck/doe ratio associated with light pressure are obvious. The 1:1.5 ratio equates to 40% bucks and 60% does, meaning there are 40 bucks in the population of 100 adult deer. This compares to 30 bucks in the moderate pressure example (1:2.5 buck/doe ratio) and only 20 bucks in the heavy pressure example with a 1:4 buck/doe ratio. Had you rather hunt a population of 100 deer with 40 bucks or with 20 bucks? The numerical advantage speaks for itself.

Buck Age Structure

The buck age structure will determine how many of the bucks are potential trophies, i.e., 3½ years old or older. The 35% mature bucks in the light pressure situation compares to 15% in the moderate and 5% in the heavy. In our examples, this translates to 14 mature bucks in the light pressure case versus five in the moderate and one in the heavy. How much do your chances improve when hunting 14 mature bucks as opposed to five or to one? The value of a good buck age structure is clear, especially when combined with a low buck/doe ratio.

No. And Size Of Mature Bucks

These graphs say it all!. The dramatic impact of hunting pressure on the number of mature bucks is clearly shown by the height of the curves. The righthand entension of the curves speaks to buck size. The actual size of the mature bucks in a population, given the genetic potential of that location and existing nutritional conditions, depends on how well bucks are distributed throughout the mature age classes, i.e., 3½ through 9½. A population with a limited distribution of mature bucks may consist almost entirely of 3½-year-old bucks in the mature age classes. This would limit both the average and top-end size of the mature bucks in that population to the size achievable by 3½'s. In a population with well-distributed age classes, not only will there be more mature bucks but these bucks will average larger because their average age is greater. In addition, the top-end size will be larger since there will be more bucks in the 5½-year-old and older, peak-size age classes.

Looking at the light hunting pressure example, we see a bell-shaped curve spanning the graph, depicting the presence of all size bucks because of good age distribution. Also, we see both a higher average size and more larger-than-average bucks. The moderate hunting pressure graph reflects the predominance of 3½'s among existing mature bucks and the lack of appreciable numbers of larger 4½'s, 5½'s or 6½'s. In a heavy hunting pressure situation, nearly all the few surviving mature bucks are 3½'s, reducing both the average size and the likelihood that older, larger bucks exist. 🦌

percent of the buck harvest might be yearlings. The percentage of the buck population harvested each year would range from 30 to 65 percent. Depending on the doe harvest and the reproductive rate, a buck/doe ratio from 1:1.5 to 1:4 would be expected. Somewhere around 1:2 or 1:3 would probably be average since buck pressure usually exceeds doe pressure. Deer movement would be somewhat suppressed and altered, depending on the intensity of the pressure. Overall daytime activity would be largely limited to early morning and late afternoon hours. Mature bucks would tend to be primarily nocturnal, especially outside the rut. The rut would be evident and fairly well defined, depending of the buck/doe ratio and the age structure. Buck sign would be present and huntable, though inconsistent. "Serious" buck sign might be hard to find at higher pressure levels. Moderate pressure is the most prevalent trophy hunting situation in the United States today.

High hunting pressure seriously reduces, and in some cases virtually eliminates, a hunter's chances for a trophy buck. Less than 10 percent of the bucks will be 3½ years old or older. That number will drop below five percent in many areas. The few mature bucks that do exist are nearly all 3½'s. High pressure can result in an annual harvest of 65 to 95 percent of the buck population. High pressure areas are nearly always characterized by buck/doe ratios significantly weighted toward does. A range of 1:3 to 1:6 would be expected. Most deer activity will occur at night or very early or late in the day. Since daytime movement is so limited, forced movement often accounts for a big part of the harvest in high pressure areas. The rut is a pretty sad affair. Rutting activity and buck sign are spotty and inconsistent.

OTHER FACTORS

Independent of hunting pressure, a couple of other considerations influence the trophy prospects of a place. One is herd density. This is a two-sided issue. On one hand, more deer can mean more trophy bucks and greater odds of success. It's simple arithmetic. If 30 percent of the bucks on two separate 1,000-acre tracts are mature but one tract carries 100 deer while the other supports 50, which tract offers you the best chance to see a 3½-year-old buck? All things being equal, the tract with 100 deer offers you twice the odds! The sheer number of deer present is an important consideration. On the other

The huntability of the habitat plays a big part in hunter success. Some places are just plain hard to hunt. Still, I had rather hunt difficult country with trophy bucks than easy country without them. Photo by Mike Biggs.

hand, too many deer means overpopulation, which reduces antler size due to poor nutrition. So for the trophy hunter, the abundance of deer and where the herd stands relative to the carrying capacity of the land are both important concerns.

Another consideration is the huntability of the habitat. This is different from the huntability of the deer due to behavioral changes brought about by hunting pressure. Here, we're talking only about how the characteristics of the country affect the huntability of bucks. There are some places that are just plain hard to hunt. Thick cover, rough terrain, swampy conditions, inaccessibility, etc., can reduce your odds even though the trophy bucks are there. I once hunted an 8,000-acre plantation in South Carolina that had been completely clearcut and replanted in pines some eight years earlier. Apart from the access roads through the property, it was nearly impossible to find a place with visibility over 10 yards. Even dog hunting couldn't dislodge the many mature bucks from the impenetrable pine thickets. We had no success until we located a couple of relatively open hardwood bottoms with the aid of aerial photos.

Though the nature of the habitat can be a limiting factor, I much prefer tough hunting country with trophy bucks than easy country without them! More and more today, appreciable numbers of trophy bucks are only found in places that are hard to hunt for one reason or another. On a local basis, these inaccessible or difficult-to-hunt places can be an important part of a trophy hunter's strategy.

TROPHY PROSPECTS WHERE YOU HUNT

Now that we've examined some of the factors influencing trophy prospects, let's look at your hunting territory. Some pertinent questions should have been raised about your chances for a trophy there. One is whether or not bucks meeting your trophy standards exist in huntable numbers in the general area you hunt? There is no great mystery in determining this. Simply look at what's being killed areawide. If you live there, chances are you already know. If you are new to the area or if for whatever reason you are unsure about what is being taken, talk to your local game warden or biologist or drop in on check stations during hunts. Local deer contests or area taxidermy shops are also very good sources of information. The search will reveal something of the number and size of the trophy bucks currently being taken. A historical survey also will give you a good indication of the genetic potential of the area your hunt.

Once you have some idea about the trophies being shot in the overall area, apply this information to your personal situtation. Given the number of trophy bucks killed in your area that meet your trophy standards, what does that say about your individual chances of shooting such a buck? Remember, you are just one hunter among many. A handful of trophy bucks spread among hundreds, perhaps thousands of local hunters doesn't speak well of your chances. You must decide if enough bucks meeting your requirements for a trophy are being killed to represent a reasonable chance for your own success. If the answer is clearly no, hunt elsewhere or lower your standards. If the answer is yes, then the time has come to size up your chances of shooting a trophy on the actual place you hunt.

First, what about the size of the property you hunt? Is it large enough to be buffered to some degree from the effects of hunting pressure on surrounding land? If the property is less than 1,000 acres, the answer is probably no. However, the level of pressure, the nature of the habitat and many other factors go into that answer. A negative answer means your property is subject to the influences of pressure on surrounding land regardless of how much hunting is actually done on your property. In this case, your thinking must expand to include all the surrounding area since you are, for better or worse, a part of it and controlled by it. The "pressure signs" on your property will tell the story.

If your property is large enough to be at least partially buffered from the effects of outside pressure, the pertinent questions must be applied directly to the place you hunt. What is the level of hunting pressure there? What is the buck age structure and buck/doe ratio like? What do deer patterns, movement and sign tell you about pressure? What is the deer density there? Is the population above or below the carrying capacity? Do habitat conditions work to your advantage or disadvantage? What's a realistic trophy goal there? Do sanctuary areas exist that might be buffered from the full impact of hunting pressure? The answers to these questions will largely determine whether your time is spent "hunting kudu in Georgia" or hunting trophy whitetails in a place where they haven't all been shot!

Chapter 6

The Different Faces
Of Trophy Hunting

B ECAUSE OF ITS INCREDIBLE ADAPTABILITY, the whitetail is the most abundant big game animal in North America and one of the most widely distributed. Only the black bear can claim a wider distribution, but it is no where near as plentiful. Best estimates place the total whitetail population in North America at 20 million. Odds are good that it's even higher. Better than four million are harvested by hunters each year. Every indication is that there are more whitetails today than ever before in history.

Whitetails are supposedly present to some degree in all the Lower 48 states. However, California, Nevada and Utah have no hunting season for whitetails, and they are so rare there that they are practically nonexistent. But, the northwestern states of Washington, Idaho and Montana have good to excellent populations. Oregon has a huntable population in the northeastern corner of the state. Colorado and Wyoming, famous for their elk and mule deer, are home to some fine whitetails, particularly along riverbottoms in the eastern part of the states.

Whitetails are present in the Southwest as well. Arizona and New Mexico both have good populations of the diminutive Coues whitetail, a small desert mountain dweller that offers a unique and

No other big game animal is more adaptable than the whitetail. He not only survives in the presence of man, he thrives on the results of man's activities, mainly timbering and farming. Photo by Mike Biggs.

demanding hunt more akin to hunting desert bighorns than whitetails. New Mexico also has huntable, but localized, populations of the Texas subspecies of whitetail.

From the eastern borders of Montana, Wyoming, Colorado and New Mexico to the Atlantic, the whitetail is found virtually everywhere. It has, in fact, pretty well saturated this, the heart of its range. Many areas, especially in the South and East, are at or above carrying capacity. The fact that the whitetail has been restored so completely to its original home range and beyond is a credit to hunters, whose concern and money provided the will and means, and to dedicated biologists and game wardens, whose long hours and hard work saw the restoration through. But in the end, it is the whitetail's incredible adaptability that made it all possible.

Canada has a large and growing whitetail population. Because of timbering and farming, the range of the whitetail in Canada has increased tremendously in the last 50 years. Today, whitetails are present in huntable numbers in all the southern Canadian provinces.

South of the border in Mexico, whitetails exist in a harsh environment and, in many places, despite constant harassment. The small Coues deer occupies a large range in northern Mexico, extending several hundred miles south of the U.S. border along the western desert mountains. Aside from the Coues deer, whitetails are found primarily within 100 or so miles of the border with Texas up and down the Rio Grande River.

Obviously, any animal that can exist in the blistering, arid thorn-bush country of South Texas and Mexico as well as in the unforgiving, snow-covered evergreen forests of Ontario is adaptable. This same animal can get along equally well in the remote backcountry of western Montana or in the suburbs of New Jersey. No other animal is as versatile and able to live in man's presence quite so successfully as the whitetail. In fact, the whitetail prefers to live within the sphere of man's influence and thrives on the results of man's activities, mainly timbering and farming.

Scientists tell us there are 30 recognized subspecies of whitetails, 17 of which are found in the United States, Canada and northern Mexico. Frankly, this is not of great concern to the hunter since not even scientists can always tell the difference. Years of subspecies mixing through transplanting or expansion of one subspecies into the range of another have pretty well confused the picture. The hunter just wants to know where in North America the best bucks are likely to be found. Additionally, the hunter may be interested in a unique whitetail variety that justifies its own trophy category. In my mind, there are two such subspecies that are huntable.

First, the widely recognized Coues deer of Arizona, New Mexico and northern Mexico is given a separate trophy status from other whitetails by the Boone & Crockett Club and Safari Club International (SCI). This is justified since the Coues is geographically isolated and since it differs from other whitetails in that it is smaller and has larger ears and a bigger tail relative to its body size. The second distinct category, the

Scientists claim that there are 30 subspecies of whitetails, 17 of which live in North America. This huge buck is of the Dakota subspecies, which shares the title of being the largest with the northern woodland and Kansas subspecies. Photo by Dick Idol.

Carmen Mountains whitetail, is very similar to the Coues but of less significance. It is found in the Big Bend region of West Texas and just across the border into Mexico. This small whitetail is not given its own listing by Boone & Crockett or Safari Club International. But because of its isolated habitat and small size, it is looked upon by the handful of hunters who care as deserving a separate trophy category.

Let's now survey the trophy prospects across North America and try to paint a picture of the different faces of trophy hunting. The following maps and their accompanying comments will begin the process. Next, we'll divide the United States, Canada and Mexico into geographic regions based on similarity of habitat, current trophy opportunities and hunting traditions. Then, we'll explore each region indepth. While there are many similarities within each region, differences certainly exist. Our purpose is to draw a broad picture of trophy hunting across the continent, not to deal with countless exceptions.

Whitetail Deer Populations In The United States

T his map, created from data submitted by state game departments, provides a good overview of whitetail densities in the United States and the distribution of huntable populations. As is evident, the greatest concentrations are in the South, including Texas, and up the Atlantic Seaboard to southern New York. Parts of Michigan and Wisconsin also have high numbers of deer. The Midwest shows pockets of moderate to high concentrations, but overall this area has relatively low deer populations, which partly accounts for the large deer there.

The Plains and Prairies Region is shown to have low populations on the whole. But as some of these states reflect, most deer are concentrated in the available cover along rivers and streams in this otherwise open countryside. Deer densities in the riverbottoms can be remarkably high. Deer populations in the northwestern states of Washington, Idaho and Montana, represented as being low overall, also tend to be somewhat localized along rivers and in major valleys and their associated hillsides. As the map reflects, local populations can be quite high.

The Coues deer in Arizona and New Mexico is represented. The pocket of whitetails shown in south-central New Mexico is a herd of the Texas subspecies in and around the Mescalero Apache Indian Reservation. In Texas, the large area where deer are shown to be rare or absent does not accurately tell the whole story. Actually, within that area, especially in the central and eastern sections, there are some substantial deer herds. Whitetails are more scarce to the west and north in Texas, however.

(Author's Note: You may order a 23x35-inch copy of this map, laminated for durability, from: Information Outfitters, Inc., 1995 Daniel Lane, Yulee, FL 32097, (904) 277-4046. The price is $6.95 U.S. per map, plus $3 for shipping and handling.)

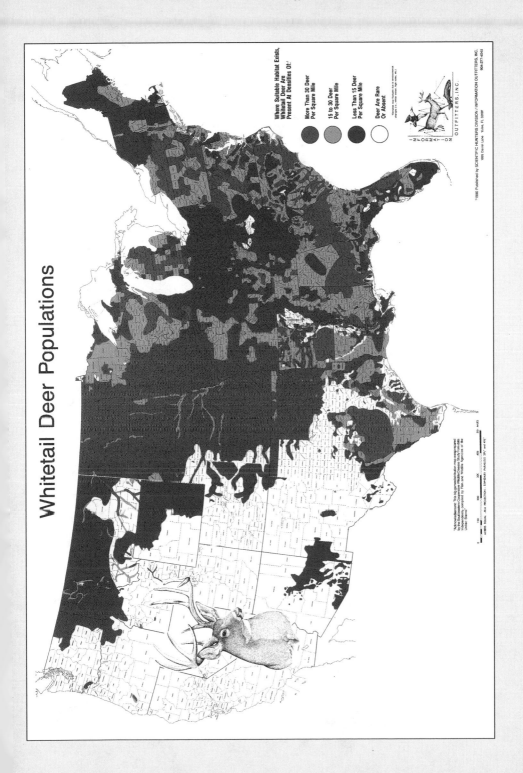

Whitetail Deer Populations

Where Suitable Habitat Exists, Whitetail Deer Are Present At Densities Of:

More Than 30 Deer Per Square Mile

15 to 30 Deer Per Square Mile

Less Than 15 Deer Per Square Mile

Deer Are Rare Or Absent

The "Where" Of Boone & Crockett Bucks

A s the map clearly shows, Minnesota and Wisconsin dominate the record books. There are reasons for this. One, they are incredibly productive states for big bucks. More B&C bucks are added to their tallies each year despite considerable hunting pressure, especially in Wisconsin. Two, these states have had deer throughout the 20th Century, giving them a longer time to mount impressive totals than many other states. Third, in the last decade, both these states have seen a proliferation of whitetail shows, seminars and big buck contests that have brought reams of B&C bucks out of closets. The result is that a high percentage of their existing B&C's have ended up in the record book. This is in contrast to No. 3 Saskatchewan, where only a small percentage of the B&C's killed there — especially those killed by local hunters — ever get recognition in the record book. This is the case throughout Canada. Fortunately, this is changing today, especially in areas where the whitetail outfitting industry is growing and people are becoming more aware of their unique resource.

Texas comes in fourth with 108 B&C's. Like Minnesota and Wisconsin, Texas has a long and illustrious whitetail history, and many of its record bucks were killed long years ago. Since 1980, 17 record bucks have been shot in Texas, representing only 16 percent of the state's total B&C entries. That compares to 42 recorded in Kansas since 1980, a whopping 70 percent of its B&C total! Kansas obviously is coming on strong.

Most of the top B&C producers are clustered in the Midwest. Along with Minnesota and Wisconsin, Iowa (with 78 B&C's) and Illinois (with 66 record bucks) top the list of a host of premier trophy states. Ohio is the easternmost state in this trophy region and has earned the reputa-

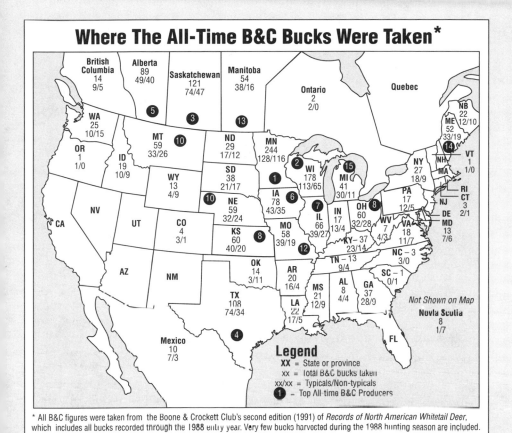

Where The All-Time B&C Bucks Were Taken*

British Columbia 14 9/5

Alberta 89 49/40

Saskatchewan 121 74/47

Manitoba 54 38/16

Ontario 2 2/0

Quebec

NB 22 12/10

ME 52 33/19

WA 25 10/15

OR 1 1/0

MT 59 33/26

ND 29 17/12

MN 244 128/116

WI 178 113/65

MI 41 30/11

NY 27 18/9

NH 1 1/0

VT 1 1/0

ID 19 10/9

WY 13 4/9

SD 38 21/17

IA 78 43/35

IL 66 39/27

IN 17 13/4

OH 60 32/28

PA 17 12/5

MA

RI CT 3 2/1

NV

UT

CO 4 3/1

NE 59 32/24

MO 58 39/27

KY– 37 23/14

WV 7 4/3

VA 18 11/7

NJ

DE

MD 13 7/6

CA

KS 60 40/20

OK 14 3/11

AR 20 16/4

TN – 13 9/4

NC – 3 3/0

SC – 1 0/1

AZ

NM

TX 108 74/34

MS 21 12/9

AL 8 4/4

GA 37 28/9

Not Shown on Map

LA 22 17/5

Mexico 10 7/3

FL

Nova Scotia 8 1/7

Legend
XX = State or province
xx = Total B&C bucks taken
xx/xx = Typicals/Non-typicals
1 – Top All-time B&C Producers

* All B&C figures were taken from the Boone & Crockett Club's second edition (1991) of *Records of North American Whitetail Deer*, which includes all bucks recorded through the 1988 entry year. Very few bucks harvested during the 1988 hunting season are included.

tion as the place for giant non-typicals. The famous "Hole-In-The-Horn" buck, the No. 2 non-typical scoring 328⅞, focused national attention on the state when it came to light in 1983. Also, Ohio's four non-typicals over 250 points top any other state or province for bucks of that size.

On the all-time B&C map, note the strong tendency toward non-typicals in the northwestern United States. In Wyoming, Montana, Idaho, Washington and Oregon, a total of 117 B&C bucks are listed. Fifty-nine, or 50 percent, of them are non-typicals! For sheer numbers of non-typicals, however, the Midwest and Canada have the edge.

The "Where The Giants Are From" chart (page 103) offers only a couple of mild surprises. One is the strong showing of Texas, the southernmost of the great trophy states. With five 190–plus typicals *and two non-typicals over 250, its seven all-time biggest bucks are bettered only by Minnesota's 10 — eight typicals and two non-typicals. New York's 198⅜ typical, killed back in 1939, and Maine's 192⅞ typical, taken in 1920, somewhat break the pattern for where the giant bucks are from. It is significant that all three of Indiana's 190-plus typicals were killed in the 1980's, promising of great things in the future. Other places producing typicals in the 190's since 1980 are: Minnesota (three), Saskatchewan (three), Kansas (one), Manitoba (one), Michigan (one), Ohio (one) and Wyoming (one).*

On the non-typical side of the giant buck listing, a couple of interesting points also come through. Ohio's strength for giant non-typicals is evident. Nova Scotia slips in with two all-time great non-typicals. This small maritime province clearly has something going for it in the way of non-typicals. Of its eight total B&C's listed, seven are non-typicals! Neighboring New Brunswick has only 12 typicals versus 10 non-typicals, a very high percentage of non-typicals. Maritime Canada is certainly worth watching, and hunting, for big non-typicals. Kansas and Alberta both have three giant non-typicals to their credit, and each produced one in the 1980's. Both of Missouri's two non-typicals topping 250, including the 333⅞-point world record, have turned up since 1980. With one each, Ohio and Illinois were the only other states to produce a 250-plus non-typical from 1980 to 1988.

*T*he listing of "Top Recent B&C Producers" once again reflects the dominance of the Midwest in recent years. Along with Minnesota and Wisconsin, Illinois, Iowa and especially Kansas may offer the best chance in the United States for a B&C buck right now. Kentucky's 21 book bucks since 1980 are impressive. Alberta and Manitoba have good recent numbers, as does Saskatchewan. But as good as these numbers appear, they do not reveal anything near the true trophy opportunities in these places. Maine continues to produce B&C's because of good age structure. Despite an overall lack of age among its bucks, Georgia turned out 17 B&C's from 1980 to 1988, several of which were only 3½ years old! Montana recorded 15, but even today, many B&C qualifiers in the West are never entered in the record book.*

Where The Giants Are From

Typicals Over 190			Non-typicals Over 250		
Location	No.	Biggest	Location	No.	Biggest
Minnesota	8	202	Ohio	4	328$^{2/8}$
Saskatchewan	5	200$^{2/8}$	Alberta	3	277$^{5/8}$
Texas	5	196$^{4/8}$	Kansas	3	269$^{3/8}$
Wisconsin	4	206$^{1/8}$	Missouri	2	333$^{7/8}$
Nebraska	3	199$^{2/8}$	Texas	2	286
Kansas	3	198$^{2/8}$	Iowa	2	282
Indiana	3	195$^{1/8}$	Minnesota	2	268$^{5/8}$
Missouri	2	205	Nova Scotia	2	264$^{5/8}$
Alberta	2	204$^{2/8}$	South Dakota	2	256$^{1/8}$
Iowa	2	200$^{2/8}$	Nebraska	1	277$^{3/8}$
Montana	2	199$^{3/8}$	Idaho	1	267$^{4/8}$
S. Dakota	2	193	Illinois	1	267$^{3/8}$
Illinois	1	204$^{1/8}$	Saskatchewan	1	265$^{3/8}$
Ohio	1	201$^{1/8}$	Maine	1	259
New York	1	198$^{3/8}$	Manitoba	1	257$^{3/8}$
Manitoba	1	197$^{7/8}$	North Dakota	1	254$^{6/8}$
Michigan	1	193$^{2/8}$	Montana	1	252$^{1/8}$
Maine	1	192$^{7/8}$			
Wyoming	1	191$^{5/8}$			

Top Recent B&C Producers (1980-88)

Location	Number From 1980-88	Percent of Location Total	Location	Number From 1980-88	Percent of Location Total
1. Minnesota	72	30%	9. Saskatch.	24	20%
2. Wisconsin	51	29%	10. Ohio	23	38%
3. Kansas	42	70%	11. Kentucky	21	57%
4. Alberta	39	44%	12. Georgia	17	46%
5. Illinois	38	58%	13. Maine	17	33%
6. Iowa	36	46%	14. Texas	17	16%
7. Manitoba	26	48%	15. Michigan	15	37%
8. Missouri	24	41%	16. Montana	15	25%

Relative Trophy Prospects In North America

T his map is intended to provide relative size comparisons of representative trophies from across North America. The sizes given are based on information from trophy hunters throughout the continent and reflect the size buck most experienced hunters would consider a trophy in the various areas.

To understand this map, some points need to be made. First, our definition calls for a trophy to be at least 3½ years old and among the best bucks consistently taken in the area. Without the minimum age requirement of 3½, the second part of the definition (among the best bucks consistently taken) would dictate that the representative trophy size be lowered in high-pressure areas. For example, in the most heavily hunted areas of the East, a 2½-year-old buck scoring 100 points would surely qualify as one of the "best bucks consistently taken in the area." Here, the 3½-year-old requirement automatically elevates the representative trophy size and makes trophies hard to come by because so few survive to age 3½. This is also true of parts of the South.

Second, the figures shown represent typical B&C gross scores for the size bucks actually being taken under current conditions, not the true size potential of the area. In many cases, overharvesting and/or overcrowding have significantly reduced the size of the bucks harvested. Genetics are what they are, but the age structure of the buck population and the quality of nutrition available determine how much of that genetic potential is actually realized in a location.

An example of reality versus potential can be seen in the 140 zone across southern Minnesota, Wisconsin and Michigan. This zone is enveloped by the 145 zone. Does this mean that the 140 zone has less

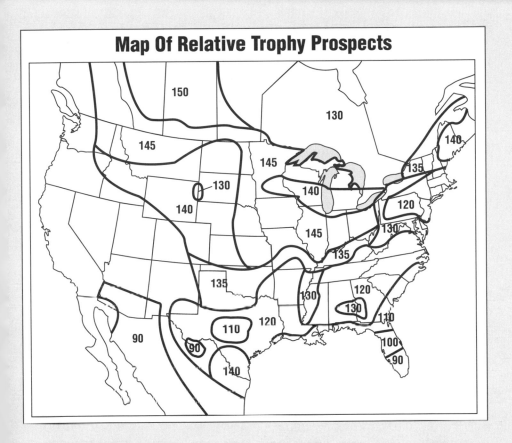

Map Of Relative Trophy Prospects

potential than the 145 zone surrounding it? No! The potential there is every bit as good, but high hunting pressure has reduced the number of older bucks. The current reality is that most bucks qualifying as a trophy there are, in fact, 3½ years old. Therefore, the average age of trophies there is younger than in surrounding areas, thus the representative trophy is somewhat smaller because of age, not lower size potential. The fact that this area produces many B&C's despite relatively few bucks surviving to older ages speaks to the tremendous potential there.

Third, the map reveals nothing of the number of trophy bucks in an area or of the odds of getting one. For instance, parts of Texas and Maine show a trophy size of 140. Yet, your odds of killing such a buck in Texas are much higher than in Maine, where the number of 140's is lower and their huntability is considerably less than in South Texas. Another example would be the 110 zone in Hill Country

Texas compared to the 110 zone in the coastal South. Higher numbers of deer, a greater percentage of older bucks and more huntable terrain in the Hill Country would give hunters there a significant edge.

Fourth, the sizes given do not reflect the top-end size of an area or even its relative top-end as compared to other areas. For instance, 120 is pretty much the typical trophy size in the South, but 180-point bucks or larger show up there from time to time. A 208⅝-point non-typical was shot in South Carolina's 110 zone, and Texas' Hill Country produced the former world record non-typical scoring 286 points! The 130 zone on the South Dakota/Wyoming border is the Black Hills. This area has produced several B&C's in the past, particularly non-typicals from the Wyoming side. Now, overcrowding and increased pressure have reduced the average trophy size in the Black Hills. Yet, a buck topping the Wyoming non-typical record of 238⅞, which was taken in the Black Hills, could be shot there next year.

A couple of other comments about the map. South Texas stands out as an obvious anomaly. Age class for age class, South Texas bucks differ little in size from those of the best areas of the South or East. Its relatively large trophy size comes mostly from the sheer number of mature animals in the region. The average mature buck in the Brush Country probably would score 130 points; however, there are so many mature bucks there that a hunter can hunt for the exceptional mature buck and stand a very good chance of getting him, at least on the better ranches.

The 145 zone in the Midwest extends into the northwestern part of the United States and into Canada. Actually, the trophy potential of the Midwest, with its nutritious agriculture, is somewhat greater than that of the Northwest. Again, this is a case where hunting pressure has reduced the average size in the Midwest, though it is still the highest in the United States. The slightly lower potential of the Northwest is offset by its advantage of more older bucks.

In Central Canada, we have the only 150-point area on the continent. For the visiting hunter, this overall area is quite likely the best place in North America to kill a 150-plus buck, and certainly a 160-plus buck. But on the other hand, there are areas in the Midwest where local hunters familiar with the land and the deer have every bit as good a chance for a 150-plus buck as anyone in Canada. Often, the hunter is after one specific deer, and given time, skill and the right set-up, his odds for success are enviable. Select ranches in Texas and Mexico also can yield 150's with regularity, as can the right ranches in the plains and prairies. Bucks topping 150 are present in good numbers in the Northwest and in Maine and New Brunswick, but the remoteness of the country and difficult nature of the terrain lower both the local and visiting hunter's chances of finding and killing them. For record-class bucks, Central Canada would be my choice ... unless I lived in Iowa, Illinois or Kansas.

In Texas and the South especially, deer management on individual land tracts causes considerable variance in the trophy prospects. In Hill Country Texas, for example, one ranch may produce trophies in the 110 class as shown, but the ranch next door may consistently give up 125's. Protection of bucks and game management make a big difference. Actually, exceptions of all kinds exist throughout the continent. The map reflects the relative trophy prospects on a broad scale.

Region-By-Region Trophy Survey

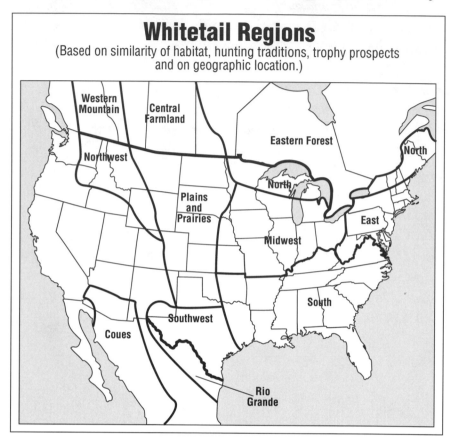

Whitetail Regions
(Based on similarity of habitat, hunting traditions, trophy prospects and on geographic location.)

Western Mountain

Central Farmland

Eastern Forest

North

Northwest

North

Plains and Prairies

East

Midwest

South

Southwest

Coues

Rio Grande

UNITED STATES

North Region

A land of snow and deep evergreen forests, the North Country personifies the romance and tradition of American whitetail hunting. Names like the Upper Peninsula and the Adirondack Mountains and, yes, even Maine and Wisconsin are synonymous with deer hunting to all whitetail aficionados. When deer were

North Region

North

North

rare or absent from much of the rest of the United States during the early and mid 1900's, this relatively unsettled region was home to the whitetail. In fact, efforts to capitalize on the vast timber resources of the region in the 1800's and early 1900's actually improved the deer habitat by encouraging secondary growth, and the logging operations provided limited access to this otherwise inaccessible country. Hunters trekking north behind the timber crews found deer populations in many places higher than they were before the white man first left his mark. For those willing to work at it, trophy bucks were plentiful during the early days, though most hunters then were more interested in venison than antlers.

Today, much of the North Country remains untamed by American standards. This is still "big woods" country. Expansive, unbroken tracts of mixed hardwood and evergreen forests spread across the northern reaches of the states comprising this region. Huge national forest holdings assure much of this wilderness environment will be there for years to come. Actually, the protection afforded some of these public holdings has resulted in a decrease in deer populations in recent years. In northern Minnesota, the moose and wolf have moved back into the maturing woodlands. In fact, in parts of the Superior National Forest in northeastern Minnesota, there are now more moose than whitetails. Maine's vast northern wilderness, much of which is owned by large commercial timber companies, is also home to many moose, as well as to some of the largest bodied whitetails in the United States.

Deer hunting is rooted in time-honored traditions and methods in the North. Hardy hunters brave cold, harsh conditions in this snow-covered landscape every fall in much the same way they did 50 years ago. Most hunting is done from the ground, though the use of portable tree-stands has grown in favor in recent times. Snow tracking is a favored method when conditions allow. Hunting in the North is not easy. Snow and cold, rugged terrain, inaccessibility and low deer densities in many areas make the going hard and success uncertain, but some of the country's biggest bucks can be the payoff.

Most firearms seasons last about two weeks, but Maine and Upstate New York seasons are longer. Liberal archery seasons are the rule, nearly all running a month or longer. Special muzzleloader seasons are common throughout the region. The bag limit is pretty well restricted to one buck. This is the home of the "brush rifle," and

Even today, the North Region remains relatively untamed. In the vast woodlands of this region live some of the country's best whitetails. Photo by Bill Kinney.

many are the .30/30 Winchester 94's that see action there in the fall.

Overall, the North Region has more public hunting available than any other region except the Northwest. This has given rise to a fair-sized whitetail outfitting/guiding industry, especially in Maine. Many hunts offer only the basics, that is, a place to stay and some help in the field and around camp, which usually is shared by several hunters. The success of the hunt is largely dependent on the hunter's skills. A few complete package hunts are available. Historically, the industry has largely catered to regional hunters. Since the hunts are usually pretty basic and hunter success runs fairly low, the price seldom exceeds $1,200 for a week's time.

Low deer densities are usually associated with the North Country, but there are exceptions. Parts of northern Wisconsin and Michigan have relatively high deer populations, some as high as 30 or more deer per square mile (640 acres). Other areas of the region have populations from 15 to 25 deer per square mile. Basically, where timbering and land clearing have improved food availability and cover, deer densities tend to be higher. In places with large stands of mature timber and little disturbance from man, deer populations are lower, running from 5 to 15 deer per square mile. A severe winter and deep snow can play havoc with deer in the North Region.

Hunting pressure takes an interesting slant in the North Region. In areas with good road access, hunting pressure can be high. But even in those same areas, a hunter willing to walk a couple of miles usually can get away from the crowd and the major effects of pressure. Some areas, like northern Maine and parts of northern Minnesota and Michigan's Upper Peninsula, are so remote that hunting pressure is hardly a factor. The area of Michigan's Lower Peninsula lying in the North Region receives moderate to high pressure, except in the most inaccessible pockets. The roaded areas of Wisconsin get high pressure. Access, terrain and remoteness control the region's pressure, which ranges from low to high. No other region has such a wide spread. On balance, moderate would probably best characterize the pressure overall. Correspondingly, the buck age structure would range from fair to excellent and would average in between. The buck/doe ratio is quite good regionwide.

The North Region is big buck country. The genetic potential is present for world-class bucks. Indeed, the current world record typical scoring 206⅛ was killed there in 1914 by James Jordan in Burnett County, Wisconsin. A Maine buck shares the title of the "heaviest buck ever officially weighed," 355 pounds field-dressed, with a buck from, surprisingly, Georgia. The subspecies inhabiting the entire region is the northern woodland whitetail, *Odocoileus virginianus borealis*, which, together with the Dakota and Kansas whitetail, is the largest of its kind. Minnesota is the No. 1 B&C state with 244 record bucks reported through 1988. Wisconsin follows a close second with 178. Michigan and New York both weigh in with a very credible 41 and 27 record bucks respectively as of 1988. Maine has yielded 52. Oddly, Vermont has only one B&C buck and New Hampshire none, but they both produce some real heavyweights. While not all the record-book bucks cited above have come from the North Region sections of these states, many have.

The size of a representative trophy varies considerably within the region. Minnesota, Wisconsin and Michigan, with an average trophy size of around 145, are right at the top in the country. But, the average trophy size in northern New York, Vermont and New Hampshire drops to 135 or so. With a representative trophy size of 140, most of Maine falls in between. Bucks in the 150 class or larger are a real possibility in Minnesota, Wisconsin, Michigan and Maine. All in all, this is one of the best trophy regions, especially for top-end bucks.

East Region

Like the North Region, the East is steeped in whitetail hunting tradition. Deer never completely disappeared from this region. The rolling hardwood hillsides and picturesque fields and meadows hosted autumn deer hunters when deer were hard to find in the South and Midwest. Because of this long tradition, the East has some of the most avid deer

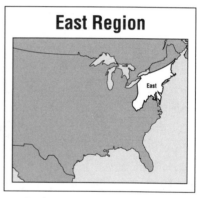

hunters in the country. Where else can you find school closings and business shutdowns just because deer season is open? This comes from a valued tradition passed down through the generations.

The East Region has tremendous variety in habitat, as would be expected for a place stretching from the beaches of the Atlantic to the mountains of West Virginia. Hunters chase whitetails in the thick Pine Barrens of New Jersey to the open fields and orchards of southern New York to the sprawling hardwood hillsides of western Pennsylvania. Throw in the flat, open farmland of Maryland's Eastern Shore and the suburban hunting in Massachusetts and you have diversity unrivaled elsewhere.

Hunting methods vary as much as the habitat. Traditional methods,

This high-jumping eight-pointer is a good trophy for much of the East. Many of the bucks taken there are shot either directly or indirectly as a result of forced movement. High hunting pressure is the rule, but some areas are remote enough to escape the brunt of the pressure and harbor trophy bucks. Photo by Denver Bryan.

such as stand-hunting, "stalking," field-watching, etc., are all employed in the region. Snow tracking is certainly a part of the tradition from Pennsylvania northward. But, the hunting method that most sets this region apart is "party hunting," where groups of people hunt together in either organized drives or loose association. More than anywhere else, deer hunting here is a social affair. Because of this, the majority of the bucks killed in the East Region fall either directly or indirectly as a result of forced movement. There is, of course, one-on-one hunting, especially on private land in the northern and southern extremes of the region, but party hunting symbolizes the East.

The East Region has an abundance of public hunting land, mostly in and around the mountainous areas. Hunting pressure is intense on much of this land. In fact, pressure in the East overall is the highest of any region. Even private land receives high pressure in the more popu-lated parts of the region. Only the remote, roadless areas or large private holdings escape the high pressure from the region's many avid hunters. Parts of West Virginia and Maryland receive the least pressure. The East is not a prime destination for visiting trophy hunters for obvious reasons, though there are a handful of hunting operations around, patronized mostly by area hunters.

The high number of hunters dictates short seasons and limited bag limits. Generally, firearms seasons run from a week to two weeks in length. A couple of places allow three weeks. A one-buck limit is the norm most places. Archery seasons are rather liberal, lasting from three to eight weeks. Muzzleloader hunting is popular, and special seasons are in place throughout the region. The use of centerfire rifles is allowed in much of the region, but the more populated areas, especially in the coastal states, are restricted to shotguns only.

The East supports a lot of deer, even in suburban areas. Deer populations run from a low of 15 deer per square mile in the open farm country and more settled deer habitat to a high of around 60 deer per square mile. In the inland areas, winter kills can be a factor. The moderating influence of the ocean makes severe winter weather less of a problem along the coast.

Trophy bucks are hard to come by simply because few reach 3½ years old; therefore, almost any 3½ can rightfully be considered a trophy. Less than three percent of some herds make it to maturity. In places with lower pressure, that number may climb to 15 or 20 percent. Region-wide, 4½, 5½ or 6½-year-olds are rare indeed. The buck/doe ratio favors does, but not as badly as one might think. A tradition of doe hunting and high reproduction prevents the balance from getting too far out of hand. Still, the pressure on bucks reduces their numbers significantly each year, resulting in buck/doe ratios commonly in the 1:3 to 1:5 range.

Though the obvious lack of age and, to a lesser degree, overcrowding are problems, the best areas of the East are capable of producing some good bucks. The genetics are present for B&C bucks. New York and Pennsylvania have the best potential, but the number of trophy bucks produced there has declined in recent years owing to high pressure. Today, Maryland and West Virginia offer the top trophy prospects, followed by the sections of Vermont, New Hamsphire and New York in the East Region. Some surprisingly good bucks are also found in Connecticut and Massachusetts, if you don't mind hunting in the shadow of civilization.

The South Region

Hunters in the South ply their trade in rugged mountains and vast river swamps and in rolling hills and flat piney woods. They hunt deep, unbroken forests as well as open farmlands. While Southern hunting is most often associated with palmetto-covered flatlands and moss-laden swamps, gently rolling pine hills laced with hardwood bottoms and dotted by fields and pastures probably best characterize Southern deer habitat.

Traditions in the South run deep, and so it is with deer hunting. Interestingly, much of the South was devoid of deer until the 1950's. During that time, reforestation of former agricultural land was well under way and deer restocking began. The tradition of dog hunting for deer sprang up in those early days when access to land was free and easy, deer densities were low and hunters were relatively few. This tradition survives today in many Southern states, especially those bordering on the coast where cover is thickest. But in the last 20 years, a new hunting tradition has emerged revolving around deer leases and stand-hunting and "stalking." Dogs don't understand property lines, and in many places, the old and new have come into conflict. It remains to be seen how dog hunting for deer will fit into the South's future, but one thing is for sure — deer leases and one on one hunting are here to stay. From a trophy hunter's viewpoint, that's just as well.

The South may have been late coming back onto the deer hunting scene, but it has more than made up for lost time. Well-distributed agriculture and young, dynamic forests combine with a long growing season to produce a great abundance of food. Thick cover throughout the region provides more than adequate protection for deer. Plus, the mild climate and plentiful rainfall eliminate weather as a limiting factor to deer population growth. So, the deer herd in the South has exploded. This has led to the most liberal seasons and bag limits in the country. Seasons last from a month to as long as 4½ months, and bag limits run from two bucks to no limit at all. Both rifles and shotguns are used in the South, but the preferred weapon is the rifle. In addition, special archery seasons

The South receives moderate to high-moderate pressure overall. As a result, most trophy bucks are 3½-year-olds like this 130-class nine-pointer I shot in Georgia.

and, in some cases, muzzleloader seasons extend the hunting opportunities in the South. Combine the long seasons and liberal bag limits with a deep-rooted hunting tradition and a growing human population and the result is substantial pressure on the South's deer herds.

The great majority of the land in the South is privately owned. Some public hunting is available on state and federal wildlife management areas, refuges and forests. However, most hunting takes place on private land, with commercial timber companies and private farms and holdings being of equal importance. Deer clubs and leases of various sizes, ranging from 100 acres to several thousand acres, control the deer hunting on this private property. Deer management, or the lack thereof, varies greatly from one tract to another. As a result, there are tremendous differences in the quality of hunting, especially trophy hunting, from tract to tract. Except for Texas, more deer management effort is being put into individual tracts of land in the South than in any other region. The results can be impressive, but the small size of most landholdings limits what many clubs can do. Yet, as the remaining pockets that are not either overshot or overcrowded shrink, management on individual tracts must be depended on more and more to provide good trophy hunting.

In recent years, the South has seen a proliferation of deer hunting operations. Most people are attracted to Southern hunting because of high hunter success (often upwards of 50 percent on a three-day hunt), a long season that extends their hunting opportunities, a liberal limit (a second buck can sometimes be taken at little or no charge) and the mild climate. Most do not come for the sole purpose of shooting a trophy buck, and that's good. The truth is that less than 25 percent will shoot a buck qualifying as a trophy even on the best operations. Hunts are often priced by the day so a hunter can control his total cost. Rates of $150 to $300 per day can be expected. Three-day, all-inclusive package hunts normally run from $800 to $1,200. Hunting there is not physically demanding, and the hunter can set his own pace and work as hard or as little as he chooses. Accommodations range from adequate to excellent.

Deer populations in the South are high, so high that overcrowding and habitat damage are serious detriments. Only in recent years has the "sacred doe" concept in the South been sufficiently dispelled so that widespread doe harvests can address the overcrowding problem. Deer densities run from 20 to 80 deer per square mile. Generally, the lowest populations are in the relatively infertile mountains and the highest along the major rivers. Because of the abundance of deer, hunter success in the South is quite high, upwards of 40 percent in some states, but it has come at the cost of antler size.

Hunting pressure ranges from moderate to high-moderate. A few places would have to be rated high, mainly because of long seasons and high hunter participation. Light pressure conditions are limited to protected private tracts or remote areas. Across the board, the buck age structure is fair to poor. That means 3½-year-old bucks are present, but they are not easy to come by. Older bucks are a major challenge. The buck/doe ratio tends to be fairly high but varies greatly because of differing doe harvests and reproductive rates. Some places would be in the 1:1.5 area while others would exceed 1:8.

The genetic potential for big bucks in the South is better than most people realize. Extensive restocking from other parts of the country is part of the reason. Georgia in particular appears to have benefited from this. Except for Texas (of which only a small part lies in the South

In the better areas of the South, bucks can reach impressive size ... if they get the necessarey age. This 150-class eight-pointer is one such buck. Photo by Mike Biggs.

Region), only Kentucky can match Georgia's 37 record bucks as of the 1988 B&C listing. Kentucky shares some of the excellent trophy hunting found in the neighboring Midwest Region and is the hottest place in the South for trophies at this time. In fact, 21 of Kentucky's 37 record bucks have been killed since 1980 compared to 17 in Georgia. Mississippi follows in recent production with 10 of its 21 B&C bucks coming since 1980. Florida has never yielded a record buck, and South Carolina has but one. North Carolina broke into the records in the 1980's for the first time with three. The other Southern states turn out B&C's with varying degrees of consistency. Many of Oklahoma's and most of Texas' record bucks have come from outside the designated South Region.

Although Alabama has only eight record bucks listed with Boone & Crockett through 1988, a couple of bucks have come to light recently that have caused considerable excitement in trophy circles. In 1989, a huge non-typical was shot by Jon Moss that has since been scored at a whopping 259⅞ points, placing it high in the records. Another giant non-typical has recently been uncovered that was shot by David Melton in 1956. Incredibly, the Melton buck was first scored at 287⅝, but after being scored by the B&C Judges Panel in May 1992, the buck's final score was reduced to 239⅛. Still, both the Moss buck and the Melton buck are world-class non-typicals and elevate the status of Alabama as a trophy whitetail state.

The size of a representative trophy varies considerably by locale. In Florida, a buck scoring 90 to 100 would make trophy status, but it would take a 135 in Kentucky. Regionwide, the average trophy size is a 120-point buck, reflecting both overcrowding and an age weighted toward 3½. Bucks in the 130 to 135 class are probable in the better areas, and something topping 140 is a possibility. Anyone looking for a 150 would be fighting long odds. Obviously, record-class bucks are killed in the South, but your chances of being one of the lucky few are slim indeed.

Midwest Region

The Midwest has emerged in the last two decades as the top producer of giant whitetails in the United States. Only the central farmland region of Canada can rival it. The reasons are simple — great genetics, sufficient age and a super abundance of high-quality food.

The fertile soils of the Midwest farm country make it the nation's breadbasket. Expansive fields of corn, soybeans and small grains broken by woodlots, timbered bluffs and wooded waterways characterize the region. Most of the land there is privately owned, and the countryside is fairly populated by those working and living on the farms. Generally, the farms are relatively small, from 150 to 500 acres. The deer are accus-

tomed to living near man and can exist undetected in places with surprisingly little cover. Since cover, not food, is most often the limiting
factor in the Midwest, short seasons, low bag limits and shotgun-only
restrictions are the norm in much of the region. For the most part, gun
hunters have from 5 to 15 days to find their buck. One is the normal
limit. Most of the region is limited to shotguns only (or muzzleloaders),
but rifles are allowed in some places.

One of the unique things about hunting in the Midwest is the great
emphasis on archery hunting. Long seasons, up to 3½ months, give
serious bowhunters added time to try for big bucks. Around this long
archery season and the high stakes for record-class bucks have emerged
some of the best whitetail hunters on the continent. That they successfully challenge big whitetails with a bow is testimony to their skill. These
bowhunters have accounted for some of the top bucks in the country in
recent years.

Two primary hunting methods are employed in the Midwest. One
is deer drives. With the limited cover available, hunters can often sur-
round or cutoff a woodlot or a strip of timber most effectively. This
method accounts for many of the region's big bucks. The other common
method is hunting from treestands. Hunters, especially the archers, locate
major trails, scrapelines, etc., position a stand, often a portable, and wait.
If they've done their homework, an opportunity is likely to come their
way. Slipping quietly through the cover or along field edges is also a frequent hunting method.

Overall, Midwest deer densities tend to be rather low, mainly
because of the lack of cover. In large wooded areas, found primarily in
association with hills or rivers, populations are higher. Such places may
carry 20 to 50 deer per square mile. However, the typical farm country
is home to fewer deer since only a portion is actually year-round deer
habitat. A range of 5 to 15 deer per square mile would probably apply
to most Midwest farmland.

Because of the lack of cover and the fact that much of the existing woodlands consist of open hardwoods, the deer are exposed to
pressure in the Midwest. Actually, the crops themselves, corn in particular, provide some of the best cover until harvest time. The large rural
population and the proximity of large cities assure plenty of people to
pursue these deer. What the deer have going for them is a short gun

Because of limited cover in the Midwest, deer drives are a popular and highly effective way to hunt the region's trophy bucks. Photo by Denver Bryan.

season, private land with limited access and the fact they are accustomed to living near humans and staying out of their way. The net result is moderate to high hunting pressure. The high pressure is mostly centered around the limited public land and the more heavily wooded areas. Most of the farm country per se sees moderate pressure, leading to a fair to pretty good age structure. Because the harvest includes a healthy percentage of does and reproduction stays high, the buck/doe ratio is good in most places.

The lack of age in the Midwest does handicap the otherwise tremendous genetic and nutritional advantages of the region. Still, enough bucks reach the mature age classes to make the average size of Midwest trophies most impressive. Southern Minnesota, Wisconsin and Michigan have tremendous potential, but high hunting pressure hurts the buck age structure. The best trophy prospects are in Ohio, Indiana, Illinois, northern Missouri and especially Iowa and eastern Kansas. This is home to some seriously big bucks. The average trophy there probably would

A soybean field, a record-class whitetail, a hunter with a shotgun ... this photo says a lot about Midwestern hunting. Photo courtesy of North American Whitetail.

be 145! Bucks topping 150 are not at all uncommon. A person hunting the right piece of land would have a reasonable chance for a 160. And, the odds of killing a record buck here are better than anywhere else in the United States and compare favorably with those of Central Canada.

Unfortunately, there is limited opportunity in the Midwest for a visiting trophy hunter. The land use and ownership patterns as well as the relatively high human population make it very difficult for an outfitting industry to exist, although a few outfitters are trying to put something together on leased land. For the most part, a hunter is on his own there. It is necessary for him to know exactly where he is going to hunt, preferably even the buck he's after, in order to take full advantage of the region's trophy opportunities. For this reason, local hunters with access to the land and time to scout have a far better chance at these mega bucks than visiting resident or nonresident hunters. Your best hope is to know or get to know a local.

According to B&C records, over 50 percent of both the top 20 all-time typicals and non-typicals have come from states lying in part or in total in our designated Midwest Region! Even more amazing, the top three bucks in both categories are from Midwestern states. The current world record 206⅛-point typical is from Wisconsin (even though it is from just across our designated North Region line); the No. 2 typical scored 205 and was shot in Missouri; and No. 3 is a 204⁴⁄₈-point typical from Illinois. As for non-typicals, the world record is the 333⁷⁄₈-point buck from Missouri and No. 2 is Ohio's famous "Hole-In-The-Horn" buck scoring 328²⁄₈. The unofficial No. 3 non-typical has not yet been listed in the record book, though it has been measured by an official scorer. This buck scored 288⁴⁄₈ and is also from Ohio. It should be apparent that the genetic potential of the Midwest is essentially unlimited. And, the good news is that almost half of the B&C bucks taken in the "core" Midwestern states have fallen in the last decade!

Plains And Prairies Region

To a hunter east of the Missis-sippi, The Plains and Prairies Region bears no resemblance to whitetail country. Wide open spaces interrupted only by strips of trees and brush along waterways or blocks of timber planted for windbreaks seem to hold little promise for whitetails. As far as the wide open spaces are concerned, that is largely true. But, those scattered strips and blocks of cover are indeed home to the whitetail!

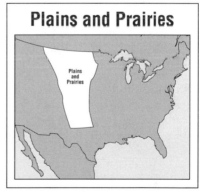

Depending on where you are in the region, you may know the plains and prairies for their endless wheat fields or their shimmering grasslands or for their stark sagebrush-studded landscape. On the eastern edge of the region, windbreaks, hedgerows and woodlots add to the cover available to whitetails. To the west, brushy and timbered draws finger out

If you can gain access to one of the better ranches in the Plains & Prairies Region, your chances of shooting a buck like this are very good. Photo by Denver Bryan.

into the rugged breaks along the major waterways to extend the range of the whitetail beyond the riverbottoms. But for the most part, the whitetails of this region are concentrated along the many watercourses networking through the vast plains and prairies of the United States. This pattern is broken only by the scattered pockets of timbered hills and forested areas here and there, most notably the Black Hills straddling the South Dakota/Wyoming border. Although public hunting land is present, by far the majority of the whitetail hunting is on private ranches, some of which are very large.

Much of the riverbottom habitat of the Plains and Prairies Region is in association with agriculture. These fertile floodplains are flat and productive. For the whitetail, the presence of agricultural crops is an important factor in this harsh land. Winters there are severe. Howling winds and subzero temperatures take their toll. The food availability represented by agriculture gives the deer an edge in surviving the long, hard winter.

Because of the farming, the already limited cover is made even more critical. Additionally, the timbered areas, most often consisting of cotton-woods and ash, that do exist are often quite open. Only where tall grass, cattails or low-growing willows, wild rose or cedars provide good ground cover does the whitetail find secure shelter. Islands in the rivers are favored and somewhat protected haunts of whitetails. Big bends in the rivers and low-lying areas subject to flooding are where the largest tracts of cover are found ... and where the greatest concentrations of deer are located. The brushy or timbered breaks extending out from the rivers into the drier, open uplands are also frequented by whitetails, especially when they are pressured. In fact, there are places where whitetails seem to be spending more and more time in the drier, open country, possibly in response to hunting pressure or overcrowding in the preferred riverbottoms.

Having painted this picture of limited cover and high exposure, it is understandable why I say this region is one of the easiest places in the country to hunt whitetails, once you find the deer. It's a fairly simple matter to find cutoff points along the waterways to intersect their linear movement. Deer there orient to the agricultural crops. A few afternoons of staking out an alfalfa or sugar beet field will pretty well reveal what's there. Deer drives are also understandably effective. Another advantage hunters often have in this region is that the deer, after spending the summer and early fall feeding and living over a large area, are forced to concentrate in the limited remaining cover during the late fall when hunting season is underway.

Season length averages about four weeks overall, though shorter and longer seasons do exist. One buck is the norm, with a couple of exceptions. Archery hunting is more popular in the eastern tier of states than in the western. In areas with a long gun season and a one buck limit, archery hunting is less favored for obvious reasons. Muzzleloader hunting is not very widespread, but a few states do have special seasons in areas. The wide open spaces and relatively low human population make this rifle territory, preferably of the long-range variety.

A spotty but fairly widespread whitetail outfitting/guiding indus-try exists in the Plains and Prairies Region, mainly in the northern reaches. Many ranches will sell access rights to visiting hunters, but getting the names of such places is difficult unless you know the ranch-ers or someone who does. Even then, the ranch may or may not be worth hunting. For most visiting hunters, hiring an outfitter or guide is a better way to go, at least to start with. If a hunter has access to some of the better hunting in this region, the trophy prospects can be excellent. Most visiting hunters stay in hotels in nearby towns. Prices for week-long hunts normally fall within the $1,500 to $2,500 range.

Deer densities vary greatly across the region. The greatest concentration of deer I've ever seen was there. A 325-acre stretch of timber in a big bend in Montana's Missouri River harbored around 300 deer, nearly a deer per acre! In one afternoon, my wife and I counted 180 deer in an adjoining sugar beet field, and that was not the only field adjacent to the woods! On the other hand, I have hunted places in this regions where only a handful of deer were scattered up and down long stretches of creek or riverbottoms. It's all a matter of cover and food, with emphasis on the cover. Because the best hunting is on private land and the deer herds are very localized, a visiting hunter must know exactly where he's going to hunt. The difference between adjacent ranches can be startling.

Measured in volume, hunting pressure would have to be considered low to low-moderate overall in the Plains and Prairies Region. However, measured by effect, it would get a higher rating. First, pressure here is concentrated in a relatively small area. Second, the deer are very vulnerable. The combination of these two factors means that a little pressure goes a long way. Relatively few hunters can exert moderate to high-moderate pressure on a somewhat fragile resource. I've seen the top-end shot off a place in just a year or two with relatively light pressure by Eastern standards. The saving grace from a trophy hunter's viewpoint is that many of the ranches allow only limited hunting, thus protecting the age structure.

Regionwide, the buck age structure is fair to good. Enough bucks reach the older age classes to make things interesting. Because of high hunter success for bucks and the one deer limit in most places, the pressure is often much heavier on bucks than does, resulting in an imbalanced buck/doe ratio. I've hunted areas in this region with ratios that seemed upwards of 1:6 and as low as 1:2. Winter kills and predators can hamper fawn survival, contributing to bad buck/doe ratios when there is heavy emphasis on shooting bucks.

Deer in this region have the potential to get big, both in body and antler size. A good number of B&C's hail from the region, but not as many as one might think. The reason is because the overall number of whitetails in the region is relatively low due to the localized nature of the herds, not because of a lack of potential. Many of the B&C bucks from states making up the Plains and Prairies Region have come from areas of the states designated to be in other regions. For instance, in Nebraska and Kansas, the majority of the record bucks were shot in the eastern part of the states, which we have designated as the Midwest Region. Most of Texas' record bucks are from the Brush Country to the south. Oklahoma has about an equal split between its two regions. About half of Montana's record bucks originated in the mountainous Northwest Region. Still, the right ranch in the Plains and Prairies Region offers as good a chance for a record-class whitetail as just about anywhere. Overall, I would say a 140 is a representative trophy, but there are ranches where a 150-class buck or better is a reasonable goal.

Northwest Region

This is Rocky Mountain country. Snow-capped mountains and picturesque evergreen valleys dotted by farms and fields dominate the landscape. Here, the bugle of elk fills autumn mornings, the grizzly still rules the wilderness beyond the roads, moose forage in hidden beaver ponds, mule deer feed in alpine meadows and the awesome buffalo still roams ... right alongside big whitetails!

Yes, the northern Rockies are home to a large and growing population of whitetails. In fact, some people are concerned about their impact on mule deer since whitetails seem to be displacing them in some traditional muley areas. Currently, the whitetail is widely distributed throughout western Montana, northern Idaho and eastern Washington. Oregon has a fair population in its northeastern corner, and Wyoming has scattered pockets of whitetails in its western half.

Historically, whitetails have not been hunted much in this region, though that's changing now. One reason is that hunters are usually limited to one buck, and many Westerners either prefer to hunt mulies or find them easier to shoot than whitetails. A large herd, low pressure and the great availability of public hunting land make the Northwest Region one of the last frontiers for trophy whitetails. But like the Plains and Prairies Region, whitetail populations vary considerably between locales. Even a matter of a mile or less can make a big difference. Also, whitetails living in and around the mountains can be truly migratory, both in terms of elevation and general location. In places, mature bucks tend to stay at surprisingly high elevations until either the rut or severe weather pushes them down. Plus, entire populations can migrate dozens of miles in response to winter.

One of the most popular ways to hunt deer in the Northwest is to ride around in a vehicle until one shows up. The legalities of this are questionable, but it's done. When the truck is left behind, most hunting is done from the ground. But as whitetail hunting increases in popularity, treestands, mainly portables, are gaining in favor, as is rattling. Snow tracking is also practiced here but does not seem to be as prevalent as in the North Region. Some of the best hunting is in and around agricultural crops, but that means private property, which can be hard to get permission to hunt. Most public hunting is done in a "big woods" environment. The terrain can be demanding and the distances great. Also, the weather can be cold or wet, or both. Because of the remoteness of some of the country, a hunter should be in shape and equipped for any contingency. All this is to say that whitetails there are not particularly easy to hunt.

Hunting seasons in this region are amply long, from two to five weeks. Hunters are allowed one buck of any species in most places. That forces a choice and spreads the pressure between mulies and whitetails, and even blacktails in the Pacific Coast states. Bowhunting is gaining ground but is not as popular as in some other regions. Some muzzleloader opportunities exist. Rifles are, of course, the preferred weapon.

Many visiting hunters take advantage of the great abundance of public land and go on do-it-yourself hunts. The results are mixed. Some stumble upon good areas and are successful. Others never get it together and have a miserable hunt. Because of the localized nature of whitetail populations, the vastness and ruggedness of this country and the difficulty in finding and hunting the better bucks, an outfitter/guide is recommended. Currently, not very many specialize in whitetails, but that's changing. Most run small operations, and their hunters stay in nearby

A large herd, low pressure and loads of public hunting land make the Northwest Region one of the last frontiers for trophy whitetails. This record-class buck was shot in western Montana by Richie Manos of Kalispell. Photo by Dick Idol.

motels. There are a few large, traditional western outfitters catering to whitetail hunters. Prices for a week-long hunt run from $1,500 to $2,500 on the average. If you are fortunate enough to get one of the better guides, a hunt there can be a good value considering the trophy possibilities and the quality of the experience.

Deer populations are concentrated primarily in the valleys and associated hillsides near human activity, like farming, ranching or timbering. Whitetails also exist in some of the wide agricultural valleys that have no direct association with mountains. Hunting in such places is much like that of the Midwest or Plains and Prairies Region. The remote wilderness country supports few if any whitetails.

Deer densities vary considerably from place to place. The highest concentrations seem to be in western Montana and northern Idaho. It is often difficult to get a handle on deer density since a herd may scatter over a huge chunk of country during the summer but concentrate in a much smaller area in the winter. I have hunted large areas with relatively few deer. Judging from sign and sightings, a density of 5 to 10 deer per square mile seemed reasonable. But 20 miles away in the same type habitat, sign and sightings pointed toward an apparent density of around 20 to 30 deer per square mile. One notable characteristic of this country is that deer tend to bunch up on desirable food sources rather remarkably, even in places that don't appear to have all that many deer. Near a small ranch I own in western Montana, anyone spending time in the woods would estimate the deer population at about 25 deer per square mile. Yet on any given afternoon prior to hunting season, 100 to 200 deer show up in a nearby 100-acre alfalfa field. They must come from miles around!

Because of the remoteness of the country, the relatively low human population and the other hunting options available, pressure on whitetails across the region is low. The most heavily hunted areas would only be rated as moderate. Even when a lot of hunters are in an area, most tend to hunt on or near the road so overall pressure may still be fairly low. One other factor is that the older mature bucks often hold up in areas away from the bulk of hunting pressure. For instance, during the first three weeks of the season around my ranch, most pressure is along the roads in the valley, but many of the big bucks are still high on the unroaded mountainsides, some even at or above timberline. They remain there until the rut kicks in before Thanksgiving. During the early days of season, does and young bucks are the focus of most of the pressure. The older bucks escape the initial hit. The result is a good buck age structure. An encouraging number of 4½, 5½, 6½ and 7½-year-old bucks are present, yielding excellent trophy prospects. The buck/doe ratio is good as a whole.

Some great bucks have been taken in this region. Western Montana has put a couple of 190-plus typicals in the book, the largest of which scored 199$^3/_8$. Several very impressive non-typicals have been taken there, including a 267$^4/_8$ from Idaho and a couple in the 250 class from western Montana. In fact, one of the most notable things about big bucks in the Northwest is the frequency that record non-typicals show up. Wyoming and Washington have more non-typicals in the B&C records than typicals. Montana and Idaho also have an unusually high percentage of non-typicals. Overall, a buck in the 140 to 145 class would represent a trophy in the region. A 150 is a definite possibility. Bigger bucks are there, but owing to the difficulty of hunting this big country, they are never easy.

Southwest Region

The Southwest is unlike any other place in the United States. The two principle areas from the whitetail hunter's perspective are Texas' Hill Country and Brush Country. These two places adjoin each other but are worlds apart in appearance and deer resources. The Hill Country is a land of limestone hills covered with live oaks and cedar trees. Clear streams

Southwest Region

flow through deep canyons, and beautiful wildflowers paint the landscape blue, yellow and red in the spring. The Hill Country is all of this plus home to the greatest concentration of whitetails in the world!

By contrast, the Brush Country, also known as the South Texas Plains, is essentially gently rolling plains, although some striking outcrops and geological formations are found there. This is a land covered by thornbrush, cactus and mesquite trees. Its rivers are muddy and slow-moving, and the ground as often as not is parched and bare. Heat waves dance over the land, and rain is precious in this hot, dry southern extremity of the United States. The Brush Country is indeed a most unlikely place to find the greatest concentration of trophy whitetails in the world. That's a strong statement, I know, but I'll stick by it. Area for area, there are more trophy whitetails in South Texas than any other place! They may not average as big there as in the Midwest or Canada, but there are more of them!

Texas is a strange land. In this vast state, you find the highest number of deer and the greatest concentration of trophy bucks. Yet to the north and west of these incredible deer areas, whitetail populations dwindle. As you leave these areas, deer numbers first begin to drop as the land becomes more arid and open. Next, herds become localized along rivers and pockets of cover. Finally, as you move farther west and north, whitetails practically play out. So, on the very fringe of the whitetail's range, extremes exist, ranging from virtually no deer at all to the continent's greatest concentration of whitetails!

Other than the Brush Country and Hill Country, a couple of other notable places should be mentioned. First, there's the upper coastal region of Texas where the brush gives way to a vast coastal plain consisting of marshes, agricultural fields and oak motts. This is Texas' famous goose and duck country, but whitetails also live there in impressive numbers, if not size. To the west along the border with Mexico, the Carmen Mountains whitetail of the Big Bend Country survives in rugged, arid mountains. In New Mexico, in addition to the Coues whitetail in the southwestern corner, a substantial but little-hunted herd of the Texas subspecies of whitetail is found in and around the Mescalero Apache Indian Reservation in the south-central part of the state.

The deer hunting tradition in Texas is deeply rooted and unique. It was there that the concept of leasing hunting rights first developed. Today, leases are the basis of a huge hunting economy in Texas, and the idea has spread to most other states, especially in the South. Texas is where "horn-rattling" for bucks originated, or at least its widespread use. And, the Lone Star State is one of the few places where hunting from a vehicle is not only widely practiced but legal. In South Texas, it has become highly specialized. Known as "high-racking," hunters ease along roads on the sprawling ranches in elevated platforms mounted high above the bed of the pickup or atop other specially rigged vehicles, much like tuna towers on offshore fishing boats. From this lofty perch, hunters can see into the dense low-growing brush.

Stand-hunting is also very popular in Texas. Tripod stands provide elevation in places where no suitable trees exist. Covered blinds, from the most basic to extravagantly elaborate, loom above the Texas skyline. Baiting deer is also legal and much practiced in Texas. Many bucks meet their end every year as they blissfully eat corn.

Texas is the focus of the most intensive deer management programs in North America. Game-proof fences are a common sight. The buck age structure and buck/doe ratio are managed for maximum trophy production on many ranches. Helicopters whirl overhead as deer herds are censused. Genetic work is under way to improve trophy potential. In Texas, deer hunting is big business, and some ranches have the money and land to do it right.

What makes Texas so unique? First, the mentality of Texas hunters and the game department is bent toward quality deer, not just numbers. Secondly, the land is fertile and deceptively productive. Thirdly, and most importantly, nearly all the Hill Country and South Texas consist

The South Texas Brush Country and one of its more notable residents. Though seemingly bleak and unproductive at first glance, this region has the greatest concentration of trophy whitetails on the continent. Photo by Mike Biggs.

of large privately owned ranches. Many have the will and the means to protect and manage their deer. The Brush Country in particular has huge ranches, ranging in size up to more than 800,000 acres, as is the case with the famous King Ranch.

There's another unique factor regarding the Brush Country: Reproduction is very low during most years because of the combined effects of periodic droughts and predation. This, oddly enough, can be an advantage in trophy management. Low reproduction can result in a relatively stagnant deer herd maintained at or below carrying capacity and consisting of a high percentage of mature bucks. In effect, mature bucks can be stockpiled. In places with high reproduction and low hunting pressure, the population would become severely overcrowded and antler size would deteriorate. This is basically what has happened in the Hill Country, where deer size has been hurt due to increased numbers.

Texas allows a hunter two bucks and gives him two months to shoot them. About the only thing you can't do is shoot them at night or off a public road. Trespassers, however, are dealt with most harshly in Texas.

Without a doubt, Texas is the No. 1 destination state for visiting whitetail hunters. Extremely high hunter success for trophy bucks draws hunters from across the country. Outfitters and ranchers offer everything from do-it-yourself day hunts to complete package hunts lasting several days. For bucks scoring 100 to 125, the Hill Country is the place to go. Hunter success approaches 100 percent on the better ranches. The cost of a typical two to three-day package hunt is $800 to $2,000. Hunters looking for bucks in the 130 to 150 class will find no better place than South Texas. Success rates run extremely high, and the high cost reflects the large size of the bucks. Expect to pay $3,000 to $5,000 for a fully outfitted South Texas hunt. In both the Hill Country and South Texas, the hunter will see plenty of deer and find accommodations ranging from adequate to plush. The weather is mild, and hunts are not physically demanding. The hunter does not have to work any harder than he likes, but the level of his effort will determine to a large degree the size of his buck. A second buck is sometimes available for an additional trophy fee.

The Hill County, also known as the Edwards Plateau, carries an incredible number of deer, too many in fact. Deer densities there range from 40 to over 100 deer per square mile! That, my friend, is a bunch of deer! Some estimates say that the Hill Country carries 10 percent of all the deer in North America! The Brush Country supports fewer deer, but this area is by no means a slouch in numbers, either. From 20 to 40 deer per square mile would be representative of most South Texas ranches.

Moderate hunting pressure describes that of the Hill Country. Because management and hunting practices differ so much, individual ranches in the Hill Country vary greatly in their buck age structure and buck/doe ratio. Overall, a fair to good age structure can be expected. Generally, the Hill Country tends to be heavily weighted in favor of does because of disproportionate buck pressure and low reproduction stemming from overcrowding. There are ranches with 8 to 10 does for every buck. Something in the 1:3 to 1:5 range would be more typical. Emphasis on shooting does has increased lately and is helping in a number of ways.

Hunting pressure in South Texas is low. Even where pressure is relatively high in terms of hunter days, the harvest may be low because only trophy bucks are taken. Some ranches have age structures with considerably more bucks over 3½ years old than under! Many ranches try

Above: The buck in the rear is world-class! The great non-typical was photographed in South Texas by Mike Biggs, who figures the buck will score about 220 points. The "little" 10-pointer in the lead is a 145-point buck, a very good deer in most places.

Right: This buck is a giant of the species. Tall tines and great mass give him a gross B&C score in the 180's and a net typical score in the mid 170's, putting him solidly in the record book. Photo by Curt Helmick.

Above: I shot this remarkable eight-pointer in South Texas. The buck's gross typical score is 172, and his net is 167 ⅜. The brow tines are nine inches long; the first primaries are 16 inches; and the second primaries are 12 inches. Only the "sticker" points on the first primaries keep the buck out of the Boone & Crockett records.

The Midwest is home to some of the nation's biggest whitetails. Bucks like this 155-class 10-pointer are a real possibility in the best areas. Photo by Mike Blair.

Right: Yeah, he's heavy and tall but look at the middle of the buck's forehead... there's a bonus third antler on this trophy! Photo by Curt Helmick.

Below: If you ever see a buck this good, skip the judging and go straight to the shooting. This is a near-record non-typical. Photo by Curt Helmick.

Long tines, exceptional main beams and good spread run up the score on this trophy Midwestern buck. Photo by Mike Blair.

I shot this 187-point non-typical in the waning minutes of a week-long hunt in South Texas. He was worth the wait! My longtime hunting buddy, Steve Spears, poses with the 15-pointer.

bove: Canadian whitetail
nting can be cold and tough,
t the big bucks are there.
skatchewan produced this
8 point typical for me on a
gid Thanksgiving morning.

Right: Huge bodies and
heavy antlers characterize
mature northern bucks like
this one from Wisconsin.
Photo by Bill Kinney.

Bucks like this have made South Texas famous for its trophy whitetails. This 25-inch-wide (outside) buck will score in the 160's. Short brow tines are his only weakness. Photo by Mike Biggs.

Look at the neck on this buck! Although he's not built to score real high, any trophy hunter would be proud to claim this buck as his own. Photo by Bill Kinney.

Early morning mist and the silhouetted rack of a big white-tail … this is a scene straight from the dreams of a trophy hunter. Photo by Mike Biggs.

The North Country is a land of deep forests, snow and trophy whitetails. Photo by Bill Kinney.

This 13-pointer is my best Georgia buck. His basic 10-point typical frame scores 155. The matched pair of six-inch drop tines makes the buck one of my favorites.

Trophy whitetails live in the limited cover along streams and rivers throughout the plains and prairies of the United States. Photo by Denver Bryan.

I had to try every trick I knew to get a shot at this big Brush Country 11-pointer. He was almost totally nocturnal. Four days of hard hunting passed before he finally made a mistake. Photo by Dick Idol.

to harvest nothing but 5½-year olds and older. Of course, there are ranches that hammer the bucks pretty hard, but many don't. Overall, South Texas undoubtedly has one of the best buck age structures in North America. Buck/doe ratios are just as impressive. Some ranches actually have more bucks than does, which results in intense rutting competition. This explains why antler-rattling works so well. Most South Texas ranches have ratios of from 1:1 to 1:2.

With well over 100 bucks in the record book, Texas stands as one of the top trophy states in the United States. The great majority

These two bucks hail from the Hill Country of Texas, an area that supports tremendous numbers of whitetails. The 10-pointer on the left is an exceptional buck for that part of the world. He'll score in the upper 130's. Photo by Mike Biggs.

of Texas' record bucks hail from South Texas. The Hill Country has a few record bucks to its credit, including the former world record non-typical, a 286-point monster dating back to 1892. In fact, the state's No. 2 and No. 4 non-typicals are from the Hill Country, and they scored a very high 272 and 240 respectively! And not only has Texas given up some world-class non-typicals, its five typicals topping 190 are second only to Minnesota's eight.

The representative trophy for the Hill Country is a buck scoring in the 110 class. Yet, I have a friend whose Hill Country ranch, which is under high fence and intensively managed, yields a buck topping 160 nearly every year. This is under ideal conditions, however. Overcrowding and cropping of the upper age classes have reduced the reasonable top-end prospects on most Hill Country ranches to around 130, though bigger ones are occasionally taken.

The Brush Country is another story altogether. Because of the tremendous number of mature bucks, many of which are 5½, 6½ and older, the representative trophy for this region is an impressive 140 or so. A 150 is a possibility on many ranches and a probability on the best. Such a buck would represent the exception in a herd, but high numbers of mature bucks cause exceptions to show up frequently. A 160 is definitely in the minority, but every year many are killed. Book deer represent a tiny fraction of the mature bucks, but Texas' B&C record speaks for itself. All in all, I consider South Texas to be the best place in North America to shoot a buck scoring from 130 to 150. For bucks between 150 and 160, it's a toss up between Canada and the top ranches in Texas. Over 160, Central Canada gets my nod ... unless I had a very dear friend in a prime area of the Midwest or unless I had access to one of the very best ranches in Texas!

MEXICO

Mexico can be divided into two major regions — the Rio Grande Region and The Coues Region. The Coues Region is, of course, named after the small subspecies of whitetail inhabiting the desert mountains of southwestern New Mexico and southern Arizona southward several hundred miles into Mexico. Our discussion here will include both the U.S. and Mexican sides of the Coues Region. The Rio Grande Region is essentially a 100-mile wide extension of the South Texas Brush Country into Mexico from the Big Bend area of Texas south to the state's southern tip.

Coues Region

For most whitetail hunters, the Coues deer is relatively unimportant. Compared to other whitetails, even a record buck is not big enough to turn many heads. But for those who live in that region or for those who have hunted this down-sized buck, he's something special. His attraction lies in the challenge of hunting him in remote, rugged and entirely unique

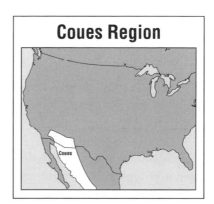

Coues Region

These are two of the bucks a group of us from North American Whitetail *shot on a trip to Mexico. Note the barren ground from overgrazing. This is a common situation there. The Sierra Madre Mountains are in the background.*

country. The Coues (pronounced "cows") is thoroughly whitetail, so he's no pushover. Put him in country so rough it is home to desert bighorns and so hostile it is unsettled by man, and the challenge begins to take shape.

This region is made up of deserts and mountains. In this exotic land, there's an interesting role reversal — the desert mule deer lives in the lower elevations, the desert environment, while the Coues inhabits the high country above the mulie. In the Coues' remote and trying high terrain, known to ecologists as the "Upper Sonoran Zone," a greater abundance of cover is more to the whitetail's liking. There, live oaks, grama grass, manzanita, junipers, mountain mahogany and an assortment of other indigenous plants provide cover for the Coues. Hunting is difficult at these altitudes, often over 5,000 feet above sea level. Just getting to the hunting grounds requires stamina. Horses or mules are sometimes employed to reach the best territory. Obviously, good conditioning is necessary for hunters serious about pursuing these deer.

Qualifying scores for B&C records are 110 for a typical and 120 for a non-typical. A buck in the 90 class is a trophy. These deer are small, but not as small as one might think. The average field-dressed weight of a mature Coues buck is about 90 pounds. An exceptional one will top 115 pounds. Frankly, that's not much different from most Texas Hill Country bucks and Central and South Florida deer. Arizona dominates the record book for Coues. Interest in Coues in recent years has created a small outfitting industry for them in the Southwest. Costs for a week-long hunt usually run from $1,500 to $2,500. Do-it-yourself hunts are possible but not recommended for first-time visitors. For a whitetail fanatic looking for a trip with all the adventure and romance of a classic Western mountain hunt, Coues may be the ticket.

Rio Grande Region

As I said, this region is basically an extension of the Texas Brush Country into Mexico. The main difference is that the quality of the habitat varies tremendously in Mexico because of land clearing and over-grazing by cattle. Rather than a fairly universal distribution of deer, as is found in South Texas, Mexico's deer hunting comes down to individual

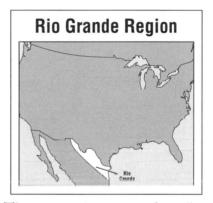

ranches, some of which are quite large. The resource is not spread evenly.

Even in suitable habitat, deer populations in Mexico tend to run lower on the average than in Texas. There are a couple of reasons for this. One, the habitat historically has been grazed heavier and is not in as good a condition. Two, poaching is more widespread and is largely nonselective, meaning does, fawns or bucks are shot with equal abandon. This latter factor acts to hold the population down and results in a low buck/doe ratio. Since overcrowding is not a problem, if a buck can get some age on him in Mexico, he's subject to be very good. While not nearly as many mature bucks exist there as in South Texas, the average size is at least as large. Heavier mass seems to be especially representative of Mexico's top-end bucks.

The best ranches seem to carry from 10 to 25 deer per square mile. Like South Texas, the average trophy size on these ranches is around 140. Bucks in the 150's are commonly taken. Mexico had recorded 10 B&C's as of 1988, and that number is growing. This is partially because of increased American involvement in deer management as Texas hunting and leases have gotten more expensive.

Mexican whitetail hunts tend to cost somewhat less than in South Texas due to the logistical problems and lower hunter success. Something around $2,500 to $3,500 is normal for a fully outfitted hunt. Anyone interested in hunting whitetails in Mexico should plan the trip carefully. Check out the ranch thoroughly. Cover all details of the hunt and the arrangements. I once arrived in Mexico on a hunt only to find out that the season had been unexpectedly closed. The owner of the ranch somehow talked officials into reopening it on his ranch. This 70,000-acre ranch was supposed to be virtually unhunted. On two occasions, however, I saw a truckload of Mexicans lay down indiscriminate volleys at deer while cruising the ranch roads. As it turned out, they were guests of the owner down for a couple of days of hunting. The deer were understandably the wildest I've ever hunted. I spent my time well away from the roads and found some good bucks. One buck I couldn't get a shot at must have been in the 160's. I finally shot a 140 after seeing several in that class. That ranch probably carried about 10 deer per square mile, but there were huge areas with very few deer as well as pockets with fair concentrations. The ranch next door, which we drove through to reach our ranch, was nearly devoid of any cover … or deer. So it goes in Mexico.

CANADA

There is much that is good about Canadian whitetail hunting — friendly people, interesting and diverse country and low hunting pressure to name a few. But, the one thing that sets Canada apart is the incredible size of its whitetails. If a hunter is after a record-class whitetail and is willing to risk going home empty-handed after paying his money for a reasonable chance (in relative terms) to get one, then Canada is the place to go. For instance, over 400 potential record bucks have been identified in Saskatchewan alone by Canadian trophy enthusiasts, although only 118 had been recorded with Boone & Crockett as of 1988. Every season, 25 to 40 more known record qualifiers are shot. The racks of many more end up nailed to the side of a barn or discarded behind the shop without ever coming to light. The best farmland deer country in Alberta and Manitoba compares favorably with Saskatchewan.

There are, however, some notable drawbacks to hunting Canada.

First, cold weather takes on a whole new meaning there. A hunter must be dressed and prepared for the extreme cold, or he cannot endure it. Strange things happen when the temperature is below zero. Safeties and firing pins freeze in place. Hands simply refuse to work. Vehicles don't start. Binoculars frost over, and buck lure turns to ice in the bottle. Heaven forbid hitting your fingers during a rattling session.

Second, deer densities are generally low in Canada. This problem can be further compounded by the fact that deer concentrations, such as they are, tend to be localized. It is possible to be a mile or more from the nearest deer while hunting seemingly good deer country. This is why choosing the right outfitter is so critical in Canada. He should have some bucks located so you can spend your time hunting deer ... not hunting the place where deer can be hunted. Even when the outfitter does his part, hard hunting is the order of the day.

Third, Canadian whitetail hunts are not cheap. Just getting there is expensive. Most people must buy special clothing to cope with the snow and cold, adding to the actual expense of the hunt. Week-long Canadian whitetail hunts range from $1,000 to $4,500, depending on what the outfitter provides and the size and reputation of the operation. Some of the best deals and best hunting are with the small outfitters who take only a handful of hunters and give personal attention.

Fourth, game laws in Canada can be restrictive and complicated. One of the most frustrating laws to the trophy hunter has to be Saskatchewan's and Manitoba's legal shooting hours regulation. Their hunting regulations booklets include official sunrise and sunset times and state, "Legal hunting time for big game includes that period of the day from one-half hour before sunrise until sunset." All serious trophy hunters know that the best time in the afternoon is from sunset to dark. Mature bucks seldom move prior to that time. This law eliminates nearly 50 percent of a day's prime time and probably causes more "honest" hunters to violate the law than any other regulation. At least one province requires solid orange or white outer garments from head to toe, literally. On some public lands, it is illegal to take a 4WD vehicle off a public road before noon. The guide laws are so confusing in one province that even the guides don't know for sure what is and is not legal. Hunting on Sunday is illegal in most provinces. Oddly, baiting deer is legal in places. Tagging and transporting trophies can be complicated and confusing.

Cold weather takes on a whole new meaning in Canada. But, one brief moment can make all the shivering worthwhile. Dick Idol shot this buck in Alberta.

Other laws, most of which are perfectly reasonable, are in direct conflict with the two most popular methods of hunting — deer drives and road-hunting. For instance, in most provinces, you are required to have prior permission to hunt private property whether it is posted or not. In one province where driving deer is very popular, it is illegal for more than four people (it was two until recently) to hunt together in concert. Despite the widespread popularity of road-hunting, it is generally a violation for the hunter to have cartridges in the magazine, let alone the chamber, of his rifle while in a vehicle. In one province, it is illegal to even have an uncased rifle in a 4WD truck or on an all-terrain vehicle. Shooting across or along a "provincial highway or grid road" is unlawful everywhere I've hunted in Canada.

Given these laws, there is practically no way to road-hunt legally. Think about it. A hunter can't ride with a loaded rifle, which I certainly agree with, or even with cartridges in his magazine. In some places, the rifle must be cased. He cannot shoot from a public road. Couple these considerations with the fact that a big whitetail is not going to stand around while a vehicle skids to a halt and the hunter steps out of the vehicle, uncases and loads his rifle and walks off the public road to take a legal shot, and you see the problem. Even if a hunter does all this, he still has to get permission from the landowner in most cases!

Deer drives theoretically could be conducted legally in most provinces by gaining advance permission from landowners. In practice, it usually doesn't work that way. Because of the relatively low number of deer and scattered cover, it takes a lot of land to meet the driving needs of 8 to 12 hunters. Season is long for the outfitters. Some run dozens of hunters through, each expecting a trophy buck. An outfitter would need permission on a large number of prescouted farms. Logistics make that difficult; therefore, it is seldom done. Most often, the "scouting" is done while road-hunting. When a guide finds a likely place, he contacts other members of the party and they converge to "push the bush." When the landowner hears the shooting and comes over to investigate, he is not particularly happy to find a party of nonresidents who have paid some guy big money to let them shoot his deer.

Because road-hunting and, to a lesser degree, deer drives so often violate game laws and create problems for landowners, the continued employment of these two forms of hunting actually threatens the nonresident's right to hunt in parts of Canada. True, resident hunters use these methods even more than nonresidents, but like it or not, the blame will fall on nonresidents. After all, not a lot can be done about resident violations, but something can be done about violations by Americans — they can be prevented from hunting there. So, what's the solution?

First, all parties need to recognize that everybody loses if U.S. citizens are further restricted from hunting whitetails in Canada. The greater burden, however, is on the visiting American, who must see to it that he hunts legally and in no way abuses landowners. On the other hand, the outfitter and guide must run a legal and responsible operation. And, I believe that a change from traditional hunting methods — road-hunting and deer drives — is necessary. The right change could make hunts more enjoyable and perhaps even more successful. During recent trips to Canada, I have still-hunted and stand-hunted almost exclusively and enjoyed far better success than I ever experienced riding the roads or driving in large groups. I would like to see Canadian outfitters offer one-on-one hunting on either public land or private property where they've gotten hunting permission as the norm, not the exception. Both the game law violations and the landowner abuses would be greatly reduced, if not eliminated. Happily, the trend seems to be moving in this direction.

Still, Canada remains the best place in North America for the visiting hunter when the goal is a 160-plus whitetail. Even at that, don't expect a sure thing. Hunter success for bucks topping even 150 probably doesn't exceed 25 percent with the most reliable outfitters. Hunters satisfied with bucks in the 120 to 150-point range would be better off going to Texas or the western United States. They'll see more deer, have better weather and enjoy much higher success. But if you're after a shot at a giant whitetail, Canada is the place.

For our purposes, Canadian whitetail hunting can be divided into three general regions: the Eastern Forest, Central Farmland and Western Mountain regions. Each is unique in its habitat, deer size and hunting traditions.

Eastern Forest Region

From Ontario eastward to the Maritime Provinces, this is "big woods" whitetail hunting with only scattered pockets of agriculture, mostly along the U.S. border. Whitetails in Ontario and Quebec are found in appreciable numbers only in the southernmost reaches of the provinces, where agriculture and timbering have made harsh conditions

Eastern Forest Region

more tolerable. The endless forests of interior Ontario and Quebec are more suitable to moose than whitetails. Relatively few whitetail guides and outfitters operate in Ontario and inland Quebec, though the number is on the upswing.

To the east along the Atlantic, the ocean's moderating temperatures result in a wider distribution of whitetails. Quebec's huge Anticosti Island, located at the mouth of the St. Lawrence River, has gained fame among whitetail hunters because of its abundance of deer, liberal bag limit, high hunter success and long season. An excellent whitetail outfitting industry has emerged there. A week's hunt with full services and good accommodations runs from $1,800 to $2,500. Travel expenses are

Big bucks in eastern Canada are often characterized by short tines, non-typical points and great mass. Photo by Curt Helmick.

in addition, and they are considerable.

New Brunswick, Nova Scotia and the part of Quebec lying east of the St. Lawrence River have widely distributed deer herds, though deer densities are relatively low on the whole. Guided whitetail hunts are growing in this part of Canada, and some outstanding trophies are turning up there. Most hunters stay in nearby hotels or in fairly basic camps. Hunts there are among the lowest priced anywhere. Most week-long hunts are well under $1,500, but some are higher, depending on the guide situation and services. While conditions are tough and hunter success low, the top-end prospects are considerable.

The Eastern Forest Region is home to some of the biggest bodied whitetails in North America. The body size can be simply enormous. Bucks topping 300 pounds live weight are not unlikely. A few will weigh over 300 pounds field dressed! Throughout the region, 200-pound-plus bucks are common. The racks, however, don't usually match their body size. That's not to say there aren't some big-racked bucks in the region. There are. A respectable number of B&C whitetails have been taken in the Maritime Provinces of eastern Canada, especially in New Brunswick. On the average, however, these bucks do not "score" as well as those from Central and West Canada. Note I said "score," because big bucks from eastern Canada are often characterized by short tines, non-typical points and tremendous mass. Main beam palmation is common. So, even when true monsters are killed in this region, it is not uncommon for them to fall short of the record book because of short tines and deductions from abnormal points. The odds of killing a non-typical record buck there may be better than for taking a typical record. As of the 1988 B&C listing, New Brunswick had 10 non-typicals against only 12 typicals. Nova Scotia brings the point home even more convincingly with only one typical versus seven non-typicals!

Much of the hunting in this region is done either from a stand or by walking. Snow tracking is a common practice. Guides sometimes position their hunters in treestands over agricultural crops or clearcuts. The lack of roads limits road-hunting in eastern Canada. Cold weather and physically challenging country place great demands on the hunters.

Central Farmland Region

Stretching from south-central Alberta through all the southern half of Saskatchewan into western Manitoba, the Central Farmland Region is home to some of the biggest antlered whitetails in the world. Like the U.S.'s Midwest, this is farm country and the agricultural crops make possible the huge bucks inhabiting this region. It is a land of

Central Farmland

expansive grain fields broken by various-sized woodlots, known locally as "bluffs." Some big woods areas are found in the region, particularly up and down the major waterways, along the northern fringe of the farm country and in areas of hilly or rough terrain.

This region is where most visiting whitetail hunters come in search of trophy bucks. A flourishing outfitting industry exists in Alberta, where there are less restrictions on where the nonresident may hunt than in the other farm provinces. Hunting whitetails in Alberta, however, is the most expensive of the Canadian provinces. Nonresident hunting in Saskatchewan is limited to the northern fringe of the farm country. Frankly, I believe this area offers the most interesting, if not the best, hunting in the province. More cover and fewer roads mean less pressure from road hunters there. Manitoba also limits nonresident hunters to the northern part of the farm country. Plan to spend $2,000 to $4,500 a week in the Central Farmland Region for a fully outfitted hunt. Some small, no-frills operations are cheaper, especially in Saskatchewan and Manitoba. Don't look for plush accommodations or a lot of creature comforts on Canadian hunts. Just the hope of a huge buck allows the high prices.

Much of the Central Farmland Region is cut by north/south and east/west "grid" roads, lying primarily along section lines (a section is one square mile) and along further subdivisions of sections. This network of roads, along with the open fields, makes the set-up ideal for road-hunting. A hunter in a vehicle can look over a lot of countryside in a day. This is one of the most widespread methods of hunting white-tails there, its questionable legality not withstanding. The other favored method is deer drives. A group of hunters will gather at a bluff and position standers to watch escape routes while the drivers walk through to push out deer. This is a very effective way of hunting this country, and many big bucks are taken this way. A few hunters sit on fields, hunt from stands or slip slowly through good deer territory. Hopefully, these forms of one-on-one hunting will increase in popularity.

Hunting pressure in the Central Farmland Region is the highest in Canada. Even at that, it does not compare with high pressure in the United States. Pressure in this area of Canada could be termed moderate, perhaps even low-moderate in the northernmost farm country where nonresidents are typically allowed to hunt. In areas close to population centers or with little cover, the buck age structure can be knocked down

I shot these two whopper bucks on a recent hunt in Saskatchewan. (Two bucks are legal.) The buck hanging up weighs over 300 pounds. He is the heaviest whitetail I've ever killed, but even larger ones live there.

148

to the point where older bucks are scarce. Because many of the deer there are taken for meat, does are fair game where legal. This favors a good buck/doe ratio. All in all, this region stands as the best place on the continent to shoot a record-class whitetail.

Western Mountain Region

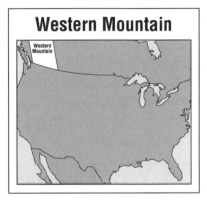

The Western Mountain Region consists of southeastern British Columbia and southwestern Alberta. This is the land of towering Rocky Mountains. Whitetails are found in the valleys, particularly those with agriculture, and on the wooded mountainsides that border or extend into farm country. This region is basically a northern extension of the Northwest Region of the United States. Hunting in the Western Mountain Region is rather localized but can be very good. The trophy potential is excellent, although the top-end is not as great as in the Central Farmland Region. Book-class bucks are present and an outside possibility.

Much of the hunting in this region is conducted around agriculture and in woods near agriculture. Most hunters ply their trade from the ground, as opposed to treestands or vehicles. Hunters slip slowly along field edges, through clearcuts or through likely places in the "big woods." Sitting on agricultural fields is also a common practice. Road-hunting is done there but on a limited basis.

Hunting pressure for whitetails is low, partly because of the popularity of the many other big game species in the region. Relatively few outfitters specialize in whitetails, but as in other places, the number seems to be growing. A very good buck age structure and buck/doe ratio is the standard regionwide. A visiting hunter will pay from $1,500 to $3,000 for a guided whitetail hunt. He should be prepared for a physical hunt in difficult terrain and trying weather.

Chapter 7

Planning A Trip
For Trophy Whitetails

S O, YOU WANT TO TAKE A TRIP for trophy whitetails. You're willing to spend the time and money to hunt a place that offers you a legitimate chance for a really good buck. Hopefully, after our survey of the different regions and their trophy prospects, you have a pretty good handle on where you want to go based on the size buck you're after, the money you're willing to spend and the type hunt you want. Now what?

Judging from the calls and letters we get at *North American Whitetail*, many people are at a loss about how to proceed after deciding to take a trip and perhaps even after deciding on where they would like to go. That's understandable. There are many things to consider if you want to get the most from your hunt. Let's look at some of the first considerations and then at the step-by-step process of selecting that all-important outfitter/guide.

FIRST CONSIDERATIONS

M atch your goals to the hunt. Generally, as your trophy standards increase, your options of where to go decrease, the cost is higher, your chances for success are reduced and the skill and effort required on

If you plan your hunt well, do everything right and get very lucky, a B&C buck like this 174⅜-point typical could be yours. **North American Whitetail** *publisher Steve Vaughn killed this 7x7 typical in Dimmit County, Texas, in 1987.*

your part are greater. It helps to keep this in mind as you plan your trip. For instance, say you're a fairly experienced hunter from somewhere on the East Coast with several "nice" bucks to your credit but nothing really good. Assuming you would be happy with a buck in the 140 class, you probably would not want to choose Central Canada. There, the cost might be $3,500 or more, and your odds of success for even a 140

Hunters spend lots of time and money and travel long distances in hopes of shooting a buck like this. But all too often, they have not properly prepared themselves to make the most of the opportunity when it comes along. This buck will easily make the B&C records. Photo by Curt Helmick.

wouldn't be much better than 50 percent, if that. If you want to hunt a northern environment, a ranch in the Plains and Prairie Region might be a better choice. A buck of that size would be a good bet on one of the better ranches, and the cost would probably be in the neighborhood of $2,000. In South Texas, a 140 would be virtually a shoo-in on a good ranch, but the cost would be at least $3,500. On the other hand, if you are a long-time trophy hunter with a hankering for a 160-plus whitetail, pay your money and go to Alberta, Saskatchewan or Manitoba. Prepare to hunt hard in bone-chilling conditions and hope you'll have the luck of a Las Vegas jackpot winner!

Having said this, if there's an area you just want to hunt, whether or not other cheaper or higher percentage places exist, go there! Maybe your dream has always been to follow the track of a trophy buck through the snow-covered woods of Maine or Minnesota. If so, head to the North Country, even if you could go to Texas and stand a better chance of shooting a trophy for the same money. Don't lose sight of the fact that deer hunting is a sport. The aim is satisfaction and enjoyment ... not just a buck!

The cost of a hunt can be a very deceiving matter. Most of the prices we've talked about are only the outfitter/guide's fee. That's just the beginning. First, you may not have the right clothing, boots, foul-weather gear or other equipment. The cost of outfitting yourself can be very expensive. Figure in that. Next, a hunting license in many places totals to a tidy sum, sometimes over $200. Then, you still have to get there. Often that involves a substantial air fare plus a car rental. Travel costs to remote areas of the West or to Canada can exceed $1,000. That's not all. There are sometimes additional costs once you arrive. Many hunts, especially those in Canada and the North, Plains and Prairies and Northwest regions of the United States, require that you stay in a hotel and buy your own meals. Another few hundred dollars can be tacked on there. Throw in tips and other odds and ends, and the associated costs of a hunting trip can rival the cost of the actual hunt itself! That's why you must look at the total expenses involved when comparing hunts. A $2,000 package hunt in Texas may be cheaper in the long run than a $1,000 New Brunswick hunt, where the extra cost of travel, meals and lodging can really add up.

Another thing to consider is what do you really want from the hunt? What kind of experience are you looking for? For example, if you are looking for a relaxed, enjoyable trip where you can take a passive role as events unfold before you, don't go to the Northwest Region or to Canada. And, forget Coues deer. You have to put forth effort and depend on your own skills to successfully hunt these places. Texas or the South may be more to your liking. There, you can work as hard or as little as you like. Much of the work necessary to put the deer in front of you will be done in advance, such as scouting, stand selection, planting food plots, etc. Of course, the more you bring to the table, the greater your odds of success ... and of shooting a top-end buck.

Perhaps it's important for you to see lots of deer. Maybe you want to hunt in a classic one-on-one chase, just you against the buck. You may not be willing to tolerate extreme cold. A physical limitation may make hunting from a vehicle or a stand attractive. It may be necessary for you to actually kill a buck to consider the hunt, and the cost, worthwhile, which would eliminate any hunt from consideration that is not a sure bet. Know your preferences and choose the hunt that will come closest to meeting your goals. Obviously, it will be necessary to quiz your outfitter or guide to be certain he can meet your expectations.

SELECTING YOUR OUTFITTER/GUIDE

How do you find the outfitter/guide that's right for you? Upon deciding where you want to go, this becomes the question of the moment. Selecting the right one will largely determine the success and enjoyment of your hunt. Perhaps the best way to find an outfitter or a guide is through someone you know who has recently hunted with him. Your source must be reliable and able to accurately relate what can be expected. A hunter of limited experience will often exaggerate, even though it may be unintentional.

If you don't have the advantage of a credible personal contact, then some research is called for. Start by identifying as many potential outfitter/guide candidates as possible. Phone calls or letters to knowledgeable hunters, perusing magazine articles and ads and contacting reputable booking agencies for names are good ways to begin. If the location you've chosen to hunt does not have "visible" operators, then local game departments are a good source of names. If possible, try to talk to a biologist, game warden or someone in the field rather than to a person bound to a city desk. The field people have a much better idea of what's going on. Also, they may be able to put you in contact with some of the smaller, more personally involved operators. Both small and large operators can be good, but as a general rule, I prefer to trophy hunt with someone who takes only a handful of hunters and gives each one personalized attention. Although this individual attention can also exist in bigger operations, it is harder to find.

Another excellent way to find the right outfitter/guide is to attend sporting shows where they are promoting their hunts. Because you can see what they are offering through photos, videos or brochures and talk to them directly, a lot of time can be saved. The shows also allow for

Although there are many do-it-yourself trips available for trophy whitetails, the services of a reputable outfitter/guide greatly improve anyone's chances for success when hunting unfamiliar territory.

comparison between outfitters. Many of the shows are held early in the year so the better hunt dates are often still available. Regional shows in the area you're hoping to hunt are sometimes attended by outfitters you won't find at major national shows.

Once you have a list of possible candidates, write them a letter outlining exactly what you are looking for and asking very specific questions that call for specific answers. Most importantly, ask for phone numbers and addresses of references in your area and beyond. Be sure to ask the outfitter/guide to identify all costs associated with the hunt once you get

Success like this is no accident. It comes from advance planning, selecting the right place to hunt, choosing a reputable outfitter/guide and hard work and determination. A group of us from **North American Whitetail** *magazine took these bucks in South Texas in 1985.*

there. Obviously, if he has photos or a brochure, that will be helpful. If the outfitter/guide is too busy or has too little interest to answer your questions promptly, he probably won't have sufficient time or interest during your hunt, either. From the replies to your letters, you can narrow down your candidates. How well your original letter specifies your desires and directs exacting answers to your questions will largely determine the accuracy of your assessment of those who respond. Fortunately, most reputable operators do not want anyone to hunt with them who they know in advance will not be satisfied with their operation.

After your list has been pared down to the few who seem to offer what you want, start checking references. I prefer to call rather than write. It seems to save time and is less bother for all concerned. But most importantly, you get far more accurate and detailed information by talking directly to the person. The enthusiasm in their voice or the tone of the conversation is almost as important as what is said. You will also be able to establish their level of expertise in trophy hunting, which is more difficult to do through an exchange of letters. I have always found serious hunters to be willing to share their experiences on a hunt with fellow hunters. These personal contacts are key to the final selection.

With your reference check complete, now's the time to contact the outfitters or guides who make the final list. Again, I much prefer to talk to them over the phone rather than to write. Have a list of topics to be covered before calling. Go over your criteria for the hunt in detail, asking as many questions as necessary to flesh out your understanding of exactly what he has to offer. Discuss such important points as the size bucks he takes, hunter success, hunting methods, the number of hunters in camp and per guide, the guide's role in the hunt, the land he hunts and, very importantly, the timing of the hunt. My preference on any hunt is to be there just before or during the rut. If he recommends another time, be sure you are satisfied with his reasoning.

Try to get to know your prospective outfitter/guide and his attitude toward hunting big whitetails and toward his clients. Reach a comfort level about whether his sense of aesthetics and sportsmanship is compatible with yours. A week cooped up with a guy who has an entirely different set of ethical or aesthetic values will definitely take the edge off the hunt. In short, learn all you can about the hunt and the outfitter/guide. Fortunately, it's not hard to tell if someone is shooting straight or feeding you a line, especially over the phone. Invest now in your hunt so you won't have to "pay" later.

If an outfitter/guide is still a candidate after talking with him awhile and examining his hunt, then it's time to talk business. Cover the subject of money with him thoroughly to avoid any future misunderstanding. How much is the hunt? Are there any additional costs? What are his deposit and cancellation policies? Are accommodations and meals included in the price? If not, get an estimate of these costs from him. Write down the information as you discuss the points. Find out about transportation to and from the nearest airport. Will he pick you up at the airport, or do you have to rent a car? How much does a hunting license cost? How do you get it? Is a second buck possible? If so, at what price? What does the outfitter/guide provide? What are you responsible for? What specialized equipment costing significant money will you need that you might not otherwise have? You must clearly identify all direct and indirect costs so you can make the right decision, and so you won't be surprised later.

FINALIZING YOUR DECISION

Armed with all this information, you should have made your decision. After notifying the outfitter/guide of your desire to hunt with him, a letter recapping the precise terms of your agreement and understanding is needed. I've found this to be very important. Outfitters and guides by nature are not usually great business men. That's fine. I'd rather them be great hunters, but somebody needs to spell out the costs and expectations in writing. Your confirmation letter will allow any misunderstanding to be identified and hopefully resolved. And, it will serve as a written record for both you and your outfitter/guide to use as your hunt approaches. You may assume he writes everything down, but experience has taught me differently. Along with the money issues, be sure to include your hunting dates; arrival and departure dates and times; and the transportation arrangements. Don't assume anything. Spell out the details. There's nothing quite so frustrating as waiting for hours for your host to pick you up at some faraway airport while he's in camp 200 miles away wondering where you are.

GETTING YOURSELF READY

The hunt is arranged at last. You're anxiously awaiting the time. But, there are still things you need to do. One, don't let a license application deadline slip by you. Two, get your gear and clothing together. For me, this is part of the fun of the trip. It heightens anticipation and extends overall enjoyment of the hunt. What clothes do you need for the expected weather conditions? Do you need rattling horns? Daypacks or backpacks? Waterproof boots or hip waders? Does the country you'll be hunting dictate a certain rifle/scope combination? Do you need a soft gun case to transport your rifle during the course of the hunt? Should you carry a sleeping bag? What about trail food during the hunt? What are the hunter orange or other legal clothing requirements? What headgear is needed? Should you bring any survival gear? Compass? Waterproof matches? There are many things to consider in preparation for your hunt. Your outfitter/guide can help determine what you'll need.

Are you physically prepared? If the hunt will be physically demanding, are you in shape? Are your feet toughened up so you don't get blisters the first day out? A hunting partner of mine once got such bad blood blisters after two days of hunting that he had to soak his socked feet in a stream just to get his socks off! Don't let that happen to you.

Are you ready to make the shot when the moment of truth arrives? Have you spent time on the range and in the field with your rifle? Are you confident in your rifle and your ability to use it? If all goes according to script, there will come a time in the hunt when everything boils down to that one shot. Have you done all you can to assure the bullet will fly true?

Your preparations before the hunt, all of them, will go a long way toward determining whether you return home with a heavy heart and an empty bag or with memories of a great experience and the buck of your dreams in tow!

The "When"
Of Hunting Trophy
Whitetails

Chapter 8

Unraveling The Mysteries Of Deer Movement

"A LITTLE KNOWLEDGE IS a dangerous thing," and so it is with thinking you understand deer movement. Many years ago, I decided that I could spend my allotted time afield more fruitfully if I could learn when deer activity is greatest. Thus, I embarked on the mission of doing just that.

I began by having the biologists on a 13,000-acre hunting plantation in Georgia I'm involved with keep detailed deer sighting and kill records. The moderate hunting pressure there allows the deer to remain relatively undisturbed throughout season. After collecting data for several years, I related every imaginable weather condition (plus moon phases) to every way of measuring deer movement I could think of — daily hunter success rate, average number of deer seen per hunter-day, bucks seen per hunter-day, to name a few. When I put the computer to work on the figures, I was surprised and delighted to see distinct deer activity trends relative to certain weather conditions. For a brief while, I operated under blissful ignorance, not knowing enough to know what I didn't know. Then, as my hunting experience expanded beyond Georgia

Forced movement accounted for this 13-pointer with double drop tines. He was bedded in a small island of cover in the middle of a 500-acre field when I jumped the buck and shot him at 2 p.m. one cold, blustry afternoon.

and the Southeast, my "absolutes" gradually became clouded with exceptions. Days that should have been "good" for deer movement turned out to be not so good and vice versa. I began to question my theories.

Undaunted, I again set out to understand deer movement and sort out the factors influencing it — not just bits and pieces of the puzzle but the whole picture. To this end, I have been partially successful. I have gained a pretty fair understanding of the major trends and a limited grasp of some of the factors contributing to the total picture. Yet, I do not hold these things out as hard-and-fast rules, only trends.

With that, let's attempt to unravel some of the mysteries of deer movement and the many factors controlling it. We'll start with the non-weather factors that play a major role in influencing deer movement. Then, we'll look at the effects of weather. But before we do, let's identify the types of deer movement of interest to the hunter.

FORMS OF DEER MOVEMENT

Essentially, there are three forms of deer movement of concern to hunters — forced, rutting and feeding movement. Forced movement, such as when a hunter jumps a deer or dogs run one, is involuntary and has no bearing on natural deer activity. There are times, however, when forced movement offers a hunter his best chance of connecting. Rutting movement is any deer activity revolving around the fall breeding urge and is of paramount interest to trophy hunters. Obviously, feeding movement is activity associated with a deer's ongoing need to feed itself. Feeding activity is important to the trophy hunter but accounts for the downfall of fewer trophy bucks than does rutting movement.

NON-WEATHER FACTORS

Hunting Pressure

When pressured by man, deer can run; they can hide; they can become nocturnal or any combination thereof. The one sure bet is that they will do something to counteract the pressure. And, whitetails catch on quickly. It only takes a day or two of high pressure for deer to abandon their normal feeding or even rutting activities and concentrate on avoiding contact with man. The more the pressure, the more the change. Enough pressure will limit deer movement to the twilight hours of early morning and late afternoon or even cause them to move only under the cover of darkness. Yes, hunting pressure is a key controlling factor in deer movement and will override nearly all other factors.

Generally, as hunting pressure increases, forced movement becomes ever more important to hunters. In some of the most pres-

Hunting pressure pushes both feeding and rutting activity into the low-light periods of early morning and late afternoon ... or into the cover of darkness altogether. This old buck is slipping out to feed at last light. Photo by Mike Blair.

sured areas, the majority of the deer killed fall as a result of forced movement. Deer drives are one way hunters try to force movement in a more or less controlled fashion, but forced movement in heavily hunted areas is often a result of the sheer number of hunters in the woods. In such cases, deer are moved randomly, although there are certain strategies that boost a hunter's likelihood of encountering a buck. From the standpoint of effectiveness and safety, still-hunting is not a recommended tactic in highly pressured areas. Stand-hunting and noisy drives are the favored methods. Wearing enough orange to make yourself look like a neon pumpkin is also recommended.

While hunting pressure per se is the most common and important form of pressure affecting deer movement, it is not the only one. Predators such as wolves, coyotes and especially feral dogs also can impact deer movement. In Canada, I've seen deer behavior change abruptly when a pack of wolves moves into the area. In the South, large numbers of free-ranging dogs harassing deer can have pretty much the same effect on deer movement as heavy hunting pressure. Deer become increasingly nocturnal, very nervous, unpredictable and generally hard to hunt. Deer also commonly behave like this in areas of the South where dog-hunting is legal and widely practiced.

Man does not have to be actually hunting deer to affect their movement and their behavioral patterns. Just the presence of humans is enough. For instance, in densely populated farm country, deer often adopt a permanent nocturnal lifestyle in order to live among man, especially if the deer are not overcrowded and forced by hunger to move during the day. Obviously, temporary non-hunting disturbances like timber operations, land clearing and such also will disrupt normal deer movement for a period of time.

The Rut

The rut is the time of peak activity for deer, particularly bucks. The distance bucks travel, the amount of time they spend on the move, the speed and caution with which they move and the type of movement (i.e., what bucks are doing while moving) are all positively impacted by the rut from the hunter's perspective. Big bucks in particular move more and are more vulnerable under the influence of the breeding urge than at any other time. Trophy hunters must take advantage of the rut if they have any hope of consistently taking mature whitetails. Because big bucks are preoccupied with their amorous duties, this is an especially good time for an accomplished still-hunter to cover a lot of ground in search of breeding parties.

To help better understand rutting movement, let's look at the two different aspects of the rut — rutting activity, the ritual activities associated with the rut, and breeding, which usually takes place without the hunter ever being aware of it.

The ritual activities are important to the hunter because they put a buck on the move and, hopefully, in the hunter's sights. Making rubs, checking scrapes, trailing does and rambling around in search of does are all part of the ritual activities of the rut. The level of ritual activity is tied to the weather, hunting pressure, herd composition and density and other factors, not the least of which is time of year. Without this rutting activity, truly big whitetails would be largely creatures of legend and myth because few hunters would ever see one firsthand.

During the rut, bucks are more vulnerable than at any other time. Here, a hot doe has lured this buck away from the security of thick cover. Photo by Mike Blair.

On the other hand, the actual breeding, which is the reason for the rut, will take place at practically the same time every year whether or not rutting activity is visible to the hunter. When a doe comes in estrus, chances are good she will be bred, even though visible signs of the rut may be suppressed by unfavorable weather, hunting pressure or the like. Breeding most often takes place at night.

Another interesting aspect of increased deer movement associated

Rutting activity causes bucks to move more during daylight hours and to be less wary. This buck is preoccupied with making a scrape. Photo by Mike Biggs.

with the onset of the rut involves 1½-year-old bucks. As the rut approaches, yearling bucks begin to wander around rather aimlessly. They move great distances and at all hours. I call this the "fall shuffle." The young bucks could be feeling the rutting urge but may be at a loss as to what to do about it. It is more likely, however, that they are reacting to social pressure from other deer, either matriarch does or more dominate bucks. Whatever the cause, these yearlings move — a lot, often and long distances. This seemingly aimless wandering is also true to a much lesser degree in some of the older, subordinate bucks. They are apparently displaced by competition from other bucks or by some other type of social pressure.

Feeding Movement

For the trophy hunter, feeding movement is an important aspect of his fall strategy, although of less importance than rutting movement. In the fall, a couple of significant changes take place in the deer's feeding patterns. One, with the arrival of cooler fall weather, deer tend to expand their daytime feeding movement beyond the early morning/late afternoon pattern so prevalent during the warmer months. Two, there is often a shift to new food sources as the green summer browse, which previously was widely available throughout the deer's range, gives way to more concentrated fall food sources such as agricultural crops, acorns, wild grapes, persimmons, apples, etc. As deer concentrate on the new food sources, feeding movement can become more visible to the hunter, if not actually intensify. This usually works to the hunter's advantage, but there are situations where abundant fall foods may make hunting more difficult.

It is a widely held belief, one that I tend to go along with, that during years of very good acorn crops deer can be harder to hunt. The reason for this is limited exposure of the deer to hunters. Why? First, during good acorn years, acorns are often distributed throughout the deer's range, thus the deer don't tend to concentrate in any one place as they might on, for instance, a cornfield. Second, even when the deer do move to feed, they seldom have to leave cover since the acorn-bearing trees most likely are located in protected woods. Even the oaks themselves provide some cover. Third, bedding cover is sure to be nearby, cutting down on the distance necessary for deer to travel and making it convenient for deer to feed any time. Fourth, the concentration of food makes it easy for deer to satisfy their hunger relatively quickly. All this can reduce the exposure of deer and the visibility of feeding movement, resulting in difficult hunting.

This concept is not limited only to acorns. Any widely distributed, abundant food supply located in cover can cause the same situation to exist. I've seen this occur in the South Texas Brush Country, and in other browse-dependant places, when sufficient rain has allowed the fertile desert to produce a super abundance of widely available browse. Under such conditions, feeding movement will take place but hunters can't see much of it. It takes the rut to make the deer show themselves.

Whatever the fall feeding movement should be, it will be disrupted by high hunting pressure. I believe that hunting pressure affects feeding patterns even quicker and to a greater degree than it affects rutting activity. This speaks to the power of the rutting urge. Plus, day-to-day feeding movement is greatly impacted by weather conditions, moon phases, etc., even more so than rutting activity.

Feeding movement is important to the hunter, especially before and after the rut, but frankly, trophy bucks are hard to kill on a feeding pattern if pressured much. Photo by Mike Biggs.

The Moon

The moon definitely does affect deer movement, especially when movement takes place during any given 24-hour period. There are four moon phases: new moon (completely dark), first quarter (half moon), full moon (completely bright) and last quarter (half moon). Each of the moon phases is considered to be in effect over a seven-day period, the day the phase actually occurs plus three days before and three days after. As far as deer movement is concerned, the two quarter moons can be overlooked. Their influence on deer movement is minimal and easily overridden by prevailing weather conditions. The impact of the new moon and full moon is worth considering, however.

During the new moon period, the nights are dark. You might assume that deer can't see well on these dark nights; therefore, they move less at night and more during the day. That assumption is partly correct. Deer do seem to move more during the day on a new moon, especially during the early and late hours of the day. However, from doing legal deer studies at night, I have found that deer do move at night on a dark moon, or at least they feed in open fields then. Those same studies have resulted in mixed reviews on deer movement at night on a full moon. Admittedly, my exposure to night activity during the fall is limited. Since we don't hunt deer at night, what they do in the darkness is not all that important anyway. What is of interest, however, is the fact that on a new moon deer seem to move more freely in the early morning and late afternoon hours. These times happen to be prime movement hours for whitetails anyway, as opposed to the bright midday hours. The new moon seems to intensify deer activity during these natural peak movement periods. The result is concentrated and predictable movement that is advantageous to the hunter. Other conditions can and very often do override the new moon's full influence.

A full moon seems to have the opposite effect on deer movement from that of a new moon. On bright nights during the full moon phase, deer do not usually move well during the early and late daytime hours. What daytime movement there is tends to take place during the midday hours. This has a negative effect on deer hunting, especially on hunting feeding patterns. Hunters lose the advantage of concentrated movement during the prime early and late hours, and activity becomes more scattered and less predictable. It does, however, give the hunter a chance to hunt longer hours, even if those hours are not as productive.

When the peak of the rut (the time of actual breeding) falls on a full moon, there is opportunity for the hunter, again mainly during midday hours. I believe that when the full moon corresponds with the breeding period of the rut, bucks actively engage in breeding on brightly lit nights. One of the reasons for this could be that visual contact between the pursuing buck and the receptive doe seems to be important in the breeding process. Full moon nights allow this visual contact under the security of dim light, and these nights offer freedom from the harassment of hunters or other daytime nuisances. After a busy night of courtship, the amorous bucks may cease proceedings at first light only to later succumb to mounting desire during the midday hours. This midday rutting activity may again be followed by a lull in late afternoon movement, awaiting the startup of festivities under the moonlight. Whatever the cause, hunting during the peak of the rut when the moon is full can

The effects of the full moon on deer movement have long been pondered by hunters. It is my belief that a full moon results in less deer activity during the prime early morning/late afternoon hours and more (although limited) movement during midday hours. Photo by Mike Biggs.

be quite productive. It certainly allows the hunter a chance to hunt throughout the day with some hope of success at any moment. As with the new moon, other conditions can minimize the effects of the full moon.

Over the years, I have developed a pet theory about the full moon that I'll pass along. Even during the full moon phase, the moon is not necessarily "up" all night. For instance, the moon may come up at 9:30 p.m. and remain up past dawn. Or, it may already be up at dusk and go down at 3 a.m. It is my belief that the greatest effect of the moon on deer movement relates only to the time the moon is up. Based on this assumption and my observations and limited records on this matter, I have theorized: Daylight movement tends to be significantly reduced within five hours of a bright moon at night. For example, if the full moon goes down at 3 a.m., one might expect increased activity (though it may be limited) around 8 a.m. But if the full moon is up at 6 a.m., it may be 11 a.m. before deer activity, such as it is, begins. This is most difficult to pin down since midday movement is not very great anyway, but I plan my hunts based on this theory. Several seasons of application haven't yet proven it wrong. Whether or not heavy cloud cover neutralizes the effect of the full moon is unclear. Generally, I think that it does, but there are times when I'm not so sure.

This is a good time to talk about solunar tables. Though I often refer to them while bass fishing, I have limited experience with solunar tables in deer hunting. The few times I have tried to correlate solunar table predictions to whitetail movement, there was nothing to discredit the accuracy of their predictions. Several hunters I respect believe solunar tables can help identify the best feeding times for deer. In the absence of overriding factors, that may be true. But personally, I feel other things such as hunting pressure, the rut, the natural tendency of deer to move early and late in the day and weather conditions are far more important in predicting deer movement. Unlike bass fishing, where feeding times are very important if you want to catch fish, deer hunters are not concerned just with the deer's feeding times. They want to know when deer are moving for any reason. Feeding is only one reason deer move, and to me, it is not the most important reason — the rut is!

Other Non-Weather Factors

There are some other non-weather related factors that affect deer movement. One is the deer population density. In areas where deer numbers exceed the carrying capacity, deer tend to spend more time moving in search of food since it is in short supply. From a hunter's standpoint, the result can be rather dramatic. Often, deer can be seen feeding at all hours of the day. On a badly overcrowded farm I used to hunt in West Alabama, two 15-acre oat plots served as major food sources for deer in the fall. Despite constant pressure and a high harvest from those plots (over 50 bucks a year were shot there), you could find 100-plus deer on either plot almost anytime of day! When the deer were run off the plots, they would return in full force within the hour!

High deer densities can also bring about more activity during the rut, or at least more visible activity. Just the frequency of encounters between deer brought on by the concentrated presence of animals picks up the pace of the rut. Herd composition also directly impacts rutting activity. Herds with a low buck/doe ratio and a good buck age structure

In areas with thick cover, bucks are more likely to move freely during daylight hours, even though the hunter may not be aware of it. Photo by Mike Biggs.

will, as we've said before, experience a more competitive rut. This increased competition results in more movement, especially during the day. Feeding movement is not swayed much by herd composition.

Cover is also a consideration in deer movement. In areas with thick cover, deer tend to move more freely during daylight hours, although the hunter may not be aware of this movement. The importance of thick cover to daytime movement can be particularly obvious when hunting fields. Fields with a "hot" food source bordering on thick cover, which provides a secure approach for the deer, are likely to see activity during daylight hours. Whereas similar fields bordering on more open cover might see only nighttime use because of the reluctance of deer to expose themselves en route to the fields.

WEATHER

As I said earlier, I have conducted a rather extensive study of deer movement based on data gathered over several years at a large Georgia hunting plantation. The weather data used was taken directly from records published by the National Oceanic and Atmospheric Administration (NOAA). Their "Local Climatogical Data" sheets provided daily and even hourly weather conditions throughout the season. I compared this weather information to the many different ways of measuring deer activity. In addition, I looked at the time of day deer were seen and killed in relationship to weather and moon phases. I gave special consideration to when the biggest bucks were killed. Then, I factored in my own experiences and observations from across North America and those of other experienced hunters to reach big-picture conclusions, or at least opinions. Here, rather than examining the detailed figures and data, we'll look at the general trends I uncovered.

The General Trends

When I first pulled all my Georgia movement data together and related it to weather, a clear pattern emerged. I thought I had deer movement pegged. In time, however, my airtight theory sprang a few leaks. Now, I know I was on the right track, but incomplete information led me to incomplete conclusions. Let's backtrack, and you'll see for yourself.

When I applied weather conditions to the best deer movement days in Georgia, the following trend was overwhelmingly clear. The best movement took place when:
- Temperatures were normal or below normal for the date.
- Relative humidity was low (50 percent or below at 1 p.m.).
- Barometric pressure was high (above 29:00 inches).
- The day was bright and sunny.
- Wind was out of the northwest.
- Wind was steady and less than 10 mph.
- A light drizzle was falling. (This was the one exception to the pattern established by all the other "best movement" factors. During a drizzle proved to be an excellent time to shoot a buck, especially a trophy buck.)

By contrast, the worst weather conditions for deer movement in Georgia were as follows:
- Temperatures above normal for the date.
- High relative humidity (above 50 percent at 1 p.m.).
- Low barometric pressure (below 29:00 inches).

- Cloudy, hazy or foggy days (particularly after two or three days of constant cloudy weather).
- Wind gusty and over 10 mph.
- Wind from the east.
- Heavy rain.

From this, I saw a clear pattern. With the exception of a light drizzle, the best conditions for deer movement took place a day or two after a cold front pushed through Georgia and the trailing gusty wind had died down. From that, I concluded that deer move best during the cold, dry, clear days following a cold front and that cold temperatures, low humidity and light wind are controlling factors in deer movement. Actually, all of that is true in part. But when my theories were applied to other regions, I found out there is more to it.

A couple of examples of breakdowns will show what I mean. When the occasional severe cold front pushes through South Texas and the temperature in that normally semitropical region drops into the low 20's, deer do not move much, especially early in the morning. Once things start to warm up during the day, deer begin stirring around. To make matters worse, some of the best movement I've seen in South Texas has been on cloudy days, which is contrary to the Georgia pattern. In Canada, I've noticed a distinct slowdown in deer movement during periods of extreme cold. In fact, I have seen good deer activity there on days when the temperature was "moderate," at least for that part of the world. From such experiences, it became apparent that colder isn't always better. And, what about good movement on cloudy days in Texas?

With these breaks in the theory to ponder, I thought at first that there might not be a universal standard. Then, one day it hit me. The guiding principle was so obvious and simple that I couldn't believe I hadn't recognized it earlier. All other things being equal, deer move best when weather conditions are the most comfortable and invigorating for them, relative to what they are used to and what they are prepared to face.

Let me explain. Being warm-blooded animals, deer are not a whole lot different from us. When the weather is pleasant, cool and sunny for example, we feel good and like to participate in outdoor activities. Like-wise, there are certain weather conditions that cause deer to "feel good" and be more active. While a deer's "comfort zone" and ours share certain similarities, they are somewhat different, at least in degrees. For one

Although deer generally prefer temperatures that humans would consider cool to cold, the mercury can drop too low for good deer movement. The temperature is below this buck's "comfort range," and he has chosen to sit it out until temperatures moderate. Photo by Denver Bryan.

thing, deer are accustomed to being out in the cold and are better prepared to face it; therefore, they not only can tolerate more cold but they are comfortable in lower temperatures than we are. Also, we can dress up or down for the weather. But once deer put on their winter coats, not to mention the fat they normally put on in the fall, they are "dressed" for the cold. Since they can't shed their coat, warm weather is uncomfortable for them. On the other hand, extreme cold, relative to that region and that time of the year, is at best unpleasant. Thus, both unseasonably warm weather and unusual cold curtail deer movement. Conditions in the comfort zone, which varies by region, encourage good deer move-

In most of the South, deer movement is suppressed on cloudy days, but this is not necessarily so in South Texas. Apparently, cloud cover provides some relief from the blistering sun and high temperatures so common there. Who would have believed this big Brush Country buck could have gone under the fence? Photo by Mike Biggs.

ment. Once I understood this, not only did Georgia's cold front pattern make sense, but the seemingly contradictory situations in Texas and Canada became clear. Let's look at them again with an eye toward the "comfort zone concept."

In Georgia, deer have to cope with oppressive heat and humidity throughout the summer. Even in the fall, Georgia weather is naturally fairly warm and humid. It takes the introduction of air from elsewhere, i.e., cold fronts, to cool off the state and lower the humidity. Autumn ushers in cold fronts of varying intensity. By October, the deer have replaced their light summer coat with a heavier winter coat in preparation for the coming cold. Unfortunately for Georgia deer, fall weather varies from summerlike heat and humidity to temperatures in the low teens when a very severe cold front blows in. Nature has prepared the deer for something in between, hedging in favor of the cold for survival reasons. With the deer equipped for cool weather, cold fronts are usually needed to cool the air to the deer's comfort zone and lower the oppressive humidity. Only when the rare cold front plummets temperatures into the teens does it get too cold for good deer movement, and then only for a short time.

In South Texas, deer seldom experience severe cold; therefore, they are ill-prepared when it comes. Over much of the year, they face a dry, blistering heat and burning sun. This explains why the occasional "norther" pushing cold air into this semitropical region can suppress deer movement if the temperature drops below the deer's comfort zone, which is even higher than that of Georgia deer. This also explains why South Texas deer often move well in cloudy weather. Such conditions provide some relief from the otherwise hot sun and high temperatures. Notably, cloudy weather in arid South Texas does not necessarily bring with it high humidity. Additionally, I have noticed that South Texas deer move more on windy days than most other deer I've hunted. Perhaps the wind also provides some relief from the heat and sun, or the deer may simply be accustomed to wind since it commonly blows there.

The reluctance of Canadian deer to move in extreme cold also can be explained by the relative comfort zone concept. Even though Canadian deer are more accustomed to and better prepared for cold weather than deer anywhere else, it does get too cold in this harsh land for them to be comfortable. During such times, the deer simply hold tight to conserve energy and body heat.

Based on this concept, it obviously is difficult to draw hard-and-fast conclusions about the ideal comfort zone for good deer movement for every region in North America. It's all relative to what's "normal" for that region. Mexico and Canada, for example, could not be more different in their norms. The burden, then, falls on the individual hunter to determine what specific conditions make up the comfort zone for good deer movement where he hunts. However, I do think some general principles can be identified regarding relative weather conditions and deer movement that can be applied most any place.

Temperature

As is probably obvious by now, temperature is one of the most important factors governing deer movement. It is safe to say that deer movement is best when the temperature for a given place

Cold, clear days following a cold front usually bring good deer movement. This fine non-typical is taking advantage of such a day. Photo by Curt Helmick.

and date is normal or below normal. At what point does the temperature fall below the deer's comfort zone and curtail movement? Clearly, that "too cold" mark varies with different locations around the country. In Georgia, my guess is that anything much below 20 degrees slows activity. In South Texas, that number is higher, maybe in the low to mid 20's. In Canada, I'm not exactly sure where the breakpoint is, but from my experience on days when the temperature dropped to around minus 20 degrees, the deer didn't seem to move much. Both the relative humidity and wind can affect the "feel" of cold (we know it as the chill factor) and move the zone. Anything you recognize as being extremely cold for that area threatens to be too cold for good deer movement.

On the top side of the deer's comfort zone are temperatures too warm for good movement. I had much rather hunt when it's too cold than when it's too warm. At least when it's too cold early in the morning, there's always the chance temperatures will rise during the day, especially in the more southern latitudes. In such cases, I find deer movement to be quite good when temperatures warm into the comfort zone. If high humidity joins with unseasonably warm temperatures, which it often does, then things can get very difficult for the deer hunter. A drizzling rain represents the biggest exception to cooler weather and low humidity being better for overall deer movement. More on this later.

Relative Humidity

I'm convinced that relative humidity has a direct impact on deer movement, at least in some places. We're all familiar with the difference in how we feel cold or heat under "dry" versus "humid" conditions. Everyone has experienced the oppressive weight of hot, humid days when the air hangs thick and heavy and your energy and enthusiasm are sapped. Surely you've felt the bone-chilling discomfort of cold, damp days when it's hard to get warm no matter what you're wearing. On the other hand, "dry" heat is not nearly as oppressing and energy-sapping. "Dry" cold can be invigorating and does not penetrate the very core of your body like damp cold will. Basically, deer respond to humidity the same way we do.

Hot, humid weather is right at the top for the worst possible time to deer hunt. During the fall, these conditions are often accompanied by cloud cover. Unusually warm temperatures and high humidity (over 90 percent) seem to hang like an oppressive haze, bringing deer movement to a low ebb. If such conditions persist for several days in succession, deer activity will progressively worsen. Often, by the third or fourth day, all movement practically ceases. At times, it will seem as if the deer have disappeared all together. They don't even make tracks! This may be the worst of all times to hunt deer. They hold tight in cover and are even hard to jump.

However, all is not lost. Once these conditions give way to cooler, drier weather, as is normally the case following the passage of a cold front, deer activity peaks, often immediately. The amount of movement seems to be directly proportional to the length of time the hot, humid conditions persisted. That is, deer activity is greater after prolonged periods of "bad" weather. The deer seem to try to catch up on lost time. Again, if strong gusty winds and extreme cold accompany the clearing weather, deer movement will be limited until these conditions moderate.

High humidity in cold weather does appear to inhibit deer activ-

High humidity normally spells poor deer movement, but trophy bucks sometimes move in the fog, especially if the fog is accompanied by mist. Photo by Mike Biggs.

ity but not as much as high humidity in hot weather does. As we've said, the greatest impact of humidity in cold weather may be to elevate the temperature range of the deer's comfort zone since humidity increases the "feel" of cold.

I feel relative humidity is a controlling factor in deer movement, not just a symptom. Symptoms may be cloud cover, haze or fog, which are most often associated with warm, humid weather. The level at which relative humidity becomes a limiting factor in deer movement depends both on the region and the temperature. In the Southeast, relative humidity of only 70 percent may be a relief to deer. Whereas in South Dakota, 50 percent relative humidity may slow deer movement. The key is what the deer are used to in that region. Generally, I would say that relative humidity below about 60 percent encourages deer movement and anything above that is likely to cause a slowdown.

There is no better time to shoot a trophy buck than during a light, drizzling rain. I rattled in this 24-inch nine-pointer on such a morning. He was only 15 yards away and still coming when a bullet from my .270 Win. halted his progress. Drizzle stands as a major exception to the general rule that deer movement is suppressed during warm, humid weather.

Drizzle, Rain And Snow

So far, we've said that the best deer movement takes place when the temperature is normal or below normal for that time of year and when the relative humidity is low. And, we've said that the worst time for deer movement is during periods of hot, humid weather, which is often associated with cloud cover, fog, haze and, one would assume, rain. And, that's all true ... with one big exception — a light, steady drizzle. This can be an excellent time to shoot a trophy whitetail!

During a drizzle (or even a substantial mist), especially if there is little wind, the chances of killing a trophy whitetail may never be better. Frankly, I'm not convinced that overall deer movement is the best during a drizzle, but the trophy bucks are sure likely to be on the move. Experience has taught me that wise old bucks are less wary and more likely

This excellent buck is on the move during a light snowfall, which has much the same positive effect on buck movement as drizzle. Photo by Denver Bryan.

to leave thick cover on such days. Maybe it is the low-light conditions combined with the cooling effect of the drizzle and the quiet, soothing nature of the wet woods that cause good movement during a drizzle. Whatever the reasons, this is a choice time for trophy hunters, especially the skillful still-hunter.

Even a drizzle is not foolproof. First, when does a drizzle become a rain? This is hard to determine, but when I'm hunting, I can tell. Deer will move in a fairly brisk drizzle, but when it gets too heavy, movement all but ceases. If in doubt, go and let the deer decide if the rain is too heavy. It seems the best time to hunt a drizzling rain is the first day it starts. After that, movement becomes spotty. Like people, deer may get tired of it. Also, gusty winds, which sometimes accompany a drizzle, will nullify its advantages.

Heavy rain definitely reduces deer activity. Depending on how hard and how long it has been raining, deer movement can be almost completely halted. During rain, deer tend to hold up in the thickest places they can find, preferably evergreens. Also, deer frequently stand during a rain. The combination of holding up in predictable places and the fact that deer are often on their feet can mean there is opportunity for a still-hunter to slip up on a buck in the rain. The wet woods and the noise from the rain allow the hunter to move with less concern about being detected. And when a deer does hear or see a hunter in the woods during a rain, he usually stands a few seconds and stares in disbelief. When the rain stops, even for brief periods, deer often move around.

Snowfall pretty much has the same effect on deer movement as rainfall. A light snowfall is a good time for deer movement, especially for mature bucks. During periods of heavy snowfall, activity is slowed. I believe one reason for this is that the movement created by falling snowflakes makes deer nervous. Regardless of why, deer respond to heavy snowfall much as they do to heavy rain, except they tend to bed down rather than stand.

Wind

Like temperature and relative humidity, wind is a controlling factor in deer movement. The harder the wind blows, the less deer move. Also, variable and shifting winds, even if fairly light, will cause problems both for the deer and the hunter. The noise and movement created by high winds make deer nervous and impair their senses.

Deer will move in light to moderate wind, provided it is reasonably steady in its velocity and direction. This can be beneficial for the still-hunter. The wind can mask the hunter's movement and sound and can be used to direct his scent away from the deer. Even high winds can be hunted despite poor deer movement, although it clearly is not an optimum time. On windy days, deer tend to hold up in thick evergreens or in areas with low, thick ground cover, such as clearcuts, fallow fields,

Bucks, particularly big bucks, will occasionally run into an open field during times of high wind. Perhaps the wind and the noise in the woods play havoc on the bucks' nerves. Photo by Mike Blair.

etc. A good still-hunter can move with little fear of being heard, smelled or seen. I have shot several bucks on windy days by walking up on them in pine thickets or by jumping them in fallow fields.

There is an odd situation related to strong winds. Bucks, particularly big bucks, occasionally will run into open fields during times of high wind. They seem to be spooked and nervous. I can only speculate that the wind and noise play havoc on the bucks' nerves. They apparently seek relief in the quieter open fields. I've seen this several times, but it can't be depended on to put a buck in your sights.

In areas where wind is the norm rather than the exception, it has little effect on deer movement. An example of this can be seen in the Plains and Prairies Region where the wind blows almost constantly. There, the deer go about their normal routine in winds that would seriously suppress movement in other parts of the country. Also, the wind generally has less impact on deer in open habitat than on deer in more wooded areas.

Barometric Pressure

Much has been written about the effects of barometric pressure on wildlife activity. In fact, there is a mystic quality attached to barometric pressure, probably because it is something that cannot be seen by humans. As far as deer movement is concerned, barometric pressure in itself is probably more a symptom than a cause. Actually, it's an early alarm system. What barometric pressure really does is forecast coming weather changes, some of which deer react to in advance. For instance, when the barometer starts dropping in the fall, a cold front is likely to be on the way. The passage of a cold front may be preceded by days of cloudy, rainy or otherwise inclement weather that results in low deer activity. The deer may react to the falling barometer in advance of the arrival of the cold front while the weather is still fair.

Generally, deer movement is best on an unstable barometer or during high pressure, which is often associated with cool, dry air in the fall. A falling barometer normally foretells of bad weather; a rising barometer usually promises improving weather. In both cases, deer will sometimes move in advance of the visible change. From my experience, movement is greater after bad weather than before bad weather. Often, activity in advance of a weather system is not markedly greater than normal. The severity of the system will determine the level of pre-frontal and post-frontal deer movement.

SUMMARY

Best Movement

- Low to moderate hunting pressure.
- Rut approaching or underway.
- Concentrated food sources found in limited, identifiable places. (Hopefully in places requiring the deer to expose themselves.)
- Good age structure and low buck/doe ratio. (Increases rutting activity only.)
- Dense deer population. (Movement best if overcrowded, but trophy size is reduced.)
- Thick cover. (Movement is better, but deer sightings and hunter success may be low because deer are not exposed.)
- Temperatures in the "comfort zone" of deer. (Normal or below normal for that time of year.)

- Low relative humidity. (60 percent or less, depending on what is normal for the area.)
- Light drizzle or light snow. (A major exception to the general pattern, and one of the best times for trophy bucks.)
- No wind or light, steady wind. (Less than 10 mph.)
- Unstable or high barometric pressure. (Unstable pressure indicates coming weather changes, which often cause advance movement. High pressure usually accompanies fair weather.)
- New moon. (Movement is likely to be concentrated and predictable in prime early morning and late afternoon hours. During the breeding period, the full moon can offer good hunting since some rutting movement may take place during the midday hours.)

Poorest Movement

- High hunting pressure.
- After the rut is over.
- A lack of identifiable, concentrated food sources. (Widely distributed food sources in cover or an overall absence of identifiable food sources limit visible feeding movement.)
- Poor age structure and high buck\doe ratio. (Adversely affects rutting movement only.)
- Low deer populations. (Movement is less when the herd is below carrying capacity, but trophy size is good.)
- Open or limited cover. (Deer movement is less, but sightings and hunter success could still be good because of the deer's exposure.)
- Temperatures above or below the deer's "comfort zone." (Movement is reduced when temperatures are unseasonably warm or exceptionally cold for the area.)
- High relative humidity. (60 percent or more, depending on what's normal for the area.)
- Foggy or hazy days. (However, bucks will sometimes move in fog, especially when the fog is accompanied by mist.)
- Heavy rain or heavy snow.
- Three or more consecutive days of warm, humid weather. (This is one of the very worst times.)
- High, gusty and/or variable winds. (Especially in areas where such winds are not normal.)

This buck is up and moving the morning after a big snow storm. Notice the snow still clinging to his antlers. Changes in the barometric pressure foretell of coming weather systems, some of which deer react to in advance. Photo by Bill Kinney.

- Low barometric pressure. (Most often accompanies turbulent or warm, humid weather.)
- Full moon. (Results in somewhat unpredictable and limited midday movement. Especially bad for feeding movement. Rutting movement in midday can be pretty good during the full moon.)

Remember, no one factor controls deer movement. You have to look at the overall situation and try to figure out how all the related factors might impact activity. If all this sounds complex and confusing, do as I do … go deer hunting every chance you get. If you go often enough, you'll be there when the deer move!

Chapter 9

Fall Activity Patterns
The Big Picture

M Y WIFE IS A GOOD WOMAN. You see, I like football, and in the fall, when I'm not hunting deer, she sometimes indulgently joins me to "look at" the game. Notice I didn't say "watch" the game. That would imply too much interest and involvement on her part. Actually, she more or less observes the individual plays but seldom has a clue about what they mean to the overall game. First quarter, second quarter, third, fourth — they're all the same to her. Game plans, strategies, tactics — she could care less. It's not that she can't understand football; she's just never bothered to learn. Basically, she knows when the game starts and ends and when a big play happens, mostly because of the crowd noise. Otherwise, the game is just one continuous, unstructured event with a beginning and an end and the occasional moment of chance excitement in between. And, you know what? For many deer hunters, that's exactly what deer season is to them!

Many deer hunters fail to realize that there are distinct and predictable patterns in the fall, each different, each requiring its own

The rut is the most important feature of the whitetail's fall activity patterns.
This critical time can be divided into two periods — the scraping period and
the breeding period. The big buck pictured here is taking in the full aroma of a
doe about to come into estrus. The distraction of the rut is the one chink in the
trophy buck's armor that hunters can take advantage of with any consistency.
Photo by Curt Helmick.

strategies and bringing its own advantages and disadvantages. Just as the game plan and tactics in a football game must change in response to advancing time, game situations and what the opponent is doing, or not doing, so it is with deer hunting. If the opponent starts off running the football up the middle every play, a defense with eight men on the line may work fine. But, if the other team suddenly starts sending five men down field for passes, do you keep defending the run or change your strategy? Of course, you change ... or lose.

Seems obvious, doesn't it? Yet, many deer hunters fail to adapt to major changes by the deer. Some will scout around opening weekend and, after finding some sign, set up to hunt that site. Then, as days and even weeks pass, they continue to hunt that same spot, even though the deer have long since changed their pattern. It doesn't take much of a coach to notice that the opponent has stopped running the ball and is now passing every play. Unfortunately, a change in deer patterns is not quite as obvious; however, the evidence is there if you look for it. And even better than that, hunters actually can predict the changes before they occur, just as a football coach knows the other team will start passing once the running game is shut down. But as with football, deer hunters must understand the basics of the game before they can predict what will happen and react accordingly.

SEASONAL PATTERNS

With that, let's take a look at the seasonal changes that take place in the world of whitetails. We will only be concerned about the time of year deer are hunted. But because seasons vary so much over North America, that almost encompasses the entire time bucks have "hard" antlers, from the first of September through February on average.

For whitetails and whitetail hunters alike, there is no time more important than the rut, which is the time when breeding and its related activities take center stage in the deer's life. The rut causes the normally super cautious trophy buck to temporarily drop his guard. It is the one chink in the buck's armor hunters can take advantage of with any consistency. Because of its importance, we'll use the rut as the basis for our seasonal divisions. These divisions are the **pre-rut period**; then the two periods of the rut — the **scraping period** and the **breeding period**; and

During the time of year deer are hunted, whitetail activity follows predictable patterns. These patterns can be divided into four distinct periods that encompass the entire time bucks have "hard" antlers. The first of these four periods is the pre-rut period, which begins when the bucks shed their velvet around early September. The last period, called the post-rut, ends when bucks drop their antlers, which normally occurs in February in most places. Photos by Bill Kinney.

finally the **post-rut period**. My friend Dick Idol, to whom I give a lot of credit for my own understanding of deer patterns, divides the fall into exactly the same four periods, although he refers to three of them by different names. Regardless of what they're called, these divisions represent distinct, predictable periods of whitetail activity and patterns. In this chapter, we will briefly identify these periods, but before doing so, some qualifications are needed.

ADVANCE QUALIFICATIONS

First, a deer's seasonal biological clock is controlled by the length of day. This is called photoperiodism. As with anything triggered by daylength, the timing of the period is almost exactly the same from year to year in a given place. Obviously, some deer will precede the majority and some will trail, but the peak activity will occur on a predictable timetable. It is this peak that we are most interested in, not exceptions or the minority, especially in regard to the critical scraping and breed-

193

ing periods of the rut. Once you know when these peaks have occurred historically in your area, it's an easy matter to dependably predict their arrival, barring major changes in the herd.

Although the timing of a period, its duration and the deer's behavioral patterns during a period are quite consistent from year to year in any given area, considerable differences exist from region to region across the country. We've already examined the great impact of hunting pressure, which can affect the buck age structure, buck/doe ratio and deer behavior. In addition, the latitude, physical condition of the deer, herd density, habitat and terrain are important factors influencing how these periods are played out where you hunt. Also, local weather conditions play a major role in determining the level of activity and sign associated with these seasonal patterns.

The four periods of fall deer activity we will discuss represent the ideal under "normal" circumstances. The combined effects of hunting pressure, weather and other factors may significantly alter the patterns, sign and level of activity locally during any given period. However, the concept of the four distinct periods is valid everywhere. They simply may not be as well defined, true-to-form or as visible in some places as in others. You must find out when these periods start, how long they last and what their characteristics (and sign) are where you hunt to take full advantage of the opportunities offered by each.

The one key date you must determine is the start of the breeding period. The time when the major wave of does comes in estrus is well defined and seldom varies more than a day or two from year to year by locale. Your local game department can almost surely tell you this. If not, seek out experienced local trophy hunters. Chances are they'll know. As you will see, from this one date you can pretty well map out the four periods. This is possible because the duration of the two vital rut periods — the scraping and breeding periods — is normally fairly consistent across the country, even though when they begin isn't. Over time, experience will help you refine the timing of these periods where you hunt.

Hunting seasons don't always overlap all four periods. Still, the need to understand the overall patterns is there for every serious trophy hunter. Only by knowing the "why" can a hunter make good, consistent judgment decisions about the "what," "when," "where" and "how."

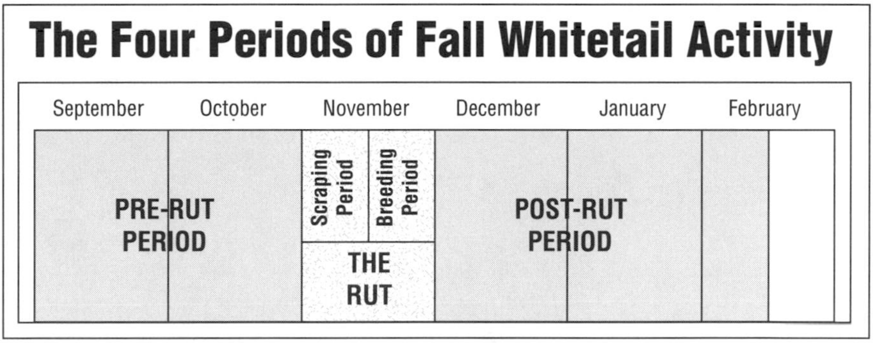

The Four Periods of Fall Whitetail Activity

September	October	November	December	January	February

PRE-RUT PERIOD	Scraping Period	Breeding Period	POST-RUT PERIOD	
	THE RUT			

THE FOUR PERIODS

With those qualifications, the accompanying graph depicts the "average" timing and length of the four periods. Following that, we'll look at how the beginning and ending points can be identified and at the primary characteristics of each period. Then, we'll explore each period indepth in the following chapters.

Pre-Rut Period

Beginning Point — When bucks shed the velvet from their antlers.

Characteristics of the Period — Predictable early morning/late afternoon feeding patterns predominate, gradually giving way to increased rutting activity, such as scraping, checking scrapes, etc. Bucks use the pre rut to build up body fat by feeding heavily and to prepare for the approaching rut by rubbing and mock-fighting bushes and trees.

Ending Point — When the focus of the buck's activities shifts from feeding to rutting, signaled by an increase in the number of serious scrapes. The end of this period and the beginning of the scraping period is gradual, usually occurring over the course of a few days.

Scraping Period of The Rut

Beginning Point — When bucks are more motivated by rutting than feeding activities and the number of serious scrapes and accompanying rubs clearly increases.

Characteristics of the Period — Rutting activity dominates the bucks' routine. Daytime movement increases as bucks, which now alter and expand their range, make their rounds to doe group hangouts, where they make and check scrapes. Travel patterns are now fairly pre-

195

David Goodchild of Dunwoody, Georgia, shot this 160-class 10-pointer in South Texas during the breeding period, which is undoubtedly the best time to shoot a trophy buck.

dictable. This is an excellent time to find and hunt one particular buck on a scrapeline.

Ending Point — When does come in estrus and breeding begins.

Breeding Period of The Rut

Beginning Point — When the first major wave of does enters estrus and breeding begins. Occurs rather suddenly and at a predictable time each year, barring major changes in the herd.

Characteristics of the Period — A marked reduction in scraping activity and scrape maintenance. Tracks of running deer are commonly seen on woods roads and along field edges. Bucks are either with a doe or looking for one. Travel patterns are very unpredictable, and bucks range a great distance at this time. It's hard to hunt a particular buck, but the chances of bumping into a mature buck rambling around in a rather careless manner are good. This is when most trophy bucks are killed.

Ending Point — When the majority of the does have been bred and are no longer in estrus.

Post-Rut Period

Beginning Point — When most does are no longer in estrus and breeding activity yields to feeding activity and "resting."

Characteristics of the Period — When the frenzied peak breeding activity is over, deer movement slows noticeably. Bucks initially become reclusive and nocturnal as they recover from the rigors of the rut. Does and young bucks tend to hold up in thickets near food sources and feed at night and during first and last light. Daylight movement is greatly reduced. After a period of rest, bucks gradually return to a feeding pattern, although they remain largely nocturnal, depending on hunting pressure. A secondary rut can initiate limited rutting activity as the unbred does (primarily yearlings and six-month-old fawns) come in estrus a month or so after the start of the breeding period.

Ending Point — When the bucks drop their antlers.

Chapter 10

The Pre-Rut Period
Food Is The Key

S UMMER IS A TIME of abundance and leisurely living for deer in most places. The does are busy tending their fawns and feeding on the lush vege-tation. Bucks of similar ages have banned together in bachelor groups and spend the hot midday hours loafing in cool places. As the shadows lengthen and the air cools, they start their daily feeding forays. On

Fall Whitetail Activity

September   October

PRE-RUT PERIOD

and off throughout the night and into the early morning hours, bucks go about the task of nourishing both their bodies and their developing antlers. For does and bucks alike, their summer routine revolves around food, shelter and water and their home range is only as large as is nec-essary to meet those basic needs.

In late summer, after their velvet-covered antlers are fully devel-oped, a change begins in the bucks. Triggered by changes in daylength, the testicles, which have been withdrawn and functionally inactive, begin to swell and drop back into the scrotum. Testosterone, the male hormone,

During the summer, bucks of similar ages ban together in bachelor groups and live with each other in relative harmony. Photo by Mike Biggs.

is produced and starts to flow through the buck's body, bringing both physical and mental changes. First, the buck's antlers harden. Then, the velvet dries and is soon shed. And just as significant, the buck's shy and retiring attitude changes. He becomes more aggressive and restless. These changes, marked by the shedding of velvet, usher in the beginning of the pre-rut period, which usually lasts 8 to 12 weeks depending on the region.

The start of this period varies by location but is very consistent from year to year in a given place. In Middle Georgia, most bucks shed their velvet a few days either side of the first of September. According to Texas biologist Bob Zaiglin, the majority of South Texas bucks shed their velvet between September 10 and September 15. Dick Idol, who lives in western Montana, says that velvet-shedding there peaks from September 5 to September 10. Wisconsin bucks shed their velvet the first week in September. Most whitetail bucks in North America probably loose their velvet between August 20 and September 20. Of course, within any herd, some bucks shed earlier than the majority and some later. Here, we're interested only in the peak time.

Most whitetail bucks in North American shed their velvet between August 20 and September 20. The shedding process, which marks the beginning of the pre-rut period, is usually completed within 24 hours. To remove their velvet, bucks rub their antlers on saplings as this one has just done. Photo by Bill Kinney.

The shedding process is usually completed in a surprisingly short time, normally within 24 hours from start to finish. Some bucks will carry strips of remaining velvet longer, especially in hard to reach places on the antlers. To remove the velvet, bucks rub their antlers on saplings, often with great zeal. Some have been observed to completely strip their antlers of velvet in one rubbing session.

Velvet-shedding marks the beginning of progressive changes in the buck that culminate in a masculine, big-necked animal ready to vie for breeding rights. This "combat-ready" physique differs greatly from the buck's more feminine, delicate features at the beginning of the pre-rut period. The catalyst for these changes is testosterone, which pours into the buck's bloodstream at an ever-increasing rate from velvet-shedding to breeding. During this time, his muscles grow larger as he rubs his antlers and mock-fights bushes and trees. This also allows a buck to get the "feel" of his new antlers. The increased amounts of testosterone in a buck's bloodstream have the same effect that steroids have on an athlete in training.

THE PERIOD IN OVERVIEW

From the beginning of the pre-rut period, the bucks within a bachelor group start showing aggression toward each other and the time of social harmony winds down. Bucks begin posturing and vying for dominance as the hierarchy is established. The pre-rut is not, however, the time of serious fighting, only occasional sparring contests to establish a pecking order. As time passes, the bucks, especially the older, larger ones, separate and retire to their own core area, which is chosen largely based on security and seclusion. The core areas of mature bucks are likely to be well away from the doe groups living near the prime food sources.

Early in the pre-rut, mature bucks have little interest in does and don't intentionally interact with the doe groups, although their feeding excursions surely will take them into the home ranges of the doe groups.

From the beginning of the pre-rut period, bucks, especially the older bucks, become increasingly aggressive and start vying for dominance. His ears laid back and his head cocked menacingly, the big buck above has assumed a threat posture and is letting the smaller buck know who's boss. During the pre-rut, threats and posturing are usually enough to establish the pecking order. Photo by Mike Biggs.

Since bucks frequently bed some distance from food sources during the pre-rut period and because the days are still fairly warm, bucks often reach their feeding grounds very late in the afternoon or at night. Photo by Mike Blair.

Young bucks tend to hang out together or stay in loose association with the doe groups, mainly because of the nearby presence of food and because they have nothing better to do. They do not yet follow the behavioral pattern of a mature buck.

After settling into their core area, bucks establish a routine. Most of their movement is from their bedding area to feeding grounds and back again. Along the way, they hone their fighting skills on bushes and small trees and do some preliminary "pawing," leaving rubs and "boundary scrapes" in the areas where they spend the most time. (Simply speaking, a rub is a section of tree with the bark rubbed off by a buck, and a scrape is a place on the ground pawed clean by a buck.)

Since bucks frequently bed some distance from food sources this time of year and because the days are still fairly warm, bucks often reach their feeding grounds very late in the afternoon or at night. Many factors affect this, such as hunting pressure, herd density, weather, terrain, cover and the distribution of prime food sources. Although a buck does not necessarily feed in the same place or travel the same trails every day, his travel pattern is repetitive and fairly predictable. However, a hunter must constantly watch for changes in a pattern, which can occur rather abruptly if a food source peters out or a better source becomes available.

As the end of the pre-rut period approaches, bucks start to rub with more aggression, sometimes shredding bushes and small trees. Their scraping activity, which largely has consisted of haphazard pawings, takes on added seriousness. Bucks begin to show some interest in does. When they encounter other bucks, they will threaten and posture — their hackles up and ears back. The feeding pattern becomes less predictable. Bucks start traveling farther from their core area and move more often in daylight. Testosterone coursing their veins, bucks will shift their focus from food to females over a period of only a few days. Now, instead of heading to feeding areas, their travels take them far and wide to doe groups, where they make serious scrapes and sometimes vicious rubs in the "living rooms" of potential girl friends. The rut has arrived, and the pre-rut has drawn to an end.

THE SIGN

During the pre-rut, rubs, trails, tracks, boundary scrapes and droppings are all usable sign. Rubs, however, most dependably identify the presence of a big buck. While not 100 percent reliable, the general rule that bigger bucks make bigger rubs is worth planning against. A more accurate way to say it would be that large, medium and small bucks can make small or medium-sized rubs, but big rubs are almost always made by big (at least big-bodied) bucks. There are always exceptions, but they don't invalidate the general rule. I have seen small bucks rub large, well-worn trees, but upon examining the rubs, I felt certain these small bucks were not responsible for making the rubs originally. They were just contributing their "mark" to an already established rub. I believe this situation is the basis for many stories about small bucks making exceptionally large rubs.

At any rate, I depend on rub size to point out the presence of a trophy buck. I then try to verify that fact by checking for big tracks and large droppings. My decision on whether or not a buck is worth hunting is made on the weight of the evidence. Short of having seen the buck, which is by far my first choice, rub size is the most important consideration. And, I'm not talking about hunting one rub, but rather, hunting

Of the pre-rut sign available to hunters, rubs most dependably identify the presence of a big buck. While not 100 percent reliable, the general rule that bigger bucks make bigger rubs is worth planning against. Photo by Curt Helmick.

rublines consisting of several large, fresh rubs, indicating frequent use of the area by a big buck. Rubs, unlike true scrapes, don't necessarily promise of a buck's imminent return. But, an abundance of them does indicate a buck has spent time in the area and may do so again in the future.

What constitutes a large rub? That varies by location across the continent. In Canada and Montana, I've seen rubs on fence posts and road-sign posts, as well as on 8 to 10-inch trees! On two occasions, I've seen fence posts rubbed in half — one in Canada, one in Montana! The big-bodied bucks all across the northern climes, including the Midwest, rub impressive trees and leave large scars on them. Trees with a diame-

No matter where in North America, this rub would be considered very large and would be worthy of a hunter's time and attention. Photo by Mike Blair.

ter of two to four inches, and sometimes larger, would be the usual rubbing size for trophy bucks up North.

In the more southern regions, rubs tend to be smaller, mainly because the deer are smaller, but the bigger bucks make respectable rubs. Along the Flint River in Georgia, large landholdings provide age for some of the state's purest gene pools of Wisconsin deer. These bucks are very large-bodied with antlers to match. I've seen rubs there comparable to those of big northern deer. On the whole, though, rubs on trees over four inches in diameter would be unusual in the South. Rub trees in the 1½ to 3-inch range would be the average target for mature bucks there. Because of the extreme resiliency of the tough South Texas brush, big bucks commonly rub one to two-inch stuff there, but I've seen some hefty mesquites worked over, too. Remember, however, it's not only the size of the tree rubbed that indicates a buck's size. The depth of the tine gouges, the amount of broken and twisted limbs, the length and height of the rub and the overall degree of damage are all clues to a buck's size.

In conjunction with rubs, halfhearted scrapes often will be found during the pre-rut. These pawings are called "boundary scrapes." They are not as large or as well defined as the clean, yard-long "breeding scrapes" to come later. The pawings of the pre-rut are probably made instinctively by the buck as a foreshadowing of future serious scraping activity. Or, perhaps boundary scrapes, like rubs, are visual or scent markers serving notice of a particular buck's presence. Whatever their purpose, they are not in themselves an indicator that the buck will return to that place unless their number alone points to high usage. Boundary scrapes can be good places to find clear tracks, which may tell you something of the buck's size. Big tracks aren't foolproof by any means, but they usually do indicate good body size. What's on the buck's head may or may not bear much relevance to track size.

FEEDING AREAS

Major feeding areas are excellent starting points when trying to sort out a pre-rut pattern. Fortunately, they often are easy to find and identify. The ideal situation for the hunter during the pre-rut feeding pattern is when there are only a few major, distinct food sources. An example would be where several square miles of woodlands adjoin only a handful of fields planted in desirable agricultural crops, such as corn, soybeans, winter wheat, oats, alfalfa, etc. Deer would feed heavily on these crops, especially if other attractive alternatives like acorns or clearcuts didn't compete. The worst situation is an expansive tract of timber without any concentrated food sources. In such cases, deer will disperse throughout their range to feed, and their daily travel patterns will not be very predictable since they have no specific destination points. It is also possible to have too much of a good thing. Areas that offer too many choices of concentrated preferred foods can make predicting travel patterns difficult. A widely distributed acorn crop can cause this. So can

Mature bucks usually avoid the exposed major food sources used by does, fawns and young bucks. Often, they prefer out-of-the-way secondary food sources or feeding grounds with some protective cover. The buck pictured here has plenty of food available, and cover is only a step away. Photo by Denver Bryan.

an abundance of agricultural crops to choose from, as is commonly the case in parts of the Midwest and Central Canada. Yet, food sources remain the best beginning point for finding pre-rut bucks.

But alas, there is a hitch in the get-along. Mature bucks sometimes avoid the exposed major food sources used by does, fawns and young bucks, at least during daylight hours. Hunting pressure will surely cause this. Instead of exposing themselves in the open or "eating out" with the crowd during the daytime, trophy bucks might opt to feed at secondary food sources, perhaps ones closer to their bedding areas or ones with some protective cover like a clearcut. Or, they may indeed feed at the hotspots with other deer ... but at night. Many hopeful trophy hunters waste precious time watching food sources filled with does and fawns while mature bucks feed at out-of-the-way secondary sources or sleep away the day. While hunting pressure will nearly always cause this, it can happen even when pressure is light.

Near my ranch in Flathead County, Montana, where hunting pressure is fairly low, several large alfalfa fields are located in the valley one to two miles from the base of the mountains. During the pre-rut period, these fields load up with does, fawns and young bucks. A few trophy-sized bucks are seen there, but on the whole, they are noticeably absent. Most big bucks seem to bed on the side of the mountains away from the doe groups, roads and people. The distance from their bedding areas to the alfalfa fields is not insurmountable for whitetail bucks. Still, they seldom frequent these prime spots, preferring instead to feed on secondary food concentrations nearer their beds. From a hunter's standpoint, clearcuts are the most important and identifiable of these secondary sources.

Once you've located a feeding area, there are a couple of places to look for big rubs. First, rubs may be found in or around the feeding area. In the case of agricultural fields, rubs are frequently made along the edges. When deer are feeding on acorns or in other areas of cover, the rubs may be seen in the feeding area itself. Second, deer commonly will stage (hold up) some 100 to 200 yards inside cover before entering a field or exposed food source just before or after dark. To identify these staging areas, look for evidence of heavy overall deer use such as droppings, tracks, browse sign and trails, particularly intersecting trails and trails running parallel to the food source. Bucks often make rubs in these staging grounds.

BEDDING AREAS

Discovering where a buck is bedding helps in figuring out his travel pattern. Unfortunately, this is not always easy to do. The degree of difficulty is determined by such things as the terrain, cover, the distance the buck is traveling, the amount of sign (specifically rubs and trails) and your access to all the buck's range. In reality, you will usually know only part of the travel pattern of the buck you're hunting. You will have to make an educated guess at the rest. Happily, bedding areas have certain common characteristics that will allow you to predict where they are likely to be located.

A buck's bedding site is within a his core area, the fairly small acreage where he spends most of his time. In hilly country, bucks seem to choose elevated places to bed, most commonly on the side of hills rather than right on top of them. If possible, they will bed facing

In hilly country, bucks seem to choose elevated places to bed, most commonly on the side of hills rather than right on top. Photo by Denver Bryan.

downhill and downwind in a place that gives them a decent view. This allows the bucks to use their incredible sense of smell to detect danger coming from their uphill blindside. Anything approaching from below and downwind will be seen. By bedding thusly, a buck can escape over the hill when he sees a threat below and down the hill when he smells a problem on top.

In relatively flat country, bucks usually bed in out-of-the-way places with thick cover. They are particularly likely to bed where there is good ground cover such as dense underbrush, blowdowns, low-growing evergreens, tall grass, cattails, cane, etc. I've also found that bucks like to

In relatively flat country, bucks frequently bed in areas with good ground cover. This giant non-typical has found protection in tall grass. Photo by Curt Helmick.

bed near beaver ponds, sloughs and other such places with standing water. This is probably because dense cover is usually found around these places. Plus, the water side of these bedding sites provides the bucks with partial protection from approaching danger and a secure escape route if needed.

Flatland bucks often employ a similar strategy to that of bucks in hilly terrain when choosing where in a piece of cover they'll bed. As in hilly areas, they use the wind to protect their blindside behind them and try to bed where they can see some distance downwind. The best examples I've seen of this have been in the small woodlots in

Canada. There, snow allowed me to read sign in ways impossible in non-snow areas. After hunting this country awhile, I began to notice that deer tended to bed on the downwind side of woodlots. A little thought explained why. The deer could smell any danger approaching through the timber, which offered limited visibility. By laying where they could see downwind into the open fields, they could detect danger there immediately and escape unnoticed. Once I figured this out, I could predict with some accuracy where deer might be bedded. But, even knowing this didn't mean I could slip up on them. Most of the time, warm beds and departing tracks were all I found to prove my prediction correct. I am convinced that this same scheme holds true for bucks bedding in thick cover inside an area of thinner cover.

CONNECTING TRAILS

Obviously, the trails that connect bedding areas to feeding areas are of importance to the hunter. However, you'll be lucky indeed if you can backtrack along visible trails and reconstruct a buck's travel pattern. The trails are normally too indistinct to follow all the way. Or, a profusion of intersecting trails and overall deer sign may make the whole deal too complex and confusing to allow you to unravel the travel pattern of any particular buck. Snow, of course, would be a great aid, but it's seldom present during the pre-rut. Usually, the best I can do is to follow trails a short distance or find bits and pieces of what I think is the same buck's trail. Yet, this partial information is often enough to reveal a general pattern. From this circumstantial evidence, I can speculate on what the buck is doing.

Food sources are a good place to start the search for trails. The number and complexity of trails will depend on the importance of the food source and on the herd density. One of the first things I look for at a food source is a concentration of tracks. In open food sources like agricultural fields, deer usually have preferred entry points, such as corners of the field, behind islands of cover and secluded parts of the field. These entry points will be heavily tracked, and trails will be nearby. In a major feeding area, does, fawns and young bucks are sure to be feeding there, creating their own rather elaborate network of trails. Check for big rubs and other evidence that a good buck is using the trails. Also, don't limit your search to the major entry points; trophy bucks sometimes enter a feeding area well away from the crowds.

After locating the trails leading into the feeding area, try to back-track them to the staging areas inside the cover. Do this whether or not you've found big rubs on the trails entering the food source. Staging areas, which are not always easy to find and identify, are excellent places to hunt night-feeding bucks since they may arrive there before dark. The presence of big rubs will tell you if a staging area holds promise.

Once you've found a trail marked with promising rubs, follow the trail out to learn as much as possible about what the buck is doing. Try to fit the section of the trail you've found into the buck's overall travel pattern. Determine whether the trail is a "going-to-feed" trail used in the afternoon or a "back-to-bed" trail used in the morning, or both. The rubs themselves will help you decide this. If all the rubs along a trail are on the same side of trees and bushes, you can assume the buck is traveling in only one direction on that trail, from the side with the rubs. If rubs are on both sides of trees, the buck is using the same trail coming and going, assuming it's the same buck. To be honest, in places with high deer populations, it's hard to sort out one particular buck from all the sign. But, big rubs will tell you that at least one good buck has been there.

Trails between bedding areas and feeding areas are well worth hunting if you can find one with an active rubline. The advantage connecting trails offer is that bucks often travel them in the daylight. Mature bucks tend to use their own trails this time of year. Heavily used trails with lots of tracks and only small rubs don't hold a lot of promise for trophy hunters. Lightly used trails with large rubs are the ticket. Look for rubs at the intersection of trails or along noticeable "edges," such as old logging roads, breaks between timber types, streambeds or the edges of small clearings. If anything funnels deer movement along the trial, you may have found the place to wait out a trophy buck.

As trails lead farther from feeding areas, they become fainter and harder to read. By the time they reach a buck's core area, they will have fingered out and pretty much dissipated. However, rubs may be present along the faint trails near a bedding area and are almost certain to be found in the bedding area itself. When a buck gets up in the late afternoon or returns from his nightly feeding excursion, he

This huge buck is traveling a connecting trail between the bedding area and feeding grounds. It would be very unusual for a buck of this size to travel such an open trail in areas with much hunting pressure. Photo by Curt Helmick.

frequently loiters in or near his bedding area and makes rubs.

If the presence of rubs in combination with the right conditions for a bedding area indicate you've found the buck's "bedroom," be careful. Too much disturbance there may cause him to relocate. If I can help it, I don't like to jump a buck I'm hunting from his bed. It's best to scout the surrounding area and find a place to set up for him outside of where he actually beds. The advantage of hunting near his bed is that he may be on his feet there earlier in the afternoon and later in the morning. The disadvantage is the danger of running him off. Generally, your chances of killing a buck in his core area diminish with time. You had better get him quickly before he knows he's being hunted.

DOE GROUPS

I have referred a couple of times to doe groups. Dick Idol calls them "family units," and that's an appropriate name for them since they probably consist of related deer, at least in part. The doe groups can be made up of from a half-dozen to 30 or more does and fawns. Young bucks often hang out with them, mainly because food is inevitably nearby. The doe groups are lead by a matriarch doe, called the alpha doe by biologists. In low density herds, doe groups are distinct and spend much of their time apart from other groups. In high deer populations, they are far less distinctive and are in frequent, if not constant, contact with other doe groups. In fact, in the highest densities, it is virtually impossible to tell that a doe-group structure exists at all. Doe groups occupy the best habitat in an area, and their home range is closely associated with prime food sources. The mature bucks know where the doe groups are in their neck of the woods. When the rut arrives, they head to them.

An interesting new theory has emerged in regards to doe groups. I mentioned the "fall shuffle" of yearling bucks in an earlier chapter. This is a time when yearling bucks disperse over a wide area and wander around aimlessly. New evidence strongly indicates that the alpha does are actually the ones that kick these young bucks out, running them away from the doe groups as the rut approaches. Conventional wisdom has held that the more dominant bucks ran the yearling bucks out of their home ranges. The theory that it is the alpha does makes sense based on the social makeup of the herd at that time of year. Whatever is responsible, there is a good biological reason for the fall shuffle. By dispersing the young males from groups of related does, inbreeding is largely prevented.

HUNTING THE PRE-RUT

Assuming the existence of an adequate number of mature bucks and an absence of high hunting pressure, the pre-rut period offers what I would term a "fair" chance for a trophy. To be honest, it is not

The doe groups consist of distinct units of does and fawns and play an important role in the whitetail's social structure. Doe groups occupy the best habitat and are usually found in close association with prime food sources. Photo by Mike Biggs.

easy to shoot a top-end buck then. In the face of high hunting pressure — which nearly always means there will be few mature bucks anyway — the pre-rut can be an extremely difficult time to shoot a trophy. The bucks will be mostly nocturnal and difficult to pattern. High deer populations can also make patterning a particular buck difficult during the pre-rut, although your chances of randomly bumping into a good buck may improve.

Before going on, a word about topographic maps and aerial photographs is in order. These indispensable tools will allow you to quickly identify potential feeding and bedding areas, travel routes, bottlenecks, ambush points, etc. They will save you considerable time and effort and provide "access" to land you don't have permission to go on. By their use, you can postulate a theory about what a buck is doing over his entire range and then make efficient use of the leg work required to prove out your theory. We'll talk more about topo maps and aerial photos later.

Now for some hunting application. The first thing I do during this period, after obtaining topos and/or aerials, is find and scout major and secondary feeding areas. I look for overall deer activity, rubs, trails, staging areas and general travel patterns. If I can't locate any big buck sign, I hunt hot food sources or the staging grounds near them. I continue scouting during midday in an effort to find big buck sign along trails, near bedding areas or at secondary food sources, especially those "in cover" like acorns and clearcuts. If the area has much hunting pressure, I move farther from the food sources and hunt bottlenecks, powerlines or other odds-on intercept points along what I believe to be the major travel routes from bedding to feeding areas.

Once I find big rubs or other hopeful sign, I try to learn as much as I can about what's going on without overly disturbing the place. Where pressure is light, my preference is to hunt near the food source. As the destination point, this is the most dependable place to wait out a buck. Depending on the sign, I may watch the food source directly or set up in the staging area.

If hunting pressure is too heavy for consistent daytime use of food sources, I would hunt the next highest concentration of big buck sign I could find, preferably an active rubline in cover. If I wanted to hunt near the known bedding area of a big buck, I would wait until conditions are most favorable. I would go in well before daylight, probably hunting from a ground blind to hold down noise, and stay until late morning. I would return mid-afternoon and stay until well after dark. If I failed to shoot the buck there after two or three tries, I would likely hunt elsewhere, fearing that I had spooked the buck from his bedding area.

During the pre-rut, I usually hunt from either treestands or ground blinds once I've found big buck sign or a good ambush point. About the only still-hunting (slipping around) I will do during this time is while hunting/scouting prospective new places. Even then, I spend a lot of time sitting and leaning against trees, especially during prime hours and when I'm in a good location. General deer movement during daylight hours is not all that great during the pre-rut period. Plus, visibility is usually limited because of thick vegetation since the leaves may not have yet fallen. Mature bucks tend to have a specific place to go when moving now, and the best plan is to wait for them at a destination point or to hunt them while they're en route to one. Stand-hunting is the best way to do this. Also, bucks tend to be cautious and careful during the pre-rut. It's not easy to slip up on them.

Deer drives can be a good alternative tactic during the pre-rut, especially during warm spells when deer movement is low. Known bedding areas are good places to roust out a trophy buck during midday

Here's proof that trophy bucks can be killed on major food sources during the pre-rut ... if hunting pressure is low. This big-bodied buck was shot on a grain field early in the Alberta season. Photo by Dick Idol.

hours. Early morning drives near feeding areas can be productive if you can get set up without spooking all the bucks from the area. The main drawback to drives is that they disrupt natural movement in the area. If you are limited to a small tract of land or hunting one particular buck, take that into account.

Rattling during the beginning and middle of the pre-rut period is spotty at best. A passive form of rattling seems to work best then, if it works at all. Just tickle the antlers together very gingerly a few times and wait. A little mild rubbing on trees might help. If you're in a place frequented by a mature buck, he may ease over to see what's going on. Response to rattling picks up toward the end of the pre-rut period. This is when a buck's interest starts to shift from food to does and the frosty autumn nights usher in a new time in the life of the whitetail — the scraping period of the rut.

Chapter 11

The Scraping Period Of The Rut

The First Chink In The Armor

T HE DAYS ARE SHORTER now; the nights colder. The smell of frost-cured hay is in the air, and the rustle of autumn leaves rides the chill north wind. On the ridge a mile beyond the alfalfa field, a thick-necked whitetail buck rises to his feet just as woodducks whistle overhead in the orange glow of last light. The buck stretches, relieves himself and

Fall Whitetail Activity

November

Scraping Period | Breeding Period

THE RUT

then stares in the direction of the alfalfa field where he's spent most of his nights over the past few weeks. He tests the air, his nose raised high. Something is different tonight. It's been coming on for several days — a new urge, strong and obsessive.

    He suddenly pivots and walks menacingly toward a small pine. The first powerful upstroke of his massive two-foot-wide rack rakes deep

His massive neck muscles bulging, this trophy buck is ready to enter the rut, which can be divided into two parts — the scraping period and the breeding period. Photo by Bill Kinney.

gouges in the trunk of the 2½-inch tree and snaps off two thumb-sized lower limbs. The buck leans the full weight of his 240-pound frame into the "fight." His head twisting from side to side and his eyes rolled back in heated frenzy, long tines strip bark and rip limbs from the tree. Sharp, thrashing hooves cleave the ground, sending leaves and debris flying 15 feet behind. Froth appears at the corners of his mouth, now open and gasping. The tree, after three minutes of unabated assault, yields and breaks in half, leaving the seven-foot top section cradled in the buck's sap-stained rack. Walking forward defiantly, he shakes his head violently, casting aside the mangled treetop.

His sides heaving, he again stands and stares to the south, toward the alfalfa field beyond the gathering darkness. He then looks to his right. Something's over there ... something from the past. A smell, a memory, an urge he can't resist. Suddenly, the buck wheels and heads west at a trot. He gives no heed to the slight hunger pain welling up inside. Tonight, something else draws him irresistibly onward, beyond his home range. His unrelenting pace first takes him to a small clearing near a cornfield two miles away. Then, he presses on southward for another mile to a streambottom coursing a soybean field. Next, his quest takes him eastward to an abandoned apple orchard. Finally, the buck returns to the familiar alfalfa field, but there will be little time to feed this night. The great buck has yielded to a timeless call. For the next four weeks, he will be driven by the desire to breed. For this buck, the rut, specifically the scraping period, has begun!

WHEN AND HOW LONG

Unlike the beginning of the pre-rut period, which is marked by the specific and easily identifiable event of velvet-shedding, the start of the scraping period is not so obvious or as neatly defined. Yet, like any daylength-controlled function, it occurs at a predictable time each year at a given location. Actually, the scraping period "emerges" from the end of the pre-rut period. Increasing testosterone levels doing its work, the bucks become more restless, aggressive and preoccupied by their sexual desires with each passing day. Finally, the bucks sell out and shift their priority from food and security to the urge to reproduce.

The start of the scraping period is directly related to the start of the breeding period, the timing of which varies greatly across the country.

As the scraping period arrives, bucks become more restless, aggressive and pre-occupied with rutting activities. They range farther and farther from their core areas and spend more time on the move. His mouth agape, this buck is on the prowl, probably making or checking scrapes. Photo by Bill Kinney.

Therefore, when the scraping period gets underway is likewise variable. Fortunately, however, the length of the scraping period is quite consistent over the whitetail's range. Given this, if a hunter can determine when the breeding period starts where he hunts, then the timing of the scraping period can be forecast quite precisely ... if its duration is known. Let's pin that down.

Although I have occasionally seen significant scraping activity three or more weeks before the start of breeding, my experiences and those reported by experts throughout North America lead me to the conclusion that the scraping period lasts roughly two weeks in most places. Serious, consistent and predictable scraping activity, the trademark of this period, simply cannot be counted on much earlier than two weeks prior to the start of the breeding period. And oftentimes, things don't really heat up until about 10 days before breeding starts. From then on, the pace picks up daily. The last week is a time of frenzied activity, provided the weather and other conditions are favorable.

If the scraping period lasts two weeks, then a hunter can accurately project when it will start by determining a beginning date for peak breeding and backing up 14 days. Local game departments should know when peak breeding begins in their area. The timing of the scraping period, like that of the breeding period, can differ from place to place by up to several weeks, even months. Across Canada and the northern United States, the scraping period usually begins in late October and early November. Hill Country Texas sees this period begin in early to mid October. The South Texas startup is much later, usually around the first of December. Surprisingly, South Florida bucks start serious scraping in August. But, parts of Alabama don't see the scraping period get underway until well into January. You must find out for yourself when it starts where you hunt.

PERIOD OVERVIEW

Let's look at the buck patterns that might be expected during this period. The patterns discussed here represent the ideal. Heavy pressure on a herd or changes in key population parameters will threaten the social order and alter patterns, possibly even preventing the bucks from engaging in any significant scraping activity at all. Bucks start out the scraping period using their core area as their base of operations. Instead of traveling mostly to and from their feeding grounds, their destination is now doe groups, some of which may be a mile, two miles or even more from their core area. Because of the distance, the excitement of the rut and perhaps even cooler weather, bucks not only travel farther but they're on the move more hours of the day. Some of these travel hours spill over into the daytime. That alone is a big advantage for hunters.

Early in this period, bucks make scouting passes through the home ranges of doe groups, checking out the territory, locating the high-activity areas, making preliminary "test" scrapes, rubbing and maybe even feeding a bit. Over time, they will establish a relatively fixed route and have a specific purpose. Their excursions will take them directly to the

This buck has just finished reworking a scrape (the pawed-out patch of bare ground in front of him) and is now scent-checking or "flehmening," something bucks commonly do around active scrapes or hot does. Photo by Curt Helmick.

"social hub" of a doe group's home range for the purpose of leaving alluring "calling cards" for would-be girl friends. These calling cards are scrapes, and they should not only attract does but also wise trophy hunters!

As the scraping period wears on, bucks continue their predictable routine of making, checking and maintaining scrapes at the social hubs of the various doe groups. Hormones running high, bucks now will engage in some rather vicious rubbing, leaving behind shredded and mangled trees and bushes called by some "breeding rubs." They are distinguished from earlier rubs by their freshness and the increased extent of damage from the bucks' mounting aggression and frustration. They are most often found near scrapelines but also can be found along trails connecting scrapelines. These rubs are of value in helping to piece together a buck's travel pattern or, obviously, in determining something about his size.

The growing aggression also leads to challenges and fights between bucks of similar size. Mature bucks are now ranging well beyond their familiar home range where a hierarchy has been established among area bucks. During their travels, they encounter other mature bucks that offer challenge. Threats and posturing ensue, and out-and-out fighting sometimes follows.

The younger bucks randomly work the doe groups and check their own half-baked scrapes, as well as those of the mature bucks, in hopes of getting in on whatever action may occur. Does continue to feed, but their schedule is now disrupted both by their own restlessness and by the evermore persistent bucks. Bucks not only check their scrapes, but they also seek out does in hopes of catching their first whiff of the coming estrus. With their heads held low and outstretched, hopeful bucks rush any prospective doe they come across. The does, their tails tucked and their bodies hunched and low to the ground, scurry away from their aggressive suitors. Should the doe urinate, the buck excitedly sniffs the discharge, sometimes raising his head high and curling his upper lip. Their strange act is called "flehmening" and is apparently an attempt by the buck to concentrate the doe's odor near his nostrils.

The buck's routine starts changing as breeding time draws closer. It becomes more erratic and less predictable. He spends more time near the doe groups, even bedding near them, returning to his core area less frequently. His travels take him feverishly from one doe group to another, sensing the time is near. He eagerly checks each doe he encounters. The promising scent of soon-to-be-ready does causes him to focus his attention on certain doe groups, further disrupting his travel pattern and routine.

Finally, the unmistakable scent of a hot doe rises from his scrape. Nose to the ground, the buck searches frantically for the departing trail. Moments later, he hits it and weaves back and forth along the trail for 10 yards before locking on to the alluring scent with unwavering certainty. Intent on one thing, he goes off in a short-gaited trot. Unerringly, his nose takes him to the doe. She is ready but teasingly unwilling to receive his advances. A chase follows. This same scene is played out

The actual process of pawing out a scrape is underway here. Bucks are very intent on the task at hand when making and checking scrapes. This spells opportunity for the hunter. Photo by Mike Biggs.

The buck is now leaving scent from his forehead and preorbital glands, and even his saliva, on the characteristic overhanging limb nearly always found in association with a scrape. Photo by Mike Biggs.

With his head held low and outstretched, this hopeful buck rushes a prospective doe. Not yet ready to accept his advances during the scraping period, the doe scurries away from the lustful buck. Photo by Mike Biggs.

across the land. The first major wave of does has entered estrus, the scraping period has ended and the breeding festivities have begun.

With this profile of the scraping period, you probably see why this time of year offers hunters their best opportunity to successfully hunt one particular buck. On a fairly predictable travel pattern while working their scrapes and distracted by the lure of the rut, trophy bucks that seldom expose themselves to danger in daylight hours are now more vulnerable. This is a time trophy hunters do not want to miss.

All-Important Scrapes

As we've seen, scrapes perform a very specific function in the whitetail breeding scheme, which is unique in the animal world as far as I know. The serious scrapes made by mature bucks during this time are called "breeding scrapes." Every hunter should know what they look like and how to tell if they're in use.

Breeding scrapes are usually oval in shape and about 36 x 30 inches. Some are larger; others smaller. About 4 to 4½ feet above the scrape, there will virtually always be an overhanging limb, usually a half-inch or so in diameter. This limb will be mangled and broken, the aftermath of the buck's sometimes violent attempt to leave scent on the limb from his forehead or preorbital glands, or perhaps even from his saliva since he frequently will bite the small branches and pull them through his mouth. (Bucks will also deposit their scent on limbs, known as "licking branches," at places other than scrapes. These licking branches appear to be an important form of scent communication, and some hunters even seek them out and hunt them.) As with rubs, a scrape is usually a part of a series called a scrapeline.

An active scrape will look fresh. It will be pawed clean of leaves or debris. The "plowed up" ground in the scrape will be freshly turned and will often be damp and have a musky odor. This is because both bucks

Bucks often make vicious rubs near scrapes. These rubs can give the hunter some idea about the size of the buck making the scrapes. Look closely and you can see this buck's scrape in the foreground. Photo by Curt Helmick.

and does urinate over their tarsal glands (located on their hind legs) onto the scrape. The overhead limb will be significantly damaged. The area immediately around the scrape will show considerable disturbance, such as overturned leaves, fresh dirt flung from the scrape, tracks, etc. Droppings will be in evidence near the scrape and in the immediate vicinity if the area has high usage.

How can you tell what size buck is using a scrape? The size of the scrape, the damage to the limb and the general disturbance of the area surrounding the scrape are good indicators. An excellent clue to the magnitude of the buck is the size of the rubs associated with scrapes. When working scrapes, bucks get excited, sometimes frenzied. It's the exception when they fail to take on a bush or a tree along scrapelines.

Who uses scrapes? It may surprise some hunters to know that both bucks and does frequent scrapes. They are created by bucks to serve their purpose, and they are maintained primarily by bucks. However, does do check scrapes, probably to see who's in the market for action, and they come to them to signal their readiness as estrus approaches. Does will actually paw the ground in scrapes and, as we discussed earlier, they will urinate in them. When does come to scrapes, they tend to spend more time in the vicinity than do bucks. After all, does do live in the area. Mature bucks, on the other hand, probably don't. Plus, they are usually in a hurry to check out some other place.

More than one buck will use a scrape. I'm not yet convinced that it is a common practice for more than one dominant buck to use the same scrape. In fact, I rather doubt it. But, I do know that smaller bucks will check and "touch up" the scrape of a larger buck. An active scrapeline in a soon-to-be-hot area is a focal point of deer interest and activity. It's only logical that young or subdominant bucks keep an eye on the local "pickup corner" when Mr. Big is away.

When do bucks use scrapes? There's good news and bad news on this subject. The bad news is that 70 to 80 percent of a buck's visits to his scrapes are at night. This is based on studies done over 24-hour periods using infrared cameras to record nighttime activity. The good news is that the remaining 20 percent or so represents far more daytime movement than normal, not to mention bucks are now less cautious. Yet, high hunting pressure or too much harassment on a scrapeline will cause bucks to either abandon the area or work the nightshift altogether.

When do bucks make scrapes? Research has shown that 70 to 80 percent of a buck's visits to his scrapes are at night; however, the remaining 20 or so percent represents more daytime activity than normal. Photo by Mike Blair.

And even in the absence of high pressure, there's no guarantee a buck will return to his scrapes, at least during legal shooting hours. Hunting scrapes is like any other hunting method — you pay your money and take your chances.

Researchers in Missouri found there were three peak times for daytime scrape use in their study area, which received light to moderate pressure. The first and most active peak was from 8:45 to 10:15 a.m.

This is an active breeding scrape in South Texas. Note the three-foot patch of "plowed-up" ground and the twisted and broken limbs. Photo by Mike Biggs.

Their studies showed that mostly does came to scrapes the first half of this period. The majority of the visitors during the last half of this period were bucks, but most "winded" the scrapes from a distance and did not actually come to or attend the scrape.

Interestingly, the researchers found that they could coax some of the winding bucks nearer the scrape by grunting or by emulating a long deer snort (not the short, sharp snort which is an alarm call). They said that the drawn-out deer snort is a "who's there" identification snort and that the bucks sometimes would come to see what's going on near their scrape.

According to the Missouri study, the second most favored time for scrape visitation was from 3:45 to 5:15 p.m. This period of scrape activity differed from the morning peak in that bucks showed up first, followed later by does. Also different in the afternoon peak was the fact that the bucks actually came to the scrapes then and worked them.

The third period of scrape activity, which involved far fewer deer, was from 11:15 a.m. to 1:15 p.m. Mostly bucks visited during this midday time. About half of the bucks winded the scrapes and half actually worked them. The researchers did not differentiate between the sizes (or ages) of bucks visiting scrapes during their study. My experience has been that trophy bucks are more likely to visit scrapelines during the low-light hours. But, these three peak times do clearly show a couple of advantages inherent to the scraping period — daytime movement is greater and possible at all hours.

How and where do you find scrapes? Breeding scrapes will be near doe groups, which normally will be found near food sources. Like rubs, scrapes are practically always found along an edge of some type. Old logging roads, the edge of clearings or fields, old homesites, the break between two timber types and around ponds or lakes are some of the places scrapes are frequently put down. Areas where rubs were found in the earlier pre-rut period are likely spots for scrapes. Scrapes are commonly made in the same places year after year, barring changes in the deer herd or the habitat. Check the areas you've seen them in previous seasons. There's no secret to finding scrapes. Just look along the edges and walk, walk and walk some more. If you find a hot scrapeline, your scouting could pay "big" dividends!

HUNTING STRATEGY

Hunting strategy for the scraping period is probably evident by now — hunt active scrapelines. Since bucks could be moving any time of the day, the old "grind-it-out" theory of hunting long and hard works well now. Even if you can't find a scrapeline you feel is active, which is a realistic possibility in heavily hunted locations, take heart. The increased buck activity alone greatly improves your odds even if you have to hunt "blind." In such cases, hunt close to the best buck sign available and/or powerlines, bottlenecks and other advantageous sites near or on the way to food sources. But, the best way to capitalize on the unique opportunity presented in the scraping period is to hunt active scrapes.

Let's assume you've found a series of breeding scrapes along an abandoned logging road near a soybean field. The evidence says they are active, and the rubs you've seen nearby spark visions of a hoss whitetail. First, try to get an idea of how this scrapeline fits into the buck's overall travel pattern. Where's he coming from? Where's he going? What do his trails or the direction of the scrapeline tell you about his approach? Because of the distance bucks will travel this time of the year, it's unlikely that you can reconstruct his entire route. Still, put together as much as possible so you can determine where you should set up.

When you're around active scrapes, be very careful not to smell the place up any more than necessary. Bucks depend heavily on their noses now. Your scent won't go undetected. The use of cover-up scent may be helpful. Also, wear rubber-bottomed boots if possible. They don't pick up and transfer odor like other boots. Try not to let your clothes or body rub against vegetation near the scrapeline or approach route. It is surprising how long deer can detect human odor. A buck with several seasons behind him will not tolerate much interference from humans.

As you probably have gathered, stand-hunting is the best way to hunt scrapes. I prefer portable stands over permanent ones. The portable should be one that can be hung quickly and quietly. A ground stand is also fine, but you are more likely to be seen or smelled on the ground than if you're up a tree.

In their excited state, bucks can approach scrapes from anywhere, regardless of the wind direction. But, they do have a tendency to come in from downwind or crosswind. Even when they approach from crosswind, they'll usually end up downwind, especially if they are winding the scrape rather than actually working it. For this reason, it is best to locate your stand well downwind of scrapes, or better yet, downwind but to the opposite side of the buck's suspected approach route. I like to be as far away from the scrapes as is reasonable. This reduces the likelihood that other deer investigating the area will give me away to the buck I'm after.

When hunting scrapes, you must be constantly on the alert for a change in patterns. Just hunting a scrape in itself increases the odds that activity will fall off. Deer will eventually smell you or your approach trail, even though you may never be aware of it. Unless your

Guy Shanks, Jr. of Bigfork, Montana, was hunting from a portable stand over-looking an active scrapeline with plenty of big rubs when he shot this near record whitetail during the 1990 season. The 25-inch 11-pointer grossed 178 and netted 166. Photo by Dick Idol.

stand is located just right, two or three days of constant pressure may cause an old buck to either shift to nocturnal activity or relocate altogether. Scrapelines near fields are much more sensitive to pressure than secluded scrapes in the woods. Also, watch for changes in the use of a food source by does. If they shift their feeding pattern, bucks may be forced to relocate their scrapes.

Because scrapes are usually hunted in close quarters and because of the deer's sensitivity to human pressure, I try to choose a day to hunt an active scrapeline when weather favors good deer movements. However, time and other limitations don't always allow this. Anytime you're hunting right on top of a big whitetail, your best chance at him is usually the

I was watching an active scrapeline when I rattled in this buck. When he responded, the excited buck immediately started working the scrapes and viciously rubbing bushes. He's a 160-class buck. The scraping period is an excellent time for antler-rattling. Photo by Jim Goodchild.

first couple of tries before he knows he's being hunted.

Though stand-hunting is normally the most effective technique to hunt scrapes, slipping slowly and quietly through areas with buck sign or around food sources can also be good. The bucks are on the move and off their guard. Until I find an active scrapeline I want to hunt, this is my preferred hunting method. It allows me to hunt and to scout, and I've killed many good bucks this way. Unless the pressure is high, which means nocturnal activity, or time is running out, I don't like to drive deer during the scraping time. This can disrupt their natural movement patterns.

The scraping period is the best time for antler rattling. Bucks are "wired" and full of themselves. When they hear the sound of a "buck fight," their aggression takes over and they come looking for action. You don't have to be bashful about rattling now. I do start off slowly so I don't startle nearby deer. But by the time the sequence is over, the rattling horns — and usually my knuckles — have taken a pretty good beating. I like to add realism to the process by rubbing trees, breaking limbs and stomping the ground. To me, this is one of the most exciting forms of hunting. There's nothing like seeing a wild-eyed buck come charging in on top of you. If that doesn't blow the cholesterol out of your arteries, you need to take up another sport ... like spearfishing for great whites!

Chapter 12

The Breeding Period
Of The Rut
The Time Of Greatest Vulnerability

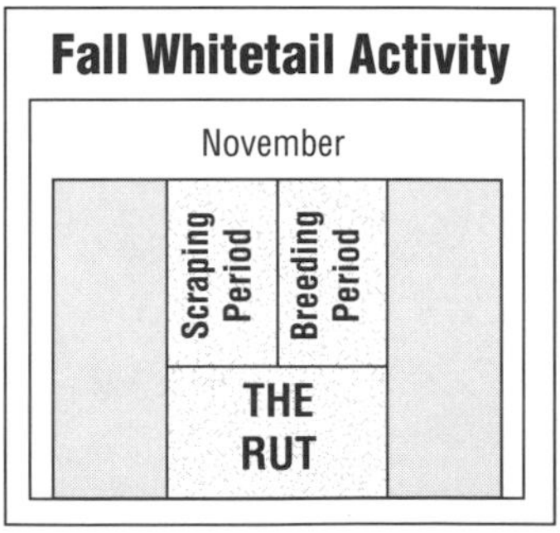

I COULDN'T IMAGINE a more unlikely or foolish situation for a grown whitetail buck to be in. And despite his current state of stupor, he knew it. There he lay, right smack dab in the middle of an endless snowfield somewhere in Alberta, his head stretched out as far as it would go and pressed hard against the snow. He was trying his best to become invisible, indeed burrow into the white stuff. His lady friend, who had gotten him into this mess, sat next to him with no apparent concern, looking alternately at her hapless suitor and then at me. Through my 10X binoculars, I watched in disbelief from a distance sufficient to cause a 130-grain .270 bullet to drop two feet, as I was about to find out.

The buck did an admirable job of hiding himself ... all but his

Fall Whitetail Activity

November

Scraping Period | Breeding Period

THE RUT

When the breeding period finally starts, anything can and does happen. Then, even the wisest trophy buck can make a foolish mistake — like following his girl friend into the open in the broad daylight. Photo by Mike Blair.

ample antlers. And, it was his antlers that interested me most. They were heavy and dark but not too wide. I couldn't tell how many points they sported. As I tried to figure that out, the frustrated and crestfallen buck lifted his head, knowing the jig was up. He turned and looked at the doe in utter disdain as if to say, "Look at the fine mess you got me into now, you hussy." With that, he lay his head back down, nothing else to do. Though entirely justifiable, that scolding of his running mate was a bad idea. It had revealed 10 good tines, enough to start me on the search for a rifle rest.

The buck was quartering toward me, but in his dug-in position, he didn't offer much of a target. Even in his stricken state, I didn't think he'd hold for me to get any closer. After all, I was as much out in the open as he was. My best bet was to put a little "Kentucky windage" on the shot and try him where he lay. As I leveled on the visible top half of his body, I must confess to feeling a little guilty about shooting a buck so handicapped. But, I shook it off as I remembered the countless times his kind hadn't given me much of a chance.

The crosshairs had a sliver of light between them and the buck's back when I fired. The distance allowed me to recover from the recoil in time to see the bullet strike ... a foot in front of the buck's nose! I don't know why he did it. Maybe the snow the bullet kicked in his face momentarily blinded him. Maybe the doe, who led the way, was tired of him and wanted him out of her life. I'll never know why, but the buck, following the does' every move, jumped up and ran ... straight toward me! The second 130-grain Nosler flew straight and true. He was a fine 10-pointer, and I still feel a tinge of guilt when I look at him. Such an incredible event could only happen during the rut, and more specifically, during the breeding period of the rut!

When the breeding period finally starts, all bets are off. Anything can and does happen. Mature bucks that have spent most of their waking hours trying to avoid danger now cast caution aside and frequently expose themselves to high-risk situations for the sake of love. The woods, and often the fields, are astir with chasing, trailing and other rites of the rut. Normal and predictable patterns are out the window, making it difficult for a hunter to hunt one particular buck. No matter. Random though it may be, there is no better time to bump into a trophy whitetail than during the breeding period of the rut! This is when trophy bucks are most vulnerable and when the bulk of them fall to the hunter's bullet.

SOME BASICS

Let's lay some groundwork for understanding the critical breeding period. As we've said, the first wave of does enters estrus rather suddenly and on approximately the same date each year. True, some does come in heat earlier and some trail the majority, but it's the first big wave we are most interested in. This major group of does, most of which are 2½ years old and older, spurs frenzied breeding activity and brings on what is generally called the "peak of rut." This peak period is of paramount importance to trophy hunters and when breeding activity is most visible. This is the time we define as the breeding period.

In healthy deer populations, 20 to 50 percent of the doe fawns like the one pictured above may come into estrus at six months of age. This can contribute to ongoing rutting activity well after the peak of breeding. Photo by Mike Biggs.

Breeding doesn't end after this first rush of hot does is over. About 26 to 28 days after the start of the peak period, a second group of does will enter estrus, signaling what is normally called the "secondary rut." This second batch of does is much smaller than the first and is made up mostly of 1½-year-old does, along with any older does that did not conceive during the peak period. The secondary rut, which occurs during the time we've designated as the post-rut period, is not nearly as important or as visible to hunters as the first breeding cycle.

This buck has gotten a nose full of hot scent and is doggedly trailing his would-be lover. Photo by Curt Helmick.

Following the second cycle, a third minor time of breeding, the "tertiary rut," often will occur when six-month-old fawns enter estrus for the first time. In healthy deer populations, 20 to 50 percent of the doe fawns may come in estrus at six months of age. Also, adult does that have not conceived at this point will get another chance. Does will cycle every 26 to 28 days up to three or four times until they conceive. For this reason, barren does are quite rare.

So, we see a relatively brief peak breeding time when most does are bred followed by minor secondary breeding periods spread over two to three months. The big peak breeding period is the way nature assures that most fawns are born during the ideal time for maximum survival. The secondary periods are nature's way of spreading a lesser fawn drop over two or three months to avoid putting all the "eggs in one basket." If something catastrophic were to happen during the prime window for fawning, enough fawns would be born outside this time to prevent a complete year-class loss.

The length of the ideal window for fawning differs from place to place based on environmental conditions. In areas with harsh conditions that limit fawn survival, such as extreme cold, drought, flooding, etc., the ideal fawning window is narrower. In areas without severe limiting factors, the window conducive for best fawn survival is wider. Where the window is narrow, nature compensates by having briefer peak breeding periods and/or a higher percentage of the does in estrus during the peak. In part, this explains why the rut tends to be more spreadout in much of the South (Texas being an exception because of drought limitations) but more defined and concentrated in the North. On the whole, however, the duration of the peak is fairly consistent throughout much of the country. Only a few unique locations significantly deviate from the norm.

Besides environmental conditions, factors within the deer herd itself also impact both the peak breeding period and the secondary cycles. Three of the most important are the number of 1½-year-old does in the deer herd, the health of the individual animals and the buck/doe ratio. Let's look at each of these factors.

First, the number of 1½-year-old does in the herd is important since most of them will not enter estrus until the second cycle, which affects both the peak and secondary breeding times. In high hunting pressure areas where a substantial percentage of the does are cropped each year, the percentage of the doe population made up of 1½'s can be high, like 25 to 40 percent. In such cases, the secondary rut may be fairly well defined and of some importance to hunters, while the peak period would be correspondingly weakened. Middle Georgia is an example of this. The secondary rut, which starts there at the end of November, is a pretty good time for a trophy.

Interestingly, bucks killed in Middle Georgia during the secondary rut tend to average larger, though fewer in number, than bucks taken during the peak period. Why? In the peak of rut, the relatively few mature bucks present can't get around to all the hot does; therefore, bucks of all ages and sizes get in on the action. Many area hunters are nonselective and will shoot the first buck that comes along behind a receptive doe. Since all sizes of bucks are involved during the peak breeding time, all sizes are shot. In the secondary rut, a higher percentage of the bucks trailing hot does are mature since they dominate the limited supply of receptive does. As a result, the average size of bucks shot in pursuit of does then is greater.

Second, the physical condition of the deer contributes to the timing and duration of the rut. If the does are in poor condition due to drought, undernourishment or the like, they are less likely to come into estrus on the first cycle. Even if they do, they may not be on time. This causes a "soft" or spreadout rut, which works against the hunter. I have seen this happen in overcrowded, mast-dependant deer populations when acorns fail. These deer need acorns to put on weight in the fall. Without them, they go into the breeding period in poor condition, and the rut seems to never really materialize. Drought and disease can also cause the same problem. Also, when the deer are undernourished, fewer six-month-old doe fawns will enter estrus their first fall, negatively impacting the secondary rut.

Third, a poor buck/doe ratio can spreadout the rut. This is largely a mechanical problem. There simply may not be enough bucks around to service all the does during the 24 hours each doe is in estrus. When this happens, the does cycle again about 26 days later, and they all try once more. Unfortunately, when the buck/doe ratio is this bad (which is seldom), the overall rut is adversely affected in other ways as well, such as poor daylight movement because of low rutting competition and a disrupted social structure leading to unpredictable behavior. You can start to see why so many heavily hunted populations simply do not show a distinct and predictable rut.

WHEN AND HOW LONG

Great differences exist across North America as to when the breeding period begins. The earliest breeding period I'm aware of starts in August in South Florida and the latest begins in late January in Alabama. Interestingly, both of these extremes very likely represent a different response to the same environmental limitation — flooding. Throughout most of the northern climes, peak breeding starts around the middle of November. Farmland Canada, for instance, sees the first wave of does come in estrus around November 12. Dick Idol figures November 18 is the kick off for the magic time in western Montana. Peak breeding in Wisconsin can be expected to

Once breeding is underway, predictable travel and movement patterns are pretty much a thing of the past. Bucks now blindly follow hot does wherever they lead them, shadowing their every move. Photo by Curt Helmick.

begin about November 14. November is, in fact, the dominant month for whitetail breeding across the continent.

Most notable exceptions to a November breeding period are in the South. For example, I plan my South Texas trips around a breeding startup date of December 14. Oddly, the Texas Hill Country just to the north usually heats up in late October. Coastal regions over much of the South have an October breeding period, while the inland areas may be as late as December or January. For instance, peak breeding starts in early October along the coast of Georgia, about November 3 in the central part of the state and around December 15 in the southwestern corner. It is possible that the introduction of deer from areas outside the South has contributed to such diversity, but I think it would exist whether or not foreign deer had ever been stocked there. Unlike much of the rest of the country, climate is not the shared controlling factor in the South; unique localized conditions like flooding are.

Because the timing of the breeding period does vary so, it becomes incumbent on each hunter to find out for himself when it starts where he hunts. Again, a call to your local game department will probably get the answer. If not, talk to experienced local trophy hunters. They'll know.

How long does the breeding period last? From the hunter's view-

Serious fights take place during the breeding period. Our party from North American Whitetail *came across this incredible sight on a hunt in South Texas. The buck on the ground was half eaten by coyotes. Photo by Chuck Larsen.*

point, I'm going to say two weeks. I know breeding can go on at some level almost nonstop for a month or longer after it starts. But under our definition of the breeding period, we're only concerned about the first peak cycle, which pretty much runs its course in two weeks. The truth is that the very best time is the first 7 to 10 days. The breeding period usually starts with a sudden, rather dramatic burst of does entering estrus during the first few days. Then, the number of receptive does gradually declines over the following days. Toward the end of the two-week period, action slows down significantly. I wouldn't be surprised if the buck's enthusiasm isn't beginning to wane a bit by that time from both fatigue and too much of a good thing.

THE PERIOD OVERVIEW

As the scraping period draws to an end, bucks are spending more and more time near their scrapes and the doe groups, often bedding nearby. They are ready to breed and have been for a long time. On and off throughout the day and night, bucks anxiously check their scrapes for the first hint of coming estrus. Any doe they encounter is hazed and harassed.

A day or two before a doe actually comes in estrus, she starts showing signs of its approach, urinating on her tarsal glands and emitting the telltale scent of coming heat. She may well begin to seek out a buck now by visiting and hanging around scrapes. One thing is certain, she won't have long to wait. As she nears estrus, her fragrance is evermore alluring. Whether in a scrape, on her trail or wafting along on a gentle forest breeze, her siren scent will reach the seeking nostrils of a lovesick buck in short order. However it happens, he will find her, and she will help him do so. Some experienced hunters even believe a hot doe actually selects a specific buck, particularly that the alpha doe chooses the most dominant buck promoting himself in her range. That's possible, but I can't say for sure it's so. But, I do know this — does entering estrus will make their presence and their readiness known, usually by visiting active scrapelines. And, area bucks will be drawn to the hot does like politicians to a baby kissin'.

When the first wave of does comes in, things get crazy in the white-tail woods. Dominant bucks get first choice. If the buck/doe ratio is low, there usually aren't enough does in heat at any one time to go around. This means young and subdominant bucks watch from the sidelines in utter frustration as the "big boys" get all the action. I've seen five or six desperate subdominant bucks look on longingly as the old man feverishly guards his lady and fends off advances from the lesser hopefuls. The younger bucks constantly test and probe, hoping to find an unguarded moment to get to the sweet-smelling doe. The doe sometimes seems to enjoy exasperating her suitor by trying to break free of his defenses. In such cases, it's common to see the buck working the doe back into position exactly like a quarter horse works a cow. To avoid such situations, bucks often take the doe off to isolated spots away from potential competition. This accounts for some of the ridiculous places you sometimes find bucks during the breeding period.

As the buck/doe ratio widens, the competition for does decreases. Still, it takes a very high buck/doe ratio not to have some competition. The reason is that all the bucks are ready to breed but only a certain percentage of the does are in heat at any given time even during the peak

These two bucks are displaying the classic threat posture — ears back, hair stand-ing on end, tail tightly tucked, stooped in the rear, head held low and moving in a stiff, sidling walk. Photo by Mike Biggs.

of breeding. For the purposes of illustration, let's assume that the breed-ing period lasts 14 days and that 70 percent of the does are bred during this time. That would mean an average of only five percent of the does, which are each in estrus for only 24 hours, would be receptive on any given day. In actuality, there is a peak time toward the beginning of our 14-day breeding period. So, some early days will see a higher percent-age of does in estrus, perhaps as high as 10 to 15 percent. The spreading out of does entering estrus even during the two-week peak breeding period is perhaps a built-in mechanism to give dominant bucks every chance to do most of the breeding. However, the buck/doe ratio and the buck age structure can get so badly out of whack that the available mature bucks simply can't get to all the does. When this happens, young or inferior bucks participate in breeding at an unnatural level.

Once breeding is underway, predictable travel and movement pat-terns are a thing of the past. Bucks now blindly follow hot does wherever they lead them, shadowing their every move. When a buck picks up a doe, he'll usually remain with that one doe as long as she's in estrus, unless he gets run off by another buck. After the doe

As though on a silent, invisible signal, the bucks lunge at each other and the fight commences. The smaller-racked eight-pointer won the combat and ran off the big non-typical. Dominance is not always based on antler size. Photo by Mike Biggs.

is out of cycle, the buck will head off in search of another receptive doe. (The pattern of a buck staying with a doe throughout her cycle tends to breakdown in high-density populations. There, a buck may breed a doe and leave her well before her cycle is over, perhaps lured away by another hot doe. In such cases, it is not unusual for several bucks to breed the same doe during her estrus period.)

Between flings, a buck usually starts checking the doe groups again and may even return to his scrapes if he doesn't first come across a beckoning doe. Which doe group he'll end up with and when is anybody's guess. Bucks without does, especially the young and subdominants, spend their time harassing unreceptive does, pestering bucks with willing girl friends and trailing promising scent trails. All in all, it's a chaotic time in the deer woods!

Any time you have a bunch of lovesick males and only a few accommodating females, you're sure to have fights, especially when the ladies are only open for business once a year. This is certainly true of whitetails during the breeding period. I believe the most serious fights of the year take place when two dominant bucks lay claim to the same hot doe.

When this happens, the two bucks, perhaps strangers to each other and both claiming dominance, can engage in mortal combat.

My partner in *North American Whitetail* magazine, Steve Vaughn, was a witness to just such an event during the breeding period a couple of years ago in South Texas. A big-bodied, 145-class 10-pointer chased a hot doe into a small clump of dense mesquite. Moments later, a heavy-antlered nine-pointer eagerly trailed them into the mesquite thicket. The sound of fighting and a bunch of general commotion ensued. Three or four other smaller bucks soon came over to watch the proceedings. After several minutes, all fell silent and the 10-pointer slipped out the back of the thicket with his lady friend. Not interested in shooting any of the bucks, Steve continued on his hunt. The next day, a gathering of coyotes around the clump of mesquites sparked an investigation. The heavy nine-pointer lay dead among the mesquites, nearly all eaten by the coyotes. He had undoubtedly been killed in the fight with the 10-pointer the day before even as Steve looked on!

On that same trip, we also came across one of the most incredible sights I've ever encountered in the wild. Chuck Larsen, another partner in *Whitetail*, found two 160-class bucks locked in deadly combat. When he came upon them, only one buck was alive, his antlers locked to those of a dead buck, which had his entire back half eaten away by coyotes! Imagine the horror of the surviving buck as he watched, exhausted and helpless, while those feared predators ripped and tore at his adversary's body! Chuck recruited help. After considerable effort, the live buck, now gaunt and spent from the ordeal, was freed from his grisly burden. There's no way to know how long the two had been locked, but from the condition of the surviving buck, it must have been days — days of terror for the "lucky" one. Though I can't say for sure, I'll bet a doe was the start of it all.

Not all fights over does end in death; indeed, that is the rare exception. Even the intense battles usually do little real damage to the combatants. The worst is normally a chipped or broken tine or two, although I've seen main beams snapped in two, and a few gouges in the face and neck. In Texas, where brow tines tend to be rather weak anyway, it is very common for bucks to loose one or both brow tines in battle. But, antlers are formidable weapons and injuries do happen. Dick Idol and I once rattled up a very respectable non-typical that had a six-inch

Another great fight sequence. These two bucks actually became locked temporarily. They were lucky to escape without injury. Photos by Mike Biggs.

section of another buck's tine protruding from his skull! Why he wasn't dead from this injury I don't know. Despite the wound, he obviously remained interested in either fighting or hijacking an onlooking doe!

Many encounters don't even get beyond the threats and posturing, which see the two bucks square off with their hair standing on end, ears laid back, eyes rolled, their bodies stiff and stooping and their heads cocked menacingly. Just the sight of a challenger so posed is sometimes enough to cause the faint-hearted to give way.

In all my days afield and despite the countless bucks I've seen with receptive does, I've only seen whitetails engage in the actual act of breeding a handful of times. The act itself takes place very quickly, but I don't think this explains why it's so seldom observed. Undoubtedly, much of the breeding takes place at night or in the seclusion of their lovers' hideaway.

Toward the end of the breeding period, the hectic pace begins to wane. The number of does in estrus declines, and the fervor of the bucks abates somewhat, their pent-up lust now partially satisfied. The amount of daylight movement lessens as the intensity wears down. Gradually, the initial big wave of does passes through the first cycle and the breeding period draws to an end.

Bucks and does alike welcome the calm that follows. The does use the time to catch up on feeding, mostly late and early in the day and at night. The bucks, weary and perhaps 20 to 30 percent lighter from their relentless pace, spend less and less time pursuing does and evermore time resting. Eventually, the bucks will return to their quiet, solitary lifestyle, first putting rest above food then slowly returning to a feeding routine. Only the scent of a doe coming into estrus late or during the secondary rut will call them "out of retirement" and rekindle their enthusiasm for love. While these secondary flings can be intense, they are isolated, sporadic and usually undependable from a hunter's viewpoint.

HUNTING STRATEGY

The most important strategy during the breeding period is to spend as much time as you can hunting. Exposure alone swings the odds your way. The bucks will do a lot of the work for you since they're active and careless now. Aside from this, there are some specific things you can do to tilt the scales your way.

The basic strategy during the breeding period is to hunt near doe concentrations. The bucks are sure to be nearby, or they soon will be. Even during the peak of the rut, a scene like this is too much to expect but it is possible. Photo by Mike Biggs.

To start with, my basic game plan is to hunt near doe concentrations. The bucks are sure to be nearby, or they soon will be. Major food sources again become important since doe groups are usually found in association with them. Look for places with good overall deer sign and preferably some promising buck sign. The presence of scrapes, even if they are not well maintained, tells you that bucks use the area to hook up with does. Chances are the bucks will return. They will continue to work scrapes sporadically throughout the breeding period, though scrapes are much less dependable now than before. Running tracks on woods roads, along field edges, etc., are evidence that bucks are chasing hot does in the area.

Snow, of course, makes the whole process of figuring out where the deer are and what they're doing a lot easier. At times, hot does can even be identified in the snow by their trails. During estrus, they sometimes drip a dull-reddish fluid that can be seen in association with their tracks. Occasionally, even excited bucks give themselves away in the snow by dribbling yellowish-brown droplets of urine over the tarsal glands on their hind legs.

When I find a place with good general deer activity and encouraging buck sign, I adopt the hunting technique best suited to the situation. A hunter now has a wide range of options. Still-hunting, stand-hunting and even rattling and deer drives can be successfully employed.

If conditions allow, my preferred hunting method during the breeding period is still-hunting, which is more accurately described as slipping and sitting. Bucks are on the move and distracted by the pressing urgency of the moment. This is an ideal time to ease silently through the woods and look over a lot of prime country. I try to hunt areas with good visibility because bucks are likely to expose themselves now in relatively open cover and because the chances of being picked off by deer are lower when you have some distance to work with.

Still-hunting during the breeding period is an aggressive form of hunting that gives the hunter a unique opportunity to react to a buck's moves and cause things to happen. For instance, breeding parties are sometimes moving pretty fast during the rut. A stand-hunter may have limited opportunity to judge and shoot fast-moving bucks from his stationary position. A still-hunter, however, can use his mobility to move on the preoccupied deer and very often can get a look and a shot at a buck he otherwise would have only glimpsed. Good visibility and favorable slipping conditions, such as damp, quiet woods or the presence of logging roads, streambeds, field edges or other aids to quiet, concealed movement, are needed for the best still-hunting results. I have killed more trophy bucks while slipping around during the breeding period than by any other method and at any other time. A memorable hunt in Mexico a few years back will show the advantages of flexibility while "slip-hunting" during the breeding period.

The large ranch I was hunting had a low deer population, and I soon realized my best hope was to look over a lot of country. On this particular day, I was easing along a ridge back in the boonies when I saw a good buck top a distant hill and disappear over the horizon. One buck, way off … I didn't think much of it and kept moving. A few minutes later, I saw another buck top the same hill going in the same direction. I decided to investigate. As I crawled through the low brush on the hilltop, I heard repeated snorting from below, something often heard from breeding parties. When I finally peered into the narrow and rela-

Giant bucks like this one killed by Barry Lundy of Calgary, Alberta, are most likely to slip-up during the breeding period. Only his drop tine kept this 26-inch-wide whitetail from making the record book. Photo by Dick Idol.

tively open canyon beyond the hill, I was shocked to see the valley floor alive with bucks — nine of them! Eight bucks milled around excitedly as the best one, a good 10 pointer, stood imposingly between them and a very harrowed doe, undoubtedly in heat. From the pestering the 10-pointer was receiving from the other bucks, I almost considered it a mercy killing when I shot him. Had I been stand-hunting, I never would have found this gathering.

If thick cover or noisy conditions prevent still-hunting, my second choice is stand-hunting. I try to set up in places where I can look over as much good deer country as possible because of the high level of movement, the speed in which a breeding party may be traveling and because bucks aren't as hesitant now to leave the security of thick cover. Power-line right-of-ways and other cutlines are excellent. Relatively open hardwood bottoms, clearcuts, especially those with some cover, isolated openings and fallow fields are all possible ambush points. The stand site

This 160-class 11-pointer practically committed suicide. I stumbled upon him and a hot doe late one morning. They ran before I could get a shot, but the doe stopped about 150 yards away. The buck followed her every move. When he stopped, I fired. Photo by David Goodchild.

should, of course, be located in high-activity areas with buck sign or on major travel lanes between doe groups. If possible, I also like to locate in bottlenecks that physically funnel activity.

Deer drives work very well during the breeding period. When deer are on their feet and moving, they are far easier to drive than bedded deer. Plus, mature bucks, which normally don't drive very well, preferring instead to sneak and circle or to hold tight in cover, now follow the does into more vulnerable situations than they would choose of their own accord. Drives are particularly effective in the snow because of the great advantage snow affords in reading sign and tracking. In areas with limited or broken cover, such as the Midwest, Central Canada and the Plains and Prairies Region, a handful of experienced hunters aided by fresh snow can drive deer with deadly effectiveness. Many farm-country trophies in both the United States and Canada fall to this technique.

Rattling works during the breeding period, though results can be unpredictable. Some hunters believe that the most likely respondents will be young or subdominant bucks. The logic is that the more dominant bucks will be with does and that they are seldom willing to abandon a hot doe to traipse off to a fight. I agree with this only in part. The reality is that trophy bucks sometimes can be rattled in during the breeding period. There are some simple reasons for this. First, there's always the chance of catching a trophy buck between does that might want to look in on a fight. Second, dominance is not always based on antler size, and it is very possible that a subdominant buck will qualify as a trophy. Several times I've watched fights where the better buck (based on rack size) was defeated by a bigger-bodied but smaller-racked buck. Finally, anything can happen during the breeding period!

Chapter 13

The Post-Rut Period
A Mixed Bag

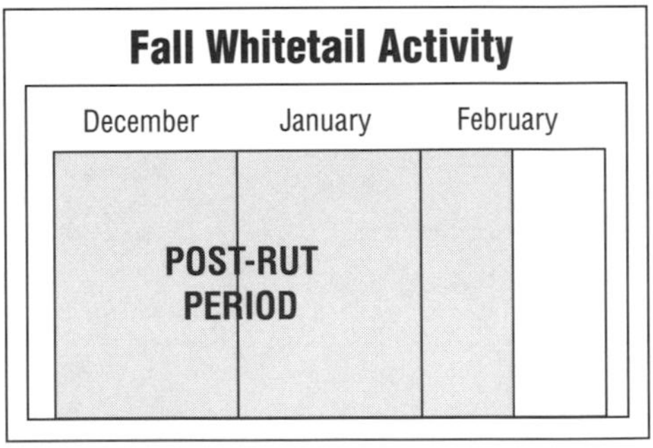

I've got to come clean with you. The post-rut period is not an easy time to hunt trophy whitetails, especially if they're subjected to much hunting pressure. They are now perfectly content to limit their movement to night-time hours if bothered by man.

Fall Whitetail Activity

December	January	February

POST-RUT PERIOD

In fact, even if not disturbed, daytime movement of older bucks during this time can be pretty scanty.

The post-rut can be divided into three different behavioral patterns or stages. The first is what I call the "waning rut." This stage includes both the tail-off breeding activity immediately following the peak breeding period and the relatively minor secondary rut. The greatest impact of the waning rut generally occurs during the first three to four weeks of the post-rut period. These last flurries of

The post-rut period comes to an end when the bucks drop their antlers. Depending on the part of the country, this can occur from early January to late April but February is the most common time. Photo by Mike Biggs.

breeding activity probably represent the best chance a hunter has for a trophy during the post-rut period.

The second stage can be accurately termed the "lull stage." During this time, bucks lay low in thick cover and recuperate from the rigors of the rut. Good luck trying to kill a buck at this time.

The third and last stage occurs when the bucks return to a feeding pattern. Depending on hunting pressure, the availability of prime food sources, herd density and the severity of the winter, the prospects for success brighten once bucks settle into a feeding routine again. Before looking at these three stages, let's explore the timing and length of the post-rut period.

THE START AND THE FINISH

Under our definition, the post-rut period starts when the two-week breeding period ends, making the timing of the post-rut totally dependent on when breeding first starts in earnest. This obviously means that the timing of the post-rut period differs from place to place by weeks or even months. Just as the start of the scraping period could be determined by backing off two weeks from the start of the breeding period, the post-rut period can be timed by adding two weeks to the starting date of the breeding period. Once again, we see that the breeding date is the key to timing all four periods of fall deer activity. The beginning of the post-rut period is marked by a dramatic decline in breeding activity, though remnant breeding does continue for a while as we've discussed.

The post-rut is brought to a close by a specific event — antler shedding. When do bucks drop their antlers? This, too, varies greatly. Bucks in the northern latitudes usually shed their antlers in January or early February. Montana whitetails, for instance, have pretty much lost their antlers by mid January. Southern deer tend to drop later. One of the latest antler-shedding times I'm familiar with occurs in South Texas, where bucks drop their antlers in March and even as late as early April. Oddly, bucks in Middle Georgia drop their antlers early, usually by late January. This could reflect their northern bloodline from early stockings of deer from Wisconsin. Bucks in neighboring Alabama don't normally lose their antlers until March. Frankly, when the post-rut period ends and exactly how long it lasts are of little concern to hunters since few places have hunting seasons extending to the end of the period.

THE WANING RUT

Once the frantic breeding period has passed, breeding and its related activities begin to wind down. With fewer does in heat, the general chaos eases, though competition for the few remaining receptive does stays high. The diminished supply of willing does means that the spoils go to the more dominant bucks. At this late stage of the game, a hot doe often will be pursued by several lustful suitors, the dominant buck having to fend for his rights. Serious fights occasionally break out now between bucks of equal status.

During the first 14 days or so of the post-rut period, breeding activity is dependent upon the straggly does that enter estrus after the

After the peak breeding time is over, limited rutting activity continues for a while. Often, this "waning rut" is perpetuated by young does, both 1½-year-olds and six-month-old fawns, coming into estrus a month or two after the older does. This long-tined eight-pointer has picked up a receptive young doe well into the post-rut period. Photo by Mike Biggs.

peak breeding period is over. The number of these latecomers diminishes steadily as time passes. Still, the bucks are hopeful and remain focused primarily on breeding. When the bucks start having trouble picking up hot does, they range far and wide looking for receptive does, anxiously checking the doe groups. Their travel pattern is somewhat like that of the scraping period, only less predictable. They pass through the social hubs of doe groups quickly and spend little or no time making or checking scrapes. They are now looking directly for a willing doe and depend on their noses to reveal her presence.

About two weeks into the post-rut period, the dwindling breeding activity can get a shot in the arm by the arrival of the secondary rut. If this second cycle, made up mostly of 1½-year-old does, is significant, the breeding ritual is again played out on a mini-scale of the peak rut. But, overall activity is far less widespread. Much of the limited breeding activity probably will take place at night, the cumulative results of growing weariness and ongoing hunting pressure. From the hunter's perspective, visible rutting activity will be isolated and sporadic and fresh buck sign will be sparse.

For all practical purposes, the waning rut is pretty much over about a month into the post-rut period. From this point on, fewer and fewer does enter estrus. With each passing day that a buck doesn't score, his enthusiasm wanes. Gradually, the time devoted to rutting activity gives way to resting or brief periods of feeding. His travels become less extensive. Doe groups drop off his route. The buck soon drifts back to his core area and starts passing the daylight hours bedded in his familiar territory. Slowly, the urge to breed looses its grip on him and the need to rest and recover from the rigors of the rut takes priority. Only the alluring scent of a hot doe can rekindle the fire in a rut-weary buck. Maybe it's an isolated late doe that comes into estrus and rearranges his schedule. Or, perhaps it's the minor third cycle, which usually hits about six weeks into the post-rut period and consists mostly of six-month-old doe fawns, that brings that familiar, all-powerful scent back to the deer woods. Even then, the effects are limited and short-lived.

THE LULL

As the power of the rut relaxes its hold, the post-rut lull sets in. Deer begin the shift to a quieter, more settled lifestyle. By now, the cold, rain and/or snow have reduced the amount of secure cover available to deer. The leaves have fallen off the trees. The underbrush has been denuded and the tall grass laid low. Also, the food supply, once fairly well distributed over much of the deer's range, is now much more limited both in quantity and distribution.

The deer, haggard and skittish, have regained their wits and have begun to feel the stress and fatigue brought on by the frantic pace of the previous weeks. Their priority now becomes rest and food. They seek refuge in the remaining pockets of thick, secure cover and devote ever-more time and attention to nourishing their neglected bodies.

Does, fawns and young bucks come through the rut in fairly good shape physically. Because they don't need as much time to recuperate, does, fawns and young bucks quickly return to a more or less regular feeding pattern. Their routine might call for bedding in the thick pockets of cover in their home range during the day and feeding at first and last

During the "lull stage" of the post-rut, exhausted bucks seek out thick, secure bedding areas to recover from the rigors of the rut. Photo by Mike Blair.

light and at night. Since their bedding area is probably near some type of food source, some daylight feeding is likely because of the short travel time between bedding and feeding areas. Hunting pressure will determine the level of daytime activity.

Mature bucks adopt a different pattern immediately following the last of any significant breeding. Having neglected both food and rest, they find themselves exhausted once the rutting urge has left them. For a period of time, their drive to feed is secondary to their desire for rest and solitude. The older bucks, already back in their core area, seek out the thickest or most secure areas to bed. Their privacy and rest assured, they will feed some during the lull time but mostly at night and near their beds. During the lull, it can appear as though the mature bucks have completely disappeared, especially in areas with substantial hunting pressure.

It's hard to say how long this lull period lasts. The impact of remnant breeding activity tends to override and confuse the pattern, as does hunting pressure. It's often difficult to figure out what deer are doing because both movement and sign are so limited. The severity of the

Once the bucks have regained their strength following the rut, their routine slowly shifts to a feeding pattern. Photo by Mike Blair.

climate (the cold), the physical condition of the deer and, of course, hunting pressure are all factors in how long it takes adult bucks to return to a consistent feeding pattern. My guess is that this recuperation time usually lasts from one to two weeks before giving way to a consistent feeding pattern.

RETURN TO FEEDING

Slowly, rut-weary bucks regain their strength by resting long hours and feeding on food sources convenient to their bedding areas. Winter is coming on, and the bucks feel the need to nourish themselves in preparation for the hard times ahead. Gradually, their daily routine shifts. They venture out farther and farther from their core areas in search of quality food. If preferred agricultural crops are in the area, you can be sure that most bucks eventually will end up feeding there. Clearcuts and other concentrated food sources will also draw attention. In the absence of concentrated feed, the deer scatter over the entire range and forage as best they can. The feeding pattern now is much like that of the pre-rut period except that the bucks are more nocturnal, food sources are fewer and more localized and the deer may have to travel even farther to

This high-scoring 10-pointer fell to a bullet from my 7mm Rem. Mag. during the peak of the South Texas rut. His gross typical score is 179, and his net is 169⅛.

While their antlers are in velvet during the summer, bucks get along with each other pretty well. But in the fall after the hormones kick in and their antlers harden, the bachelor groups break up. Photo by Mike Biggs.

Bucks usually shed the velvet in early September by rubbing their antlers on trees and saplings. This is a very good buck. Note the blood stains still on his antlers. Photo by Bill Kinney.

This heavy-racked buck is making a scrape and leaving his scent on the overhanging limb When the scraping period begins in earnest, bucks are fairly predictable in their travel patterns. Photo by Curt Helmick.

A big buck in the wide open during broad daylight ... only during the rut are you likely to see such a thing. Even then, it takes a hot doe to lure him out. Photo by Mike Blair.

The male hormone testosterone coursing their veins, bucks build massive neck and shoulder muscles from rubbing and mock-fighting bushes and trees in the fall. The high levels of testosterone have much the same effect on bucks that steroids have on an athlete. Photo by Bill Kinney.

With a live weight of 300 pounds, this Canadian farm-land buck is the heaviest white-tail I have ever shot. He's a 10-pointer scoring in the low 150's.

Chuck Larsen of North American Whitetail *magazine photographed this incredible scene during a hunt in South Texas. Coyotes had eaten half of the dead buck while the survivor undoubtedly watched in terror. The live buck was freed of his grisly burden by our hunting party. Both bucks scored about 160.*

This mid-160's 12-pointer is performing a lip curl, or flehmening. This is done to concentrate the scent of a prospective doe at the entrance to the buck's nostrils. Photo by Mike Biggs.

Above: The first time I rattled this buck in, I passed him up. About an hour later, he came in a second time. The temptation was too great for me to let him go again. He grosses a shade over 160 and nets 158 ⅞. Photo by Jim Goodchild.

Left: The West is gaining a reputation for big whitetails. This 150-class, 10-point whitetail is perfectly at home with elk, mule deer, antelope and buffalo as his neighbors. Photo by Denver Bryan.

Which one of these two bucks would you shoot? While they are both very good, the one on the left is better. He's a 160-class 11-pointer. The buck on the right is a 150-class nine-pointer. Photo by Mike Biggs.

While a potential girl friend looks on, a trophy 10-pointer leaves his scent on an overhanging limb and makes a scrape. As wise trophy hunters know, scrapes play an important role in the whitetail's rutting ritual. Photo by Mike Blair.

You've got to like this buck. He's wide, heavy and long-tined. Add in a sticker, a fork and a couple of lengthy drop tines, and the result is a 180-point non-typical. Photo by Mike Biggs.

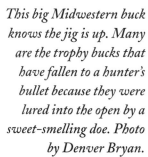

This big Midwestern buck knows the jig is up. Many are the trophy bucks that have fallen to a hunter's bullet because they were lured into the open by a sweet-smelling doe. Photo by Denver Bryan.

You're looking at a very happy hunter. Although this is not my highest scoring buck, I consider him to be the best whitetail I've ever taken. I hunted the buck for four years before finally catching up with him when he was 8½ years old. The 10-pointer's outside spread is 28½ inches. His typical score is 168 4/8 net and 174 gross.

Many people consider this to be the most impressive whitetail in the world. He is the famous "Hole-In-The-Horn" buck from Ohio. The 45-pointer is the No.2 all-time non-typical and scores 328 2/8. The buck was found dead along a railroad track in 1940. Photo courtesy of North American Whitetail.

prime feed. The hunting prospects during this time depend largely on the presence of major food sources that concentrate deer and on hunting pressure.

In the cold northern latitudes and in overcrowded populations anywhere, the emphasis on food and the potential to concentrate deer during the post-rut are great. I've seen situations where I'm certain deer from miles around have converged on a major food supply. Their quest for food may even cause them to abandon their core areas for a time and relocate miles away near prime food sources. An extreme example of this is the actual whitetail migrations that takes place in the mountainous regions of the West.

Photographer Mike Blair found this large shed antler stuck in the bale of hay. The buck was obviously feeding on the hay when he lost his antler. Bucks will sometimes travel long distances to preferred agricultural crops during the post-rut.

A friend of mine in a farming community in Wisconsin tells me that bucks nobody in those parts has ever seen before show up there to feed on the agricultural crops after the cold and snow arrive in late fall. He's certain these bucks travel down from heavily wooded areas many miles to the north. A farmer I know in South Dakota, who has a largely coverless farm a couple of miles from a forested state park, says that deer pour out of the park around Christmas to feed on his hay bales and alfalfa fields. Upwards of 100 deer can sometimes be seen in one field! In overcrowded populations throughout the South, remarkable concentrations of deer appear on prime food sources during the late fall and winter. I once counted (or tried to) over 200 deer on a 30-acre oat field in Mississippi late one January afternoon. Most of these exceptional gatherings take place — at least during the daylight — after season is over and hunting pressure ceases.

Severe winter weather and deep snows also can cause deer in harsh northern climates to concentrate in the limited protective cover. This phenomenon is called "yarding." We won't focus on yarding per se since deer are seldom if ever hunted at such times. I mention it because this extreme behavior is somewhat indicative of what deer across the country do in the late post-rut period. They will bunch up in the best available cover, although to a far less exaggerated degree than in classic yarding. In Middle Georgia, for instance, deer "herd up" in pockets of thick ever-greens in impressive numbers after winter has "burned" the cover back. They spend most of their time in these protective pockets of cover, ven-turing out only to feed. I've seen this same situation everywhere I've hunted, except in places such as South Texas, Florida and the coastal "jungles" of the South where widespread cover is maintained even during the winter. This tendency toward yarding during the post-rut period creates an ideal situation for driving deer. The only problem is that trophy bucks aren't always bedded with the large concentrations of deer found in the obvious pockets of cover.

HUNTING STRATEGY

Let's start this discussion by stating that hunting pressure affects the odds of shooting a trophy buck more during the post-rut period than during any other time. If pressure has been high previous to the pre-rut, the deer probably have been shot at, run off their feeding grounds, kept awake during their daily nap times and even disturbed on "hot dates." Under such conditions, even does, fawns and young bucks will resort almost totally to nocturnal sorties. In the face of heavy pres-sure, you will find little evidence that mature bucks still exist. You certainly won't see them up and about of their own accord in the daylight. The more pressure there is, the more the deer — especially trophy bucks — become reclusive and nocturnal and the longer it takes them to return to normal daytime activity.

During the first three to four weeks of the post-rut period, the best game in town is the low-level rutting activity brought on by latecomers from the first breeding cycle and by the secondary rut. The strategy is about the same as for the breeding period: Hunt the social hubs of doe groups, hopefully those offering some evidence that bucks are around. Unfortunately, bucks don't leave much sign during the post-rut. The best evidence of rutting activity is to actually see a buck trailing or chasing. If you see this, hunt the area hard. There could be several bucks, includ-

This fine 11-pointer was shot while in pursuit of a yearling doe on the last day of the Georgia season, which was a month after the peak of breeding. The last flurries of breeding activity probably offer the hunter his best chance for a post-rut trophy.

ing the local "big cheese," working the vicinity in hopes of connecting with one of the relatively few does now in heat.

If I believe a hot doe is in the area, I prefer to slip quietly through the woods in search of the breeding party. Stand-hunting is better if no rutting activity is evident since deer are very skittish now. Rattling can work during the waning rut, but results will be spotty. My Texas hunting buddy, Amos Dewitt, and I once rattled up 11 bucks in one session during the secondary rut on the King Ranch. We had seen a couple of bucks in hot pursuit of a small doe. Unfortunately, none of them were good enough to shoot. If a really big buck was after the young doe, he preferred her to the sound of two brawling bucks.

If forced movement is ever the best way to hunt trophy whitetails, it is during the post-rut lull. I employ two different hunting tactics to

The peak of rut was over when I shot this record-class buck on a typical post-rut feeding pattern. He was feeding in a small clearing back in a thick, roadless section of the ranch I was hunting. Photo by Amos Dewitt.

force movement during this time. One, I slip ever so slowly through thickets that are likely big buck bedding areas. Three good things can come from this. I may jump a buck and get a quick shot. A buck may stand up and hold momentarily for a shot upon hearing a slight noise or seeing an unidentifiable movement. Or, I may catch an unsuspecting buck loitering around in his bedding area. Of course, a number of bad things can happen, and they considerably outweigh the good. That aside, I have killed a couple of trophy bucks using this rather desperate tactic. However, I confess my return on investment is not so great when invading a buck's bedding area.

The other tactic to force movement is deer drives. There is no other time of year when deer drives are as justified. There are times and situations during the post-rut period when deer simply won't move unless you move them. The success of deer drives now depends on knowing where big bucks might be bedded.

Aside from forced movement, the best strategy for trophy bucks during the post-rut lull is to hunt them right in the thick cover. If the bucks move at all during legal hours, they'll move in the security of thick cover. Hunting in close quarters leaves no room for mistakes. A favorable wind and total quiet are essential. I'll often just take a seat next to a sizable tree rather than risk making noise while hanging a stand. Hunting like this is a slow and tedious way to go. But if you want to shoot a big buck now, hunting them where they are — in the thickets — is not a bad idea. As always, don't pick a stand site randomly. Find some sort of sign that says a good buck is frequenting the area.

I know a couple of patient souls who specialize in thick-cover hunting during the post-rut. They spend many a boring day in cover with the visibility of my grandmother's black bean soup. Their record over the years proves their patience has paid off handsomely. While I'll do it if I have to, I freely admit that sitting for hours in thick cover is too nerve-racking for me. Besides, I've got claustrophobia!

When mature bucks settle into a feeding pattern during the post-rut period, a hunter's options increase, assuming season is still open. The hunting strategy called for is essentially the same employed during the pre-rut period. In pressured areas, emphasis should be placed on hunting the staging grounds near major food sources or trails leading to and from bedding/feeding areas. As a general rule, the higher the pressure, the closer to the bedding area and the denser the cover you'll need to hunt. Conversely, the lower the pressure, the closer to the food source you should hunt. In very low pressure situations, even hunting open food sources may be productive.

Considerable scouting is needed during the post-rut period to determine the best place to wait out a buck headed to food. Stand-hunting is the most reliable way to hunt bucks on a feeding pattern. Still-hunting can be effective also if conditions are right, but deer are spooky now and difficult to sneak up on. Hunt to the last legal minute of the day and be in position in the morning before first light. Try to find bottlenecks or some physical feature to help funnel a buck your way. Things are going to be tough in the post-rut period so use every advantage you can!

Section V

The "How"
Of Hunting Trophy
Whitetails

Chapter 14

Arming Yourself With

The Trophy Hunter's Edge

L IKE THE ANIMALS THEY SEEK, trophy hunters are a different breed. They have a unique perspective that drives them in their pursuit of trophy whitetails. All successful trophy hunters — men like Dick Idol, John Wootters, Gene Wensel, James Kroll, Greg Miller, Randy Bean, Bob Zaiglin, Steve Vaughn, Larry Weishuhn, Noel Feather and Stan Christiansen, to name a few — have certain things in common that contribute to their success. Certainly, one of the foremost factors is that successful trophy hunters all hunt where trophy bucks exist in significant numbers. It could be no other way since by definition "successful" trophy hunters must shoot trophy bucks. This requires that they hunt where trophies live. Otherwise, a person may be a great hunter, but he will have "little" to show for it. Yet, it does take more to be a successful trophy hunter than just hunting places with trophy bucks. Let's examine some of the things that account for the trophy hunter's edge.

First, true trophy hunters have a deep respect and admiration for the whitetail, as represented by the most worthy symbol of the species — the trophy buck. Contrary to what today's pseudo animal-righters

Dick Idol shot this 175 class non typical in Oklahoma in 1991. Like all successful trophy hunters, Dick has a deep respect and admiration for the whitetail.

would have you believe, trophy hunters do not hunt for the enjoyment of killing. If they did, they would be very foolish to go after trophy bucks, the hardest of the clan to find and to shoot. Why would someone interested in just killing let lesser legal bucks walk by unscathed, not knowing whether a trophy will show up at all that season or even the next? He wouldn't! He would shoot the first legal deer he could. And, the odds would be long indeed that it would be a trophy buck!

Based on a foundation of respect, fascination, admiration, call it what you will, perhaps even love of the whitetail, successful trophy hunters have made a conscious commitment to hunt only the best bucks a place has to offer. Without such a commitment (and a tangible trophy goal to go with it), a hunter will find it very difficult to resist the temptation of the moment when a so-so buck walks by. Or, he might never be motivated to seek out better trophy hunting grounds than he is presently hunting, where every antlered buck may be shot on sight. A commitment means that the trophy hunter plans for success. He will eliminate deer hunting options that don't bring him closer to achieving his trophy goals. A commitment leads to a mind-set ... an attitude. He begins thinking like a trophy hunter. When a person reaches this point, he has taken a major step toward becoming a successful trophy hunter.

Frankly, trophy hunting is not for everybody. And, there's nothing wrong with enjoying the sport of deer hunting at any level. But if you want to be a successful trophy hunter, you must be prepared to pay the price. You must be willing to work harder, hunt longer and, perhaps most difficult of all, pass up lesser bucks, even at the risk of ending the season empty-handed. No, trophy hunting is not for everybody. But for some, nothing else will do!

The logical byproduct of commitment is determination. Determination then leads to hard work, which is a function of both time and intensity. In other words, successful trophy hunters put in long hours and are "focused" on what they're doing. Within the limits of the law and good sportsmanship, they are prepared to do whatever it takes to get the job done. Sure, some luck is needed. But, determined trophy hunters make most of their "luck" by hunting harder and longer, sticking with it in all kinds of weather and concentrating intently on the task at hand, even when things look bleak. As much as anything, dogged determination and old-fashioned hard work are required to turn your trophy hunting goals into reality.

Many people think there is some kind of magic formula or a secret tactic that brings success. It is their belief that if only they could find the right secret they, too, could shoot trophy bucks like the experts. This belief is reflected in the ongoing quest for a better buck lure, a super-duper deer call, a totally invisible camo pattern, a mineral block that grows instant trophies, etc. At best, these things are only tools, helpful aids. Gimmicks and gadgets won't bring down trophy whitetails; lots of hard work will!

A trophy hunter must be keenly observant. To a large degree, the

Nothing replaces dogged determination and old-fashioned hard work when trophy hunting. Steve Vaughn hunted hard for six days before finally shooting this 160-class 10-pointer on a 1991 hunt in the Texas Brush Country.

power of observation is related to the level of interest one has in what he's doing and to his ability to concentrate. Both of these things go back to commitment. Successful trophy hunters intently study what's going on around them. They pick up on the subtleties, like a barking squirrel, a screaming jay, the faint snap of a limb, the direction of tracks, the backward glance of a doe, etc. They have an awareness of the big picture and how everything they see and do fits into that big picture. Their senses are fully attuned to the hunt. Through their observations, they are constantly gathering new information to help them in their pursuit.

Anyone who consistently takes trophy bucks must possess knowledge and skill. These two things are related but different. Up to a point, knowledge can be gained secondhand from books, magazines, videos, seminars and by talking to other people. Extensive experience is not required. Skill, on the other hand, depends on knowledge but can only be fully developed through experience. As for knowledge, I don't know of a single trophy hunter of any repute who isn't a student of the white-tail, and not just during the season but year-round. And, his knowledge is not limited only to secondhand sources. It is tested, expanded and put into context by field experience. This time in the field studying and hunting whitetails hones his skills to a fine edge. Even then, the trophy whitetail is still more than a match for the most skilled trophy hunter.

What I lack in skill and knowledge, I try to make up in determination and hard work. These two things can cover a multitude of weaknesses. Most of my own trophy bucks have fallen as a result of stubborn persistence and long hours, not fine-honed skills or super-duper tactics. No buck better represents that fact than one that led me on a merry chase starting in one Canadian province and ending in another.

A few years ago, Dick Idol called and said he had found an area in western Manitoba that was home to some big bucks. I was on the next plane headed that way. Since we were to hunt along the border with Saskatchewan, I bought licenses for both Manitoba and Saskatchewan. About three days into the hunt, a snow storm dumped several inches of fresh powder on the foot of snow already covering the ground. The storm showed little sign of letting up when my guide and I pulled into a farmer's yard to ask permission to hunt a quarter-mile-square woodlot on his property. The farmer okayed our request and said he had seen a good "jumper" (as whitetails are called in those parts) enter the timber the afternoon before. He suggested that my guide "push the bush" and that I take a stand at the far corner of the block of timber.

"The jumpers always head to the big bush over there in Saskatchewan," the farmer offered, pointing to the woodline some 300 yards away. "If you jump him, he'll probably come out near that corner and go straight over there, eh."

After a few more minutes of conversation, I took up my position. My guide hiked to the far end of the woodlot to start the drive. For 30 minutes, all was quiet. The snow continued to fall and limited visibility to about 200 yards. A shout from my guide was the first hint I had that something was on the move. Minutes later, a doe broke cover about 150 yards to my left, almost at the limit of my vision. She was half way to Saskatchewan when a buck exploded into the open on her trail. Through my snow-smeared scope, I could see he was good. In the deep snow, the buck ran in lunging leaps. I fired just as he made one of those leaps. From the sight picture, I feared a low hit ... if I hit him at all. My second shot held little more promise.

Almost immediately, my guide emerged from the woods on the tracks of the buck. He quickly reached the spot where the first shot had intercepted the fleeing buck. As I approached, his shout relayed some not-so-good news. "I see a lot of hair and a few drops of blood. Looks like you just grazed him."

I stumbled around the scene a few minutes and had to agree with my guide's conclusion. Maybe the second shot had better results. We hurried along the bounding buck's tracks another 50 yards. There, we found the identical thing — lots of hair and a little blood. The sign was not very promising, but the buck was definitely hit. Despite the continuing snowfall, the buck had left a trail in the deep snow that my grandmother could follow. As the farmer had predicted, the trail lead straight to Saskatchewan. There was only one thing to do ... track him down. It was only 9 a.m. I had all day. Sooner or later, I would catch up with the buck.

"I'm going after him," I told my guide. "No telling how far he might go. You'd better let the others know what has happened. They'll be concerned if we aren't at the store at noon. I've got my compass and a sandwich. I'll be back as soon as I can."

With that, I struck out. As I neared the timber, the amount of blood increased on the buck's trail. My hopes rose. Perhaps I'd hit him better than I had first thought. The trail was easy to follow. The deep, soft snow made for silent but difficult travel. Under normal circumstances, I might have given the buck time to lay up for awhile before following him. But, I was pretty well convinced the buck was not severely wounded. Besides, I was concerned that the falling snow might obscure the trail if I waited too long. The woods were fairly open. I felt my best bet was to stay hot on the buck's trail. With any luck, I figured to catch him in the open and get a shot.

About a half-mile into the chase, I caught a glimpse of a deer slipping away from a small stand of spruce trees. The sign told the story. It was my buck. He had stood among the spruces and watched his back-trail, as evidenced by his tracks and two small pools of blood. I pushed on even faster. After about 200 yards, the buck's tracks told me that he had stopped running and was again walking. It was interesting to see that he frequently stopped and turned around, apparently watching for me. I felt sure I was staying very close to him. The right terrain — an opening or a stretch of open timber — was all I needed for a shot.

An hour passed before I encountered him again. The buck was standing about 125 yards away, but I didn't see him until he ran. I could have kicked myself for not watching ahead any better. That was my chance for a relatively easy shot ... if I had only seen the buck before he ran. His running tracks slowed to a walk after only a 100 yards this time. That was encouraging. Maybe he was beginning to feel the effects of his wounds. I pressed on, although the deep snow was also beginning to take its toll on me.

The snowfall began to let up about 11 a.m. The buck had begun to turn from his westward heading and drift to the south. His trail revealed that I was right behind him. Every 200 to 300 yards, he would pull up and turn to face his backtrail. He would then bound away for 30 to 40 yards before resuming a walking pace. I took this to mean that the buck was seeing me and then running a short distance. If that was so, all I needed was the right set-up to see him before he ran. I knew that time would come.

About noon, the buck's trail led me to a high bluff. Beyond the bluff was a 200-yard-wide strip of timber and then a huge frozen-over lake. Through my binoculars, I could follow the buck's tracks to the edge of the lake. I scanned the lake. I was shocked to see the buck plodding along like a work-weary mule in the middle of that half-mile-wide sheet of ice. I bailed off the bluff and ran to the lake. When I got there, puffing like a over-revved locomotive, the buck was about three-quarters of the way across the lake. I figured I had nothing to lose by attempting a shot, even though I had no idea how far away he was. Trying hard to control my gasping breaths and overcome my pounding heart, I rested the .270 against a poplar tree, held the crosshairs even with the top of the buck's back and let fly. I saw snow explode short of the buck. He ran about 50 yards, stopped and looked back. I held two feet over his back this time and tried another shot. Again, snow erupted under the buck's belly. He

Bob Zaiglin proudly displays an outstanding South Texas buck he took in late December 1990. As one of the top biologists and game managers in Texas, Bob, like so many other serious trophy hunters, is a year-round student of the whitetail. Photo courtesy of Bob Zaiglin.

galloped the remaining distance to the woodline and disappeared.

Although I was disappointed I had not gotten the buck, I knew from his reaction that he was wearing down. There was no doubt in my mind ... I would get that buck. I started across the lake on his trail. A few yards out, the ice began creaking. I looked down to see about an inch of water on top of the ice. Georgia boys don't know a whole lot about frozen lakes and the do's and don'ts associated with them. But, the thought of falling through the ice on the backside of nowhere was enough to cause me to look for an alternate route around the lake. The west end of the lake was two miles away; the east end a half-mile off. I struck out for the eastern end.

An hour later, I was back on the buck's trail. He had stopped running as soon as he reached the timber … a good sign. After a mile or so, I stopped to take a compass reading. I was surprised to find that the buck was heading to the northeast. We were going in a big circle. The buck was undoubtedly headed back to familiar territory.

On two or three occasions, the buck had milled around in stands of evergreens. I was sure he was looking for a place to bed. After all, the buck was wounded to some degree and had been pushed hard for several hours. He had stopped checking his backtrail as he had done earlier. He may have felt he had lost me at the lake. The delay caused by going around the lake seemed to be working to my advantage.

At 3 p.m., I came to an open slough. Across the slough was a steep hillside. At the base on the hillside was as thick stand of spruce trees into which the buck's tracks lead. I glassed the open poplar hillside beyond the spruce thicket. No tracks lead out. The buck was bedded in the thicket! The time had come.

I stood there several minutes trying to figure out the best strategy. Finally, I decided to stay on the buck's trail and try to sneak up on him in his bed. If I jumped him, I would have to react to the circumstances of the moment. I entered the spruce thicket in the slipping mode, my rifle at ready. The buck's tracks bore out my theory. Several times he had walked up to likely spruce trees and circled them, obviously looking for a suitable place to bed. Unraveling his winding trail was slow and tedious. I was constantly concerned about whether I had already spooked him. For the better part of 30 minutes, I trailed him from one spruce to another. Tension was running high when I eased up to a small clump of spruce trees near the center of the thicket. Without warning, snow erupted to my left as the buck burst out from under a snow-laden tree. Before I had a chance to shoot, he was gone.

In desperation, I charged out of the thicket and up the steep hillside, hoping elevation would allow me to see the escaping buck. Thirty yards up the slope was all the distance time would allow … and all my weary legs could take. I spun around and searched frantically for the buck. Movement at the far end of the thicket drew my attention. About 125 yards away, the buck was running stiffly through the open poplar trees. My first shot was little more than a hope and a prayer. The bullet centered a big poplar right in front of the buck. The crack of the striking bullet just off his nose must have startled and confused him. The buck stopped, his head pivoting right and left in search of his pursuer. I took a deep breath and squeezed off another shot. After seven hours, the hunt was finally over.

I stood over the buck, a fine 10-pointer, with mixed emotions. I had gotten to know and respect this animal. He had proven himself to be a worthy and noble opponent. It wasn't my skill or hunting savvy that had brought him down. Rather, he had fallen to nothing more glamorous or mysterious than stubborn determination and hard work — a trophy hunter's true secret weapons!

Chapter 15

Aerials, Topos and Scouting
*Mapping Out Success
Before The Hunt*

URING MY DAYS AS A BASS GUIDE long ago on Lake Eufaula, the famous 45,000-acre reservoir shared by Georgia and Alabama, I learned the importance of topographic maps and aerial photos. With them, I could quickly and accurately predict where the bass would be concentrated along the creek and river channels, ditches, underwater islands, sunken pond dams and other "structure." After determining a number of likely spots while in the comfort of my house, I would then hit the lake and use my depthfinder to "scout out" these places. In a matter of hours, I could pinpoint a dozen or more potential bass hotspots and eliminate the ones that didn't have the right structure or sufficient cover. That process would have taken me days in a random search. The use of topos and aerials (taken before the lake was impounded) allowed me to spend a far greater percentage of my time fishing for bass instead of looking for places to fish for bass.

Rather than "viewing" the lake from the monotonous sameness of the surface perspective, I learned to "see" beneath the surface. My mind's

Whether reconnoitering with aerials or topos or on the ground scouting, one of the first things I look for is major food sources. If preferred agricultural crops are present, deer are sure to be concentrated in the immediate vicinity. Photo by Bill Kinney.

eye picture of the lake was three-dimensional. I "saw" the varying depths of the lake plus the structure and cover on the lake bottom. By understanding the "lay of the lake," I could forecast where bass might be found and what they were likely to be doing at various times and under different conditions. Given enough time, I could have learned all that without the aid of topo maps and aerial photos, but they saved me countless hours and allowed me to catch many more bass than I would have caught without them. These tools can be just as valuable in deer hunting.

While most deer hunting places aren't 45,000 acres, or underwater, topos and aerial photos nevertheless can improve your chances of shooting a trophy whitetail. With them, you can save valuable deer hunting time by concentrating your efforts on potential hotspots. And, you can quickly gain an overview understanding of the place you're hunting that otherwise would take long hours on the ground to uncover. Topos and aerials are also invaluable in communicating with other hunters about the property. Trying to describe to another hunter where to go can be very frustrating. A picture is certainly worth a thousand words when the words are "turn at the big oak tree" or "go to the third fork in the stream" or "the stand is on the little hill

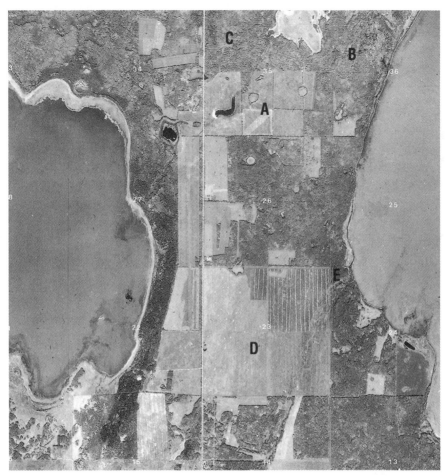

This is an aerial photo of a place I hunt in Canada. The large squares evident are mile-square sections (640 acres). Area A represents a series of alfalfa fields that are a major food source. Deer from all around feed there, including deer drawn out of the provincial forest lying a half-mile north of the fields. Points B and C are stand sites set up to intercept deer moving from the provincial forest to the fields, and vice versa. Both points B and C are located in bottlenecks of a sort, but Point B sees heavier deer traffic and is where I usually hunt. To the east of Point B is an expansive lake, and to the west is a large, marshy meadow. Together, these two barriers funnel deer through the half-mile-wide bottleneck. Area D is also an alfalfa field and an important food source. Point E is a classic bottleneck. Most deer moving in a north-south direction will pass through this 250-yard-wide stretch of woods. However, this may be too much of a good thing — big bucks tend to avoid this bottleneck during the day, perhaps sensing their exposure there.

beyond the second big hill." I've spent many an hour looking for hunters who failed to figure out those "woods directions."

TOPOS AND AERIALS

As the name implies, an aerial photo is simply a photograph of a tract of land taken from the air. Unless the country is hilly or mountainous, aerial photos are usually more revealing and useful than topographic maps. Aerial photos can be obtained from the Aerial Photography Field Office, User Services, P.O. Box 30010, Salt Lake City, UT 84130. The phone number is (801) 521-5856. To identify the location of your hunting property, include your state and county name along with a legal description of the property or a good topographic or county map with the property clearly marked. Don't send an atlas or state map as a reference. If you choose, your local Agricultural Stabilization and Conservation office (ASCS) can order aerials for you. U.S. Forest Service aerials can be ordered directly through that agency or from the Aerial Photography Field Office. Aerials come in several sizes, ranging from 10x10 inches up to 38x38 inches. I find the 17x17 size to be the best compromise between convenience and detail. The cost of maps varies by size from around $7 each to about $35 each.

Topographic maps are renderings of a tract of land with contour lines showing the elevation above sea level, usually at 10 or 20-foot intervals. They are very useful in hilly areas since they show the relief (topography) of the land. Topos also depict other major features such as roads, waterways, timbered and open areas, buildings, section lines, etc. They can be used to great effect when negotiating unknown country with the aid of a compass. Topos can be obtained by writing the Earth Science Information Center, U.S. Geological Survey, Mail Stop 507, Reston, VA 22092 or by calling (703) 648-4000. Request the free state index first. From that, you can identify which topo maps are applicable to your area and find instructions on how to order. Each topographic map costs around $2.50.

SCOUTING

As helpful as they are, topos and aerials can't replace actual scouting. Looking an area over firsthand is necessary in order to learn what it is really like. Also, deer and deer sign can't be seen on aerials or topos.

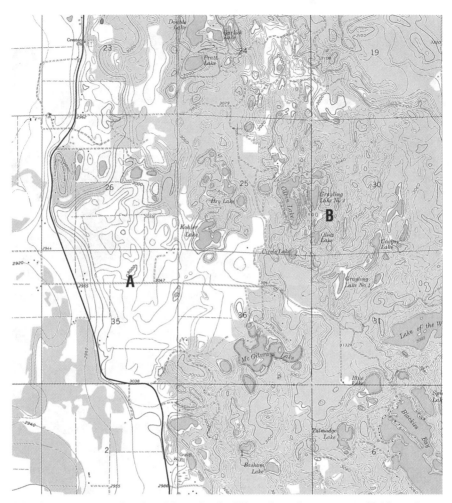

This is a topo map of a place I hunt in the West. Area A represents alfalfa and winter wheat fields that serve as the major food source for deer throughout that locale. Area B is one of several areas of low hills (as evidenced by the tight contour lines) where the deer spend most of their time. Because there are few access roads into Area B and because the woods there are thick, this seems to be a preferred bedding area for trophy bucks in that vicinity. Over the years, several record bucks have been shot in and around Area B.

That takes scouting. Nothing can replace it.

There are essentially two forms of scouting. The first is simply getting to know the property and its topography, features, habitat, access, boundaries, etc. Here, aerials and topos are invaluable, especially in the beginning. This form of scouting can be done well before season. As you become more familiar with a tract of land, the need for this type of scouting diminishes.

The second form of scouting is to look for deer and deer sign for the purpose of deciding exactly where to hunt. Aerials and topos can really speed up the process on unfamiliar property. Scouting for a place to hunt is best done just before going after your buck since deer patterns can change rather abruptly. This type of scouting should be ongoing throughout the season and from year to year.

Often, I find myself hunting new and unfamiliar places with limited time. In such cases, after referring to any available aerials or topos, I try to combine the two forms of scouting while still getting in some hunting. This means spending my first day or two both scouting and hunting. During the prime early morning and late afternoon hours, I usually hunt the best spot I can find, but the rest of the day is spent getting to know the property and looking for deer, deer sign and deer movement patterns. The time spent studying aerials and topos and scouting may cost some hunting time at first, but the returns can be well worth the investment.

The object is to make the most effective use of your hunting time. The best way to accomplish this is by doing some homework in advance of the hunt. Fortunately, there are certain identifiable features you can look for during your advance work that play a big part in hunting success. Let's look at them.

FOOD SOURCES

The first thing I look for on the land I'm hunting is agricultural crops. Studies have found that deer concentrations can be up to 10 times higher in the immediate vicinity of agricultural crops than in the more remote wooded areas. These same studies reveal that the deer disperse once the food is gone, but whitetail hunting is normally done when agricultural crops are most attractive to deer. Fortunately, major agricultural crops are among the easiest of all features to identify on aerials and topos and by scouting.

Food sources other than agricultural crops are also important. Clearcuts or even freshly thinned woodlands are excellent places to find deer feeding. The length of time a cutover area will remain attractive to

I shot this fine Georgia eight-pointer in a three-year-old clearcut. Clearcuts are excellent in-cover food sources and are prime places to catch trophy bucks feeding.

deer and huntable after the initial clearing depends largely on where it is located. In the South with its long growing season, a clearcut is usually huntable for about three or four years. After that, the deer will continue to feed in it but you can't see them for the overgrowth. Farther north, clearcuts may be huntable 6 to 10 years before they grow up enough to conceal a deer's presence. Damage from fire, bugs or storms also can open up the forest and encourage the growth of low-growing plants desirable to deer. Where hunting pressure is a factor, these in-cover feeding areas can be good bets for trophy bucks.

Acorns are an important food source in many places. Aerial photos usually show hardwood areas quite clearly, but you'll have to scout them to know where the hotspots are located. Old homesites are worth checking for food sources. Many homesites had fruit trees planted around them. Or, there may be ornamentals, honeysuckle, grasses or other plants attractive to deer growing in the openings around old home places.

When looking for huntable food sources, you must find out something about the feeding habits of local deer since differences exist from place to place. What are their preferred and secondary foods? When are these foods in-season? What kinds of places do they grow?

BEDDING AREAS

My search for potential bedding areas starts with thick cover, usually either evergreens or low ground cover. Such places are normally visible on aerial photos. In areas with some relief, hills can be important bedding sites. Topos, of course, are excellent for revealing these.

TRAVEL LANES AND MOVEMENT PATTERNS

With food sources identified and potential bedding areas located, the travel lanes between these two areas can be anticipated. As far as trophy bucks are concerned, these trails will follow routes that provide the bucks with the greatest security. Typical travel routes include such places as thick streambeds, swamp edges, pine ridges, etc. In open country, brushy draws, windbreaks and hedgerows provide security for a buck's travels. Big bucks are especially fond of traveling thick streambeds. That's why rubs so often are found in association with streams. Potential travel lanes are sometimes easy to find on aerials and, to a lesser degree, on topos, but you still have to verify their presence by scouting.

Some tracts of land lay out in such a way that overall deer movement tends to follow a distinctive pattern. For instance, on a 1,000-acre tract I used to hunt, a major creek ran north and south lengthwise through the middle of the property. Deer could cross the creek, but its steep banks and fairly deep water discouraged it. Besides, one side of the creek was pretty much like the other. Cattle pastures and roads bordered both the eastern and western sides of the tract. On the northern end of the property, a couple of big agricultural fields attracted deer. The center of the property consisted primarily of hardwoods. On the southern end, overgrown clearcuts and thick pine plantations provided ideal bedding cover. Deer on this property moved in an obvious north/south pattern up and down the creek. They traveled back and forth between the bedding area to the south and either the middle section of acorn-bearing hardwoods or the agricultural crops on the northern end. This was an easy place to hunt because practically the whole herd could be patterned.

I've seen similar situations at other places where major food sources, distinct bedding areas and physical barriers tend to limit travel options.

Normally, it's not as straightforward as the example just cited, but often, some type of funnel effect can be identified. Only in the absence of dominating features is it impossible to determine general deer movement patterns. Large tracts of uniform and unbroken timber would be such an example.

BARRIERS AND BOTTLENECKS

Barriers to deer movement can physically limit travel, or they can simply discourage travel enough to cause deer to consistently take another route. Lakes, large open areas, canyons, major highways, sheer bluffs and large rivers will pretty much restrict deer movement. Well-traveled roads, open wooded areas, minor rivers or creeks, small fields, gullies and steep hills may not pose much of a physical problem for deer, but they will avoid crossing them if an easier or safer route is available. Like humans, deer invariably will take the route of least resistance. Barriers that channel movement out of necessity or convenience are important. Happily, these barriers are fairly easy to identify on topos and aerials and when scouting.

Some barriers restrict deer movement on only one side. For example, a large lake may force deer around one end of it while nothing lies beyond the end of the lake to limit how far around the lake a deer can go. These one-sided barriers are effective in channeling deer movement and can be used to advantage by a hunter. But, a better situation is found when two barriers lie close enough to each other to constrict or funnel deer movement through a defined area. This is called a "bottleneck" and can be lethal for big bucks, especially when bucks "must" move through to reach a major feeding area or hot does. Bottlenecks may be as narrow as a dozen yards or as wide as a half-mile or more. They may be complex or as simple as a saddle between two hills. It is, however, possible to have too much of a good thing. Very restrictive bottlenecks that expose a buck to obvious danger will see less daylight travel.

If at all possible, I always try to incorporate barriers or bottlenecks into my hunting strategy. Trophy bucks with options are just plain hard to predict, so I like to limit their options. On the Georgia plantation I work with, most of the best stands involve barriers or bottlenecks in some way. One particular bottleneck stand on the plantation produced 11 bucks in one year! We were forced to limit the number of bucks shot

A long, straight stretch of a woods road can provide an open "shooting lane" in otherwise thick cover. The downside is that trophy bucks often hurry across such places, leaving little time to judge and shoot. Photo by Mike Biggs.

there each year in order to preserve the buck age structure of the area. A bottleneck in Saskatchewan allowed me to look over 24 different bucks during an eight-day period. It was a classic set-up. A half-mile-wide strip of woods was sandwiched between a huge lake to the east and a large, marshy meadow to the west. Alfalfa fields lay to the south, and

Point A represents a powerline right-of-way and a classic shooting lane. Area B is a large soybean/winter wheat field and is a major food source. Area C is a cattle pasture and holds no particular attraction for deer; however, it and Area B together tend to funnel deer through the quarter-mile-wide strip of thick pines that the powerline transverses. A stand is, in fact, set up about where Point A is depicted and has accounted for several good bucks over the years.

the expansive woodlands of the provincial forest were a half-mile to the north. I took two good bucks that trip.

SHOOTING LANES

Another easily identifiable feature I look for is right-of-ways and cut-lines. Collectively, I call them "shooting lanes." They are corridors that give extended visibility in thick cover, which is key to their pro-ductivity. Powerline and gas right-of-ways are good examples of such places. In areas of oil and gas exploration, seismographic lines often are cut through the brush and woods. These cutlines are known as "senderos" in Texas and are popular stand sites with trophy hunters there. Narrow hardwood bottoms running through thick cover also can serve the purpose of extending your hunting coverage. Cleared fencelines and long, straight stretches of woods roads are likely prospects for improved visibility.

When a shooting lane transverses a well-traveled area with secure cover, it offers huge advantages to the hunter. Even during daylight hours, bucks often will move freely in the protection of thick cover, and upon reaching a shooting lane, they will have to cross it to continue their travels. This gives hunters the advantage of hunting thick cover without the disadvantage of limited visibility. The downside is that trophy bucks seem to sense their exposure in these narrow strips of open ground and often hurry across the shooting lane, leaving the hunter little time to judge and to shoot.

EDGES

Whitetails are a lot like bass in that they, too, orient to structure, better known as "edges" in whitetail lingo. Exactly as the name implies, edges are places where two different habitats or cover types meet. These edges are important to whitetail hunters, especially when looking for rubs and scrapes. The edges of fields, clearcuts, small clearings, lakes and streams are obvious edges. Old roads are one of a buck's favorite types of edge on which to make scrapes and rubs. Breaks between two different timber or cover types are less obvious edges, but they are much used by whitetails.

ROADS AND PRESSURED AREAS

If the area I'm hunting receives substantial hunting pressure, figuring out where the pressure is being applied is high on my priority list. A good topo map or an aerial photo will go a long way toward revealing the answer. Access roads are the give away. Like most folks, hunters are fairly lazy. It's a fair bet that 90 percent of them won't get more than a quarter-mile from a road, a half-mile at the most. Given this, you can almost draw lines a quarter-mile either side of roads or easy access trails, such as firelanes, cutlines, powerlines, etc., and have a pretty good picture of where pressure is being exerted. If you really want to be safe, extend your "pressure zone" a half-mile either side of roads or access trails. Then, you can be sure that the country beyond will not be heavily trodden by the boots of fellow hunters. Generally, I prefer to avoid spending much time in the pressure zone of heavily hunted places. However, the areas beyond can open up a world of promise.

SANCTUARIES

One particular tract of land I hunt consists of several thousand acres. It is fairly heavily hunted, mostly by casual weekend hunters. The majority of the bucks killed on the property are 1½ and 2½-year-olds. Most are shot from permanent stands stationed within 200 yards of one of the many woods roads within the property. Only occasionally are trophy bucks taken, and the average guy hunting there doesn't think the tract has many good bucks. He's wrong.

If you were to draw a line about 400 yards either side of all the roads on the property, you would notice two large areas lying outside the pressure zone. One of these areas is about 1,500 acres and the other about 1,000 acres. These two areas see little human traffic and are home to a multitude of trophy bucks. This is where I spend my time when hunting the property. The number and size of the bucks I see there bear little resemblance to what most hunters encounter during their time in the more pressured areas. It's a rare day when I don't see five or six bucks, a couple of which are usually 3½ years old or older. This is not because I possess special skills and know any super tactics. It's because I seek out and hunt places that have escaped the effects of pressure. Such places are called "sanctuaries." These sanctuaries quite likely represent a trophy hunter's greatest untapped advantage and resource!

All hunters are familiar with the principle behind sanctuaries, although they may not have thought about it. Most have even seen it in practice. For instance, let's say there's a federal refuge of 1,000 acres next to your heavily hunted property. This refuge is protected and allows no hunting. You and all your friends know very well that big bucks are on the refuge. You dream of what it would be like to hunt it. Trophy bucks roam the refuge undisturbed and seem to know exactly where the property line is. You may even have reason to believe that outside bucks move into the refuge to seek sanctuary once the season starts. You'd probably be right. On your heavily hunted property, nothing but does and a few young bucks are ever seen. If only you could hunt the refuge ...

Well, take heart. While an unhunted federal refuge protected by

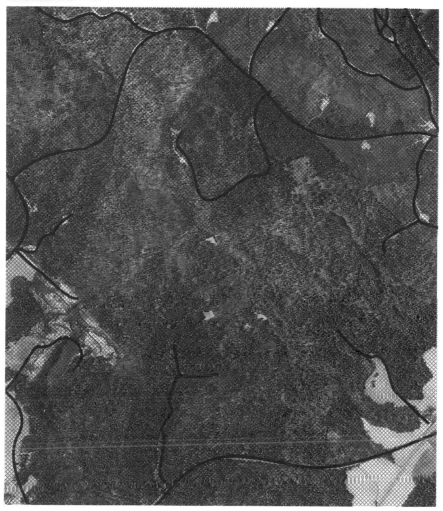

In areas of substantial hunting pressure, you can almost draw lines a quarter-mile either side of roads, open fields or other access points and have a good picture of where pressure is being exerted. The "pressure zone" is clearly shown on the above aerial photo. If possible, savvy trophy hunters will avoid hunting this area. However, the areas outside the pressure zone hold a world of promise. These "sanctuaries" offer trophy hunters a way to escape the negative effects of hunting pressure.

posted signs and game wardens may be off limits to hunters, places just as unhunted with just as many trophy bucks are available to many hunters if they are willing to seek them out. Instead of being protected by posted signs, visible boundary lines and game wardens, they are protected by distance, difficult terrain and the overall lack of easy access. And, the same thing that keeps deer on a protected federal refuge keeps them on these places. It's not the posted signs; it's not the painted boundary lines; it's not even the game wardens … it's an invisible barrier called hunting pressure! Once you get beyond that barrier, whether a half-mile from the nearest road on your hunting lease or in the heart of a protected federal refuge, the chances are good that you will find trophy bucks doing the things trophy bucks do naturally. These "protected" sanctuaries can exist anywhere distance or the lack of easy access creates areas that few hunters are willing to put forth the necessary effort to hunt.

Sanctuaries come in all sizes, shapes and degrees. A sanctuary may indeed be a sizable and virtually unhunted block of land lying deep within a larger tract. Or, a sanctuary simply may be the least accessible and least hunted part of a tract of land that sees some pressure throughout. The sanctuary concept basically involves seeking out the pockets of land that have the least hunting pressure. Obviously, the bigger the sanctuary and the less pressure it has, the better. But, even smaller sanctuaries that simply receive less pressure than the surrounding land offer hunters an advantage.

To fully understand sanctuaries, you have to understand the effects of hunting pressure. When lots of hunters invade the whitetail's domain, it is almost like an army invading someone else's territory and staking claim to it. If the deer can escape the invasion by moving to unoccupied land, they will, or certainly the trophy bucks will. Even if deer continue to live within the pressure zone, they do exactly as someone behind enemy lines would do. They try to stay out of sight by moving only in thick cover or at night. By contrast, in areas beyond the pressure zone, deer can go about some semblance of a normal routine. How "normal" that routine will be depends largely upon the level of intrusion by hunters venturing beyond the pressure zone. Basically, deer seek out the places of least pressure, or at least that's where they will be most visible. The size and shape of these lower pressure sanctuaries and the amount of relief they provide vary, but a sanctuary of any type represents opportunity for the trophy hunter.

If a hunter could look down on a tract of land and see the pressured areas, there probably would be both large blocks of land with low pressure and narrow, winding corridors with low pressure. The larger blocks of land are what we normally think of as a sanctuary, but even the corridors can be important. Bucks will use them as travel routes. In a study on a large hunting club in East Texas, deer expert James Kroll found that bucks actually "split the seam" between permanent deer stands. The bucks knew exactly where those stands were and moved with deliberate intent through the "safe corridors" beyond the sight of hunters. Obviously, these stands represented pressure and the deer avoided them. For wise trophy hunters, there is a message in that about frequently hunted permanent stands!

Aerials and topos are invaluable in identifying pressure zones and sanctuaries. The thickness of the cover, the terrain, the level of pressure, the availability of off-road paths and trails and local hunting traditions are all factors in how far hunters will penetrate the country beyond the roads. Sanctuaries do require considerable time and effort to hunt. But if they were easy to reach and hunt, they wouldn't exist in the first place.

Chapter 16

Still-Hunting
The Ultimate Expression Of The Art

DEER SEASON WAS ALMOST A WEEK OLD when the rains finally
came to Georgia. This was the day I had waited for. The steady
drizzle would quiet the noisy, dry woods. Now, I would get my
buck. Although I had never seen him, I knew him well from his sign.
His tracks were over three fingers wide. His rubs reached well above my
belt. The scrapes he left were the size of a washtub. All evidence said
he was a dominant buck.

The buck's domain included a three-quarter-mile long and quarter-
mile wide point of woods separating two large fields. Through the center
of the point ran a small stream bordered by a maze of alder and iron-
wood. This thick bottom was one of the main travel routes for the old
buck, and his trail along the stream was clearly marked by rubbed trees,
some four inches in diameter. On either side of the streambottom, the
habitat varied from open hardwoods to thick pines and from overgrown
fields to briar patches. The point ended at a fallow field overgrown with
broomsedge, briar patches and scattered young pines. Here, the buck
had made his scrapes. I had hunted his scrapes twice before but had seen
only does and a couple of young bucks. Apparently, he was working the

Still-hunting is the ultimate expression of the art of hunting and can be highly effective under the right conditions and when done properly. The hunter in this photo has but scant seconds to size up that buck and shoot.

scrapes at night. The time had come for a new strategy. The drizzling rain gave me just the opportunity I had hoped for.

After having hunted the fallow field where his scrapes were located a couple of times, I figured the buck expected danger to approach from that direction. Something different was needed. I considered taking a stand on his trail, but I didn't have a spot selected I was confident in. Plus, he had two or three trails he frequently used. Since the weather was perfect for still-hunting, I decided that's what I would do. And, I'd throw him a curve. Instead of entering from the end of the point, which was nearest the public road, I would walk the 1½ miles necessary to circle around the point and cut it off. Then, I would still-hunt back. If everything went according to plan, the buck would be between me and his scrapes at the far end of the point. I was sure he would not expect danger from the rear.

It was about 3 p.m. when I reached the place where the point of woods merged with a broad hardwood bottom. By now, the woods were completely soaked by the steady drizzling rain. It was an easy matter to move along slowly without making a sound.

At one time or another, every hunter has wished he could move through deer country unnoticed and in complete silence. This was the kind of day a hunter's wish comes closest to being answered. Everything was perfect. The hunt felt good, and I had confidence in its outcome. Even the discomfort of my wet flannel shirt and pants didn't matter. I was glad to give up the comfort of a dry but noisy rainsuit for the quietness of soft, unobtrusive clothing.

I chose to follow the buck's own route along the stream. This would give me the best view of the woods on either side of the bottom. Each step was slow and deliberate. Except for brief glances toward the ground to check for my next step, my eyes constantly searched the woods ahead and to the side. Every few minutes, my attention would be drawn to impressive rubs on the alders. Fifteen minutes into the hunt, my pace was established … one or two slow-motion steps, stop, look, another step. I was fully attuned to the woods. Squirrels and birds allowed me to approach within a few feet of them and showed little concern.

I had progressed about 200 yards when I saw movement ahead. It was horizontal movement against the vertical background of trees, obviously a deer. I reached for my binoculars. The deer moved a few feet into clear view. It was a nice buck but not the one I was after. Through my binoculars, I could see he was an eight-pointer, probably a 2½-year-old. For several minutes, I watched the buck feed on acorns on the hillside above me. He finally fed out of sight, and I resumed my hunt.

At 4:30 p.m., I came to a place where I could see the edge of one of the big fields. Silhouetted against the grey sky was a deer. My binoculars showed it to be a doe. Since the rut was approaching, I decided to check the field for a buck. Slowly, I inched my way up the hillside, stopping whenever the doe lifted her head from feeding on the tender rye.

The best time to still-hunt is when the bucks are active and distracted by the thought of love during the breeding period. Photo by Bill Kinney.

After several tedious minutes, I could crane my neck enough to see into the field. Standing about 25 yards away was a four-point buck. Still not the one I was after.

The next half-hour went by uneventfully, and I was beginning to get a little anxious. But, I felt sure the buck was ahead of me and undisturbed. In the waning minutes of the day, I approached the end of the point. Only about 150 yards of woods separated me from the fallow field. The point widened out here, and the buck, if he was around, had plenty of thickets and briars where he could hide. Then, just ahead on a sandbar along the stream's edge, I saw fresh tracks leading to my right. I quickly combed the thick pines in that direction but saw nothing. I took a couple of steps and knelt down beside the big tracks. Water was still seeping into the tracks farthest away from the stream. Now, I had him! He was just above me, probably near his scrapes along the edge of the old field.

I unslung my .30/06 Browning bolt action. Ever so carefully, I eased up the hill, taking very short steps to avoid losing my balance. The light at the edge of the field gradually became brighter, but still no buck. One step at a time, constantly stopping and looking, I crept toward the field. I could see a scrape ahead. As I neared it, my heart sank when I saw it had not been worked recently. Had I passed the buck? Had he seen me?

With no more than 30 yards of woods left, my only hope was that the buck was somewhere along the edge of the field. But now, I had a problem. An abandoned hog-wire fence hindered my progress. Wanting to avoid the inevitable squeaks that come with climbing a fence, I eased along the fence and looked for an opening. I found a spot where a fallen tree had pushed the fence down just low enough so that I could step over it.

As I straddled the fence, something caught my eye near the field. There stood my buck — 30 yards away and staring straight at me! I could see the surprise in his eyes. I could also see that he was ready to lay down some far apart tracks. His tail slowly began to rise. He turned and pranced down the edge of the field much like a Tennessee walking horse. I snapped the rifle to my shoulder and picked an open lane in the trees. When the buck passed, I fired.

I wasn't sure if I'd hit the buck, but his pace definitely picked up. He ran full tilt down the edge of the field for about 40 yards, cut into the woods, sailed over the fence I was straddling and disappeared. It all happened so fast that I was unable to get off a second shot. I didn't like the buck's reaction, but I had a clear mental picture of the crosshairs of my 1½X-5X Leupold on his shoulder when the gun went off.

Half-sick and cursing myself for getting careless at the last minute of the hunt, I walked to where the deer had jumped the fence. There was blood on the fence and the ground beyond. I hurriedly followed the blood trail 50 yards to a long-tined, 19-inch eight-pointer. The scales would later show him to weigh 238 pounds. He was a Georgia white-tail to be proud of, but my real satisfaction came from taking him on a well-planned and carefully executed still-hunt.

Over the years, I've taken more trophy bucks by still-hunting than by any other hunting method. So, it is little wonder why still-hunting is my favorite way to hunt. I confess that it is hard for me to sit patiently for long hours ... something required for stand-hunting. I like to make things happen, to stay busy and to take an active part in the hunt. Still-hunting allows this. But disregarding my own preference for an aggressive hunting style, I believe still-hunting is the greatest expression of the hunting art and perhaps the most effective of all hunting methods ... if conducted under the right conditions and properly executed.

DEFINITION

What is still-hunting? Well, the term "still-hunting" is actually an inaccurate description of the hunting method. A better name might be "slipping" or "stop-and-go" hunting. Many hunters call it "stalking," and in a way, this is a good description. Although a still-hunter does not normally stalk an animal that has previously been spotted, he does move along as if trying to sneak up on an unseen deer. Perhaps still-hunting can best be described as the tactic employed when a hunter invades the deer's domain and uses his woodsmanship, stealth and knowledge to approach and observe deer unnoticed, or at least to approach the deer in a way that offers a shot if the hunter chooses to take it.

There are proper times and places for still-hunting. And as you would expect, there are definitely times and places that are not right for still-hunting. Also, some people are physically capable of becoming good still-hunters. Others aren't. Let's explore these aspects before looking at the "how-to's" of still-hunting.

WHEN

The best time to still-hunt for trophy bucks is when they are active and distracted. That being the case, the breeding period is the optimum time to still-hunt. In their pursuit of hot does during this time, bucks are on the move and engrossed by the prospects of love. Their formidable defenses are lowered, which is a huge advantage to hunters. Since the bucks are now far less likely to pick off the hunter before a shot is offered, a good still-hunter who can slip slowly and quietly through the buck's domain has an excellent chance of running across roving breeding parties.

Still-hunting during the rut is an aggressive form of hunting. The hunter is constantly getting new information from the sign he comes across or the deer he sees. His mobility and the buck's lack of wariness allow the still-hunter to react to new circumstances. Many times, I have been able to follow a preoccupied buck or breeding party and get a shot, if I wanted it, that a stationary hunter never would have gotten. On a couple of occasions, I've even followed trailing subdominant bucks to a

During the rut, still-hunting can take on an aggressive form. When a 120-class eight-pointer trailed by me on a South Texas hunt, I followed him from a distance. He eventually lead me to a breeding party consisting of several bucks, of which this 12-pointer was the largest.

hot doe in the company of a trophy buck, which I shot. One such time took place on the Cameron Ranch in La Salle County, Texas.

I was slipping along merrily one morning when a 120-class eight-pointer crossed a sendero about 100 yards away. His nose was to the ground and his tail in the air, a typical posture for a trailing buck with a snout full of hot doe aroma. I watched him go out of sight over a small rise. I hurried over to the rise. From there, I watched the buck work the trail across a dry creekbed and up another rise, where he disappeared. I hotfooted it over there. Again, I located the buck and watched him trot along the invisible trail with unwavering certainty. Suddenly, he stopped and looked straight ahead into a mesquite-lined draw. I saw movement. A doe. Then, something moved behind her. A good buck. Moments later, another buck appeared. An hour passed before the scene was all played out. A total of five bucks were in that draw after the aromatic doe. The largest, a 12-pointer, lay dead ... all because the little eight-pointer had led me there.

Bucks are not only on the move during a drizzle, they also are less alert than at other times. Couple this with the fact that a hunter can move through the damp woods in silence, and the results spell opportunity for the still-hunter. Photo by Mike Biggs.

Another reason to still-hunt when bucks are hard at breeding is that their whereabouts is so unpredictable then. They are moving at the whim of the does and can be anywhere. Predictable travel patterns have broken down. This makes it hard for a stand-hunter to pick out the exact spot to wait out a buck. A still-hunter can hunt an area, not just a spot. This can make still-hunting the best choice if for no other reason than by default.

The second best time to still-hunt is during the scraping period. The bucks are prowling around now and are somewhat distracted, but not as much as during the rut. Since bucks are usually alone during this period and are not yet fully sold out to passion, they tend to be more alert and harder to slip up on. Their senses, though dulled, are still quick to pick up movement or strange noises. Also, during the scraping period, hunters have another good choice of hunting methods — stand-hunting. Because bucks are on predictable patterns then, a stand-hunter can pick a precise spot to ambush a buck. This doesn't make still-hunting any less effective; it is just that another good option exists.

Whether or not still-hunting is a viable hunting method during the pre-rut and post-rut periods depends largely on the terrain, cover and availability of quiet travel routes. Since the deer's senses are on full alert during these times, especially during the post-rut, no real advantages are inherent to still-hunting. Also, trophy buck movement is limited during legal hours both before and after the rut. Bedded or immobile deer are hard to sneak up on and see before they see you. Of course, stand-hunting for immobile deer is rather tough, too.

There are a couple of weather conditions that are ideal for still-hunting. One is a drizzle. (Light snowfall and even a heavy mist can have much the same effect.) Noise obviously is suppressed by the dampness and by the water dripping from vegetation. Also, deer seem to be less aware of movement then. Perhaps the light rain masks movement. And on top of this, deer are simply not as alert and as hair-triggered during a drizzle as they are at other times. They will sometimes stand and stare at a hunter in disbelief, as though to say, "What in the world are you doing out here in this weather?"

The other ideal time to still-hunt is after a period of rain or snowfall. Deer move very well then, and the dampness or fresh snow allows for silent travel.

Surprisingly, still-hunting can be a good choice of hunting methods on windy and rainy days. Deer movement will be suppressed, but a hunter can move around without much concern about being seen or heard. I have walked up on trophy bucks under these conditions and surprised both them and me. I once shot a good eight-pointer in Georgia while he stood hunkered up in a pine thicket during a driving rain. On a raw day in South Texas that saw winds gusting to 40 miles an hour, I unknowingly walked within a few feet of a big buck before I saw him. He was feeding contentedly on cactus in a shallow depression. My rifle muzzle couldn't have been over 10 feet from the buck as I waited for him to lift his head so I could see what size antlers he had. As it turned out, they were plenty big enough!

WHERE

Still-hunting can be effective just about anywhere whitetails are hunted. But, there are a couple of conditions necessary to maximize a still-hunter's chances for success. One, the cover should be

Still-hunting can be effective just about anywhere whitetails are hunted, but this tactic works best in places with good visibility. Whitetails are too cautious and well endowed to allow hunters in close proximity to them to move about undetected. Visibility gives the hunter some distance to work with. Photo by Dick Idol.

fairly open. When is the cover too thick? I generally consider cover with visibility less than 50 yards to be too dense for a steady diet of still hunting. I prefer places that have at least occasional areas with visibility of 75 yards or more. As a rule of thumb, the greater the visibility, the better bet still-hunting becomes.

Why is cover density a factor in still-hunting? Whitetails are too cautious and well endowed in their senses of sight, hearing and smell to allow hunters to move about undetected within 50 yards of them. Sure, it can be done. But, don't expect to get by with it consistently. The odds are just too long. Adequate distance tends to neutralize the whitetail's huge advantage in hearing and smell, provided the hunter plays the wind right. This makes the hunt more of a contest of sight, which is the only sense a hunter possesses that can match a whitetail's. If the hunter does his part, it becomes largely a question of who sees who first. By being extremely careful and alert, the hunter has a reasonable chance of winning, especially if the buck is preoccupied by

Woods roads provide still-hunters with a quiet route through deer country. And, you never know who you might meet on the road! Photo by Mike Biggs.

the rut instead of focusing on survival.

Other than visibility, the still-hunter needs hunting routes available that allow quiet walking and conceal his movement. In places where good travel routes exist for the still-hunter, the visibility requirements are somewhat less critical. In more open areas, the need for quiet travel routes diminishes. The best situation is where good visibility and quiet slipping trails exist together. Such places can make still-hunting the method of choice for the skilled hunter just about any time.

The classic travel routes for the still-hunter are woods roads and firebreaks. Cutlines and right-of-ways are also good routes by which to travel quietly through deer country, but the hunter must be careful to stay concealed. Even in total silence, movement can give you away. It goes without saying that the wind must be right to have any hope of sneaking up on a trophy buck.

The edges of fields and clearcuts offer productive slipping paths for the still-hunter. One of my favorite places to still-hunt is along the edges of agricultural fields where deer are concentrated. Often, roads weave in and out of the woods around such fields. These roads allow the hunter to ease around in the woods and occasionally check the field for deer.

Another excellent set-up for the still-hunter is where extended hills, bluffs or ridges offer routes overlooking large chunks of deer country. Places like this bring the advantage of elevation, which greatly improves your visibility and reduces your chances of being picked off by the deer. Also, these elevated routes tend to remove you from the immediate presence of deer since they inherently provide some distance. One ranch I hunt in South Texas has a 50-foot high, five-mile long escarpment running through it. I cannot imagine a better place to still-hunt or to rattle from. I've used elevated routes to great advantage in Canada and Montana as well. I once shot a good 10-pointer in western Montana as I eased along a high bluff overlooking a creekbottom. He was furiously making a scrape when I first saw him. Although I hit him through the lungs and had good tracking snow, I almost lost that buck. A herd of about 40 elk crossed his trail and obscured his tracks. Such are the hazards of hunting the West!

In recent years, I have come to depend on a rather unconventional but highly productive way of still-hunting … wading shallow streams and creeks. Think about it. You can move in almost total silence if the situation is right. Most streams and creeks are below ground level to some degree, which conceals your movement and breaks up the human silhouette. Plus, streams and creeks usually transverse good deer country, including acorn-producing hardwood areas. My rubber-bottomed L.L. Bean boots are sufficient for some of the streams I wade, but most often, I wear a pair of ankle-fit hip waders I bought just for this purpose. I depend heavily on this hunting method during the pre-rut feeding period when acorns are the drawing card. It also can be good during the rut, depending on the area. Hunting the streambeds is least productive in the post-rut, when winter's bite has denuded the hardwoods normally found around streams.

Two of my better Georgia bucks made their last mistake as I slipped silently down streams. One of the bucks practically walked over me while I stood in the middle of a shallow, 10-foot-wide creek. The buck, a 227-pound eight-pointer, planned to cross where I stood, but a bullet from my .284 Win. thwarted his plan. The other buck warned me of his approach as he crashed headlong through a dense stand of cane along a creekbottom while in pursuit of a doe. By the time he burst out

Wading shallow streams and creeks is an excellent way to slip through good deer habitat in absolute silence. An added bonus is the fact that most waterways are below ground level, which helps conceal movement and breaks up the human form.

of the cover 30 yards away, my nerves were shot. It's a wonder I could even find the trigger, let alone hit the buck. Somehow, the 150-grain bullet from my .308 Win. found its mark. The big 11-pointer pulled the scales to 243 pounds!

How

Still-hunting requires the greatest level of skill of any hunting method. Actually, it is an art form. Much of the expression of that art form lies in a hunter's ability to move unnoticed through the deer's domain. This depends both on natural ability and on skill developed from practice. Some hunters are simply more adept at moving slowly and silently than others. They have greater stealth and grace, and with practice, they become very proficient at still-hunting. Others can improve their sneaking capabilities with practice, but they'll never be as good at still-hunting as the hunter endowed with the necessary natural ability.

I have a friend whom we affectionately call "Thunderfoot," a name he has well earned. He is an experienced and successful whitetail hunter, but most of his bucks have been shot from treestands. He likes to still-hunt and frequently does so. But, his success is limited when he pursues whitetails from the ground. He simply makes too much noise. Try as he will, his feet fall heavily to the ground. Limbs break under his boots with "alarming" frequency. His movements are sudden and fast. He tends to plow through brushy obstacles that stand in his way. It's not that Thunderfoot can't kill a trophy buck by still-hunting. He can, but he'll never be great at it. His still-hunting should be limited to ideal conditions; otherwise, stand-hunting is the way he should go.

By contrast, my buddy Dick Idol is one of the best still-hunters I know. He fairly "drifts" through the woods. Steve Vaughn, the publisher of *North American Whitetail*, is another accomplished still-hunter. Even though Steve stands six feet, three inches and weighs 230 pounds, he moves with admirable stealth through whitetail cover, due in part to his extraordinary patience. Certainly, long hours of practice have improved both Dick's and Steve's stalking skills, but their high level of proficiency is made possible by their natural abilities. While a hunter can't do a whole lot about his natural ability, there are things he can do that will make him a better still-hunter.

A still-hunter must learn to walk and move quietly. His steps should be short so that perfect balance is maintained. Each step should be controlled and carefully placed ... the heel first, then the outside edge of the foot and finally the whole foot is brought to bear as the weight shifts gradually. Shifting the weight very slowly from one foot to the other is critical. This way, the hunter can "feel out" each step. If he feels a limb under foot as his weight shifts, he can recover and place his foot in another spot. By shifting his weight very slowly, a hunter can move with surprising quietness even through dry leaves or limb-strewn woods. Remember, deer will seldom spook at only one sound. They will usually stand motionless and wait for some type of confirmation that danger is near. When a hunter makes a mistake, he should remain still for several minutes, watching and listening.

Being quiet is more than watching where you step. A hunter must avoid tree limbs that would brush his clothes or hang on his gun barrel. He must learn to twist and turn and yield to resistance as he moves through thick cover. He has to carefully choose his routes and develop a sense for potential problems. He has to resist the temptation to clear his throat. Cartridges mustn't click together. The knife handle can't clamor against the gun stock. Clothing must be made of a quiet material.

Noise is not the only taboo for the still-hunter. Movement also draws the deer's attention to the hunter. One of the most difficult things for a still-hunter to do is slow himself down enough to move through whitetail country unnoticed. This sounds easy, but invariably, hunters are in too big a hurry and are not really hunting. Many walk along at a leisurely pace and casually scan the woods. From the whitetail's perspective, they might as well be waving the flag at the finish line of the Indy 500.

The successful still-hunter doesn't just walk, rather he "stalks," moving slowly and fluidly. He blends with his surroundings and avoids sudden or unnatural movements. He moves only to gain a new viewpoint, not to get anywhere in particular. He almost glides along with little more than his legs moving, and only at the slowest possible speed. The still-hunter moves in a stop-and-go fashion, standing more than moving. The whole purpose of the hunt is to carefully look over as much deer habitat as possible without being noticed by the citizens of the woods. To do this, the pace must be excruciatingly slow and every step deliberate.

The daily environment of the modern hunter is fast-paced and noisy. He hurries around day after day trying to meet schedules and deadlines. Time is his enemy. The game is to make every second count. Everything must be done quickly and right now, or better yet, yesterday. In his own environment, the modern hunter tunes out background noises such as trains, passing cars, radios, TV's and conversations around him. He simply doesn't hear them. He seldom experiences true quiet. Still vibrating from the rush of civilization and deaf to any sound not addressed directly to him, the modern hunter enters the world of the whitetail. There, survival is the driving force, not schedules and deadlines. Every noise, every movement is suspiciously scrutinized. Unless a hunter can slow himself down and become attuned to the whitetail's domain, he has virtually no chance of entering this world unnoticed.

One of the best ways for a hunter to slow himself down and unwind before starting a still-hunt is to sit for about 30 minutes in the woods before beginning the hunt. It's surprising how conscious a hunter will become of sound and movement, both his own and that around him, after giving the woods time to completely recover from his presence ... nay, intrusion. He will realize that the slightest noise frightens a nearby bird or a quick movement sends a squirrel scurrying up a tree. These things must be avoided if he hopes to move within range of a buck, especially a trophy buck. By sitting for awhile before starting the hunt, a hunter begins to know the meaning of silence and just how alien his presence is to the creatures of the woods. His only hope is to move with agonizing slowness and in complete silence. If a hunter is seeing only

Steve Vaughn "put the slip" on this heavy nine-pointer during a 1990 hunt. Even though Steve is a big man, he moves through whitetail cover with admirable stealth. Still-hunting requires the highest level of natural ability of all the hunting tactics. Photo by Richard Jackson.

tails and hearing only snorts, he's in too big a hurry.

There are times when try as he may a hunter cannot slow himself down enough to still-hunt. This is usually a problem of concentration. During such times, the hunter will get careless and make mistakes.

Maybe he moves too fast, steps on twigs, brushes against overhanging limbs, chooses the wrong route, ignores the wind or, worse yet, looks but does not see. He just goes through the motions. If sitting still for 30 minutes or so cannot refocus his attention on the hunt, the hunter should give up trying to still-hunt. It's time to find a place to sit and put the burden of not making a mistake on the deer. Without concentration, still-hunting is a waste of time.

Moving slowly and quietly through the woods should be for only one purpose — to gain a different look at deer habitat. Every step or two will result in the hunter having a new viewpoint of his surroundings. New "corridors" will open up that allow him to look at places previously unseen. But, just looking will not do. The hunter must thoroughly examine the woods around him, not just ahead but also to the sides and behind. Absolute concentration is needed to insure success.

Many hunters don't know how to look for deer. They expect to see an animal the size of a cow looming in the woods. Again, experience is the best teacher, but the hunter must realize that he is looking for parts of a deer rather than the whole animal — a flicking ear or tail, a throat patch, an antler or moving legs. He must quickly detect and identify every movement and every sound. Most importantly, the hunter must learn to look for the horizontal back of a deer against the predominately vertical background of the woods.

Still-hunters must be able to quickly size up and react to a situation. This, too, involves both natural ability and learned skills. Some hunters have a knack for figuring out what's going on and what to do about it in the blink of an eye. For others, it takes time to make sense of what they see and even more time to react to it. With the window of opportunity in still-hunting often measured in seconds, a hunter must be able to quickly judge the size of the buck. He must have a thorough knowledge of the animal and be skilled enough in his woodsmanship to make the right move. Plus, he must be able to handle a rifle well and shoot accurately under a wide range of conditions. These are demanding requirements considering the tension of the moment and the short span of time available.

Before I start a still-hunt, I plan out where I'm going and why I'm going there. The route is chosen according to the weather conditions, wind direction, topography, available travel routes, deer sign and deer

For the still-hunter, a soft snow is a great aid to silent movement. Photo by Tom Evans courtesy of **North American Whitetail.**

movement patterns. If conditions change or I get new information during the course of the hunt, my hunt plans are altered to meet the new circumstances. This frequently happens, but it doesn't lessen the importance of having a beginning plan and good reasons for it.

When planning a still-hunt, a hunter must be keenly aware of the wind direction. Ideally, the wind will be blowing steadily into the hunter's face. A quartering wind or a crosswind is acceptable, depending on where a hunter expects to encounter his deer. When the wind is variable, it is often necessary to speed up the hunt to avoid being smelled. It is usually better to be heard or seen rather than smelled. If there is no wind, a

Still-hunters must be able to quickly size up a situation and react. I spooked this buck when I first encountered him. I didn't think he went very far so I ran in a big circle around where I figured he might stop. I then slipped very slowly back toward his last position. I caught the buck totally unawares as he stood and watched his backtrail. Photo by Jeff Stringer.

hunter moving very slowly becomes surrounded by a cloud or scent. In close quarters, this can be a problem. A slightly faster pace or more open terrain are possible remedies.

At times, the direction of the sun can be important, especially in open country. When hunting while the sun is low in either the morning or afternoon, a hunter should try to keep the sun behind him. With the sun in the deer's eyes, it is harder for them to see the hunter. Plus, deer practically glow when a low sun shines directly on them, as do hunters. When the sun is fairly high and not directly in your eyes, hunting into the sun is not so bad. The backlighting effect causes the deer's back and especially a buck's antlers to be highlighted and to shine. From a practical standpoint, it is usually difficult to have the sun just right on a still-hunt. Other considerations such as wind direction, hunt routes and deer sign must take priority. Yet, it does pay to use the sun to your advantage whenever possible.

Still-hunting offers the hunter great flexibility. During the course of a hunt, a hunter can rattle or otherwise call deer, sit on hot sign for awhile or even attempt to force deer movement. Because new information is being constantly gathered, still-hunting is a hunt of opportunity. Mobility and flexibility are the great advantages of this method of hunting.

A brief word about clothing and equipment for still-hunting. First, the clothing must be absolutely quiet. Wool, flannel and the soft polyesters like Worsterlon and Polarfleece are my favorites. Soft cotton is good in warm weather. Be sure your headgear and hunter orange garments are likewise noiseless. The right boot is vitally important to the still-hunter. Boots should be fairly lightweight and soft-soled. Uninsulated, rubber-bottomed, leather-topped boots such as L.L. Bean's famous Maine Guide Boot are excellent when the temperature isn't too severe. Avoid hard-soled boots. They telegraph your approach.

As for equipment, a good pair of reasonably lightweight binoculars is very important to the still-hunter no matter how thick the cover. Binoculars can be used to focus out brush, to identify movement, to tell the difference between a deer and a man or to distinguish between an average eight-pointer and a trophy 10 pointer. A quick-handling, adequately powerful rifle capable of a speedy follow-up shot is best for still-hunting. The rifle should be topped with a low-power fixed scope (3X or 4X) or a variable offering low magnification, which is my preference. We'll talk more about rifles, scopes and binoculars in later chapters.

When properly executed at the right time and in the right place, still-hunting can be the most productive, challenging and enjoyable way to hunt trophy whitetails. With the hunter one-on-one against the whitetail in the deer's own backyard, still-hunting is the ultimate expression of the art of hunting!

Chapter 17

Stand-Hunting
The Universal Method That Works

WITHOUT A DOUBT, STAND-HUNTING is the most popular of all hunting methods for whitetails. As such, more trophy bucks (and whitetails in total) fall to this method of hunting than any other. And, why not? Stand-hunting is something nearly anybody can do. It is productive in all types of weather, habitat, terrain and situations. All in all, stand-hunting is a universal hunting method that works!

DEFINITION

Stand-hunting is when a stationary hunter waits in ambush for deer from a specific spot that has been selected and prepared in advance. This definition allows us to draw a distinction between "true" stand-hunting and the common practice of waiting and watching in ambush for a short time while still-hunting. The key differences are that the stand-hunter is "stationary," meaning he stays in one spot during the entire hunt period, and he has selected and prepared his ambush point in advance. Most often, the mobile still-hunter comes upon "ambush points of opportunity" and waits there for a period of time before resum-

Stand-hunting accounts for more whitetails than any other hunting method. And why not? It works in all types of weather, habitat, terrain and situations. Photo courtesy of **North American Whitetail.**

ing his stalk. With that, let's look at the major advantages of stand-hunting and at its few disadvantages.

ADVANTAGES

First, stand-hunting tends to neutralize a deer's sensory advantages. Just the fact that the hunter is stationary, whether on the ground or in a tree, greatly reduces the likelihood that a buck will see or hear him. When a hunter is in an elevated stand, the buck is even less likely to hear or see him even if he moves. This is a big advantage when a buck is nearby and the hunter needs to raise his binoculars or his rifle. The other great benefit of elevation is that the buck's primary advantage over hunters — his sense of smell — is partially negated. Depending on the conditions and situation, an elevated hunter's scent will sometimes drift beyond the immediate stand area before settling to the ground, especially if there is some wind. Because of this, deer are less likely to scent a hunter perched at bird's eye level than one on the ground, particularly at close range.

Along these same lines, stand-hunting shifts much of the burden of not making a mistake from the hunter to the buck. Aggressive forms of hunting like still-hunting and driving leave the hunter open to making mistakes that a trophy whitetail will quickly turn to his benefit. A stand-hunter who is properly concealed and who has the wind in his favor has minimized his chances of running afoul and puts the onus on the buck. That's a huge plus because the truth is that hunters mixing it up with a trophy whitetail on the buck's terms are far more likely to slip up first than the buck.

Since a properly placed stand allows the hunter to "disappear into the woodwork," deer normally are undisturbed when they approach the hunter. This offers clear advantages. Certainly, one of the most important benefits is that the hunter is likely to have the time and opportunity to judge the buck and get off a well-placed shot. The opportunity to make a good shot from a stand is further enhanced by the fact that the hunter has had time in advance to prepare a rest to steady his rifle. By contrast, still-hunters and hunters on deer drives often have to make quick judgments about a buck's size and take hasty shots at deer that are alerted and/or on the move. Frankly, if conditions are at all conducive to still-hunting, I believe that I can almost always see more deer by slipping around than by sitting in one spot. However, when it comes to how many of those deer could have been accurately judged and cleanly shot, then stand-hunting will get the nod most often unless conditions are ideal for still-hunting.

Another advantage offered by the fact that a stand-hunter often can be in the presence of deer without alerting them is the chance to watch deer do the things they do naturally. Indeed, a good stand-hunter can blend into nature and see its workings unfold in a way modern man

One of the great appeals of stand-hunting is that anyone can do it and be success-ful. My wife, Debbie, who shoots well and has great patience, stand-hunts almost exclusively. That's how she shot this eight-pointer scoring 142.

seldom experiences. Not only does this make for a relaxing and enjoy-able hunt, but it allows the hunter to learn much about the whitetail from firsthand observations.

Still another beneficial aspect of the low-profile nature of stand-hunting is that it causes minimum disruption to the deer in the area hunted. In essence, the effects of hunting pressure are minimized when hunters sit in stands rather than ramble around in the woods. Even a good still-hunter will cause more disruption than the average stand-hunter, if for no other reason than his scent trail. Deer drives obviously cause much disruption for the local denizens. Because stand-hunting generally impacts area deer less than other forms of hunting, deer hunted from stands are more likely to continue normal daylight movement pat-terns longer before reacting adversely to pressure.

Once the right stand site has been selected, which is the real secret to stand-hunting, the hunter's job is to sit perfectly still and quiet and watch for deer. This requires less skill, effort and concentration to achieve acceptable proficiency than do other forms of hunting. This is one of the great appeals of stand-hunting. Anybody can do it and be successful. Sure, a top-notch stand-hunter will enjoy much greater success than a rookie, but even the greenest novice can kill a trophy buck from a well-placed deer stand. For instance, when my old friend, Chip Gerry of Atlanta, Georgia, took his son, Jason, hunting for the first time, Chip stuck him in a portable stand we had recently hung in a grove of acorn-laden oaks on our hunting club. At nine that morning, we heard a shot from Jason's direction. We scurried over. Jason admitted to shooting at a deer that had "something on his head." What an understatement! Fifty yards away lay a 16-pointer! After nearly 10 years, that's still one of the best bucks we've ever taken on that property. Stand-hunting made it possible.

In heavily hunted areas, stand-hunting offers a couple of other advantages worth noting. One, the savvy stand-hunter can pick a strategic ambush point, preferably a place where a barrier or bottleneck channels deer movement, and let the other hunters push deer to him. This is a highly effective way to hunt and can produce any time of the day. By contrast, a still-hunter after heavily hunted deer will find it very difficult to approach them undetected since the deer are sure to be on full alert. Another major plus for stand-hunting in pressured regions is the safety factor. A stationary hunter, especially one perched in a treestand, runs less risk of being mistaken for a deer by an irresponsible hunter than someone moving around on the ground.

DISADVANTAGES

The disadvantages of stand-hunting are few and relatively minor. And, they are pretty much limited to specific situations and relate primarily to the lack of mobility. One such drawback is that a buck occasionally can get by a stationary stand-hunter without allowing him a shot, but that same deer may be killable for a still-hunter who can move on the buck. This situation is most likely to occur during the breeding period when a preoccupied buck is after a hot doe. Or at least, this is the time when a still-hunter has the best chance of successfully catching up with a traveling buck. Of course, a stand-hunter always has the option of leaving his stand and going after the buck.

Another drawback to stand-hunting as compared to still-hunting is that the stand-hunter is limited to only one place during the time he's in a particular stand. If his stand site is a good one, all is well. If it's a bad one, all his eggs are in that one bad basket. The mobility of still-hunters increases the likelihood that at least some of their time will be spent in good areas.

Also because of the lack of mobility, the wind can be an uncontrollable problem for the stand-hunter. Once in the stand, the wind can change to an unfavorable direction and leave the stand-hunter "hanging in the breeze." A still-hunter, on the other hand, can alter the course of his hunt to combat wind shifts. Also, during times of little or no

Elevation can offer big advantages to the stand-hunter, but with height comes the risk of injury in a fall. This hunter is using a portable "climbing" stand without a safety belt. Although the use of a safety belt is a bother, it would save many hunters from serious injury. Photo courtesy of **North American Whitetail.**

wind, scent clouds can form around a stand, creating an invisible barrier to approaching deer. The mobile still-hunter can move beyond this lingering scent, but a hunter sitting in a stand must either relocate or sit there and take his now-reduced chances.

Most other knocks on stand-hunting are more personal or circumstantial rather than real disadvantages. For instance, some hunters find it difficult to sit still for prolonged periods of time. Some find the passive nature of stand-hunting to be boring, especially if they aren't seeing deer. But, there is one problem with stand-hunting, specifically hunting from treestands, that is not only real but life-threatening. It is the danger of falling!

Unquestionably, the greatest cause of whitetail hunting injuries is from falling out of treestands. These accidents are far more common than most people realize, and the danger is very real. I personally have several friends who have suffered injury due to falls from treestands. Two of them were seriously injured. Steve Mason of Atlanta, Georgia, slipped on a wet rung and fell 20 feet. The result was a broken back and a crushed foot. Even now, years later, he has only partially recovered. Another friend, a well-known outdoor writer, suffered injuries from a treestand fall that eventually contributed to his death. These and many other similar cases are reason enough to take every precaution when hunting from treestands or any other elevated stand. Use common sense. Don't take any chances. Don't trust unknown stands, whether they are permanent or portable. Don't climb any stand that is physically difficult for you to negotiate. Don't go any higher than necessary. Use extreme caution in wet or cold weather. Let someone know where you are hunting. And, always use a safety belt in stands higher than about 10 feet.

WHEN AND WHERE

Stand-hunting is effective anytime and anywhere whitetails are hunted. And, the effectiveness of this method is relatively constant throughout the season and from place to place. There are, however, times and places where still-hunting or even drives can vie with stand-hunting as the method of choice. Let's look first at when stand-hunting shines brightest.

Generally speaking, stand-hunting is the preferred hunting method during the pre-rut period when whitetails are on predictable feeding patterns. This is also the case during the post-rut period, although drives can compete in effectiveness once the deer take to thick cover following the rut.

When the rut starts up, the choice of hunting methods may not be as clear. During the scraping period, the nod has to go to stand-hunting as the most dependable method but there are places and circumstances where still-hunting can be just as productive. Once the breeding period begins, I personally prefer to still-hunt if conditions allow, although I know many excellent hunters who opt to stand-hunt. At this time, the choice of hunting methods boils down to a matter of existing hunting conditions and personal preference.

About the only time I don't like to sit in a deer stand is when I have reason to believe the deer simply are not moving, like on unseasonably hot, humid days. If the deer are not moving, it's unlikely one will come

When hunting the pre-rut feeding pattern, stand-hunting is the best option, but it will still take a double dose of good fortune to catch a buck like this 150-class eight-pointer out in the open. Photo by Mike Riggs.

by your stand. During such times, forced movement — deer drives or simply walking up deer — is the best hope.

Now, the "where." Stand-hunting will produce the desired results anywhere — in open country, moderate cover or in thickets. But as a general rule, stand-hunting gains increasingly greater advantages over still-hunting as the cover hunted becomes thicker. Why? The thicker the cover, the closer the hunter has to be to a buck to see him. At close quarters, a stationary stand-hunter is far less likely to be seen or heard by a buck than a hunter moving through thick cover. Drives, of course, can be an effective means of rousting deer from thick cover ... or open cover for that matter.

THE HOW-TO'S OF STAND-HUNTING

It is interesting to contrast the skills required to be a good stand-hunter to those needed to be a successful still-hunter. Since the most critical part of stand-hunting is stand selection, the stand-hunter must be

Since the real key to stand-hunting is picking the right stand, the stand-hunter must be skilled at gathering and interpreting information and at formulating strategy that will put him in the right place at the right time to intercept a trophy buck.

highly skilled at gathering and interpreting information about the land and the deer on that land. He must then formulate a strategy that will put him in exactly the right place at the right time to intercept a trophy buck. The stand-hunter's most important contribution to success comes before the hunt begins when he chooses the right stand.

While a still-hunter needs to be able to gather and interpret enough information about the land and the deer to decide which general area he should apply his stalking skills, he is not burdened with having to pick a specific spot on which to stake his hopes. The highest level of skill required for a still-hunter does not come into play until the hunt actually begins. Then, he has to bring all his stealth, woodsmanship, instincts and self-control to bear as he enters the whitetail's world on the deer's terms. In short, the still-hunter has to be a master tactician; the stand-hunter a master strategist.

Now, I am not saying that no skill is required to hunt from a stand once it has been selected. Without question, a skilled stand-hunter will see more trophy bucks and be able to kill a higher percentage of the bucks seen (if he wants to) than a hunter with less skill. But, the fact remains that a higher level of skill is required to consistently take trophy bucks during the actual hunt while still-hunting than while stand-hunting. This is born out every year by the many trophy bucks shot by green-horns placed in good stands by the real hunters who did the critical work of stand selection. Put those same inexperienced hunters alone on the ground trying to sneak up on trophy whitetails, and the number of big bucks they would kill would drop drastically.

There are two distinct aspects to stand selection. One is finding the best area to hunt. The second is determining exactly where in that area the best spot is for the stand. We'll start with the area selection.

Choosing The Area

In choosing the best area to locate your stand, first figure out what the deer are doing. For the most part, three factors will determine this. One, the time of the year, i.e., the seasonal pattern the deer are currently on. Two, hunting pressure. Three, the nature of the place being hunted.

In previous chapters, we discussed seasonal patterns extensively. Based on deer activity, the fall was broken into four periods — pre-rut, scraping, breeding and post-rut. We looked at what deer, particularly trophy bucks, were likely to be doing during each of these periods. These seasonal activity patterns should serve as the beginning point in your search for the best areas to locate stands. You must determine where in the time line of fall activity patterns the deer are ... or will be when you hunt them. Deer movement patterns change during each of the periods, and an area that is good in one period may

In choosing the best area for your stand, first figure out what the deer are doing. Three factors largely determine this — time of year, hunting pressure and the nature of the place being hunted. This big Wisconsin buck was interrupted as he worked a scrapeline along the edge of a fallow field. Unless pressure disrupts his pattern, a stand-hunter would have a chance to wait out this buck. Photo by Bill Kinney.

or may not be worth hunting in another.

Once you understand what the deer should be doing based on seasonal patterns, another factor comes into play that will determine to a large degree what the deer are actually doing. That factor is hunting pressure. It must play a big role in what areas you ultimately select for your stands.

As we've discussed, the greater the pressure, the more nocturnal the deer become and the more they cling to thick cover. This forces the stand-hunter to adapt his strategy to the existing level of hunting pressure. We've talked much about this previously, so here we will only take a brief, general look at how various levels of hunting pressure affect stand selection during the different fall activity periods.

Where pressure is low, deer carry on their normal routine without much disruption from man. They move freely during daylight hours and may expose themselves in fairly thin cover or even in the open. A stand-hunter should focus his attention on areas in the immediate vicinity of important food sources. This is true during all four periods of fall movement. During the pre-rut feeding pattern, hunt in and around food sources that have big rubs near them. When scraping activity starts, look for active scrapelines near food sources that have heavy doe use. Hunt these same areas when the breeding period gets underway and even into the early part of the post-rut period. When breeding activity ceases and the bucks lay up to recover from the rigors of the rut, the best place to ambush a buck may be near bedding areas in thick cover. But in places with low pressure, it won't take long for bucks to return to the obvious food sources, even though they are likely to be using them less during daylight hours.

Moderate hunting pressure will cause deer, especially trophy bucks, to curtail daylight movement, to become less predictable and to be less likely to expose themselves in thin cover and in the open. This complicates things for the trophy hunter. The food sources per se become less dependable as the hub of daylight activity, but because of continued nighttime use, the areas around the food sources remain important to hunters. During the pre-rut, look for big rubs around the in-cover staging areas near food sources where several trails come together. Also, back-track the trails leading into these staging areas and look for promising rublines. These same staging areas and associated trails are likely places to locate active scrapelines during the scraping period. During the breeding period, areas with scrapes, big rubs and plenty of does are the places to be. Such places are likely to be in association with food sources, but stands must be located well back in cover. During the post-rut, chances for a trophy buck drop drastically even when pressure is only moderate. The best bet is to set up in or near thick cover. Hunt either trails leading from bedding areas, the bedding areas themselves or in-cover feeding areas near bedding areas.

Heavy hunting pressure causes deer to become almost nocturnal and disrupts their normal routines. Basically, the hunter has two options.

One, seek out sanctuaries (even if they're only small areas of thick cover other hunters seldom venture into) that escape the direct impact of the pressure. Two, turn the pressure to your advantage by letting other hunters push deer to you. This means finding bottlenecks or other high-odds escape routes that take advantage of the hunter traffic patterns.

Once you have a general understanding of what the deer are doing on the land you are hunting, focus your efforts on finding the best area to put your stand. This is when aerial photos, topographic maps and on-the-ground scouting come into play. Try to identify feeding areas, bedding areas, likely travel routes and features that tend to concentrate or funnel deer or otherwise cause them to expose themselves. I try especially hard to identify pressure zones and possible sanctuaries. Upon locating prospective areas, scout them thoroughly for deer or deer sign.

Selecting The Stand Site

When you've found an area where you hope to ambush a trophy buck, the exact stand site must be chosen. Proper placement of the stand is critical to the outcome of the hunt. This is the finishing touch on the process of stand selection that will make all your previous efforts worthwhile or a waste of time. There are many factors to consider.

Ground blind or elevated stand? In most cases, an elevated platform is far more effective than a ground blind since deer are less likely to see, hear or smell a hunter lurking high above the ground. However, there are times when elevation is not practical or necessary. In a couple of states, it is illegal to hunt from an elevated stand. Often, a low-hanging forest canopy results in better visibility from the ground than from up a tree. A person may be physically unable to climb an elevated stand. In the case of treestands, there may not be a suitable tree anywhere around. In hilly terrain, elevation can sometimes be realized while sitting on the ground. Also, distance tends to minimize the advantages of height, at least as far as detection by the deer is concerned. Occasionally, the wind blows so hard that the hunter is better off on the ground if only for the sake of his nerves. And, considerations such as convenience (a big tree trunk is mighty handy) and safety (it's a short fall to the ground from the ground) are also pluses for ground blinds. If I can hunt just as well from the ground, I'll do so, but most often, elevation gives the hunter a definite edge.

Although trophy bucks sometimes avoid permanent stands because of excessive hunting pressure, such stands do have their place. Covered blinds, for instance, offer the advantages of convenience, silent entry, size enough for more than one hunter, comfort, safety and concealment. If not overhunted, trophy bucks can be taken from even conspicuous permanent stands like this one. Photo by Mike Biggs.

What's the right height for an elevated stand? That depends. The surrounding forest canopy (if any), the ground cover, the cover available to conceal the stand, the terrain, the safety of the set-up and even the weather can all be factors. Generally, the higher you are, the better visibility you have and the less likely you are to be picked off by deer. Yet, too much elevation can result in a bad shot angle, especially for bowhunters. Also, the inherent risk factor associated with elevated stands argues against maximum height. As I get older, I find myself hanging stands only as high as is necessary to get the job done. Usually, that means a height of 10 to 12 feet. Frankly, I don't like to hunt stands much over 12 feet high. I figure I've got at least a chance of walking away from a fall of that height or less.

Permanent versus portable, which is best? Neither. I know that statement may cause many hunters to pop a collar button since it has become fashionable in recent years to slam permanent stands. But, the truth is that neither permanents nor portables are "better." They both have pluses and minuses.

It is frequently said that trophy bucks are not likely to be killed from permanent stands, especially those that have been there for a long time. The logic is that since permanent stands are in the woods all the time, and often rather poorly concealed, wise old bucks know they are there and avoid them. True, trophy bucks do avoid some permanent stands, but the reason is not just because the stands are there all the time and the bucks know it. The real problem is that old nemesis of trophy hunters — hunting pressure. Some permanent stands simply get hunted a lot. The deer detect the repeated presence of humans in the stands and learn to avoid the area. The more pressure from a stand, the more the deer avoid the area. If hunters repeatedly hunted from the same ground blind or portable, deer would soon learn to avoid those stand sites as well. Generally, it is true that a permanent blind does tend to attract pressure because of its convenience, both for the one who built it and for other hunters as well. And, a permanent blind does give the deer a specific point on which to focus their attention once they've come to suspect danger from the area. Yet, the problem does not in itself lie in the fact that a permanent stand is left year-round in the woods. It's a problem of hunting pressure being repeatedly focused on one spot.

Permanent stands have their place. They offer the advantages of convenience, silent entry (once built), size enough for more than one hunter, comfort, safety (if well-constructed and maintained) and a solid rifle rest. They can be customized to the point of being windproof, waterproof and even heated, making them comfortable enough to stay in all day. During recent years, I've grown to greatly enjoy taking less experienced hunters after whitetails. Ever tried to get two or three hunters up a tree in a portable? You also can send or take a person unfamiliar with the area to a permanent stand without a lot of hassle, and he or she has a good chance of success.

Portables certainly have their advantages, too. The flexibility they offer is a big one. With a portable stand, a hunter can freely move and precisely place his stand in response to fresh sign and changing patterns. And, the mobility of a portable allows a hunter to move around through-

The mobility of portable stands allows a hunter to move around throughout the season and constantly hunt "fresh" places. Even in the absence of suitable trees for a treestand, portables like this tripod stand are still an option. This Texas hunter, who is more exposed than I would like, is watching a "sendero," which is a type of cutline. Photo by Dick Idol.

out the season and constantly stay in "fresh" places. This is a huge benefit when hunting trophy bucks. Even in the absence of suitable trees for a treestand, portables are still an option. For instance, the movable tripod stand, though not very portable, can be used in virtually any type country and placed wherever you'd like. Happily, there's a portable design to fit just about every need or personal preference and most are fairly safe and user friendly.

Another plus for portables is that they can be used in places where a permanent stand is either impractical or forbidden altogether. Most commercial timber companies do not want nails or spikes driven into trees on their property. State and national forests usually prohibit the construction of permanent stands. Fortunately, many portables do not damage the tree.

If the place you're hunting is hunted by others, portables offer an important benefit. Since they can be taken down after each hunt, other hunters can't hunt your stand. True, they may find and hunt your area, but at least you haven't marked your spot with something as obvious as a stand. My partner, Steve Vaughn, found out the hard way that leaving a portable stand in a tree after a hunt can invite trouble. While scouting a remote part of a wildlife management area in Middle Georgia several years ago, Steve came across some good buck sign, over which he hung his Baker climbing stand. Before daylight the next morning, Steve arrived at his stand, which was hanging waist high on the trunk of a big pine. As he prepared to "hug and pull" his way up the tree, Steve got a shock.

"Hey," came a voice from above. Steve directed his flashlight toward the voice, and there sat another hunter … in the very tree Steve had hung his stand!

In disbelief, Steve responded, "What are you doing up there? Didn't you see my stand in this tree?"

A long pause followed. Then, the guy finally answered in a most accommodating manner. "Tell you what. Come on up. You can watch the pines and I'll watch the hardwoods."

Steve declined his gracious offer and left his stand-jumping buddy with a few sage words of advice to ponder.

On the negative side, portables tend to be small (or else they're not very portable) and are rather basic in their comfort amenities. They require some physical exertion and ability to put up, which can pose a problem for those less athletically inclined. Also, some portables fail to provide good rifle rests. Others are prone to be noisy while being set up, especially climbing stands. The noise factor is why I generally prefer screw-in steps (where allowed) and the lock-on type stands. The small lock-ons also tend to be more portable. If noise is not much of a consideration and the available trees don't have a lot of low limbs, climbing stands work well. Some of the ladder-type portables, though a chore to carry, are exceptionally easy to use and quite safe and comfortable.

One of the most common mistakes in stand selection is placing the stand too close to the expected deer activity. By doing so, the odds of being picked off by the buck you're after or by lesser deer entering the area are greatly increased. Such unnecessary detection also hastens the demise of that stand site since the deer will quickly learn to avoid it. Obviously, bowhunters have to position themselves pretty close to the action, but gun hunters often can set up some distance away and

Bowhunters obviously have to set up close to the action, but not so with gun hunters. One of the most common mistakes in stand selection is placing the stand too close to expected deer activity. This increases the hunter's chances of being detected and hastens the demise of the stand site since the deer will quickly learn to avoid it. Photo by Tom Evans courtesy of **North American Whitetail.**

still be in full command of the area, particularly when hunting crop fields. Therefore, I always place my stand as far from the expected deer activity as is practical for good visibility and a good shot. The beauty of this is that you very often can watch deer throughout a hunt period without them even knowing you are there. If your approach route allows you to enter and depart unnoticed and without crossing the deer's trail, such a stand can be hunted repeatedly without the telltale effects of hunting pressure.

An example of such a stand is one I hunt called the Wolf Pine. The stand itself is a roomy, comfortable structure built in a large, limby pine tree situated on top of a hill in the middle of a thick hedgerow. A 250-yard long, 150-yard wide crop field (usually planted in soybeans and/or winter wheat) begins just downhill from the stand and is bordered by thick woods. The stand can be approached and entered without the deer in the field or the surrounding woods ever knowing a hunter is around. The stand could have been situated along the edge of the field nearer the main deer activity, but if it had been, the deer quickly would have reacted to this intrusion and abandoned the field. As it is, only an occasional shot disrupts the tranquillity of that field.

Another critical aspect of selecting a stand site is the approach route. I'm always amazed how many hunters will go to great lengths to set up their stand in just the right spot only to smell up the place by walking through the middle of the deer activity. Some hunters even follow the deer's trail to the stand. Others like to check out the area immediately before getting into their stand, leaving an invisible scent barrier to turn back approaching deer. Still others choose routes to their stand that take them through bedding areas or staging grounds, spooking the very deer they hope to have amble by their stand unawares.

Two factors are important in selecting an approach route. One, choose the route that will cause the least disturbance to area deer, or at least to the buck you are after. That means the route should pass through the country least likely to harbor deer or to have deer pass through en route to the stand. Noise should be held to a minimum so try to avoid thick, difficult terrain as you near the stand. Two, make every effort to see that your approach route does not cross the trails or the activity area you expect the deer to use. You must assume that anywhere you walk an invisible wall of scent is left on the ground or vegetation you brush against. You must also assume that any deer that hits that wall of scent will smell you and become alerted. Envision how that wall of scent affects deer movement in the entire area as well as around your stand. With that in mind, pick the route that will have the least impact.

There are steps that can be taken to reduce the lingering scent problem. Cover scents, washing both yourself and your clothing with odorless soap and putting your hunting clothes outside or in plastic bags with cedar chips or pine boughs are examples of things that may help. Wearing rubber-bottomed boots definitely reduces the ground scent. Avoiding contact with vegetation reduces the scent left behind. And, there are certain conditions when scent dissipates fairly fast. Hot, dry weather is one such time. Generally, scent lingers longer in the morning than in the afternoon, mainly because mornings are cooler and more humid. But when all is said and done, always assume that a buck will smell your trail if he crosses it. You may be pleasantly surprised at times, but don't count on it.

Wind direction is another controlling factor in stand location. I operate on the simple assumption that if a deer is downwind of me he will smell me. I do not depend on cover scents or even height to alter that fact. I try to do all possible to prevent deer from getting downwind, either during their approach or upon their arrival to the area I'm watching.

If a stand is to be hunted repeatedly over a period of time, the best bet is to select a site favorable for the prevailing wind. In most places during the fall, the wind blows more often from one general direction than from others. Autumn winds in Georgia, for instance, most frequently come from a westerly direction. Most of my long-term stands are on the eastern side of where I expect the deer to show. It is not always possible to choose a stand site favorable for prevailing winds. If the place is good enough, put the stand up anyway and only hunt it when the wind is right. When hanging a stand to hunt that particular day, you can obviously position it to take advantage of the wind direction at that time.

There are some basics about wind that trophy hunters should know. First, a little wind is not bad. When hunting in close quarters, I much prefer to have a light, steady wind than no wind at all. If the stand is positioned right for the wind, the scent is blown away from where the deer are to appear. In the absence of a breeze, a scent cloud will sometimes mushroom out from the stand and encompass at least some of the area being hunted. In reasonably flat country during periods of relatively stable weather, the early morning and late afternoon hours tend to be calm even though the wind may blow during midday. This sometimes gives hunters a chance to hunt certain stands during the prime early and late hours despite the current wind direction. In hilly country, the wind is notoriously fickle but thermals can be predicted with some consistency. Thermals are winds caused by the heating and cooling of the earth's surface. As the ground warms in the morning, the air rises, causing the wind to blow uphill. In the late afternoon, the ground surface cools and a downhill wind is the result. Also, abrupt changes in major surface features, such as isolated hills and the edges of lakes and large fields, will cause erratic winds or eddies.

If possible, I like to have the sun in the deer's eyes and to my back. If I can't have the sun behind me, I at least try not to have it in my eyes. When a low sun shines fully on a deer or a hunter, either will fairly glow. I'd rather the deer glow than me. Other considerations frequently override the preference for sun position, but I always try to either take advantage of the sun or neutralize its impact.

One of the most neglected aspects of stand-hunting is preparation for the shot. Arrangements for a rifle rest should be high on the list of concerns. Can you see and shoot in any direction the buck is likely to show himself? Think ahead and prepare for success.

Stand cover and concealment are important considerations in selecting a stand site. To start with, be certain there's adequate cover to break up your outline and to conceal your movement. When hunting from a treestand, I like to have some leafy cover slightly below and in front of me if possible. Always be careful not to silhouette yourself against an open sky. When silhouetted, you become an easy target for searching eyes and even the slightest movement is quickly detected. This is a very common mistake when hunting on the edge of a field. Concealment is especially important when hunting from ground level, where you are in the deer's normal line of view. At the very least, get well back into the shadows and against a background that breaks or confuses the human form. A shining face is one of the biggest giveaways for hunters. Be sure yours is covered or obscured when hunting at close quarters on the ground. Also, I always clear the leaves and debris from ground stands so I can move without making noise.

Hunting A Stand

During my 20-year association with a large Middle Georgia plantation, something in the neighborhood of 1,500 bucks have been taken by plantation guests. Most of these bucks were shot from

Have you ever heard of a mobile elevated stand? That's exactly what a Texas high-rack is. Although easing slowly down ranch roads is the most common way to hunt from a high-rack, I generally prefer to use the high-rack as a stationary stand that can be positioned anyplace I've found good buck sign or seen a buck I want to hunt. I shot this 150-class 10-pointer from a high-rack used in just that manner.

elevated stands placed there by plantation guides. The hunters sitting these stands ranged in skill level from awful to great and everything in-between. Through both direct and indirect experience with these hunters, as well as through my own hunting experiences, I have seen about everything imaginable in stand-hunting. I've seen the things that don't work ... sleeping in the stand, forgetting cartridges, hunting upwind of the deer, walking all around the stand area before settling in, fidgeting on the stand to the point of almost dancing a jig, jumping to one's feet at first sight of a buck, going to the bathroom around and even from the stand, to name but a few. And, I've seen the things that make for success ... things like basic hunting savvy, patience, keen observation and good old horse sense. The things that lead to success are worth further discussion.

To begin with, you must prepare yourself. You need the right clothing to be comfortable during the long period of inactivity while on-stand. In foul weather, you need raingear. In cold weather, warm gloves, boots and headgear are necessary to ward off the shivers. If you're going to be on-stand a long time, lunch or a snack will hold hunger pains at bay. Think ahead about the small things that will help during the hunt. For instance, I always carry a personal pack of Kleenex tissue in my hip pocket for cleaning my eye glasses, binoculars and scope, or for more basic "emergencies." Also, a zip-lock bag can come in mighty handy when the rental time is up on your morning coffee. A small flashlight is not only useful to see by, but it provides a large measure of safety when walking in the woods when it's dark. Even yahoos who might shoot at movement or noise know deer don't carry flashlights.

When I first get into a stand, especially one I'm not very familiar with, I immediately check out the stand and study the area. Where should my primary attention be directed? What area do I give up because of the wind? Are there any long lanes of visibility that may forewarn me that a buck is coming? Where are the blind spots? Am I likely to hear an approaching deer, or do I depend only on sight? What mobility does the stand allow? Does the stand squeak or have any other booby traps to avoid? Based on stand location and stand cover, what movement latitude do I have? Are there any sun problems? Where is the best place for my gun or other equipment? What rifle rests are available for shots in different directions? I try to answer

Max Corder of Atlanta, Georgia, sat in a treestand about 70 yards from an active scrapeline for 3½ days in frigid weather before this buck finally showed. Was he ever worth the wait! The 300-pound Canadian buck grossed 183⅞ and netted 170⅞! He's a typical 14-pointer!

these questions in the beginning so I can focus fully on the task at hand when that trophy makes his appearance.

What about going to the bathroom near the stand? When you've got to go, you've got to go. Just don't go near the stand. Undoubtedly, many hunters have killed big bucks soon after having violated this advice. There's even some speculation that human urine not only doesn't spook deer but may even attract them. Anything is possible, but why risk it?

Smoking while on-stand is an interesting one. I advise against it but not for the reasons usually given. Most people think smoking is taboo because of the smell, but I believe a deer that smells the smoke would probably smell the hunter anyway. The greater problem with smoking is movement. A smoker's arm moves back and forth and is likely to draw the attention of a cautious whitetail.

Some people are not meant to be stand-hunters. They just cannot sit still for any period of time. This is one of the biggest problems we have with hunters on our Georgia plantation. Some are in perpetual motion while on-stand. Others simply get up and leave the stand after a short wait. One hunter actually beat his guide back to the lodge after the guide had put him in a stand and dropped off two other hunters! He said the deer weren't moving. Besides, there were no tracks around his stand! I have a good friend whose sitting quotient is 30 minutes — an hour at the longest. After that, he's brush-busting. And, with all his nervousness and movement comes noise. It's not always loud and constant. It doesn't have to be to keep big whitetails away.

The movement problem is not limited to wholesale activity. A more common problem is sudden or rapid movement while on-stand. Whitetails are extremely adept at picking up movement. The swatting of a mosquito, a sudden reach for a rifle, an innocent head scratch … any of these things can give the hunter away. Movement must be slow and deliberate. The hunter should always move as though a deer is within sight of him. More times than I care to remember I have heard a snort or seen a tail upon a careless movement when I had no idea a deer was anywhere around. Does that mean good stand-hunters never move while on-stand? Absolutely not. It's virtually impossible to sit for prolonged periods of time without moving, but you must learn to move ever so slowly. Make it second nature. When you control your movement, you also control your noise.

Stand-hunting requires attentiveness. I know some who read books or listen to the radio (with headphones) while waiting in a stand. They kill deer, too, but not as many or as big as they would if their full attention was focused on the hunt. A serious trophy hunter has to be ready to take advantage of any opportunity. He has to detect any noise or movement and check it out. That's not possible unless he's on a high state of alert.

A couple of years back, I walked to a stand to pick up a visiting hunter after a morning hunt. When I got about 50 yards from his stand, I saw him moving from side to side in the stand, oblivious to my presence. Closer examination revealed that he was mouthing the words to a song and rolling his head with the rhythm, his eyes almost closed. About that same time, I saw movement some 30 yards back of him. It was a suspicious acting doe. Then, a big buck walked nonchalantly into view. I waved my hands at the stander. No response. I took my orange cap off and waved it. He still didn't see me. The buck stopped no more than 20 yards behind the would-be star of the Grand Ole Opry, whose whole body was now rocking with the "music." The big eight-pointer stared first at my buddy in the tree then at me. In desperation, I yelled, "Fred, behind you!"

With that, his rifle, which was laying across his lap, set sail end over end into a briar thicket below the stand. In the calamity, the buck and doe decamped for safer parts. The melodical hunter steadfastly refused to believe a buck had been anywhere near his stand and chided me thoroughly for "sneaking up" on him and scaring the bejiminies out of him.

Many stand-hunters drop the ball when an opportunity at a trophy buck finally presents itself. That burst of adrenalin that comes when they first see a buck puts them into high gear. Forget moving slowly. Forget staying quiet. The only thought is to grab that rifle and get a shot off as quickly as possible. Many an easy shot has turned into little more than a harmless salute from over-anxiousness. When that buck comes into view, it's time for the hunter to carefully calculate each move and to avoid any noise. The rifle must be brought into play ever so slowly. With an unsuspecting buck in sight, now's the time to place that shot carefully from a rifle steadied to dampen the effects of quaking nerves. This is payoff time, but it's also the time when a hunter must quell that old foe — buck fever. That's easier said than done. After all, that feeling and that moment are what hunting is all about.

Chapter 18

Deer Drives
Forcing Success

MY FIRST REAL DEER DRIVE accounted for my second buck and taught me a couple of valuable lessons I have never forgotten. The year was 1969. Joe DuBois, my wife's cousin, had invited me to accompany him on a deer drive on their 6,000-acre deer club along the Tombigbee River in southwestern Alabama. I eagerly accepted.

As Joe and I bounced down the narrow woods road to the camphouse deep in the swamp, the headlights of the Bronco illuminated an eerie world of wafting fog, inky black pools of water and huge, grotesque tree trunks overhung by moss-draped limbs. A feeling of mystery and gloom hung heavy in the air. Suddenly, the swamp's spell over me was broken when four deer flashed across the beams of our heaving headlights. I remembered why I was there, and the feeling of impending gloom gave way to anticipation about what the morning might bring.

By daybreak, about 50 hunters had gathered at the makeshift camphouse. At least that many dogs of assorted size and origin barked and growled from their boxes, eager to get on with the morning's festivities. A group of dog men and club leaders, which included Joe, stood off to the side and mapped out the coming hunt. Just after sunrise, their meeting

Deer drives can be fun and exciting and an occasion for socializing with hunting companions. If everything goes well, they can also be very productive, even small 4 to 12-man drives. Photo by Duncan Dobie courtesy of North American Whitetail.

broke up. Joe walked over to where I stood with about a dozen other anxious hunters.

"I need four standers to go with me," he said, already walking toward his Bronco. "David, you're one of 'em. Come on."

The trek to my stand took 30 minutes through the thick, gumbo mud of the Tombigbee floodplain. On the way there, Joe gave us explicit instructions about what we were to do, foremost being not to leave the stand until he returned. He told us where the drivers and dogs were likely to come from and cautioned us to be sure of our targets.

As I stepped from the Bronco and uncased my 12-gauge automatic, Joe pointed toward the head of a cypress-studded slough filled with water black from tannic acid. "Get next to one of those big water oaks about 30 yards out from the slough," he said. "The river is only about 75 yards farther on. The deer will probably try to come between the river and the slough. You be ready."

I immediately charged my shotgun with No. 1 buckshot. For the next 30 minutes, I waited. Only wood ducks and squirrels kept me entertained. Finally, in the far distance, I heard the sound of dogs hot on the trail of a deer. A few minutes later, another pack sounded out. Then another. Soon, the excited cries of hunting dogs echoed all across the vast hardwood bottom. Shots began to boom out. My nerves were taut as my eyes scanned the grey landscape for movement.

A half dozen does and fawns were first to show up. They slipped by cautiously, maybe 30 yards away between the river and me. No dogs pursued them. They were simply moving out ahead of the commotion.

Ten minutes later, I saw a deer loping toward me along the edge of the slough. When the deer reached the end of the slough, it stopped and looked back toward the sound of the pursuing dogs, still some distance back. Small bumps on his head told me the deer was a button buck. He stared in the direction of the approaching dogs for several seconds. Then, the little buck started loping again ... back down the same trail he had come from ... towards the closing dogs! I thought he must have panicked, though he seemed calm and deliberate. About 40 yards up his backtrail, the fawn leapt from the trail and splashed into the slough. Twenty yards out and mid-body deep, he pulled up behind two big cypress trees. I watched in total fascination.

In less than a minute, four dogs burst onto the scene. They ran the trail unerringly in ragged single file. They sped past the point where the button buck had jumped from the trail. On they came, beyond the place where the buck had first stopped and surveyed the situation. For a brief moment, they seemed to hesitate but then set sail full tilt, probably on the trail of the does and fawns that had passed by earlier. All the while, the button buck looked on calmly from the slough, as though he never doubted the outcome of his ploy.

The dogs were barely out of sight when the fawn walked nonchalantly out of the water back to the trail. He sniffed the ground then looked in the direction of the now fading cries of the dogs. Satisfied, he flicked his tail, turned and walked casually out of sight in the direction from which he had come.

"Wow!" I thought to myself. "If a fawn can do that, what chance do I have of killing a grown buck?"

As I stood next to the water oak and replayed that escape in my mind, a pack of dogs cut loose nearby. A frenzied chase ensued that seemed to go first in one direction then in another. Before long, the sound took a definite direction … straight toward me. I tensed for action. Just in front of me stood a thick stand of cane. Beyond the cane, I soon heard the sound of running animals. The sound grew louder and louder. Then, the cane seemed to come alive as several bodies crashed through it. Suddenly, a buck … followed another … then three, four … then, incredibly, five bucks erupted from the cane 30 yards from me!

Maybe they saw me snap the shotgun to my shoulder, or perhaps they saw the whites of my disbelieving eyes. Whatever the reason, the bucks split. Two went to my right and three to the left. I swung right then left, trying to pick out the best buck. It was all happening too fast. I couldn't be sure. Antlers everywhere. I had to shoot now. My attention focused on the nearest buck. The bead of the shotgun tracked past his shoulder, and the deadly pellets poured forth … once, twice, three times. The buck was almost beyond my view when I saw him arc hard to the right and skid to a halt.

I ran to the buck. He was struggling to get up. Fearing damage to my prized trophy, I didn't want to shoot him again at close range. I leaned my shotgun against a nearby tree and pulled out my Puma Bowie knife, a most ample piece of steel. Frankly, I don't even know what I intended to do, but so armed, I walked cautiously toward the deer. My approach gave the buck the added impetus he needed to finally regain his feet. But rather than attempting to run away, the buck, to my great chagrin, lowered his head and charged! Suddenly, my Bowie knife seemed pitifully inadequate. No time to reach the shotgun. Only one thing to do. I turned tail and lit out, darting among the trees to elude my determined pursuer. Just when I feared my best broken-field moves weren't going to be enough, I noticed the noise behind me had ceased. The buck had gone down again … to my undying relief.

I caught my breath and tried to regain my composure … and my gun, which stood only yards from the buck. I circled slowly around the buck, trying to reach the shotgun. Once more, he struggled to his feet. Maybe it was foolish, certainly desperate, but I rushed around to the side of the buck as he turned to face me. From a distance of six feet, I threw the knife toward the buck's chest. I didn't wait to see the results. My flight carried me near the shotgun, and I grabbed it as I passed. Even as I wheeled around to shoot, I realized the buck was not in pursuit. I looked back to see his last kick. The knife had somehow found its mark.

Deer drives work. These bucks were all taken on small drives during an Alberta hunt. The largest buck was a near-record 15-pointer taken by my South Florida hunting pal, George Cooper (second from the front). George made an excellent 200-yard running shot to kill the buck.

Besides shooting a fine old buck, a 200-pound seven-pointer, on that, my first deer drive, I learned two lessons that are still with me to this day. One, if given time to maneuver, whitetails are fully capable of thwarting the best efforts of a deer drive, as the little button buck had so clearly demonstrated. Even today, I still consider the trickery of that fawn to be one of the most remarkable acts of cunning by a wild animal I have ever witnessed. Two, never approach a wounded buck when your gun rests uselessly against a tree!

Since that day many years ago, I have been on countless deer drives of all sizes and types. Certainly, not all have been as exciting or as successful as that first one. And although I would still enjoy dog hunting for deer, I seldom do it anymore. It just doesn't fit my style of deliberate, controlled trophy hunting. Instead, I prefer small, carefully planned and executed drives involving 4 to 12 hunters. Here, we will focus on this type of drive.

PROS AND CONS

Deer drives can be fun and exciting and an occasion for socializing with hunting buddies. But, the one overriding advantage drives offer is that they can force deer to move and expose themselves to hunters. Other hunting methods are pretty much at the mercy of the deer's natural, voluntary movement. With deer drives, success does not depend on whether or not deer are moving on their own. This is why the deer drive is a uniquely valuable weapon for trophy hunters in certain situations.

Deer drives are not infallible, however. In fact, trophy bucks are not easy to kill on a drive. Given any advance warning, flaws in planning or execution or breaches in the drive or stand lines, a trophy buck usually will find a way to slip the noose. If there are any miscues, the success of the drive becomes dependent upon nothing more than blind luck. That's a poor bet when dealing with a trophy whitetail.

While the forced movement of deer can be an undeniable plus for drives, this hunting method also brings with it some significant cons. First, drives disrupt the natural deer movement patterns of the area. This can cause the buck you are hunting to change his routine, become more nocturnal or even leave the area. To be fair, one drive will not necessarily result in the full realization of these ills. Much depends on the level of disruption, but expect a break in normal deer patterns for at least a couple of days following a drive of any significance. Repeated drives are sure to accelerate the negative effect of hunting pressure. In short, if a drive fails to get the desired results, the buck you're after is very likely to be even harder to kill in subsequent efforts.

Another negative associated with deer drives is that the element of individual skill is at least partially negated. Why? With several hunters involved in the pursuit of a buck on a drive, it becomes something of a

Natural deer movement patterns are often disrupted following a drive. For this reason, I don't like to stand-hunt or still-hunt an area soon after a drive. On the positive side, however, a drive can force deer into the sights of hunters whether or not the deer are moving of their own accord. Photo by Curt Helmick.

crap shoot as to who will end up shooting him. At the very least, competition is increased. It's no longer one hunter against one buck. Now, several hunters have a more or less equal chance at a given buck. Sure, certain things can be done to tilt the odds in favor of one person or the other, but when a trophy buck is forced to move, nobody really knows for sure what he's going to do. While a drive may increase the overall odds of killing a certain buck, it may well reduce your chances of being the one who pulls the trigger.

In addition, drives are logistically difficult. First, you have to get together a drive party of sufficient number and ability to properly drive an area. That's not always easy. Once you've got a group together, getting the drive underway can be something of a quagmire. Instructions aren't followed. People get lost. Everybody wants to stand. Nobody wants to drive. The principle is simple: the more people involved, the more complicated something becomes.

I hunt trophy whitetails for reasons other than just killing a buck. For me, the challenge of pitting my skills against a capable adversary in his own environment is a big part of the hunt. Also, I like to see nature work. I enjoy the serenity and peace of being alone in the wilds. Deer drives, at least the larger ones, don't allow much of the aesthetic side of hunting and observing nature. To me, that's a strike against drives.

Lastly, deer drives can be dangerous, although they don't have to be. If the hunters are experienced and follow instructions, a well-planned deer drive is no more dangerous than any other form of hunting. However, if deer are moving around helter-skelter among closely grouped, excited hunters who have little idea where the other hunters are, the formula for disaster is in place.

WHEN AND WHERE

Like stand-hunting, drives can be effective anytime and anyplace. But, there are certain times and places that are best for deer drives and there are times and places where drives are not the method of choice. Let's first look at the "when."

Because of the disruptive nature of drives, I had rather not still-hunt or stand-hunt an area after it has been driven, at least not immediately afterwards. Therefore, if I'm planning to hunt an area over a period of time, I prefer to hold off on drives until the end of the time I'm hunting. If it's a place I am going to hunt all season long, I'll wait until the tail end of the season before putting on drives. Besides, by the end of season, pressure often has suppressed natural deer movement to the point that forced movement is the best alternative anyway.

There are situations where the disturbance stemming from deer drives is not much of a factor in timing. Hunters with access to plenty of real estate can put on drives anytime and still have other undisturbed places to still-hunt or stand-hunt if they choose. In heavily hunted areas where deer patterns are disrupted from the outset of season, nothing is gained by delaying drives. This is one of the reasons why drives are so popular in certain areas of the East, most notably in Pennsylvania. There, forced movement accounts for most deer, and deer drives are the best way to create and "control" forced movement.

If disruption of the area is not a concern, when is the best time for drives? Anytime deer will not move on their own becomes a logical time to drive. There are times when deer simply lay low and the chances of catching one on the move of his own accord are slim. One such time is when several unseasonably hot, humid days fall in succession. If you want to see a buck then, you almost have to kick him up ... literally!

On a broader level, the relative effectiveness of drives compared to other hunting methods is impacted by the time of year, i.e., the seasonal activity patterns of the deer. Generally speaking, the time when drives really shine is during the post-rut period. At this time, daytime deer movement is at a low ebb. The bucks are usually bedded in the thickest cover around. This bedding cover often is fairly easy to identify, allowing a drive to focus on the most likely areas. Also, escaping deer are easier to see during the post-rut since winter's bite has denuded the trees and underbrush. In many places, snow may be available to help direct a drive to the best areas and, of course, to aid in tracking. Often, there simply are no better options than a deer drive during the post-rut period.

Relative to other hunting methods, drives also can stack up well in the pre-rut period. Oftentimes, trophy bucks will cling to heavy cover during the daylight when on their pre-rut feeding pattern. This is especially true during warmer weather. If the bucks aren't huntable on or around food sources, a drive may well be the best solution for a pre-rut buck.

During the scraping and breeding periods of the rut, drives work very well because deer movement is at a peak. And, deer on the move are always easier to drive than bedded deer, which are prone to hold tight and let danger pass. However, that doesn't necessarily make drives the best choice of hunting methods during the scraping and breeding periods. Why? Since natural deer movement is at its zenith during the rut, still-hunting and stand-hunting are also at their best then. Because of the negatives associated with deer drives, many trophy hunters, including myself, generally opt to hunt deer one-on-one when they are moving well on their own. During such times, I feel my personal chances of

The best set-up for deer drives is where accessible strips or blocks of cover can be isolated and surrounded. In eastern Wyoming, Dick Idol found that kind of situation and shot this whopper buck on a small drive. Photo courtesy of Dick Idol.

scoring are better by going it alone than as a member of a drive party Nonetheless, drives can be very effective during the rut. It's just that other methods can be as good or better.

As a general rule, morning drives tend to be better than afternoon drives. This is because morning drives usually take place while the deer arc still on the move. Afternoon drives, on the other hand, often start when the deer are still bedded, making them more difficult to move.

Deer can be driven anywhere they are found, but some places lay out better for drives than others. The best set-up is where accessible strips or blocks of cover can be isolated and surrounded without first running the deer out. With some looking, such situations can be found throughout the whitetail's range, but the farmland of the Midwest and Central Canada is the classic driving country. It's no accident that deer

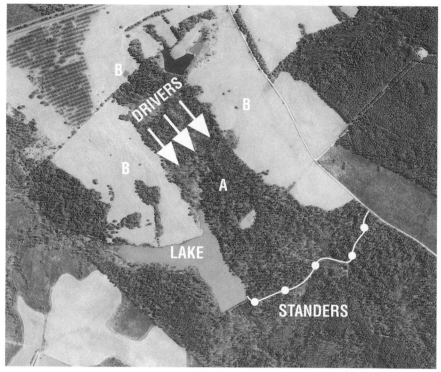

Aerials and/or topos are big aids in planning a deer drive. The drive depicted on this aerial photo is actually one of the most productive on the Georgia plantation I work with. Area A is a strip of thick woods about 400 yards wide and a mile long. This strip of woods is bordered mostly by crop fields (Area B), but a large lake provides an important barrier along part of one side. Four or five drivers are needed to push the deer, and the same number of standers can cover the escape routes. Over the years, some good bucks have fallen on this drive. The best stand is the one nearest the lake. It can get wild there!

drives are a mainstay in those regions. The riverbottoms of the plains and prairies are also ideal for drives. The agricultural regions of the South and East frequently lay out well for successful pushes.

Large, unbroken tracts of timber, especially those with limited access, are the hardest to drive. Places like this are very hard to get standers and drivers into, at least quietly. Deer often evacuate the drive area while the drive is being set up. In homogeneous woods, it also can be rather difficult to predict where the deer may be bedded or where they will go when pushed. Without obvious reference points, drive lines often go askew and both standers and drivers get lost.

When choosing a drive area, select a place that includes some thick bedding cover. Although open feeding areas, such as acorn-producing hardwoods, may be loaded with deer sign, the deer, especially trophy bucks, are not likely to be caught there at the time of day most drives take place. Thick cover is necessary for consistent success.

THE DRIVE

Let's start by examining some prerequisites for a successful drive. First, the hunter should realize that whitetails are seldom driven in a straight line for any distance. They are really just moved around or stirred up. If given much time or distance to work with, deer will habitually double back on the drivers in an attempt to bring their keen senses to bear in their evasive maneuvers. If there are any cracks in the drive line, a trophy buck is very likely to slip through. For this reason, small drives of the type we're discussing here usually are most effective when limited to distances of less than a mile.

Natural barriers offer huge advantages in driving deer. Major roads, gullies, large fields, lakes, rivers, shear bluffs and other barriers that deer are reluctant to cross or cannot cross can be used to funnel deer to standers. To a large degree, the availability of barriers will determine the number of hunters needed to effectively drive a given area (or put another way, the size area a party can drive). Barriers reduce the escape options of deer and allow both the drivers and the standers to focus only on the remaining "live areas." With the right layout of barriers, a few hunters can drive relatively large areas and accurately predict where the deer are likely to go.

Someone must be in charge of a drive. This person is called the huntmaster, and ideally, he will be familiar with the area being hunted. He must explain exactly what is expected of each hunter, and his instructions must be fully obeyed. The two inviolate rules of deer drives are to be absolutely certain of your target and to never leave your assigned position once the drive starts.

Planning and organization are critical to the success of a drive. The execution becomes fairly easy if the drive has been well designed and everybody knows what they're to do. Organization not only affects the outcome of an individual drive, but it also will determine how many

Natural barriers, such as lakes, rivers, large fields, etc., offer a huge advantage when driving deer since these barriers can be used to channel or funnel bucks past the standers. Photo by Mike Biggs.

drives a party can put on during a day. Several short, controlled drives usually are better than one or two long, haphazard drives. Because things tend to breakdown after a drive, recovery plans should be laid out for each drive so another one can be quickly organized. Certain hunters should be assigned the responsibility of gathering up the troops in their area. Determine a rendezvous point in advance and have vehicles pre-positioned to avoid long walks and delays after a drive.

Aerial photos and topos are big aids in planning a drive. No amount of words can beat seeing a "picture" of the place to be driven. A sheet of clear acetate is ideal as a map or photo overlay that can be marked with a grease pencil and later erased. Using this, each stander and driver can see where he will be and his relative position to other hunters, which is an important safety factor. Also, compasses can be helpful, especially for keeping drivers on line.

One of the most controversial subjects concerning drives is how hunters should be armed. I've heard hunters say they would not hunt on drives when rifles are used. Others say shotguns with buckshot are worthless cripplers and dangerous to other hunters. The truth is that both rifles and shotguns have a place on deer drives. Overall, the most useful weapon on a deer drive is probably a lightweight rifle topped with a low-power scope, although iron sights are also good in the hands of the right person. My personal favorite drive gun is a .308 Remington pump with a 1½X-5X Leupold on top. Generally speaking, a rifle in the hands of a competent hunter will do anything a shotgun will do and more. The reverse can't be said. However, when I am hunting with inexperienced hunters, I feel better when they carry shotguns with buckshot. Fired from a 12 gauge, buckshot is lethal at ranges of 40 yards or less and is unsurpassed in thick cover, especially when the deer are moving fast. Shotguns loaded with slugs offer no advantage over rifles and are harder to hit with than a load of buckshot. But in areas where rifles are not allowed, slugs would be my choice over buckshot in all but the thickest cover because of their added range. I would choose an auto or pump shotgun in one of the many special deer models.

It is often said that deer always run into the wind when pushed during a drive. While there is some truth to this statement, short deer drives are not necessarily governed by this popular notion. To start with, deer do not always have a chance to head into the wind on short drives. When a buck is first jumped, he will usually run directly away from the danger for some distance before regrouping to work the wind. On a short drive, that first escape run may take the buck to the stand line. Also, if a drive area is thoroughly surrounded and properly stood and driven, the pressure on a buck exists in all directions and is ever-increasing as the drive progresses. In this case, wind direction makes little difference to the outcome of the drive.

There are essentially two kinds of drives — those with both drivers and standers and those with drivers only. The bread-and-butter drive is the one with both drivers and standers, and this "standard" drive has wide application and offers limitless options. Those with drivers only are what I call "line" drives. They are limited in their application and effectiveness but can be useful in certain situations. We'll look briefly at

Big bucks have nerves of steel. While they certainly will run headlong into the unknown if pushed hard enough, trophy bucks prefer to sneak around, work the wind and pick their way through danger. This fine buck is using a hedgerow as cover to sneak out of a drive. Photo by Mike Biggs.

line drives before examining in detail the more useful standard drive. The beauty of the line drive is that it is simple. In this type of drive, hunters line up in a straight or U-shaped line, often within sight of each other, and move in unison through a designated drive area. For safety reasons, three to six hunters are about right for most line drives. Hunters need to be as quiet as possible during the drive.

I frequently use line drives when pushing fallow fields, clearcuts or other semi-open areas with enough ground cover to harbor bedding deer. In predominately timbered regions, bucks tend to be in these open places on windy days when they are nervous in the woods and on cold, bright days when they seek the sun's warmth in the low cover. In the open regions of the West and Midwest, brushy or grassy breaks, canyons and streambeds can hold bucks anytime. These are excellent places for a small party to walk out. To prevent deer from catching their scent before getting within shooting range, drivers should avoid a direct tail wind. Most shots will be at running deer that have been jumped from their beds. Rifles and shotguns with slugs are recommended since shots are sometimes beyond the range of buckshot.

The line drive can be adapted to the low visibility of woodlands by spreading the line out some and slowing the pace. Hunters must rely on their own stealth for success as they move forward very slowly and quietly. The drive is really nothing more than a coordinated still-hunt, but it offers the advantage of having other hunters helping to move deer. If all goes according to plan, a buck trying to circle back on one hunter will bump into another hunter. A crosswind or quartering wind, either front or rear, is best. Shots often are taken at sneaking or slowly moving deer, making rifles the preferred weapon. This type of drive is particularly useful in big woods where positioning standers would be difficult.

Now, the standard drive. This drive consists of a line of drivers trying to move deer toward standers positioned on strategic escape routes. It can be as simple or as complex as the situation dictates. Let's examine the different aspects of planning, implementing and executing a standard drive.

To start with, the huntmaster must evaluate the manpower available to him. How many are in the drive party? What is the ability and experience of the participating hunters? The answers to these questions will largely determine the scope of the drive and its location.

There are no hard-and-fast rules about how many drivers and standers are needed to make a drive, and the two don't have to be the same. A drive can be designed around as few as two hunters. Given enough land, a drive could be put together that would call for 100 or more hunters, but I wouldn't want to be a part of it. Fifteen people or less is a far more realistic number for the kind of drives of interest to trophy hunters. At any rate, the area driven has to be matched to the number of hunters. Too few hunters for the chosen drive area will result in an unsuccessful hunt. Too many can be dangerous. The size, shape and topography of a potential drive area are all factors in determining how many hunters are needed to drive it successfully.

Numbers alone don't determine the capability of a drive party. The ability and experience of the individuals involved are also major considerations. This is not only important in deciding which area to drive, but ability and experience will also determine who drives and who stands and where they drive or stand. Each hunter should be evaluated based on his type weapon, shooting skills, past experience, knowledge of the land, woodsmanship and his physical condition.

Next, the drive area must be selected. The number of hunters in the party and their ability must be factored in, as well as their objectives for the drive. The amount of land and the time available to hunt are considerations. The logistics of setting up the drive and regrouping afterwards go into the decision of where to drive. Attention also should be given to what barriers are available to direct deer movement.

The drive area chosen, it's time to map out strategy for the hunt. The drive routes and stand positions must be identified. The wind is a factor here. I can accept almost any wind on short drives except a direct tail wind to the standers. Given a choice, I would prefer a crosswind to the drivers and standers or a quartering tail wind to the drivers. How standers and drivers are to reach their positions needs to be clearly laid out, preferably by using aerials or topos. Safe shooting zones must be described, and all hunters must be acquainted with the safety rules. The timing of the drive should be established and a rendezvous point predetermined. Any special instructions should be given.

Now that everyone is ready, hunters must take up their positions and prepare for the drive. This is where a lot of drives go awry. It's easy to look at a map or photo and plan strategy, but it is something else to have 10 or 12 excited hunters take to unfamiliar woods in a quiet, organized manner. All of a sudden, places that seemed easy to reach and find are lost in the vastness of the woods. The standers may find themselves calling for help or wandering around lost when the drive commences, in which case the standers actually become unintentional drivers. The safety and success of the drive depend on the plans being understood and properly implemented. If the huntmaster does not have competent help in implementing the plans, he should take the time to personally oversee the positioning of everyone.

When the right number of experienced hunters drive the right place the right way, plenty of excitement is sure to follow. Photo by Mike Biggs.

In most cases, it's best to let the standers get into position first. This way, they will already be on-stand if the drivers move any deer when going to their starting points. Some set-ups, however, call for drivers and standers to move into position simultaneously so the drive area can be quickly encircled to catch any buck moved prematurely by either standers or drivers. The huntmaster has to make that call. But either way, standers and, to a lesser degree, drivers must get into position with as little disturbance to the deer as possible. Too much commotion while setting up a drive, especially a short one, may clear the area of deer before the drive ever starts. Trophy bucks have an uncanny knack of slipping out of harm's way if given any advance warning. The deer shouldn't know what's happening until everybody is in position. No talking above a whisper. No crashing through brush. No slamming car doors. Generally, the more difficult or noisy the access is, the larger the drive area must be to insure something will still be there to drive.

The beginning of the drive must be coordinated. Standers should be given a specific time by which they are to be on-stand. Once the standers are in place, the drivers can start the drive at a predetermined time and/or on a signal from the huntmaster, assuming he's driving. Normally, I like for the huntmaster to start the hunt with a yell, maybe even followed by whoops from each of the drivers. This lets everybody on the hunt know the drive has started and establishes the whereabouts of each of the drivers.

This is a good place to discuss whether or not drivers should make noise while driving. An argument can be made either way. The argument in favor of silent drivers says that they are more likely to shoot a buck themselves, they tend to confuse the deer more since the deer can't be sure where all the drivers are and they move deer more slowly, resulting in better shots. In my mind, a silent drive is only advantageous when the drive area can't be properly stood or driven, resulting in big gaps in the lines. Why? One, a silent advance might not move the deer out of the drive area prematurely, allowing the noose to tighten before the deer become too alerted. Two, a quiet driver probably does have a better chance for a shot himself, thereby increasing the overall effectiveness of an otherwise marginal drive.

The other viewpoint, the one I support, argues that drivers can use noise to keep the drive line intact and to move a greater percentage of the area deer. Also, by verbalizing during the drive, drivers can communicate special instructions or new information and, very importantly, let other hunters know their whereabouts for both logistical and safety reasons. All things considered, I feel the right kind of noise allows for effective in-drive communications and has few disadvantages.

With the drive underway, the huntmaster or someone familiar with the drive route should be positioned in the middle of the drive line so other drivers can relate to him. This is where the occasional yelp, howl or whoop comes into play in maintaining the integrity of the drive line. This does not mean the drivers should carry on like a pack of frantic hounds. Rather, they should sound off just often enough to let the others know where they are. The middle man in the drive line should be the reference point, and he should call out more often than the others. The drive line should proceed slowly and in relative unison. I commonly employ a U-shaped drive line to further encompass the drive area. Also, rather than traveling in a straight line, the drivers should meander. This allows them to cover more ground and tends to confuse the deer.

Done properly, the drivers have almost as good a chance to shoot a buck as the standers, especially on the longer drives. After all, once the standers start shooting, deer in the drive area know danger is all around and are likely to go anywhere, even back toward the drivers. For the drivers to score, they must move slowly, stopping frequently, and watch for bucks trying to slip back through the drive line. A driver also may get a shot at a buck he jumps. On one drive I was on, a driver shot a 12-point buck from a distance of only 10 feet while the buck lay, head outstretched, in a thick brushpile! The nerve of big bucks cannot be underestimated. Sometimes they will hold until the very last minute if they think they're hidden. At any rate, drivers should hunt during a drive, not just walk.

Done properly, the drivers have almost as good a chance to shoot a buck as the standers, especially on the longer drives. This lucky driver caught a buck trying to slip back through the drive line.

As the drive line nears the standers, the guy in charge of the drive line should give a prearranged signal for the other drivers to start putting up a steady ruckus. This is to prevent a stander from mistaking a silent driver for a slipping deer. With the drivers near the standers, this is the most dangerous time of a drive. By this point, however, the trophy buck you are after should already be down!

There you have it ... the basic ingredients of a successful drive. With imagination, a drive can be adapted to just about any situation. Drives are not without their drawbacks, and they are far from foolproof, as the little button buck in the Tombigbee River swamp showed me so many years ago. But when all else fails, I know of no better way to "force" success.

361

Chapter 19

Rattling In Trophy Bucks

A LIGHT SNOWFALL ADDED to the foot of soft powder already on the ground. Bundled in as many layers of clothes as I could physically get on, I waddled silently down the old woods road like an oversized Pillsbury Doughboy. My attention was occasionally drawn to fresh deer tracks that cut deep through the new snow. A scar in the postcard scenery caught my eye and caused an involuntary gasp, the cold Canadian air searing my lungs. Just ahead, a five-inch poplar was rubbed bare of bark as high as my waist. The snow at the tree's base was churned and dirty. I combed the dead-still forest around me. The buck had just left. This was where I would rattle.

I eased forward a few yards to a clump of small spruces and dropped to my knees behind them. I checked the wind. The snowflakes seemed to be drifting very slightly to the north. There, a line of low spruces bordered an alder thicket. That was probably where the buck would come from … if he came.

I checked to be sure my scope was turned down to 3X. Then, I laid my rifle across my lap, careful to keep the scope lenses clear of snow. I unzipped my heavy parka just enough to gain access to the binoculars being shielded from the snow. I reached into my pocket and pulled out a grunt call. I gave three short, pig-like grunts, paused briefly and fol-

I rattled in this 22-inch 10-pointer on a cold day in western Saskatchewan.

lowed with four more grunts. I waited about a minute but nothing moved.

I then grasped my rattling antlers by their bases and slowly scanned the surroundings one last time. Ever so lightly, I tickled the tines of the antlers together several times and then paused about 20 seconds. Then, I began rattling again, tickling the tines at first but quickly engaging the main beams. They began to ring out their solid "cracks." Steadily, I increased the tempo and volume. A minute into the sequence, I thrust the antlers into the branches of a head-high poplar. Continuing to rattle, I snapped limbs and rubbed the enmeshed antlers against the bole of the small tree. The sound of fighting bucks permeated the still north-woods. After almost three minutes, I abruptly jerked the antlers apart and dropped them to the snow. I immediately followed with three grunts on the grunt call. My rifle ready, the wait began. It was a short one.

The first hint that something was coming was the snap of a limb to my left. A blur of motion followed back in the thick alders. I tensed. Long seconds went by, but only stillness and silence rewarded my searching eyes and ears. Then, like an apparition, a buck materialized 50 yards away in an open lane. He stared intently in my direction. His thick neck and wide, dark antlers told me he was a mature whitetail. No time for binoculars. A quick look through the scope would have to tell me if he was a shooter, but with him looking dead at me, I dared not move. Then, just as suddenly as he had appeared, he vanished.

I quickly grabbed the antlers and rattled out a short sequence. I then dropped the antlers and brought the rifle to my shoulder. Looking over the barrel, careful not to breathe on my scope lens, I watched the spot where the buck had been. Rapid movement in the alders again caught my eye. The buck was returning at a trot. He exited the alders without a sound and proceeded through the small spruces. I tracked him with my rifle barrel, waiting for the right opportunity. It came when he reached a small opening 40 yards out. The buck stopped, his muscles taut and his head held high. Again, he stared my way, but this time the crosshairs of the scope were already intersecting his big chest. A quick check of his antlers was all I needed.

"Good brow tines," I thought. "One, two, three fairly long primaries on the right ... and the left beam. He's a 10-pointer. A solid 150." My focus shifted from his antlers to the center of his shoulder. The 22-inch 10-pointer's time had run out.

Rattling works... at certain times in certain places. This tactic was once associated primarily with Texas hunting, but in the last decade, hunters across the continent have found that rattling can work for them. Yet, many are the hunters who have tried and tried to rattle in bucks without any hint of success. This has led some to believe that rattling requires great skill and special technique. Actually, the real secret to rattling success is being in the right place at the right time. Basic technique has to be there, but the efforts of even the best rattler will be to no avail if the timing and the place are wrong.

To understand when and where rattling will work, it is necessary to understand why it works. Obviously, rattling imitates a fight between two bucks. Why does this attract other bucks? I believe there are essentially

Upon hearing the sound of a fight, some bucks go to the source, hackles up and eyes glaring, looking for a battle. One glance at this buck and you know he's something special — like a 24-inch, 170-class monster! Photo by Curt Helmick.

four reasons. One, they may answer in hopes of making off with an onwatching hot doe, which is sometimes the object of disputes between two bucks. Two, simple aggression. Near or during the rut, bucks, especially mature bucks, are aggressive and intolerant of other bucks. Upon hearing the sound of a fight, some bucks go to the source, hackles up and eyes glaring, looking for a fight to vent their aggression. Three, bucks may rush to clashing antlers in defense of their territory, or at least in response to what they perceive as space infringement. Four, some bucks respond to rattling simply out of curiosity. This is especially so with young bucks.

Rattling is a proven tactic in South Texas, but rattling will work anywhere with a low buck/doe ratio and a good buck age structure. Richard Jackson of Tallahassee, Florida, downed this fine Brush Country buck when he responded to rattling!

WHERE RATTLING WORKS

Rattling is a well-known and proven tactic in South Texas. Why is this so? Are the deer there uniquely susceptible to rattling? Are they different? The answer is yes ... and no. Let me explain.

The deer in South Texas are uniquely susceptible to rattling, but it's not because they are inherently different from other deer. It's because South Texas as a whole has a relatively unique deer herd composition. Why? Once again, hunting pressure comes into play, but in South Texas' case, it's the lack of it. As a result of overall light buck hunting pressure, there are lots of older bucks; the buck/doe ratio is very low; and the bucks are pretty much unmolested and very competitive during the rut. As it happens, that's the very combination required for rattling success ... anywhere.

Because herd composition is determined largely by hunting pressure, it can be safely assumed that rattling will produce just about anywhere hunting pressure is low to low-moderate. Besides Texas, I have successfully rattled in Canada, Montana, Oklahoma, Mexico and on numerous protected tracts of land throughout the South. The critical thing is not what part of the country you rattle, but rather, what the herd composition is where you rattle.

In heavily hunted areas, a would-be rattler faces many obstacles. First, there simply may not be many bucks there to rattle in. If there are some bucks around, the majority will be young. These immature bucks are not going to be highly aggressive, and aggression is required for rattling success. Second, the buck/doe ratio is likely to badly favor does. This has the effect of reducing competition between bucks, which curtails a buck's desire to "horn in" on a fight even if a willing girlfriend is the potential reward. And of course, natural deer movement is sure to be disrupted by the presence of lots of hunters, making bucks very wary and reluctant to expose themselves during the day. The end result of all this is poor rattling success in heavily hunted deer populations.

I also believe that herd density is another significant factor in rattling. Even if two places have similar herd compositions and are subject to like pressure, my experience has been that the place with the highest density population will be noticeably better for rattling. Naturally, simple arithmetic explains part of this. All else being equal, the more bucks present in a population, the more that will come to rattling. But, I believe it goes beyond this. It seems to me that rattling success is disproportionately better in higher density populations. A comparison of rattling results in Texas versus Canada provides a good example.

Some of the areas I've hunted in Texas and Canada are very similar in herd composition and hunting pressure. Yet, rattling consistently worked much better in Texas. Why? My theory is that, up to a point, higher density populations have greater competition among bucks. Perhaps it is increased territorial, social or spatial (space) competition. Regardless of what's behind it, the increased competition causes mature bucks to be less tolerant of other bucks and to be inherently more defensive of their space, characteristics favorable for rattling. In South Texas, deer populations frequently run between 25 and 40 deer per square mile and competition for space is keen. In Canada, deer populations in the 5 to 15 deer per square mile range would be common. They have plenty of space and perhaps aren't as accustomed to having to fight since perceived space infringement or aggressive encounters may be less frequent. That's not to say that bucks won't come to rattling in Canada. They will, but not as dependably (even in relative terms) as they will come in Texas or in other areas with higher densities in combination with the right herd composition.

WHEN RATTLING WORKS

Rattling success depends largely on timing. The bucks have to be in the right mood and full of themselves. When is the right time? Let's look at the expected response to rattling during each of the four periods of fall deer activity.

During the pre-rut feeding period, don't expect rattling to stir up much interest on the buck's part. The full effects of their increasing testosterone levels have not yet kicked in. They are more interested in feeding and resting than in fighting. Still, bucks can occasionally be coaxed in by rattling during the pre-rut, especially as the scraping period draws near. The best technique seems to be intermittent light rattling over a fairly long period of time. The few bucks that do answer during the pre-rut usually are slow to respond and cautious, probably coming more out of curiosity than anything else. Frankly, I seldom bother with rattling until I see serious scraping activity.

The scraping period is the most dependable time to rattle in white-tails. And, the response to rattling increases almost daily throughout the period. The bucks are now at a pitch fever to get with does, but the does are not yet ready. The bucks are active and aggressive. Skirmishes between bucks are fairly common and draw the attention of other chummed-up bucks in the neighborhood. Aggressive rattling complete with brush-beating and ground-stomping seems to work best during the scraping period. Bucks often will rush in wide-eyed and belligerent.

It is a prevalent belief that trophy bucks are unlikely to come to rattling during the breeding period because they are sure to be with receptive does. True, the more dominant bucks are at the head of the line when it comes to staking claim to available does. And, any buck smart enough to live to trophy size probably has too much on the ball to leave a "doe in the hand" to traipse off to a fight. This may be part of the reason why rattling can be inconsistent during the breeding period. Yet, I have rattled in many trophy bucks, several of which I shot, during the breeding period and consider it to be a very good time for rattling.

One of the big pluses for rattling during the breeding period is the

The scraping period is the most dependable time to rattle in whitetails. The bucks are active and aggressive then, and skirmishes are fairly common. These bucks are posturing, and the upper buck is giving way to the lower one. Photo by Mike Biggs.

fact that the bucks are extremely excited and eager to investigate any opportunity to hook up with willing does. Bucks know that the sound of antler on antler may well mean a hot doe is nearby. And at any given time, there are many doeless bucks eager to change their present status. As for trophy bucks, there's always the chance of catching them on the prowl between does. Even the subdominant bucks can be trophies. Dominance is most often determined by body size rather than antler size. It is not unusual for a bigger-bodied, smaller-racked buck to claim a doe over a bigger-racked, smaller-bodied buck, leaving the dejected trophy-racked buck vulnerable to antler-rattling.

Rattling can be productive during the early part of the post-rut period when some breeding is still underway. As during the scraping period, post-rut bucks are all dressed up for a party but few does are willing to dance. The big difference is that post-rut bucks are tired and have had their sexual appetite partially satisfied. But even though their enthusiasm is waning, some bucks, even a few trophy bucks, are willing to check out a fight, possibility in hopes of scoring one last time. As the post-rut wears on and breeding winds down, carrying around rattling antlers becomes an unnecessary burden for the hunter.

Weather has a big influence on rattling success. One of my favorite times to rattle is during a mist, drizzle or light snowfall. Trophy bucks are especially likely to be moving on such days and to respond to rattling. One drizzly morning in South Texas I rattled up 16 different bucks, 15 of which survived the morning. Nearly all were mature. Even after seeing or smelling me, several of them milled around me in apparent disbelief that a buck fight hadn't just taken place where I sat.

Weatherwise, another choice time for rattling is the cold, clear days immediately following the passage of a cold front, preferably one preceded by several days of bad weather. This is a naturally good time for deer movement, and the bucks are feeling their oats then. When days like this hit during the scraping or breeding periods, the bucks are likely to be working scrapes, looking for does or doing something else pertaining to the rut. This activity makes them susceptible to rattling.

While certain weather conditions are best for rattling, I've occasionally had good success rattling at other times as well. There have been times in South Texas when the weather was better suited for sunbathing than for deer hunting when bucks have readily responded to rattling. I've rattled in bucks on warm, cloudy days and on days so windy I could hardly hear the rattling antlers myself. Conversely, I've had times when everything seemed right, but despite my best imitation of fighting bucks, nothing showed. Rattling is never a sure thing, but when the bucks are ready, they may come running no matter what the weather.

PREPARING TO RATTLE

Obviously, you'll need a pair of rattling antlers. Hunters today have a choice between real and artificial antlers. The better artificials work very well. They are durable and easy to obtain at reasonable prices. But for aesthetic reasons more than anything else, I prefer the real thing.

Rattling antlers do not have to be from the same buck. They can be either sheds or cut from a skull plate. They must, however, be fresh, not weathered and dried out. Antlers vary in density. Some are naturally light and porous. These usually don't have good tone. I prefer dense antlers, the ones that look and feel almost like porcelain. Rattling antlers

When I shot this big eight-pointer, he was no more than five feet from the end of my barrel. He surprised me by coming in from upwind and behind me while I was rattling with synthetic antlers, which work about as well as the real thing. Note the grunt call around my neck. I frequently grunt as part of my rattling ruse.

can be from opposing sides or from the same side of the heads of bucks. Hunters favoring opposing sides say they get better tine contact. The ones using antlers from the same side argue that main beam contact is better, resulting in better tone and more volume. It's really a matter of personal preference. As for size, I believe the ideal for rattling "horns" is a set of 130 to 140-class, 5x5 antlers of average to slightly heavier than average weight.

Once you've chosen a set of rattling antlers, the brow tines should be cut off flush with the beams. I like to leave the burrs on for better grip, but some hunters cut them off to keep from chaffing their hands. To help carry the antlers, a hole can be drilled in the base of each antler and a length of cord or leather attached. Some experienced rattlers cut off the tips of the tines, but I don't recommend this. It seems to deaden the tone, especially when tickling the antlers to tease in a buck. The tone of some antlers can be improved by frequent oiling with linseed oil or the like. This also prevents older antlers from drying out and getting brittle.

Breakage can be a problem with real antlers when they are banged together forcefully, which is seldom necessary in the first place. Rattling largely consists of twisting and turning enmeshed antlers and relatively little banging. Whitetails don't butt heads like bighorn sheep. Though they occasionally engage their antlers with enthusiasm, they most often bring them together rather gingerly before starting the shoving match. I know many veteran rattlers who have used the same set of antlers for years. Yet, one morning last fall I took out a newcomer who wanted to rattle in a buck. On his first attempt at rattling, he slammed my old faithful antlers together with such force that the last two inches of one main beam shattered and the second primary tine on the other antler sailed 10 feet away! I was impressed by the guy's enthusiasm if not his style.

The need for effective and total camouflage is never more important than when rattling. When a buck responds, he comes in looking for the source of the sound. His senses are on full alert. A poorly camouflaged hunter will not go unnoticed. It is not only important to wear clothing that blends with the background, but a rattler must also cover his face and hands. Bare skin shines, especially in the sunlight, and an alerted buck will quickly see the glare of an uncovered face or exposed hands. A head net, a full beard, camo paint or, in a pinch, a hat or cap pulled low over the face will do. The hands can be covered by camo paint or gloves. I much prefer gloves since they protect the hands from taking a licking while rattling or beating brush.

In and around the breeding period, I frequently use a grunt call in connection with rattling. When a buck smells the hot scent of an estrus doe, he will sometimes verbalize his excitement by short, pig-like grunts. A grunt call duplicates that sound and sends the message that a buck is in the presence of a receptive doe. Rattling and grunting in combination can create attractive sound effects for the ears of an aggressive, amorous buck looking for action. Once the buck has been aroused by rattling, the grunt call can be particularly useful as an enticer to work the interested buck in closer and to further convince him that the ruckus he heard was for real. In my opinion, this is the most effective and dependable use of a grunt call.

Rattling is not an exact science. Being in the right place at the right time is more important than technique. Just make a ruckus like two bucks fighting and be ready. Good camouflage is very important when rattling. Photo by Mike Biggs.

How To Rattle

Effective rattling is neither difficult nor exacting. After all, the purpose of rattling is simply to imitate the sound of fighting bucks and no two buck fights are the same. Some fights last several minutes; others only seconds. Some are fierce battles with deadly intent; others are harmless shoving matches. Some are between mature, big-racked bucks; others involve yearlings. Some take place in thick cover and are accompanied by the sound of breaking limbs and crashing brush; other fights are in the open where only clashing antlers announce their existence. With fights and their accompanying sounds differing so much, it is easy to see why there is no one-and-only way to rattle. The hunter must simply imagine what two fighting bucks would sound like in that place at that time of year and try to duplicate it.

Rattling can produce for either the still-hunter or the stand-hunter. I have rattled in many good bucks by intermittent rattling from an elevated stand. Some excellent hunters specialize in this type of rattling,

The team approach works well in rattling. I was stationed about 75 yards downwind of Amos Dewitt, who is doing the rattling, when this "nice" buck showed up to investigate. We rattled in 11 different bucks at this location on the King Ranch.

citing the advantages of added sound carry, better visibility and lower chances of detection by the deer. When stand-hunting especially, the hunter must take care not to rattle too much. Excessive rattling from one place can raise suspicion. A wait between rattling sessions of at least 10 to 15 minutes, and preferably 30 to 40 minutes, is probably best when on-stand.

Most of my rattling is done while still-hunting. I prefer the greater mobility still-hunting allows, and I feel that rattling from the ground is more realistic and, in most cases, more productive. When the bucks are responding well to antlers, I like to employ a hit-and-run strategy. I'll rattle in a spot for 20 to 30 minutes. If nothing shows, I'll move 200 to 300 yards and try again. A day of this puts the sound of rattling within ear shot of a lot of bucks.

Rattling is particularly suited to a team approach. Because bucks like to work their way downwind of a rattler, they often smell the hunter without ever exposing themselves. Some bucks even slip in and see the preoccupied hunter and then tiptoe away unnoticed. Happily, there's a way to partially counter these sneaky maneuvers. A second hunter can be strategically positioned downwind of the rattler and/or in an elevated stand so he can see bucks that might otherwise go undetected by the hunter mimicking a buck fight. I have used this team approach to great effect, and it has showed me just how few responding bucks are actually seen by the hunter doing the rattling.

Now for the rattling technique. We'll start with selecting a place to rattle and assume we're rattling from the ground. I basically look for three things in a rattling set-up. One, I like to be in or near thick cover, preferably where there's an abundance of buck sign. Thick cover is more likely to harbor a trophy buck. Plus, having thick cover nearby allows cover-sensitive trophy bucks to approach within range of the rattler. Trophy bucks sometimes will cross open or semi-open cover, but they are reluctant to do so. Two, I try to have visibility for some distance downwind since bucks nearly always will attempt to get below the rattler. That doesn't mean that bucks always come in nose to the wind. I've seen them approach from all directions, though downwind is most likely. But once near the source of the noise, they invariably will work their way downwind. Three, I try to hide in some type of low cover like bushes or small trees to conceal all the movement that goes with rattling, not to mention raising a rifle. These same bushes or small trees also will serve as the object of brush-beating and antler-rubbing.

The rattling site chosen, certain preparations should be made prior to beginning the session. Clear the leaves or debris where you're sitting or standing to allow for silent movement. Position your rifle for quick, easy access. If your scope is a variable, turn it to a low power setting. Inaccessible guns and scopes set too high are major culprits in blown chances at rattled-in bucks. Finally, study the surroundings and pick out lanes that may give you a warning glimpse of an oncoming buck.

It's now time to begin the rattling sequence. If breeding is underway, I may start the sequence with a couple of series of three or four grunts on the grunt call. Then, I'll wait about a minute. If nothing happens, I'll start rattling by just tickling the tines of the antlers together for 20 to 30 seconds. Not only does this subdued beginning prevent spooking nearby bucks, but it also more realistically imitates the start of an actual fight. If I have reason to think a buck is very closeby, I'll usually stop and wait about a minute after tickling the antlers. I may even grunt again. If nothing leads me to believe a buck is in the immediate vicinity, I'll move right to a stepped-up pace.

As I've said, proper rattling technique involves twisting and turning the enmeshed antlers, using wrist action. Occasionally, I will partially disengage the antlers and snap them back together with a "crack." But, the process does not require forceful banging of the antlers. Grip the antlers firmly to get a "solid" sound. Rattle sporadically with a broken rhythm. Bucks don't fight in a steady, rhythmic fashion. It's a stop-and-go, fast-and-slow kind of deal. I'll usually keep up a sequence for two to three minutes. If a rut-charged buck is within a couple of hundred yards, he may come running well before the first sequence is over. Be ready from the very beginning.

One of my favorite tricks is to ram the antlers, while still rattling, right into brushy limbs and/or up against the trunk of a small tree. Then, I will rake the limbs with the antlers and/or rub them up and down the tree trunk as I continue rattling. This can add much to the realism of a fake fight. Many times, I've had bucks answer that were so convinced a fight was underway that they would totally ignore me — even after seeing or smelling me — and search feverishly all around the area for the combatant bucks. Also, I've frequently had bucks respond to rubbing and brush-beating before I ever actually rattled.

After two to three minutes, I will stop the rattling sequence rather abruptly, the way two bucks would disengage when one decides to call it quits. I sharply pull the antlers apart, letting the antlers slide rapidly against each other as they separate. Then, I may drop the antlers to the ground and begin my wait. Or, I may pound the butts of the antlers against the ground for about 10 seconds to emulate a running or stomping deer. I may even give another series of grunts or rake the brush a few more times. I try to do whatever seems appropriate for a concluding fight. These special effects can make the difference in fooling a wise trophy buck.

The wait that follows a rattling sequence is very important. Most commonly, the eager younger bucks show up first, often during the first rattling sequence. The older trophy bucks generally are more cautious and slower to respond. They often drift in quietly during the wait. Because I am basically impatient, I will force a wait of at least five minutes between rattling sequences by timing myself on my watch. If I have reason to believe a big buck is in the immediate neighborhood or if bucks are responding slowly to the horns, I will wait longer between sequences. Also, when I'm planning to stay in one place for a lengthy period, I'll rattle less frequently. I am convinced you can rattle too much. The time

Bob Zaiglin and Dick Idol teamed up to rattle in this 25-inch 10-pointer scoring 155.

spent waiting between rattling sequences is time well spent.

Normally, I will rattle two or three times in a spot before moving on. This translates to a 20 to 30-minute stay at each place. Sometimes, I'll rattle only once before taking off. Other times, I may stay in one place an hour. It all depends on my confidence in the place and on what pattern I've seen during previous rattling sessions. Generally speaking, I believe that most hunters, including myself, don't stay in one spot long enough.

The importance of patience both in the wait following each rattling sequence and in the length of time spent in one given spot has been driven home to me many times. When rattling alone, I've often seen patience pay off in the form of latecoming old bucks. But for me, the most convincing case for patience has been made while I watched from elevated stands as old bucks cautiously responded to the rattling of companion hunters a short distance away. What these old bucks typically do has taught me much and is worth exploring.

During the rattling sequence, an old buck often will appear in heavy cover some distance away from the rattler. He will frequently just stand there statuelike and stare in the direction of the rattling. Sometimes, he may move a bit closer or work his way slowly downwind to get a better fix on the ruckus. But most of the time, he will not try to go right in on the action. When the rattling stops and silence falls, he may continue to stare for a time then disappear. Or after waiting a minute or two, he may then begin to get restless, not knowing what's happening. Up to now, the only contact he may have had with the rattler is through sound. With the noise abated, he often will try to re-establish contact with the source of his interest. The only way to do that is through smell or sight. Often, the old buck will start drifting cautiously toward the rattling site, taking a course that will put him downwind (if there is any wind) of the now quieted action. As the buck looks for the participants of the fight, or perhaps the doe he hopes is with them, he may very well walk into view of the rattler.

Interestingly, if the hunter starts up another rattling sequence now, the buck may respond in one of two ways. He may again stop and stare without making any further move toward the hunter. Or, relieved to have relocated the fight, he may move deliberately toward the renewed battle. The odds are that the biggest bucks will opt to hold back for further scrutiny.

Having witnessed this behavior several times, I have come to appreciate the importance of patience when rattling. And, it has helped me to understand a phenomenon in rattling that I believe offers trophy hunters a unique opportunity.

Most experienced rattlers will say that success is greatest during times of little or no wind. This is when sound carries best and when deer are most likely to be on the move. I, too, feel that times of little or no wind are most productive for rattling in terms of consistency and total response. However, I have had some of my best success rattling in really large bucks during times of high wind. I've seen the same pattern enough times now to be convinced it's no fluke. I've even developed my own theory about what it takes for the windy day tactic to work and why it works.

Generally speaking, most hunters don't stay in one spot long enough when rattling. The bigger bucks are often slow to come in and are reluctant to leave the security of thick cover. Photo by Mike Biggs.

First, when I say high wind, I don't mean a breeze. I'm talking about a 10 to 15 mph wind or more. The cold, windy days that often trail a cold front are perfect. Second, the tactic seems to work best during the last of the scraping period and during the breeding period, i.e., the peak of rutting activity. Third, the set-up requirements are quite specific. Downwind visibility of 100 to 300 yards is required. This lane of visibility should be bordered on at least one side by thick cover suspected to harbor trophy bucks. It is preferable for the lane itself to provide some perceived cover for the deer. Fallow fields, cactus flats (in Texas), clearcuts and grown-up right-of-ways are good examples. Ideally, the hunter should be elevated to gain a better view and to improve sound carry.

Upon finding these specific requirements, I have rattled into view some of the largest bucks I've ever had answer my antlers. Although young or subdominant bucks typically will come in close, the exceptional bucks don't actually "come to" the rattling. Rather, they circle far downwind of the source of noise. Most will be 100 to 300 yards below the rattler, thus the need for downwind visibility. Patience is key. The real trophies seldom show themselves within the first 15 minutes. Usually, it's 20 to 30 minutes before they appear. Their approach is normally deliberate and calculated, although a big buck occasionally will trot into view. From the bucks' behavior, it is clear their intent is to get straight downwind of the noise so they can smell what they've already heard.

Why are trophy bucks vulnerable to this rattling technique during high winds? I have a theory ... but it's only a theory. First, I need to lay some groundwork. In populations with plenty of older bucks, some of the top-end animals are likely to be past their breeding prime, or at least past the time when they are totally blinded by passion. Unlike the prime, aggressive, middle-aged bucks, these older bucks refuse to cast wisdom and caution aside for a challenge fight or for the hope of stealing off with a disputed doe. Yet, the breeding urge still stirs these wizened old bucks. They may want to check out a fight ... but not at any cost. Extreme caution prevails. This would explain why the very biggest bucks are reluctant to come to rattling, and when they do answer, they do so very slowly and cautiously. It would also explain why these exceptional bucks will usually come only so close to the fight scene, often without the hunter ever being aware of their presence, and approach no closer. It's as though these wary old bucks have a "protected air space." That is, there's a limit as to how close they will allow themselves to approach anything suspicious or potentially dangerous, or allow it to approach them. Given this scenario, the theory of why rattling can work for top-end bucks on windy days can be developed.

It is possible that on days with little or no wind these cagey old bucks do indeed respond to the sound of a fight at least as well as they do on windy days ... but only as far as their protected air space will allow them to come. Then, they stop, still some distance away from the hunter and likely beyond his sight. Experienced deer hunters know that when whitetails hear something, they like to verify what they've heard by either seeing or, preferably, smelling it. Yet, cautious old bucks may be reluc-

Oddly, I've rattled in some of my biggest bucks during times of high wind. Although this is contrary to the normal pattern, I feel that windy days just before or during the peak of rut can bring special opportunity for the rattling hunter. I took this great buck on such a day. Photo by Corey Roland.

tant to come any closer or to leave the security of thick cover to see what's happening. And with little or no wind, they may innately know that they would have to violate their protected air space to get close enough to smell whatever is causing the commotion. So, they stay back ... out of sight of the hunters. But on windy days, those same old bucks, upon hearing the sound of a fight, may instinctively know that because of the wind they can circle well below the fight and use their nose to verify what they have heard ... without violating their protected air space. That could explain why these exceptional bucks show up so far downwind, usually 100 yards or more. They still maintain their caution. That's why it takes so long for them to finally work their way into view.

Like I say, the explanation for why really big bucks sometimes show up far downwind of a rattling hunter on windy days is only a theory, but I know they will. I've seen it too many times not to believe. For me, the best proof came when a 28-inch 10-pointer tiptoed into sight some 250 yards below where I was rattling. I had been hunting that buck for four years, and it took a cold, windy day in South Texas before I finally got him!

Chapter 20

Specialty Tactics
Calls, Scents, Camo And More

WE LIVE IN A WORLD OF INSTANT GRATIFICATION. Everybody seems to be looking for the quick fix, the easy way. Most deer hunters are no exception. Many are on constant lookout for a secret tactic or a gimmick that will guarantee success. You see it all the time in products designed to fool hunters rather than whitetails. The truth is that nothing can replace the basics ... experience, woodsmanship, knowledge of the animal, keen observation and practiced skill combined with determination and old-fashioned hard work. These are the ingredients for success in trophy hunting. Yet, there are some speciality tactics that can help enhance a hunter's odds. They aren't magic, and they don't work all the time. In fact, these speciality tactics only work in conjunction with the basics. They will not stand alone. But, they do have a place in the trophy hunter's arsenal. Let's look at some of them.

Calling deer is the latest rage. However, deer calls are no panacea for trophy hunting. They are only helpful aids. This hunter has grunted in a good buck, but don't expect to see such dramatic results often. Photo by Mike Biggs.

DEER CALLS

Calling deer is the latest rage in deer hunting. I'm tempted to term it a fad, but that wouldn't be quite fair. You see, calling deer does have merit; it's just not the panacea to trophy hunting many would have you believe. Overall, deer calls play a very minor role in my own white-tail strategy. Yet, they can be useful under certain circumstances.

Deer make basically three vocal sounds — snorts, bleats and grunts. When alarmed, all deer will snort. The alarm snort is a short, powerful expulsion of air and obviously shouldn't be used when trying to call deer. Deer also will snort when they are suspicious or curious in an effort to identify who's there. This "identification snort" is less forceful and more drawn out than the alarm snort. When a buck has become suspicious (but not alerted), a hunter may be able to give a rendition of the identification snort and put the deer at ease, or perhaps even draw him closer. I've tried it, but the results have been mixed. In addition, bucks will snort to vent aggression when fighting or rubbing. This aggression snort consists of a few short, shallow snorts in rapid succession followed by a

This buck is sounding out a "snort-wheeze," an aggression snort consisting of a few short, shallow snorts in rapid succession followed by a wheeze. To make this sound, the buck raises his upper lip much like he does when flehmening. Some hunters say a snort-wheeze imitation will lure in ruttng bucks. Photo by Curt Helmick.

wheeze. By imitating the "snort-wheeze," some claim aggressive rutting bucks can be lured in, especially when the hunter is around their scrapes. Since I've never tried it, I don't know if it works. I've also heard estrus does snort while being chased by bucks. They may snort from excitement or to maintain contact with the buck. Whatever the reason, I doubt if this or any other snort has much application in calling trophy bucks.

Bleats, however, can be used to call in deer, especially does and fawns. Fawns frequently bleat to locate or attract their mother, and vice-versa. For this reason, does and fawns tend to respond to bleats quite readily. While bowhunting during Georgia's early fall archery season, I have called in several does and fawns with a bleat call (actually, a converted predator call). On a couple of occasions, young bucks have wandered upon the scene after I bleated, but I can't go so far as to say they answered the call. Adult bucks are capable of bleating and are sometimes heard to do so when wounded. Still, I consider bleating to be essentially a social and bonding call between does and fawns. As such, I don't feel bleat calls, which are available commercially, hold much promise for trophy bucks.

The deer vocalization that does have significance to trophy hunters is the grunt, specially the guttural grunt of an excited buck trailing or courting a doe in heat. On rare occasions, I've heard does grunt, but the sound they make is not as guttural as that of a buck. It's really more like a cross between a bleat and a grunt and seems to be another form of communication between does and fawns. But, I've never heard a buck grunt that wasn't either with a doe or clearly looking for one. Because of this, I believe the guttural buck grunt usually is associated with the presence of a hot doe. If a buck is full of rutting passion, the promise of a nearby doe may draw him to the sound of a grunt ... and the hunter who emulates that call.

In recent years, grunt calls have become very popular with whitetail hunters. Manufacturers today make various types of grunt calls that do sound like the real thing. Stories of success while using them have been written in books and magazines and spread by word of mouth among the whitetail fraternity. Some of the stories are true; others are exaggerations at best. Many hunters looking for the easy road to trophy success have bought grunt calls expecting bucks to be drawn to them like rubberneckers to a car wreck. Alas, most have been disappointed. On the other hand, those with realistic expectations have found that grunt calls do have value when used under the right circumstances. Let's see what they are.

In my opinion, grunt calls are most effective when breeding is underway, i.e., the last of the scraping period, the breeding period and the first part of the post-rut period. When little or no breeding is taking place, bucks seem to pay no attention to grunt calls. Even when breeding is going on, bucks can be indifferent to the grunt call. Numerous times during the rut I've grunted to bucks I could see just to find out

Along the lines of calling deer, decoys have recently come onto the scene and are making waves. In the right set-up, they obviously will attract a buck's attention. It remains to be seen what their role will be in trophy hunting. The buck checking this decoy out is a mid-160's 12-pointer. Photo by Mike Biggs.

what they would do. Many would cast a glance in my direction and then continue with whatever they were doing. Some totally ignored the grunts. A few, however, responded positively. And almost without exception, these bucks appeared to have been excitedly engaged in some type of rutting activity at the time I called to them. From that and other experiences, it seems to me that a buck "turned on" by rutting lust is far more likely to answer a grunt call than a buck going about his everyday business. When a rut-driven buck is focused on does and breeding, he is susceptible to anything that might bring him closer to satisfying his sexual urge. Under such circumstances, grunts may signal the possible presence of a receptive doe, making it difficult for an switched-on buck to resist checking out the sound. Yet, if that same buck is not already sexually aroused, a grunt may hold no attraction to him … even when breeding is taking place.

As I said earlier, my favorite way to use the grunt call is in connection with rattling. It is my opinion that rattling can have the effect of switching on the rutting urge in bucks. Once aroused, these bucks are then susceptible to the lure of grunting. This is more than a theory. On several occasions, I've grunted unsuccessfully to bucks I could see, but when I rattled, those same bucks became alert and interested. Then, when I grunted as a follow-up to rattling, the excited bucks often would respond readily to the grunts. Undoubtedly, some of these bucks eventually would have answered if I'd been only rattling, but I believe the grunting helped convince some bucks to come on over.

To be honest, I've had limited success with grunting as a standalone tactic. I doubt I have grunted in more than a dozen bucks that I could positively say came as a result of the grunt call. Only a couple of these bucks were mature. Yet, I know some hunters who have grunted in and shot trophy bucks (mainly in the northern climes and especially in Canada). However, after questioning lots of hunters, I'm convinced that many of the successes credited to grunting are nothing more than unlucky bucks that just happened upon hunters after they grunted. Certainly, among the millions of whitetail hunters, many bucks do legitimately respond to grunting every year. But, the odds of you personally being one of the lucky ones to grunt in a trophy buck would not play well in Las Vegas. Still, it could happen.

As with rattling, technique is not critical in grunting. A sequence usually consists of two or three series of three to five short, pig-like grunts. Each series is spaced about 5 to 10 seconds apart. Between sequences, I'll wait five minutes or so. When grunting from one spot over a prolonged period of time, allow more time between sequences. The grunt itself should be deep and guttural, not high-pitched or quacky.

If it sounds as if I don't depend on grunt calls for success, that's true. But, I do use them, especially as part of my rattling ruse. I even use them occasionally to get a buck to look at me or to stop walking so I can judge him. And, I'll continue to use them. After all, the grunt call might be the very thing that tips the scales my way on the next trophy buck I encounter.

SCENTS

The most dramatic proof I have ever seen that scents can work came 17 years ago on a cool October afternoon during Georgia's archery season. I was hunting a harvested soybean field that had some impressive rubs along its edge. To minimize my scent trail, I parked my Jeep on the opposite side of the field from the stand so I could walk directly to the stand through the field. Just before hiking the 300 yards, I remem-

The role of scent in the whitetail's social order and communication may be even more important than we realize. We are just beginning to understand this area of a deer's life. Look carefully and you can see that this long-tined eight-pointer is leaving scent from his preorbital gland (in front of his eye) on the bush. A whitetail has numerous scent glands, primarily on his head, legs and feet. Photo by Mike Biggs.

bered the bottle of buck lure I had purchased recently. Just for the heck of it, I sprinkled some on the bottom of my boots and then headed out.

Once in the stand, I began the wait. About 6:15 p.m., I was surprised to see a buck enter the field ... within 30 yards of my Jeep! He was a good buck, well above the 125-point minimum for the Pope and Young records. Helpless to do anything, I watched and waited for the buck to see or smell the Jeep just beyond him. The buck walked well out into the field and stopped suddenly, his nose to the ground. Then, he began to walk my way ... 10 yards, 20 yards, 50 yards! Like a bolt, it hit me. He was on my tracks, following the trail of buck lure I had left behind!

I tensed and prepared for what I hoped would be an eventual shot. The buck continued to come my way. Every 50 or so yards, he would stop and smell the ground intently. Then, he would look all around, smell the ground again and continue his course. I watched in disbelief.

My nerves were frayed as he walked unerringly toward my stand. At 40 yards, I slowly raised my bow in anticipation of a shot. Then, movement and a squeak from the barbwire fence that ran along the edge of the field drew my attention to the right. A doe had jumped the fence and was now walking briskly toward the buck, who was eyeing her with interest. The doe sashayed right up to the buck, maybe even bumped him, and then turned perpendicular to the buck's course and trotted 20 yards away. The buck stared at her undecidedly. I held my breath. After what seemed like an eternity, he lowered his head and sniffed the ground, taking a couple of half steps my way. Then, he looked back at the doe. She slowly raised her tail and trotted 10 more yards. That was all the buck could stand. He broke into that short-stepping, stiff-legged gait rutting bucks have when after a sweet-smelling doe. I knew I had lost the game.

Although I have used scents quite a bit since that afternoon so many years ago, I must confess that my experience with them has never again been that dramatic. In my case, scents, like deer calls, have fallen into the category of being helpful but nonessential aids. However, my style of hunting places far greater emphasis on basic hunting skills than on trying to trick or fool whitetails with scents and such. So, I admit that my perspective on scents does not represent the final word on the subject.

Hunters today have so many different scent products to choose from that a fellow can get a headache just trying to decide which one does what. Despite some of the fantastic claims and high-sounding terminology, there are only two types of scents of real interest to trophy hunters. One is the cover or masking scent, which is intended to mask human odor. The other is the buck attractant or lure. It is supposed to attract bucks and is usually a derivative of estrus doe urine.

A whitetail's sense of smell is incredible. It is his most formidable weapon, and one we humans cannot match. We compete very favorably in sight with whitetails, and our hearing, though not nearly as good as theirs, at least allows comparison. But when it comes to smell, we aren't

During the rut, bucks will follow the trail of a hot doe wherever it leads. Buck lures made from the urine of estrus does are intended to take advantage of this behavior. Photo by Curt Helmick.

even in the ball game with whitetails. I've seen them do astonishing things with their noses. For instance, my youngest daughter, Kristin, and I sat on the ground one morning and watched for deer in a relatively open hardwood bottom. That afternoon, it began raining and continued all night. The next morning found me at the opposite end of that same hardwood bottom. About 10 a.m., a doe walked into view and began feeding on acorns near where my daughter and I had sat the day before. Suddenly, her head snapped to attention and she became very nervous. She stared hard at something. Her neck outstretched, she cautiously eased over to the exact place we had sat the previous morning. She sniffed the spot a few seconds and then discretely slipped out of sight ... this, a day after we had sat there and after nearly 12 hours of continuous rain!

There are times, however, when whitetails catch a whiff of human scent but are not spooked. Many times, I've seen whitetails react to cold trails or errant breezes only to resume their activities after satisfying themselves there was no immediate danger. But if the human scent is still hot or direct, they will quickly react by hitting the high road. In the whitetail's limited tolerance for subdued human scent lies an opportunity for hunters and the niche of masking scents. You see, it is highly unlikely that any deer scent can completely eliminate or cover human odor, at least not consistently. The best the hunter can hope for is that a cover scent will dilute or confuse his odor. He cannot count on having his scent completely masked, although it may happen on rare occasions. Yet, even the partial masking of a hunter's scent might buy him the few extra seconds or the few additional yards needed to get a shot at a trophy buck. In this hope is found some justification for the use of a masking scent in certain situations.

There are many types of masking scents on the market. Some are derived from other animals, like skunk scent, fox urine and the urine of other critters. There are products that smell like deer foods, apples and acorns for example. These food scents are not only supposed to mask human odor, but they are promoted as deer attractants as well. There are even scents that smell like fresh earth. Some masking scents are actually said to be odorless, while claiming to mask or even dissolve human scent. Besides the commercial masking scents, hunters have come up with other ways to help cover human scent. Some claim vanilla extract is a good masking scent and can even attract deer. Hunters sometimes use natural vegetation to help mask their odor. Pine, cedar, spruce and even the common weed called "rabbit tobacco" all have a strong odor that may help defuse a hunter's scent.

Despite their virtues, I still don't regularly employ masking scents to hide my presence from a buck's nose. No scent can be trusted to do it every time. The only way I can know that a buck will not smell me is by keeping my scent away from his nostrils completely. Whenever possible, I rely on the right wind direction to do that. Plus, I depend on simple basics to minimize my scent ... things like wearing rubber-bottomed boots to reduce my scent trail, avoiding contact with standing vegetation, wearing clean, unscented clothes, bathing with unscented soap and, of course, avoiding strong-smelling deodorants, colognes, etc. Only when the wind is fickle or when I'm hunting in tight cover do I buy the extra insurance cover scents may offer. If I were an avid bowhunter, I undoubtedly would use cover scents more often since shots have to be at such close range. As it is, my type of hunting doesn't call for cover scents to be a regular part of my strategy.

Scents designed to attract bucks are very popular and widely used. Because nearly all are supposedly extracted from the urine of does in heat, I am a bit suspicious about the quality control and consistency of these products as a whole. It would take a lot of hot does to supply all the companies now making buck lure of some type. Plus, I have to question whether even the real thing can hold its potency over extended periods of time. My own experience has been that there is considerable variance in the effectiveness of different brands of buck lure. Stick with the proven companies.

Despite the bowhunting experience I related earlier, I do not expect buck lure to draw bucks to me. (And believe me, I've tried.) Certainly, bucks have been lured into shooting range by attractants, but if that were the only way to shoot a trophy buck, the nation's taxidermists would go belly up after one season. Bucks simply don't come running to buck lure as some ads would lead you to believe. Still, buck lure can be useful in some situations.

Since buck lure is supposed to smell like a doe in heat, the best time to use it is when breeding is taking place. For me, buck lure has three main uses. One, I sometimes employ it as a simple cover scent. It seems to work about as well. (A word of warning: Don't put buck lure directly on your clothes unless you are willing to leave them outside or burn them. Some of this stuff smells rather rank and seems to have unlimited staying power.) Two, I use buck lure to momentarily stop or hold a buck in a certain place. For instance, when hunting a shooting lane that a buck might cross quickly, I will sometimes put buck lure at a strategic point in an attempt to get him to balk long enough to give me a shot. I have had pretty good success with this. Three, when hunting active scrapelines, I will occasionally put buck lure in or around the scrapes to "freshen" them up and to hold a buck there longer when he shows up to check the scrapes. Some hunters even create their own "mock scrapes" and dose them with buck lure in hopes of attracting bucks. Since I usually hunt pre-existing big buck sign, I've had little cause to use this technique, but it may have some merit.

Deer scents do have a place in trophy hunting, and I am convinced that much more is to come in the area of scents. As it is, they are no

When choosing a camo pattern, it is not necessary to exactly duplicate your sur-
roundings. Just be sure the color and the pattern blend with the background.
Chuck Larsen's traditional green forest camo worked well enough in South Texas
to fool this handsome 145-class 10-pointer.

more than helpful aids. They will not replace basic hunting practices.
Yet, if scents can buy you a few extra seconds or cause that buck to come
a few steps closer or stop him long enough for a shot, then the aggra-
vation of putting up with the foul-smelling stuff is well worth it.

CAMOUFLAGE

Hunters today can find a camouflage pattern to fit every situation.
No habitat type has been missed. Some camo patterns even match
specific species of plants in realistic detail. Choosing what you really
need can seem a bit confusing, but actually, it's pretty simple. The truth
is that most of today's camo patterns will work in a wide range of habitats. It is not necessary to exactly duplicate the surroundings. Just be
sure the color and pattern blend with the background. Simply avoid anything that stands out. But having said that, hunters still have to contend
with legal blaze orange requirements.

Let me hasten to say that I'm all for wearing fluorescent orange where required, though I intensely dislike it. The fact is that blaze orange is a major fly-in-the-ointment in the hunter's attempt to become completely camouflaged. I get a kick out of the great emphasis some hunters put on having just the right camo pattern from head to toe. They get all dressed up in their "invisible" suit and drive to the deer woods ... where they put on their legal requirement of 500 square inches of fluorescent orange! It does seem rather counterproductive to worry so much about having the in-vogue camo pattern when the biggest part of it is going to be covered by fluorescent orange anyway. Fortunately for all of us, deer are color blind, or at least mostly so.

In states where orange camo patterns are legal, hunters should opt for these garments rather than solid fluorescent orange outer clothing. Orange camo breaks up the solid background and defuses the human form. Also, avoid slick, shiny fluorescent orange vests or jackets. I believe it is easier for deer to see them than a softer, more textured garment. Obviously, noisy orange clothing is taboo in whitetail hunting. In the snow country where white is allowable in lieu of orange, I also prefer the white camo to solid white.

Generally, the closer a hunter is to the deer, the greater the need for camo. That's why bowhunters place such emphasis on camo. Happily, fluorescent orange is not normally a legal requirement when bowhunting. Rifle hunters in close quarters also must be acutely aware of blending in well. As I mentioned previously, the face and hands are common culprits in giving away the hunter, especially when illuminated by the sun. Take steps to cover them. A hunter should always try to stay in the shadows and keep some type of cover between him and the deer. Also, a hunter should not allow himself to become silhouetted. Even the best camo will not help if that happens.

This is a good place to talk about the latest attempt to become invisible to deer — neutralizing ultraviolet (UV) light. Research apparently indicates that deer can see UV light in much the same way we see light-colored shirts under UV lights. If this is so, then reflected UV light is shockingly visible to deer, virtually glowing. Some of the clothes hunters wear, particularly new clothes and blaze oranges, are supposed to be bad UV offenders. And, most fabric dyes and home laundry detergents are said to enhance UV light. To counter the UV problem,

In states where orange camo patterns are legal, hunters should opt for these garments rather than solid fluorescent orange outer clothing. This hoss was shot in New Brunswick. Check out the beam length and the mass. Despite short tines (which are typical of that region), this buck still scored 160! Photo by Gordon Whittington courtesy of **North American Whitetail.**

commercial sprays and washes are now available to reduce or eliminate reflected UV light. Do these products work? I'm sure they will reduce the amount of reflected UV light in clothing. But, the real question is what role does UV light actually play in the detection of a hunter by a deer? Frankly, I'm not sure. But in the overall scope of a trophy hunter's concerns, I've got to figure the UV problem is well down the list ... at least until the basics are thoroughly mastered.

WALK 'EM UP

Another scorcher was on the way. Even the early morning had been hot and balmy. The deer were unimpressed, too. All I had seen was a couple of does and fawns. Now, the midmorning sun was washing the sparse Mexican landscape. No self-respecting deer would be moving in this heat. My only hope was to make something happen. If I wanted a buck, I would have to walk him up. The hilly terrain and the low, brushy cover were perfect for this tactic. I planned to walk the ridges

The key to walking up bucks is visibility. The cover must be fairly open so the hunter can see at least some of the deer he moves during the hunt. I walked up this buck in a two-year-old clearcut. He was very old and scored in the low 140's.

and sidehills in plain view while making enough noise to alert any deer in the vicinity. With any luck, I might be able to force a buck to his feet and get a shot.

I struck out and soon reached a fair-sized valley. Walking at a comfortable pace, I worked my way along the sidehill. Every 100 yards or so, I would stop and watch, knowing the wait weighed heavy on the nerves of any bedded buck hoping I would pass him by. Before moving on, I would throw rocks into likely cover hoping to move something. On my third stop overlooking that valley, a doe and fawn burst from a thicket and started up the far hillside. Halfway up, they rousted up a small eight-pointer. He followed the doe and fawn over the ridge. Encouraged, I moved on. As I neared the head of the valley, a big doe bound down the valley floor, her hooves clicking loudly against the rocky ground.

For another hour, I continued my hunt, covering two to three miles of rugged countryside. My efforts had put to flight 8 to 10 deer, including two pretty good bucks. Had they been the size I wanted, the 150-yard running shots they offered would have severely tested my shooting skill … and my luck. At least I was seeing deer and had some chance to score.

All I needed now was the right buck and a large dose of good fortune. Both came in the next brushy draw I walked out.

I had just begun to sidle along the ridge overlooking a broad brushy draw when I heard rocks rolling below me and the sound of running deer. A point extended into the draw just ahead, blocking my view of the fleeing deer. I sprinted forward to get around the protruding point. After covering 50 yards, I could see the entire upper end of the draw where the deer had run, but no deer were in sight. They couldn't have gotten out of the draw in the time it took me to run 50 yards. I combed the far hillside. Nothing. Then, I saw movement 75 yards downhill. A doe's head stood above the brush. I brought my binoculars up and checked the brush around her. Something moved just behind the doe. A set of antlers. Big antlers. I tried to count points through the screen of brush shielding the rack. Then, the buck took a couple of steps forward, giving me a clear view of his head and neck. A good 10-pointer! I had seen enough. I hastily exchanged my binoculars for my .270. The hunt ended right there.

There are times when deer simply are not moving and when traditional hunting methods that depend on natural deer movement offer little hope. If you're hunting alone, drives may not be an option. Yet, forced movement may be the only way to put a buck in your sights. During such times, I just back my ears, set my jaw and try to walk'em up. This tactic is something of a cross between a one-man drive and a suped-up still-hunt. The hunter's goal is to aggressively cover as much ground as possible in hopes of pushing up a buck and getting a shot.

The real key to this tactic lies in where it is employed. The cover must be fairly open so the hunter can see at least some of the deer he moves during the hunt. The ideal set-up is hilly terrain with low or sparse cover. Certain parts of Texas, Mexico, the Midwest and the Plains and Prairies Region are well-suited for walking up bucks. But, localized areas that lend themselves to this form of hunting can be found anywhere. Clearcuts are universally available and can be perfect for this tactic. Fallow fields, strips of cover through agricultural fields and burned-out forests may also offer possibilities. The tactic will even work in relatively open forests, especially in hilly terrain. Visibility is essential. Walking up bucks will do no good if you can't see them.

This tactic requires considerable skill on the hunter's part. It is not as simple as just walking around and waiting for a deer to pop up. Well-conceived strategy and good hunting instincts are prerequisites. The hunter must know how to choose his areas and his routes, what cover is most likely to harbor bedding bucks, when to pause, when to make noise, etc. Instant decisions and fast reactions are required. Some hunters simply cannot respond fast enough to ever be successful when trying to walk up deer. Needless to say, good skill with a rifle is a necessity. Shots must be made quickly and often at running deer. No, this tactic is not for everyone or everyplace, but there are times when walking'em up is the best game in town.

SNOW-TRACKING

The late night snowfall in eastern Alberta had made tracking conditions ideal. I had no trouble picking up the big set of tracks just after daybreak along the edge of the alfalfa field. I had been on the tracks for two hours and probably had covered four miles. Most of that time, the buck had been traveling at a fairly steady gait and more or less in a straight line. Now, at 10 a.m., he was beginning to meander. I slowed my pace, expecting to find him bedded somewhere just ahead.

The tracks of the buck were quartering up a fair-sized hill. A series of benches stair-cased the side of the hill. I figured the buck would lay up on a bench near the top. The fresh snow allowed me to slip through the poplar and spruce forest in absolute silence. I crept slowly up to each new bench and peered over, studying the area carefully before climbing out into full view. About three-quarters of the way to the top, I found what I was looking for.

I had just gained enough elevation to see most of the new bench and all of the rise behind it. My eyes followed the buck's tracks across the bench and part of the way up the hill beyond. There, I could no longer make out the tracks. I took a step or two to gain a better view. When I did, I saw movement about 50 yards away. It was the buck. He had doubled back across the sidehill beyond the bench and bedded in a shallow depression. The movement I had seen was the buck laying his head out flat against the snow-covered ground in an effort to hide. Talk about catching a buck flat-footed! My rifle was already at portarms.

Instantly, I had the prostrate buck in my sights. Even as I checked his rack, I saw his eyes roll white and his rear end start to rise off the

A fresh snow, relatively open terrain and plenty of time and patience are important ingredients for successful snow-tracking. Of course, a buck like this one wouldn't hurt, either! Photo by Bill Kinney.

ground. He'd seen enough. So had I. The 10-pointer never left his bed.

That's one of only two bucks I've ever shot in the bed, and that snow-tracking story is far from typical. If you're lucky, snow-tracking usually leads to a split-second shot at a buck rapidly putting down fresh, well-spaced tracks in the snow. But given the right conditions and the right terrain, tracking a buck in the snow can be an enjoyable, educational and possibly even a successful experience.

Let me say up front that snow-tracking is not my field of expertise. I know guys who specialize at it, and they know a whole lot more about snow-tracking than I do. They are willing and able to track bucks in a wide range of conditions with some hope of success. I, on the other

Snow-tracking is most practiced in the North Region, where this fine buck was killed. Photo by Gordon Whittington courtesy of **North American Whitetail**.

hand, limit my snow-tracking to times when everything is just right for the tactic. Let's look at the best conditions for snow-tracking.

The first prerequisite as far as I'm concerned is a fresh snow. The fresher the better. New snow assures that the tracks you come across were recently made. The soft powder also allows you to walk quietly, which is essential if you are to have any hope of walking up on a buck unawares. Fresh snow also covers old tracks that could confuse a trail. And not to be overlooked, trophy bucks are likely to be on the move after a snowfall.

Besides a fresh snow, relatively open terrain is best for snow-tracking. If the cover is thick, you cannot realistically hope to walk up on a buck and get a shot. The odds are stacked against you. Visibility is a requirement. I prefer hilly, relatively open woodlands or broken country for tracking.

In addition, a would-be snow-tracker needs time and sufficient land to follow the tracks wherever they lead. Unless I have reason to believe the tracks are red hot, I usually limit my snow-tracking to morning starts. This not only gives me all day to stay after the buck, but he almost surely will bed down during midday, allowing me to catch up with him. If a track is obviously very fresh, I'll take it up anytime of day. Frankly, I feel the chances of killing a buck are better if you can catch up with him when he's up and moving. Then, he's easier to see and may be more preoccupied than when he's lying still and quiet in his bed. Along with sufficient time, the snow-tracker needs large expanses of lightly hunted land available to him. Bucks travel considerable distances at times, and a tracker must be allowed to follow wherever they go. This is the reason why much of the snow-tracking takes place on large public landholdings, especially those with enough backcountry to allow the hunter to get away from the crowds.

Another essential requirement for snow-tracking is a set of fresh trophy buck tracks. From this requirement, two questions arise. One, how can you know the tracks are fresh? Two, how do you tell they're made by a trophy buck?

Of course, after a new snow, any tracks you come across are fresh. Beyond that, there are some ways to tell if the tracks have been made recently. One good way to determine freshness is to step next to the tracks and compare your foot print to the tracks. This should tell you something about their age. Also, check the edges of the tracks to see if the snow has frosted over and hardened or whether the snow is still loose and granular. If the edges are hard, the tracks probably are not fresh. Are the edges of the tracks still sharp or have they rounded off with time? Has debris collected in the tracks? If leaves have been kicked up, how do they compare to leaves you turn up? If the leaves in the tracks are more dried out, considerable time has elapsed since the deer passed through. Overall, just study the tracks carefully. If they're real fresh, you'll be able to tell it. If you have much doubt, follow the tracks some distance to try to get better information. Droppings or where the deer has urinated are excellent indications of the age of sign. Fresh droppings will be soft and shiny. If the urine has not yet frozen, assuming the temperature is below freezing, the trail is still hot. Unless you can satisfy yourself the tracks are fresh, move on to something more certain.

Determining whether or not the tracks are those of a trophy buck is not always easy, but when all the evidence is considered, you can usually get a pretty good idea of what you're dealing with. The tracks themselves can tell you a lot. Basic logic dictates that big bucks make big tracks, but there can be exceptions. In fact, big tracks don't necessarily mean that it was even a buck that made them. And even if they are buck tracks, big tracks don't guarantee big antlers. Still, I don't waste my time following tracks unless they are really big. The shape of tracks can also provide information. A mature buck's tracks, especially once scraping and breeding are underway, are usually more rounded than a doe's or young buck's. This is because of the wear from pawing and all the traveling a buck does during the rut. Also, the hooves of a big buck tend to be more spayed (spread apart) than those of a lesser deer, mainly due to his greater weight. And because he is heavier, a big buck leaves deeper tracks in the ground than other deer. By the way, it's often said that tracks with the dew claws showing are buck tracks. Well, both bucks and does have dew claws, and in soft ground, the dew claws can be seen in the tracks of both. However, the dew claws are more likely to show on big buck tracks simply because of the buck's greater weight.

Much can be learned about a deer from the trail it leaves in the snow. I pay special attention to the length of stride and the center-to-center width of the track path. Big bucks take long strides. If possible, I try to compare the stride length of the deer I'm interested in to that of other deer. If it's noticeably longer, I may be on to something. Also, the legs of a barrel-chested trophy buck are set farther apart than those of does or younger bucks. Because of this, the left to right spread of a trophy buck's track path can be as much as eight inches. By comparison, a doe's may be virtually in-line. The width of the track path is one of the best indicators of a big buck. Drag marks in shallow snow also can be a signal that you're looking at buck tracks. However, if the snow is deeper than two inches, both bucks and does often drag their feet. Finally, bucks tend to travel in a straight line and at an even gait as though they have a purpose. Does tend to meander and vary both their gait and stride.

If you stay on the trail long enough, you may find proof positive you're following a buck. For instance, rubs or scrapes made along the way will tell you for sure a buck made the tracks. And, they may tell you something of his size. Occasionally, you can even see impressions of his antlers in the snow. Most often, this is the case with feeding bucks. Also, when a buck is trailing a doe, you can sometimes see where his main beams left imprints in the snow as he sniffed the doe's trail. Excited bucks often will urinate on the move, leaving streaks of urine followed by dribbling. Does usually stop to urinate and leave round holes in the snow. With a little patience and study, a hunter should be able to piece together enough evidence to decide what he's following. The trail of a trophy buck is usually exceptional in some way. If there's much doubt after a reasonable time on the trail, the deer probably is not worth following.

I know some hunters who have a well-developed, finely honed strategy for tracking bucks in the snow, but I don't. My strategy is pretty simple — persistence. I get after him and stay after him. While on the trail, my pace is determined by whatever the buck was doing at the time he made the tracks I'm looking at. If he's covering ground at a good clip, I do the same. If he slows up, I slow up. If he begins to feed or meander, then I shift to a still-hunting mode, watching not only ahead but both sides as well.

The most critical time of the hunt is when you draw near the buck. Often, you can just sense his presence. The sign, the timing or the place may all indicate that the time of reckoning is at hand. The tracks may begin to wander or perhaps circle back a bit. You may sense the time has come for the buck to end his travels. The place may be right for a big buck to feed or perhaps bed. Somehow you know, or strongly suspect, that this is the time and place the hunt will be made or lost. Then, you must call all your hunting skills and instincts into play as you go one-on-one against a superbly equipped quarry that may well know you're after him. There probably won't be a second chance, and the one chance you get may be slim. But if you do everything just right, you may have a few seconds to play out your hand and to win at one of hunting's greatest challenges — tracking down a trophy whitetail in his own snowy realm.

Making The Most Of The Moment Of Truth

Chapter 21

Cartridges, Bullets
And Rifles

I'M A GUN NUT. I freely admit it. I really enjoy probing both the real and theoretical advantages and disadvantages of different rifles, cartridges and bullets. So, I am sorely tempted to get into tedious detail when talking about guns and such. While I will make no promises, I do hope to avoid that here. Rather, I want to reach practical conclusions about arming oneself for trophy whitetail hunting that aren't so watered down by concessions to special circumstances as to be useless. To do that, we need to start with the animal itself.

The trophy whitetail is no ordinary deer. He may be as much as 50 percent larger than a younger buck. That alone means he will react less to a hit and be more difficult to kill. But more than size, a trophy buck's survival instincts, developed through years of struggle in nature's arena, give him a will to live far surpassing that of lesser bucks. When wounded, not only does this tenacity carry a trophy buck for longer distances, it also drives him to instinctively seek out protective cover or difficult terrain in his effort to escape. Without question, a far higher percentage of wounded trophy bucks fail to be

While on a hunt in Saskatchewan in 1991, I was once again reminded of a trophy buck's great tenacity. I hit this buck too far back on a running shot. After many anxious hours of tracking in deep snow over a distance of five miles, I finally caught up with the big 11-pointer and finished him. Photo by Jim Clarey.

recovered by hunters than do lesser bucks.

Only two days prior to writing this, I was again reminded of a trophy buck's great stamina. After two weeks of hard hunting in Canada, I finally saw the buck I was after. Unfortunately, he had seen me first and was making a hasty retreat across a semi-open meadow. A quartering 150-yard running shot was the only chance I had at him. I didn't lead him enough, and the 140-grain Nosler from my 7mm Rem. Mag. struck him in the hindquarters, resulting in a mortal but not immediately fatal wound. After many hours of tracking in deep snow over a distance of five miles, I finally caught up with the big 11-pointer and finished him. A lesser buck would have succumbed to such a wound in a fraction of the time and distance.

Another factor to consider in arming yourself for trophy whitetails is that opportunities for shots at trophy bucks are rare. Most often, long hours, lots of hard work and maybe even a double fistful of dollars have gone into the chance to draw down on a trophy whitetail. When that fateful moment comes, the hunter must be ready to take full advantage of it, even if the shot offered is difficult or from a bad angle. If you fail at an opportunity to kill an ordinary buck, it may be no big deal. Ordinary bucks are interchangeable and another will probably come along to replace the one missed. Not so with trophies. Each one is special. Some are irreplaceable. The stakes are too high to leave anything to chance when trophy hunting.

In selecting the right rifle for trophy bucks, make no compromises. Don't make the decision based on what outfit will also allow you to shoot woodchucks or prairie dogs during the off-season. Don't choose something too powerful just because you hope to also use it someday on a moose or perhaps a grizzly. A gun for serious trophy whitetail hunting should be the one that's right for that purpose.

Given all this, a general conclusion can be drawn about what the proper firearm for trophy whitetails should be capable of doing. (This discussion will be limited to centerfire rifles since they are the most effective and widely used gun for whitetails.) Simply stated, a trophy whitetail rifle should be able to hit and cleanly kill a trophy buck over the widest possible range of distances and circumstances (shot angles, cover conditions, etc.) likely to be encountered. In other words, the rifle should be suitable to handle both the best and worst situations a trophy hunter may run into. This criterion begins to define the requirements for cartridges, bullets and rifles.

CARTRIDGES

Whitetail deer, even the biggest bucks, can be and have been killed by everything from a .22 Short to a .458 Win. Mag. But, just because a cartridge is capable of killing a trophy whitetail doesn't mean it is right for the job. Being the gun nut I am, I've shot deer with a .222 (one), .243, 6mm, .25-06, .270, .280, .284, 7mm-08, 7x57, 7mm Rem.

A rifle for trophy whitetails must be powerful enough to cleanly kill a big buck over the widest possible range of conditions and circumstances, including a rear raking shot such as this. Photo by Mike Biggs.

Mag., .30-30, .308, .30-06, .300 Win. Mag. and .338 Win. Mag. (one). Except for the .222, which I consider too light for whitetails of any size, and the .338 Win. Mag., which is unnecessarily powerful, the others can all be classified as deer cartridges. However, I do not consider all of them to be right for trophy bucks. Right away, I would throw out the

.243, 6mm and, yes, even the venerable .30-30. The remaining cartridges — the .25-06 to the .300 Win. Mag. and others similar to them — essentially constitute what I feel is the range of trophy buck cartridges.

Narrowing this down further, I believe cartridges for trophy bucks should shoot at least a 120-grain bullet, generate a minimum muzzle velocity of 2,700 feet per second (fps) and deliver 1,300 or more foot-pounds of energy at 300 yards. The .25-06 becomes marginal on the basis of bullet weight and 300-yard energy. The 7mm-08, 7x57 and .308 don't have much room to spare on either velocity or 300-yard energy, but all are marginally acceptable for trophy bucks. That leaves the cartridges that, in my opinion, are the best for trophy whitetails. They are the .264 Win. Mag., .270, .280, .284, 7mm Rem. Mag., .30-06, .300 Win. Mag. and other similar cartridges, such as those of the Weatherby series. Rifles in any of these cartridges are capable of hitting and killing trophy bucks at ranges in excess of 300 yards ... if the hunter does his part. If I had to pick favorites, the .270, .280 (when handloaded) and the 7mm Rem. Mag. would be my choices.

Let's now examine some of the logic behind both the criteria and the cartridge selection. We've said that a trophy whitetail rifle must be capable of hitting and cleanly killing a big buck over the widest possible range of distances and circumstances. Under field conditions, I believe 300 yards is about the maximum distance even a good shot can accurately place a bullet with any consistency. For that reason, my criteria for a trophy deer rifle is based on meeting minimal performance levels at that range. If a cartridge is adequate at 300 yards, it will obviously do the job quite admirably at ranges less than 300 yards (with the right bullet).

Assuming the shooter and the rifle are capable of reasonable accuracy, one of the biggest factors in hitting a deer's vitals at 300 yards is bullet drop, or trajectory (the flight path of a bullet). The amount of drop is determined largely by velocity (along with a bullet's ballistic coefficient, which is a measure of how streamlined it is for efficient flight). This is where the minimum velocity of 2,700 fps comes into play. Applying this to a hunting situation, let's assume the chest depth of a small-bodied trophy whitetail is about 16 inches (a big northern buck can have a chest depth of more than 20 inches). A bullet with a reasonably good ballistic coefficient leaving the muzzle at 2,700 fps will

While most shots at whitetails are under 100 yards, longer shots do come along, especially in the more open country. To dependably hit a buck's vital area at extended ranges out to 300 yards, I believe a minimum muzzle velocity of 2,700 fps is required. Photo by Mike Biggs.

drop about 10 inches at 300 yards when sighted-in two inches high at 100 yards, which is my preferred sight-in point for reasons I'll cover later. With a maximum bullet drop of 10 inches at 300 yards, a high-on-the-body hold, say two or three inches under the top of the buck's back, will result in a fatal hit even at 300 yards. Any more drop than 10 inches almost dictates an off-the-body hold, which I don't like.

Driving a bullet into the vitals of a big buck from difficult angles or from long distances requires both sufficient velocity and adequate bullet weight (as well as strong bullet construction). All things being equal, a light bullet will not penetrate or kill as well as a heavier bullet traveling at the same velocity. I've had considerable experience with cartridges shooting reasonably light bullets (.243, 6mm and .25-06). Based on that experience, I believe that at least a 120-grain bullet is needed to dependably reach the vitals of a big whitetail from off angles, such as a rear raking shot. I know some people will jump and holler about taking such a shot, but the right cartridge and the right bullet are perfectly capable of delivering a fatal blow to the biggest whitetail from difficult angles. Of course, all this is predicated on a good hit that transverses the buck's vitals no matter where the entry point. A bad hit is a bad hit whether from a .243 or a .300 Win. Mag. Still, a marginal hit from a more powerful cartridge is more likely to kill or disable a buck than the same hit from a lesser cartridge. This fact leads me to opt for more power.

How much power is enough? The answer obviously depends on many factors, bullet placement being foremost among them. Operating under the objective of having enough power for the worst situation likely to be encountered, experience has taught me that a bullet needs to strike with at least 1,300 foot-pounds of energy to ensure a clean kill. With that energy, a well-constructed bullet will penetrate deeply and cause extensive damage. Our criteria for a trophy cartridge call for 1,300 foot-pounds of energy at 300 yards. That requirement limits the number of cartridges that make the grade. Many less powerful cartridges are capable of delivering the required 1,300 foot-pounds … but at lesser distances. For instance, a 150-grain bullet from a .30-30 hits with 1,300 foot-pounds of force at 100 yards. By comparison, a 150-grain bullet from a .300 Win. Mag. slams home with 1,300 foot-pounds of energy at 425 yards. Think about the striking power of the .300 Win. Mag. slug at 100 yards! You see, it's not that the .30-30 and many of the other tried-and-proven "brush" cartridges are not effective for deer. They are, but their range is limited by both power and trajectory. Why be so limited?

While on the subject of killing power, two terms are frequently associated with a bullet's ability to kill an animal. One is "knockdown power." This term is usually connected with the bigger, slower bullets that, because of their weight and large frontal area, sometimes knock the deer down on impact. These big slugs do considerable damage in direct association with their bullet path. But, the problem with these slow, poorly shaped projectiles is that they loose their energy rapidly and have a trajectory like a nine-iron shot. The .375 Win., .45-70 and .444 Marlin are examples of cartridges with lots of knockdown power.

The other term frequently used to describe a bullet's ability to kill is "shocking power." This is a term most often associated with high-speed bullets. When a high-velocity bullet strikes animal tissue, which is mostly water, violent shock waves erupt from the point of impact and spread to surrounding tissue. These shock waves can produce extensive tissue damage well beyond the actual bullet path and can result in sudden kills, particularly when induced in soft, vital tissue like that found in the chest cavity. In addition, when a bone is hit by a high-speed bullet, even the bone fragments themselves become destructive missiles.

How much velocity is required to produce this shock effect? Undoubtedly, some level of shock is produced at any velocity. While it is little more than speculation on my part, I would guess that a minimum striking velocity of something around 2,500 fps is necessary on deer-sized animals to realize the dramatic impact of "shocking power." However, I must hasten to point out that factors other than velocity contribute to the shock effect ... factors such as the size of the animal, bullet placement, bullet weight and how fast the bullet expands and sheds its energy. These are things some hunters were slow to realize after high-velocity cartridges first hit the scene in the early 1900's.

From the beginning, much was made of the dramatic kills high-speed cartridges produced. Even very light bullets traveling at high velocity from such cartridges as the .220 Swift (shooting a 48-grain bullet at 4,100 fps) and the .250-3000 Savage (shooting an 87-grain bullet at 3,000 fps) were heralded as instant deer killers. And, they were ... if the bullet punched through the deer's rib cage and entered his chest cavity. But if these light bullets hit a shoulder blade or had to penetrate much muscle to reach the vitals, a terrible superficial wound and a crippled deer were the results. Savvy hunters soon realized that adequate bullet weight and good bullet construction were still necessary for reliable penetration and sure kills. The best combination for quick, dependable kills on deer-sized animals was found to be high velocity when combined with a good bullet of sufficient weight. The .270 earned its reputation based on that principle, and the principle remains true today.

This is as good a place as any to talk about trying to force a bullet through brush. The best advice is don't try it. Even the old "brush" cartridges shooting the big, slow bullets will not dependably arrive on target after banging around on brush. The bullets most likely to hold the course when striking brush are those with high sectional density (the longer, heavier bullets of a given diameter). These bullets tend to be more stable in flight. It is generally true that bullets traveling at high velocity do tend to deflect or even breakup on brush, but much depends on the bullet itself. When I shot one of my best

The best advice about trying to force a bullet through brush is "don't try it." If possible, pick a hole through the brush or target an unobscured spot. Short of a head shot or an upper neck shot, this buck doesn't offer much of a target. A "blind shot" at his shoulder would likely result in a wounded deer. Photo by Mike Biggs.

bucks, the 140-grain Nosler from my 7mm Rem. Mag. centered a three-quarter-inch limb 10 yards in front of the buck. Although the bullet was deflected a few inches off course, it still got the job done.

Brush-bucking considerations are not worth trying to achieve at the cost of velocity, downrange energy and trajectory.

Now, a word on handloaded versus factory ammo. Over the years, hunters who "rolled their own" usually could count on better accuracy, more velocity and a wider bullet selection than were available over the counter. Today, the advantages of handloading are not as great as they once were, but depending on the cartridge, the benefits still can be considerable. Let's see why.

Given the available powders and bullet selection, each cartridge has a maximum potential. Because of economics, product liability and the strength limitations of the guns chambered for the various cartridges, the full potential of a cartridge is seldom realized by factory ammo. From an economic standpoint, ammunition makers cannot justify loading a cartridge with every available bullet option. And, the more popular options may or may not be the best for hunting trophy whitetails. Also, it has not always been economically feasible for a manufacturer to load premium bullets (which generally cost much more than standard bullets) in commercial ammo or to load to the exacting tolerances possible with handloading. Fortunately, as hunters have become more knowledgeable about bullets and cartridge performance, the ammo companies are finding they can pass on the higher cost of premium-quality ammo. This can be seen in the emergence of premium lines such as Federal Premium, Remington Extended Range and Winchester Supreme rifle ammunition. These top-of-the-line ammunitions come closer to realizing a cartridge's full potential. Still, the handloader can select the precise bullet he wants and tailor the load to his rifle, getting all his rifle/cartridge combination has to offer.

Although runaway product liability is partly responsible for the general trend of manufacturers to load below a cartridge's potential, there are also practical reasons for this. Different cartridges are linked to different rifles and actions, and the strength of these rifles and actions varies considerably. Because certain cartridges are used in weaker actions or in rifles with design flaws or inferior steel, the manufacturers have to keep breech pressure within the allowable range for the weakest guns that could possibly use their ammo. For some cartridges, this prevents factory ammo from approaching their power potential. For instance, the .280 Rem. was originally marketed as a round to be used in autoloaders to compete with the .270. Because autoloading actions aren't as strong as bolt actions, the .280 was and still is loaded below its potential. By contrast, the .270 was designed from the beginning as a cartridge for bolt actions. Factory ammo delivers much of its potential. In recent years, advances in rifle powders have allowed manufacturers to increase the performance of certain cartridges while still staying within allowable pressure limits. Yet, the handloader can milk the last bit of performance out of any cartridge. In cartridges like the .280, the difference can be substantial, which is why I prefer to build my own.

BULLETS

When it's all said and done, the planning, time, effort and expense that go into hunting trophy whitetails ride on whether or not the bullet does its job. This small projectile is the ultimate link between the hunter and success ... or failure. If the bullet performs its task, the hunt ends successfully, assuming a good hit. If the bullet fails on its assignment, not only does the hunter go home without his trophy, but he must live with the bitter disappointment of having wounded a noble animal. Despite the critical importance of the bullet itself, many hunters make little effort to select the right bullet for their particular situation.

Let's start our bullet discussion by examining the demanding and somewhat contradictory expectations placed on a trophy whitetail bullet ... and most other big game bullets for that matter. One, the bullet should expand rapidly upon contact so its energy is violently imparted to the animal. Two, it should penetrate deeply so the vitals can be reached from just about any angle. And if that's not enough, the bullet should expand and penetrate properly whether shot from a distance of 10 yards or 300 yards, regardless of a velocity difference of several hundred feet per second! This last demand, particularly, poses a real problem. You see, a bullet that would open up quickly at the reduced velocity of a 300-yard shot would likely go to pieces on a buck only 10 yards away. Conversely, a bullet built to expand properly and penetrate dependably at the higher speeds of a 10-yard shot would likely be too strongly constructed to expand well at 300 yards. And, the problem is not limited only to varying ranges; different cartridges present the same dilemma. For instance, the same 150-grain .30 caliber bullet can be fired from a .308 at 2,800 fps or from a .300 Win. Mag. at 3,300 fps. Even at iden-

Steve Vaughn shot this excellent 10-pointer with a .300 Win. Mag. Bullets fired at very high velocities can fail to penetrate properly unless the right one is selected. Steve used the fine 180-grain Remington Core-Lokt on this buck. Photo courtesy of **North American Whitetail.**

tical ranges, the velocity at impact differs drastically between these two cartridges. Again, we have the problem of the same bullet being called upon to perform consistently at significantly differing velocities. This is a problem bullet makers have grappled with for decades.

So, what's the solution? While there is no cure-all, there are some guiding principles that I use in bullet selection. To start with, between bullet expansion and penetration, I prefer to hedge my bets in favor of penetration. My primary concern is that the bullet stay together en route to the vitals, but proper expansion is certainly important. Actually, our requirement for a minimum muzzle velocity of 2,700 fps in itself almost assures adequate bullet expansion, except perhaps at long ranges. About the only way to get into trouble with expansion would be to shoot one of the heaviest bullets available for a cartridge with marginal velocities. The heaviest bullets in a given caliber normally are very strongly constructed. The combined effects of lower velocity and strong bullet construction could spell expansion problems. The solution, then, is to use the lighter or medium-weight big game bullets in the less powerful trophy cartridges with velocities under, say, 2,900 fps. For instance, in the 7mm-08 or 7x57, shoot 140 or 150-grain bullets, not 160's or 175's; in the .308, use 150's or 165's, not 180 or 200-grain bullets; and in the .30-06, choose 150, 165 or, at most, 180-grain bullets, not 200's or 220's.

While high velocity promotes expansion, it can be detrimental to penetration, especially at close and intermediate ranges. When fired at velocities exceeding 3,000 fps, some standard-grade bullets, particularly the lighter big game bullets in a given caliber, expand so rapidly that they lose much of their weight, thus limiting penetration. A few may even break up upon striking the animal, especially if a major bone is hit. There are essentially two ways to combat the problem of erratic bullet performance at high velocity. One, use a heavier bullet in that caliber, i.e., a bullet with higher sectional density. Two, use a premium-grade bullet designed for controlled expansion and limited weight loss. Let's take a closer look at these two options.

All things being equal, a heavier bullet will retain more of its weight and penetrate deeper than a lighter bullet of the same caliber. So, when using standard-grade bullets at velocities of 3,000 fps or better, penetration insurance can be bought by using heavier bullets. For instance, in the .270, use 140 or 150-grain bullets; in the 7mm Rem. Mag., use 150 or 160-grain bullets; and in the .300 Win. Mag., use 165 or 180-grain bullets. Because heavier bullets also retain velocity better than lighter ones, little is lost in trajectory or energy at extended ranges as a result of the lower muzzle velocity using heavier bullets.

The closest whitetail I have ever shot was virtually looking over my shoulder. Sitting next to a fence post and facing downwind in a virtual

This heavy eight-pointer was about 120 yards away when the 140-grain Nosler Partition arrived from my .280 Rem. There is no better hunting bullet than the Nosler Partition, which opens up quickly and penetrates dependably because of a partition across the bullet's center.

gale, I was rattling away when I saw movement just over my left shoulder. Thinking someone had walked up behind me, I spun around abruptly, only to find a big buck staring intently downwind. He gave me no more than a cursory glance before resuming his search for the bucks he was sure were thrashing out their differences nearby. While it's hard to judge a buck from a distance of about five feet while looking up at him, I could make out enough about his main beams, mass and spread to know he was a worthwhile buck. I just tilted my rifle barrel up and fired. He didn't quite fall on me, but it was close.

I don't know the distance of the longest shot I ever made on a whitetail. Suffice to say it was a long way ... too far to be shooting. I had given the shot up as a miss when the telltale "thump" finally echoed back. I would like to claim it was skill that brought the big 13-pointer down, but alas, it was not. It was blind luck.

What do my shortest and longest shots on whitetails have to do with a discussion of bullets? Well, I shot both animals with the same make of bullet and was able to recover both bullets. Even though one bullet was traveling over 3,300 fps upon contact and the other was loafing along at about 2,100 fps when it finally arrived, the two recovered bullets look almost identical and still retain almost 65 percent of their original weight! How can that be? They were premium bullets designed with a soft front end to expand quickly and with a solid partition across the bullet's center to guarantee over 50 percent weight retention. Specifically, they were Nosler Partitions, one of the finest hunting bullets available.

There are several makes of premium-grade, expanding bullets on the market today that are designed to ensure minimum weight loss and deep penetration. I have had extensive experience with the Nosler Partition and some experience with the Speer Grand Slam and Barnes bullets. All performed well. Other manufacturers also make premium bullets of good reputation, but I have not used them. It's also worth mentioning that some standard bullets are capable of good penetration even at high speeds. Remington Core-Lokt and Hornady Interlock bullets are dependable performers, but at extreme velocities, I still favor the heavier weights in these bullets. As for the Nosler, however, I have little hesitation using even the lighter big game bullets in a caliber (130 grain in the .270; 140 grain in the 7mm; and the 150 grain in the .30 caliber, etc.) at speeds over 3,000 fps on trophy whitetails. In fact, my favorite load (chosen because of accuracy) in both my .280 and 7mm Rem. Mag. hustles a 140-grain Nosler along at 3100 fps and 3350 fps, respectively. I use a 150-grain Nosler in my .270 because my rifle shoots it more accurately than it does the 130-grain.

Another consideration in bullet selection is something called "ballistic coefficient." This is just a fancy name for how well a bullet holds its velocity during flight, which is an important concern since both trajectory and downrange energy are affected. The ballistic coefficient of a bullet is determined by two factors — sectional density and shape. Simply stated, a longer, heavier bullet will overcome air resistance better than a shorter, lighter bullet of the same shape and caliber. And, a pointed, streamlined bullet will "cut the air" better than a flat-nosed or round-nosed bullet of the same caliber and weight. Since most big game bullets in the calibers we've discussed have adequate sectional density for efficient flight to start with, the shape of the bullet is of more concern to the trophy hunter than sectional density as far as bullet flight is concerned. An example will best illustrate the importance of bullet shape to trajectory and downrange energy.

A 180-grain bullet from a .30-06 leaves the muzzle at about 2,700 fps with 2,900 foot-pounds of energy. At 300 yards, that bullet in a pointed soft-point would be still traveling 2,050 fps and retain 1,700 foot-pounds of energy. Sighted-in two inches high at 100 yards, the pointed soft-point would be about 10 inches low at the 300-yard mark. If that bullet were a 180-grain round-nose, however, it would have slowed to 1,700 fps at 300 yards and would have only 1,150 foot-pounds of wallop left. Plus, sighted-in two inches high at 100 yards, the round-nosed slug would drop about 15 inches at 300 yards. The conclusion, then, is that the more streamlined pointed-nosed bullets can make a significant difference in hitting and killing a trophy whitetail at long ranges.

Boat-tail bullets are the most aerodynamic of all, but I've never been particularly fond of them when used at extreme velocities. Using boat-tails, I have shot many species of big game, ranging in size from whitetails to moose. Of the bullets I could recover, I found an alarming number had lost too much weight for dependable penetration. The lead core of some had even separated from the jacket, especially on close or medium-range shots where velocity was still high. Yet, I know some successful trophy hunters who swear by boat-tails. But almost to a man, they use the heavier bullets in their respective calibers, like the 162-grain boat-tail in the 7mm or the 180-grain in the .30 caliber. At velocities under 3,000 fps, most boat-tails would probably perform fine.

RIFLES

The rifle a trophy whitetail hunter chooses is pretty much a matter of personal preference. There are many makes and models that will get the job done; however, because of the demands of trophy hunting, some choices are better than others. The choices largely revolve around actions.

There are basically five types of actions of concern to whitetail hunters. They are single-shots, lever actions, pumps, autoloaders and bolt actions. There are, of course, double rifles, but they don't have much of a place in whitetail hunting. Because of the high stakes nature of trophy hunting, I would eliminate single-shots from consideration. Why be limited to one shot when other actions are available that will do anything a single-shot will do and allow rapid follow-up shots? Sure, the first shot is the most important one, and I realize that single-shots are chambered for some excellent cartridges and can be very accurate and well-balanced. For varmint hunting or even for big game hunting where an irreplaceable trophy is highly unlikely to show up, single-shots are fine. But when I'm after really big whitetails, I like to know quick follow-up shots are possible if I need them.

Lever actions are an American classic. They conjure up images of the Old West and John Wayne. In the deer hunting arena, lever actions are the stereotype "brush rifle" and have accounted for countless whitetails over the last century. They are quick-handling, rapid-fire guns that typically lob big, round-nosed bullets at their target. This makes them superbly adapted for close-up work in thick cover.

Historically, lever actions have lacked long-range potential. There are three primary reasons for this: limited cartridge selection, tubular cartridge feeding (which makes the use of pointed bullets dangerous since recoil can cause an accidental discharge in the magazine) and difficulty in mounting scopes. Today, these problems have been eliminated or reduced in some lever actions. Even the famous Winchester 94 now has angled ejection to allow the use of a top-mounted scope and is available in the .307 Win. (a rimmed version of the relatively potent .308). Browning and Savage, which include the .308 among their offerings, market clip-fed lever actions that can accommodate the more aerodynamic pointed bullets. Still, the lever action remains essentially a close to medium-range gun. I do not consider it to be the best choice for hunting trophy whitetails.

The pump-action rifle is a viable option for the trophy hunter. It is very fast on the follow-up shot, quick-handling and dependable. Furthermore, Remington pump-action rifles, which as far as I know are the only pumps currently being manufactured, are chambered for long-range numbers like the .270 and .30-06. Scopes can be easily mounted on the Remington, and the ones I've shot have been quite accurate. In places where most hunting is done in thick cover, the pump is worthy of consideration.

Everything said about the pump is also true of the autoloader, except the autoloader is even faster. Plus, Browning's excellent BAR is

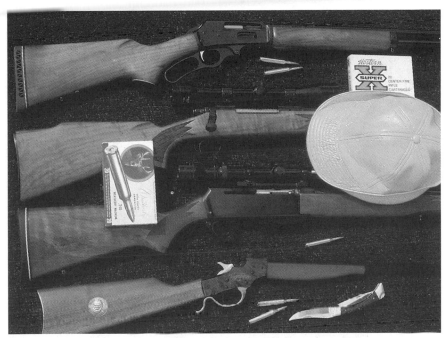

There are basically five types of actions of concern to whitetail hunters. From the top, they are the lever action, bolt action, autoloader, single-shot and the pump (not pictured). For trophy hunters, bolt actions, autos and pumps are the most useful.

available in the 7mm Rem. Mag. and the .300 Win. Mag., as well as the .270, .308 and .30-06. Today's autoloaders are dependable and surprisingly accurate. They are certainly valid contenders.

Hands down, my choice for big whitetails is a bolt action. While not as fast on the follow-up as a lever action, pump or auto, the bolt action has dependability, strength, accuracy, appearance, simplicity, cartridge selection and flexibility going for it. There is a bolt action to handle every imaginable situation or whim. Today's selection and quality of factory rifles have never been better. Some even look and perform like custom rifles. A few of the major manufacturers like Remington and U.S. Repeating Arms are even offering custom versions of their rifles from in-house custom shops … at prices that don't put the kids' college education in jeopardy. And, recent years have seen a proliferation of fine custom gun makers who can rework or build a bolt action to suit your exacting desires.

What would be the ideal bolt-action rifle for hunting trophy white-

This is my old faithful trophy rifle and one of its more noteworthy victims. The rifle is a 7mm Rem. Mag. built on a reworked Remington 700 action. It has a 24-inch stainless steel barrel that is fluted to reduce weight. The stock is a fiberglass/Kevlar composite. A 2½X-8X Leupold scope sits atop the rifle. (It now wears a 3X-9X Swarovski only because my wife gave it to me on my birthday. Good wife.) The gun, sling and scope weigh a shade under 8¾ pounds. All in all, this is pretty close to an ideal trophy whitetail rig.

tails across North America? There are almost as many answers to that as there are hunters, but in my opinion, it would shape up something like this: The rifle would be chambered in 7mm Rem. Mag. The decision of which make and model action to use is difficult. I like the claw extractor and the three-position safety on the pre-64 Model 70-type actions, but the accuracy of the Remington Model 700 is unexcelled. I would probably opt for the Remington, even though I don't like the extractor. (A Sako-type extractor would be better.) The Remington safety is a good one, but I would prefer that it lock the bolt when the safety is engaged, as was the case with the older Model 700's before product liability forced a change. I would put a premium-quality, 24-inch barrel without iron sights on the rifle. All the metal work would have a non-glare, matt finish. The stock would be classic style with a conservative cheek piece and would be made of a relatively quiet, strong synthetic with a rough finish for good grip. The trigger would be set at a crisp three pounds. I'd fit the stock with quick-detachable sling studs and hang a simple one-inch sling on it. Using Redfield or Leupold rings and bases, the rifle would be equipped with a high-quality variable, probably a 2½X-8X Leupold or a 3X-9X Swarovski or Zeiss. The whole outfit, sling and all, would weigh between 8 and 8¾ pounds. So armed, the hunter would be ready to handle anything trophy whitetail hunting is likely to throw at him.

Chapter 22

Scopes And Binoculars
Choosing The Right Optics

B EFORE I EVER MET JOHN, I had heard of his reputation. In those parts, he was looked upon as the best rifleman and hunter for a "fer piece around." Many a moose, deer and bear had fallen to his rifle, along with countless furbearers such as beavers, coyotes, rabbits, red squirrels and the like. For over half a century, John had hunted and trapped the lower fringes of Central Canada's vast forests, and he was reputed to be very good at what he did.

During a hunting trip to Canada, I finally met John and wasted no time in trying to unlock his storehouse of knowledge. It quickly became apparent that as a hunter and woodsman he had few peers. Somewhere in our conversation, I asked about his rifle. He retired to his back room and returned with an old Winchester lever action, the metal polished white from years of use. Intrigued that he had built his reputation using an ancient rifle with iron sights, I started to question him. John openly admitted that he seldom tried a shot over 100 yards. Fifty yards or so was about right. Anything over 150 yards was out of the question. "The front sight near covers the whole animal at that distance," he said, accepting the limitations of his rifle as a fact of life.

No matter how proficient someone is with iron sights, that person would be better off with a scope when hunting trophy whitetails. Iron sights cannot compete with a scope in long-range shooting, in precise bullet placement and during dim light. Chuck Larsen shot this 155-point buck from a distance of 250 yards.

Rather than fancy shooting, John depended on hunting skill and time in the woods to get his animal. He wasn't much interested in antler size; he was after meat. If an animal was too far or the light too dim for a shot with his iron-sighted musket, no problem … John would try again the next day. One day and one animal was about like another to him. He knew his chance would come in time.

Near the end of that trip, I managed to shoot a big whitetail at a distance of 394 paces across an alfalfa field. The shot was from a dead rest at a previously stepped-off distance. I was using a 7mm Rem. Mag. topped with a 3X-9X Swarovski scope. John was amazed that a shot like that was even possible. He would never consider attempting such a thing.

Does that mean I am a better shot than John? Absolutely not! I'm certain that John's innate shooting ability surpasses my own, but my equipment allows me to make shots that are beyond the capabilities of John's old Winchester. Not only is John limited by a cartridge that has the trajectory of a slow-pitch softball, but the open sights he uses prevent him from fully realizing even the modest potential of his rifle.

I grew up shooting iron sights. You couldn't get all the BB's and .22 cartridges I shot as a youth in the back of a long-bed pickup truck. I can testify that with enough practice some pretty incredible feats can be accomplished with iron sights, especially at close range and on moving targets. Shooting becomes instinctive, more of an art than a science. But no matter how proficient someone becomes with iron sights, that person would be better off using a scope when hunting trophy whitetails. Iron sights cannot compete with a scope in long-range shooting, in precise bullet placement and during low-light conditions. And as a hunter's eyes go (as they surely will), the advantages of a scope become even greater.

The first advice is to buy the best scope your checkbook and your wife will allow. Nothing will put a hunter out of business like a fogged scope or a scope that won't hold point of aim. Besides dependability, there's a big difference between the clarity of a quality scope and the hazy images of a poor scope, especially during the all-important low-light times. The old baseball saying, "You can't hit what you can't see," applies just as well in hunting. Fortunately, the overall quality of modern scopes is very good.

For years, the debate over whether to choose a variable or a fixed-power scope has been bandied back and forth. The case for fixed-power scopes has long been made on the presumption that they were more dependable, more accurate and smaller, and that by growing accustomed to just one power the hunter could better judge distances. Also, fixed-power advocates argue that variable scopes get hunters in trouble because the power is often set too high for the circumstances. The case for variables is obvious — they offer the flexibility to cover a wide range of hunting situations. I openly admit that I have always been a fan of variables.

As for fixed-power scopes being more dependable, more accurate or being smaller, forget it. That may have been the case years ago, but not now. There is a bit of truth in the contention that hunters might be able to judge distances better when looking through the same power all the time. But, I usually judge distances using my naked eye or my binoculars. Besides, if the deer is so far away that I have to worry about judging distance, I want plenty of magnification in my scope when trying to make the

This shot is makable, but it requires precision shooting. With the aid of magnification and a steady rest, a bullet could be safety squeezed between the two trees into the buck's shoulder. Photo by Mike Biggs.

shot. On such long shots, variables offer power options that would be too high to be practical in a fixed-power scope for whitetails. And yes, hunters do occasionally get in trouble by having their variables set too high. But, come on! If I were to get a traffic ticket for speeding in a 20 mph zone, that doesn't mean I need a car that will only go 20 mph!

The best power or power range for a scope has also been a lively topic for a long time. If I were forced to hunt trophy whitetails with a fixed-power scope, I would reluctantly choose a 3X or 4X. Whitetails are rarely hunted in country so open that 5X or 6X wouldn't sometimes be too much power. There are places, however, where 2X would seldom be too little power. It is probably becoming evident that power needs vary by place and by situation, which validates the need for a variable.

What variable power range is best for hunting trophy whitetails? As an overall rule of thumb, the low power setting should be 3X or less and the high setting should not exceed 9X, at the most 10X. Within those general parameters, there are two schools of thought on the best power range for variables based largely on the habitat hunted. The first is founded on the belief that low magnification and a wide field of view are most important since whitetails are normally hunted in thick cover. Variables chosen based on this theory usually have a low power setting of 1X to 1¾X and a high setting of 4X to 6X. These low-power variables tend to be compact, and because of their low magnification, they have a wide field of view, are quick in tight cover and shine on running shots. These scopes are good choices for hunters who spend most of their time in dense cover and who rarely have the opportunity for long shots, although 5X or 6X is adequate (though not the best) for work at extended ranges.

The other school of thought calls for more magnification, with upper limits of 7X to 10X. The lowest power on these scopes is usually from 2X to 3X, which is low enough for nearly all situations encountered when hunting trophy whitetails. The popular 3X-9X and the 2½X-8X, which I consider just about ideal, exemplify these higher power scopes. Despite greater magnification, most of these scopes are not much larger than fixed 4X or 6X scopes, although a few, especially those ranging to 10X, can have imposing dimensions. (By the way, the diminutive size of the new generation of compact scopes is quite remarkable, but because this reduced size usually comes at the cost of brightness and field of view, I prefer the full-size scopes.) Even though greater top-end magnification also dictates an increase in the low-end power (somewhat reducing the scope's field of view and sighting speed), it is my opinion that the benefits of greater magnification more than offset any associated negatives. Let me explain.

When hunting trophy whitetails, precise bullet placement is important. It is not enough to aim for "somewhere in the chest area." At ranges in excess of 200 yards, the added magnification allows more exacting shot placement, which can mean the difference between a lost buck and a recovered buck. Precise bullet placement is not only important at long ranges, it also can be critical on bad angles or when part of the animal is obscured by brush. Many times, I've had only a small part of the vital area as a target or I've had to squeeze a bullet through a hole in the brush. Precision shooting like this is best accomplished with the aid of higher magnification. Also, more power makes judging antler size easier on those all-too-often occasions when time or circumstances don't allow the use of binoculars. And one more thing — despite what the industry's formula for relative brightness may say, an object shows up clearer and brighter in dim light when viewed through higher magnification (up to a limit of 6X or 7X in most scopes). Just test it out for yourself any late afternoon. As for the loss of speed in sighting and the reduced field of view caused by greater low-end power, the truth is that very little is given up in practical hunting application. It is important, however, that variable scopes be kept on a lower power, like 3X or 4X, until a situation arises that dictates a change.

Another factor in scope selection is the choice of reticles. While there are many types of crosshairs, I prefer the type commonly referred to as "duplex" reticles. They consist of a coarse outer wire with a finer center wire. The coarse wire serves to quickly direct your eye to the center while the fine wire allows for precision sighting.

The diameter of the objective (front) lens is also a consideration when selecting a scope. When all else is equal, the larger the objective lens, the brighter the scope. However, if the objective lens is too large, it becomes necessary to mount the scope higher above the rifle. This I don't like. I feel that a low-mounted scope facilitates faster sighting and firmer cheek-to-stock contact, resulting in a steadier hold. For those reasons, I prefer a scope that can be mounted with low rings, which usually dictates an objective lens 40mm or less in diameter. Medium-height rings aren't so bad, but on whitetail rifles, I draw the line on high rings. (As a note, when using certain scopes on some bolt-action rifles, the scope's eyepiece can also dictate mounting the scope higher in order for the bolt to clear.)

BINOCULARS

The importance of binoculars to the trophy hunter cannot be overstated. Not only can binoculars add greatly to the enjoyment of the hunt, they can spell the difference between success and failure. I would no more consider going hunting without my binoculars than I would without my boots! As with scopes, the best advice is to buy the finest binoculars you can afford. Names like Zeiss, Leica (Leitz), Bausch & Lomb and Swarovski guarantee years of good service.

Many hunters figure they can use a scope as a substitute for binoc-

This photo was taken with a 500mm lens, which is the equivalent of 10X binoculars. The buck is obviously very good, but a close examination will show that both of his brow tines are broken off flush with his main beams. Such detail would be impossible to detect without the aid of magnification. Even a scope does not have the viewing qualities and detail of top-grade binoculars. Photo by Mike Biggs.

ulars. No way! First of all, it is a downright dangerous practice. The unknown "movement" may be another hunter; not a deer. Binoculars don't accidently fire. A scope should be used for viewing only after the subject has been positively identified. Second, a buck is more likely to see a hunter raise a rifle than a pair of binoculars. Third, scopes cannot match the viewing clarity and detail of quality binoculars. And at close ranges, binoculars — at least those with center focus — are capable of partially "focusing out of view" obstructing brush between the hunter and the buck. This is made possible by the narrow depth of field (zone of clear focus) center-focusing binoculars have at close ranges. Minor obstructions not in the sharp zone tend to dissolve from view. Scopes have a very wide depth of field, as is appropriate for their purpose. Nearly all obstructions are visible to block the view when using a scope to study deer. This is also true of the constant-focus binoculars, which is why I prefer center-focus models for whitetail hunting.

Binoculars are described based on power and objective lens

diameter. For instance, 7x35 means the binoculars magnify seven times (7X) and have a front lens diameter of 35mm. As with scopes, the greater the magnification, the higher the resolution but the lower the field of view. In binoculars of equal power, larger objective lenses translate to increased brightness. During low light, brightness greatly affects the viewer's ability to make out detail, an important consideration in trophy hunting.

The overall size of binoculars is of concern to a hunter. He doesn't want to be burdened down with a heavy, cumbersome load draped around his neck. In response to this concern, manufacturers now offer a wide range of compact or mini-binoculars, some as powerful as 9X or 10X. The better ones offer surprising clarity and are adequate for most glassing purposes. Some models can comfortably fit in a shirt pocket. But to achieve this small size, the optic makers have had to shrink the size of the objective lenses to less than 30mm. This has a price — reduced brightness. Plus, in some of the smaller models, prolonged use can cause a bit of discomfort, especially in failing light.

So, are compacts suitable for trophy whitetail hunting? Most of the time, yes. But larger binoculars, those with objective lenses in the 30 to 42mm range, are generally better. Glasses with even larger objective lenses would be great ... if you didn't have to carry them around. The more streamlined roof prism models, which have straight tubes, can deliver power and brightness with reduced size and weight, but they are generally more expensive than the standard porro prism versions.

The power of most hunting binoculars is from 6X to 10X. The lower magnification has the advantage in field of view while the higher magnification has resolution on its side. If I commonly used binoculars to search for whitetails, I would lean toward field of view. But most of the time, I call on binoculars to identify deer or movement I've already seen with my naked eye. Because of this, I opt for resolution, which is a critical factor in judging bucks. Therefore, I consider 7X to be minimum for trophy hunting. Eight power is even better. When hunting fields or semi-open cover, I frequently carry my excellent 10x40 Leitzs. I've used the very bright 7x50 and 10x50 binoculars, and they really take the mystery out of the twilight times. But, their excessive size makes them too cumbersome for all-around trophy whitetail hunting.

Chapter 23

Making The Shot
When It's All On The Line

W E'LL CALL HIM HARRY to protect the guilty. Harry had forked
out big money to hunt this great Texas ranch. During the
early part of the hunt, warm weather had slowed the rut
and big bucks were scarce. But on the hunt's last full day, a cold front
roared down on South Texas and replaced the stagnant heat with a brisk
north wind. Having already gotten my buck, I offered to help Harry get
his. As we were soon to find out, the sudden weather change had put
the bucks on the prowl. We were also about to find out that this would
be a morning Harry would very much like to forget.

Before the sun had topped the mesquites, Harry and I had rattled
in several good bucks. It was one of those mornings when the bucks
were "wired." After encounters with three or four near-shooters, our
route took us to a place where I had seen a record-class 12-pointer the
year before. If both his brow tines hadn't been broken off flush with his
beams, that buck already would have been on my wall. With this buck
in mind, Harry and I set up to rattle. I was only a minute or two into
the sequence when I looked to my left, and there, my disbelieving eyes
beheld the very same 12-pointer ... only 35 yards away ... and now com-

When that trophy buck stands before you, everything rides on the outcome of the shot. If it's good, sweet success! If the shot fails, only bitter disappointment awaits.

plete with three-inch brow tines to go with his 25-inch-wide rack!

The buck was staring directly at me. I dared not stop rattling. Harry was on the other side of a bush and had not seen the buck. "Harry, to the left," I whispered, still rattling.

His view blocked by the bush, Harry rose slowly to his feet and stepped clear of the bush. Instantly, his rifle snapped to his shoulder and he fired. Even though the buck spun around and disappeared into the brush, the thought of a miss never crossed my mind. "You may have just shot a record buck," I shouted to Harry.

Harry looked pale and gave no response. We hurried over to the spot where the buck was standing. No blood, no deer. Then, Harry uttered his first words. "I missed," he said weakly. "I shot to his left."

An hour-long search proved him right. A dejected Harry and I resumed hunting. About 10:30 a.m., we eased up to a tank where I had previously seen deer watering. Still nearly 250 yards away, we saw deer standing at the water's edge. One of them was a very good buck. My 10X binoculars showed him to be a tall-tined 10-pointer about 19 inches wide. He would easily score in the 150's ... a second chance for Harry. He settled in for the shot. The first bullet slapped the ground three feet to the right of the deer. The second one was a bit closer, as was the third. Because of the distance and a strong crosswind, the buck had no idea what was going on. He would run a few feet and stop, looking all around. Harry really steadied up on the fourth shot. It struck right between the buck's legs. That was enough for the buck. He departed, shaken but untouched.

Harry was distraught to say the least. True, a 250-yard shot in a crosswind is no "give-me," but that did little to relieve Harry's disappointment. After shaking his head and using a few choice words to punctuate his frustration, Harry said, "My rifle must be off. It must be."

"Must be," I agreed. "Mine is in the truck. Use it the rest of the morning."

"I will, but let's head in and check my rifle." Harry said, with a glimmer of hope that his rifle, not him, was behind the misses.

Fate was not through with Harry that morning. On the way back to camp, a doe stepped into the road about 125 yards in front of us. Harry hurriedly got into position for a shot should a buck be following the doe. I had hardly gotten my binoculars up when antlers emerged from the brush. The buck had good mass and three substantial tines on his near beam … and on his off beam. He turned away and gave us a rear view, revealing good brow tines and 22 to 23 inches of spread. "He's a solid 150, Harry," I said. "Take him."

By now, the buck was going straight away in that stiff-legged gait of rutting bucks. Harry sent a round down the road after him. Through my glasses, I saw hair fly from the buck's right side, at which time he cut abruptly into the brush, a white streak clearly visible down his side. The bullet had only grazed the buck!

Harry left the ranch without his trophy. Thoughts of "what if's" filled his long flight home.

Harry's story of missed opportunities is only one of countless similar stories I could recount. Even as I write this, two friends have just returned empty-handed from an expensive week-long hunt in Texas. One missed a record-class buck at less than 50 yards. The other broke the leg of a wide 10-pointer scoring in the 150's but failed to recover him. The only difference between great memories and bitter disappointment for those two hunters was the outcome of the few seconds it took to make the shot.

If one instant can make or break a hunt, doesn't it make sense to be fully prepared for that moment? Of course it does! Yet, many hunters go to great extremes in effort, time and even money to put that trophy whitetail in their sights only to leave the outcome of the shot to little more than a crap shoot. While it is true that the value and enjoyment of hunting is not found only in the kill, the object of the hunt is, in fact, to kill the quarry. Besides, we owe it to the animal. Clean misses are not the only byproduct of poor shooting; wounding is, too.

I believe the greatest opportunity for improvement among trophy hunters lies in the area of shooting. Think about it. With magazines, books and videos, hunters can sit in their homes and learn a great deal about how, when and where to hunt trophy whitetails. Once in the field, they can then quickly transform much of this knowledge into skill. It's not quite that way with shooting. True, information about shooting is available, but more than any other aspect of hunting, head knowledge is no substitute for practice. Shooting skills must be honed through repetition. A person's natural ability will determine how good a shot he can become, but everybody can improve with practice.

Adequate shooting skills for trophy whitetail hunting require more than being able to hit a buck standing broadside in the open at 100 yards. Difficult shots at trophy whitetails are more the norm than the exception. The trophy hunter must be skilled enough to have a chance of getting the job done over the full range of situations likely to come his way. Obviously, no hunter can kill every trophy buck he sees, but the greater his shooting skill, the higher the percentage of opportunities he can convert to happy endings.

ACCURACY AND SIGHTING-IN

The first step is to be sure your rifle is capable of acceptable accuracy and is properly sighted-in. Acceptable accuracy begins with good equipment — rifle, scope, rings and bases — that is set up right. We read a lot about rifles that will shoot one-inch groups (three shots with a maximum center-to-center spread of one inch) at 100 yards, but the truth is that few hunting rifles will deliver that level of performance. Even eliminating the human factor, most rifles taken to the field each fall will only group somewhere between two and five inches at 100 yards. That's not acceptable accuracy for the demanding shooting trophy hunting can require. The accuracy of many deer rifles could be considerably upgraded by tightening all the screws, proper bedding, improving the trigger pull and by experimenting to find the best ammo for that particular rifle. Even then, however, most deer rifles still would not be able to dependably print one-inch groups.

So, what is acceptable accuracy? In my opinion, a trophy whitetail rifle should consistently group two inches or less. And, even more important than group size is the ability to consistently group in the same place. Even a rifle that can shoot one-inch groups is no good if the groups move around from one shooting session to another.

Some may feel that two-inch groups won't cut it for trophy hunting. While I do require at least 1½-inch performance from my own rifles, the fact is that two-inch accuracy is adequate for nearly all situations ... if the rifle prints rounded groups in the same place each time. You see, consistently placed, circular two-inch groups basically mean that the bullets are deviating only one inch in any direction from the point of aim at 100 yards. At 200 yards, the rifle would account for no more than two inches of deviation from the point of aim. At 300 yards, only three inches. That level of variance would seldom cause a problem.

Before discussing sighting-in, a word about rifle triggers. Because of product liability, factory triggers are typically set too heavy (usually from five to nine pounds) for accurate shooting. Also, many triggers have too much travel, or creep. When a heavy trigger pull is combined with excessive travel, there is no way the shooter can predict when a rifle is going to fire. Because of the importance of trigger control in achieving accuracy, hunters should carefully examine the trigger pull on their rifles. If the trigger seems hard to pull and/or creeps before breaking, I recommend that a competent gunsmith work on it. I personally prefer a crisp trigger set to break at 2¾ to 3 pounds. Don't set the trigger much less than three pounds. Extremely light triggers coupled with cold weather, heavy gloves or the excitement of the hunt can result in premature firing.

Now, sighting-in a rifle. First, find a benchrest ... complete with sandbags, a chair and a bench. It is the only way to find out what you and your rifle are capable of doing. Be sure to have hearing protection and shoulder padding to absorb recoil. It may seem macho to shoot without these precautions, but in truth, it is sheer folly. I know of no better way to develop bad shooting habits, or to lose your hearing.

I do not intend to go into great detail about the mechanics of

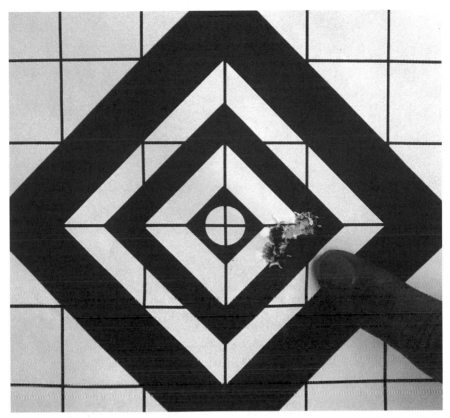

We read a lot about 100-yard groups of one inch or less, but in truth, few hunting rifles are capable of that level of performance. This group is a touch over a half-inch in size. That's great accuracy!

sighting-in, but highlighting the basics is probably a good idea. On a new rifle/scope set-up, I'll bore-sight first then shoot a 30-yard target to get close to zero. After that, I'll move to a 100-yard target and fire the necessary number of "sighters," adjusting the scope after each shot until the point of impact is roughly where I want it. At this point, I will let the rifle barrel cool for about five minutes before moving on to serious sighting-in.

To sight-in, I fire three well-spaced shots without making any scope adjustments. I make certain that the forearm and the butt of the rifle are solidly supported, as well as both of my elbows. Before each shot, I take a deep breath, release half to relax and then very slowly squeezzzze the trigger. After each three-shot group, I examine the group for size

Shooting from a benchrest is the only way to find out what you and your rifle are capable of doing. Be sure to wear hearing protection and shoulder padding.

and to determine the center of the group, assuming this "average" represents where the rifle is actually sighted-in. I then make the necessary scope adjustments to move the point of impact to my desired sight-in point. Allowing five or so minutes between each three-shot group, I continue this process until my rifle prints a group whose center is two inches above the bullseye, my preferred sight-in point.

Why sight-in two inches high at 100 yards? Why not dead-on? Or one inch high? Or even three inches high? In a word, compromise. To me, sighting-in two inches high is about the right compromise between the needs of medium-range shooting and those of long-range shooting. First, it is necessary to understand that a rifle sighted-in to hit high at 100 yards is really sighted-in to be dead-on at some distance beyond 100 yards. Using the .270 as an example, one inch high at 100 yards is really dead-on at just over 150 yards. Two high is dead-on at around 225 yards, and three inches high is on-target at about 275 yards. Obviously, the greater the distance a rifle is sighted-in for, the less drop a hunter has to contend with at extended ranges. However, this long-range benefit has a cost. Since a bullet actually begins to drop from the time it leaves the barrel, a bullet must be angled upward, causing it to "rise" above the line of sight (it crosses the line of sight twice, once at 25 to 30 yards and again at the sight-in point) in order to be on-target at extended ranges. The problem is that the farther out the zero, the more bullet "rise" a hunter has to contend with at intermediate ranges, where most chances at trophy whitetails come.

Again using the .270 as an example, a rifle sighted-in at 275 yards (three inches high at 100) will be less than three inches low at 300 yards, but the bullet will rise over four inches above the line of sight en route to the 275-yard point of aim. Because most shots at whitetails are at ranges well under 275 yards and because some shots are through holes in brush or at small parts of the animal, a bullet variance at intermediate ranges of over four inches from the line of sight is excessive. On the other hand, the bullet from a .270 sighted-in for 150 yards (just under one-inch high at 100 yards) will only climb about an inch above the line of sight, but at 300 yards, it will hit more than 10 inches low. I feel this is giving up too much at the longer ranges. Obviously, sighting-in dead-on at 100 yards would even worsen long-range trajectory. That leads to the compromise position — two inches high at 100 yards.

With our .270 example, the maximum rise en route to the 225-yard mark would be just over two inches and the 300-yard drop would be less than six inches. Those are acceptable numbers. (The figures cited are only close approximations. The actual numbers would depend on the rifle, cartridge, bullet and load used, as well as the scope height.)

PRACTICE, PRACTICE AND MORE PRACTICE

Like tennis or billiards, shooting is a game of skill developed only through practice. Nobody who is serious about winning in tennis or billiards would enter into a high stakes match without lots of practice first. Yet, whitetail hunters, even many with trophy aspirations, take to the woods each fall with the relative shooting skills of a beginner tennis player. Sure, shooting a high-powered rifle frequently is demanding. The thing kicks and bellows. It's hard to find a place to shoot. It's time-consuming. It's a bother to gather up all the necessary paraphernalia. There are always plenty of good reasons not to shoot, but there is one excellent reason to do it — shooting practice can spell the difference between having nothing but a sad story at season's end and proudly admiring the buck of your dreams.

After developing basic shooting technique on the rifle range, practice your shooting under field conditions. Learn to use whatever rests are available, like this hay bale.

Practice begins on the rifle range. Aside from simply sighting-in, a hunter should shoot frequently from a benchrest. By doing so, he develops confidence in his shooting ability and in his rifle. He learns that precise bullet placement is not an accident; it's the result of a solid rest, a steady sight picture and trigger control. These three things are the pillars of good shooting, and they are best developed on the rifle range.

Even field practice can and should begin on the rifle range, where distances are known and paper targets are available to reveal exactly where bullets hit. Leave the bench and shoot from various positions — kneeling, sitting, prone or by propping the rifle against a leg of the bench. Use your imagination. Also, try some shots offhand. This will help you understand the limitations of offhand shooting and the need for some type rest. You will learn how much wiggle is permissible if you are to make an acceptably accurate shot. You'll develop the ability to "call your shot" from the sight picture at the instant the rifle goes off. And, you'll find out why trigger control is so important since you will almost surely flinch to some degree when shooting from field positions.

One of my favorite tricks to demonstrate flinching and teach the discipline of trigger control, which is nothing more than squeezing the trigger without jerking, is to periodically remove the bullet from my companion's gun without him knowing it. If he's flinching, it will be blatantly apparent when he pulls the trigger. The degree to which some people flinch is amazing. I know of no better way to point out this problem, and to cure it, than by letting someone unknowingly "shoot" an unloaded rifle. Embarrassment is great motivation for curing the flinches. After a few times of not flinching, it seems that the discipline can be maintained. After all, repetition begets repeatability.

The final step in preparation for the hunt is to shoot under actual field conditions. Just take a stroll, and when you see a likely target, quickly find a rest, set up and shoot. Practice from all kinds of positions and at all ranges. Use whatever rests are available — a knee, a limb, a rock, the side of a tree trunk or anything else handy to steady a rifle. Pick small, well-defined targets that require some precision in your shooting. The disciplines you learn through practice are the same ones you'll call on when that trophy buck stands before you ... if buck fever doesn't make you forget everything!

SHOOTING WHEN IT COUNTS

You're playing your last card. It has been a rough five days of hunting in hot, muggy weather. The buck you're after has left plenty of sign, but so far, you've not seen hide nor hair of him. You've tried all manner of tricks, but he has thwarted your every effort. Now, on the last day of season, a light drizzle gives you new hope. You know the buck will be on the move somewhere. Rather than pin your hopes on one place, you have decided to use the silence afforded by the drizzle to slip along the edge of the fallow fields stretching up and down the riverbottom. With any luck, you might catch the buck near one of his many washtub-sized scrapes along the field edges.

Your legs are heavy from two hours of slow, careful slipping, and your nerves are taunt from unceasing concentration on the hunt. The light is beginning to fade, and a slight fog has settled over the low country. One more field to check ... the best one, saved for the prime moments of last light. You ease up slowly to the field edge. Standing well back in the shadows, you scan the far side of the field some 175 yards away with your binoculars. Movement ... a buck ... it's him! He's heavy and wide ... and at least a 10-pointer. Your heart is thumping so hard that your ears are throbbing. He's the biggest buck you've ever seen!

"Shoot!" the thought explodes brightly across your consciousness. From that point on, everything becomes kind of hazy. You instinctively bring the rifle to your shoulder. The vague image of the crosshairs wobbling on and off the broadside body of the great buck dimly registers in your mind. There is a flash of light and a muted boom as the rifle goes off, almost on its own. The sound of the report rolling down the valley

The sight of a big set of antlers can totally unnerve a hunter. Buck fever is real, and it can happen to anybody. Hunting experience, shooting practice and perhaps a few deep breaths are about the only ways to combat it. Photo by Mike Biggs.

fades as your eyes desperately probe the far side of the field in vanishing light. But, you know you look in vain. Your heart feels like lead in your chest. Your mind races, searching for alternatives that might give you another chance. There are none. You missed — plain and simple. The best buck of your life is gone forever.

Another tale of woe is born because the shot was blown. Although this scenario is played out all too often, a hunt doesn't have to end like this. Let's go back to the point in our story where the buck is standing 175 yards away. Here's another chance to do it right.

"Shoot!" the thought explodes brightly across your consciousness. But, you take a few deep breaths, trying to calm yourself and regain control of your thoughts.

"How far?" you question yourself. "About 175 yards. Dead hold. I've got to get a rest. I'm okay on time. He doesn't know I'm here."

Just ahead and to the right your eyes lock on a leaning willow partially uprooted by wind. You glance at the buck. He's still unconcerned and standing broadside, probably over one of his scrapes. You drop to your knees and shuffle to the right, putting the leaning willow between you and the buck. You hurriedly crawl the eight feet to the base of the willow and shift into a sitting position. You turn the scope from 4X to 8X. With the rifle rested solidly atop the tree trunk and cushioned by your left hand, you squirm into shooting position, leaning to the side a little so your right elbow can prop against a protruding limb. The crosshairs come to rest on the center of the buck's thick shoulder. Only a slight tremble in the rifle is noticeable through the scope as the trigger squeeze begins. There's a flash of light and a muted boom when the .270 goes off. You hear the telltale "whomp" as the report rumbles down the valley. The sight picture at the instant of the shot is burned into your mind. You know the bullet flew true. In less than 15 seconds since you first saw him, it's over. Your heart is racing in your chest and you are filled with anticipation as you trot … no, run … across the field to the trophy of a lifetime!

While this is the way we all wish our hunts would end, the truth is that making a killing shot when the time comes is not as easy as it may seem. Unexpected and uncontrollable variables are interjected into the shooting process that can make things a bit dicey for even good shots and experienced hunters. Certainly, one of the most confounding variables is this strange phenomenon called "buck fever." There is something about the sight of a big set of antlers that can totally unnerve a hunter. Logical thoughts and deliberate actions are replaced by a mindless sense of urgency to shoot before the buck gets away. Often, a shot during such frantic times is little more than a hope and a prayer.

While I know of no sure way to cure buck fever, experience with big bucks certainly seems to dampen the effects of this malady. The more big bucks you see, the less of a disruptive impact they will have on your nerves. That is why experienced hunters are less prone to buck fever. Yet, even veterans can fall victim to buck fever, especially when they see an exceptional buck or once they have decided to shoot a particular deer. It is one thing to be able to remain calm when casually observing "nice" bucks you know you are not going to shoot, but it is something else again when the "shoot" switch is turned on. Even when shooting a doe I've picked out for the table, I often feel a tinge of excitement. And, I guarantee that a sizeable dose of adrenalin floods my body when I see a whopper buck.

Unfortunately, firsthand experience with lots of good whitetails is not a viable option for most hunters. Good bucks just don't come along often enough for the majority of hunters to become accustomed to seeing them. So, what else can be done to combat the effects of buck fever?

Believe it or not, the old standby three or four deep breaths really can help a hunter regain some composure and a degree of control over his mental processes. After taking a few deep breaths, the hunter may even find on a second look not so magnified by adrenalin that the buck is not even a shooter. When hunting with inexperienced hunters, or anyone prone to overexcitement, I often use the deep-breath ploy to try to calm them down. I don't know if it's the pause, the breaths themselves or the regaining of some discipline that helps a person settle down, but I do know it works. The problem for the solitary hunter is forcing himself to do it.

In the final analysis, success at that fateful moment comes back to the shooting basics, which can only be developed through practice. Among the basics, the use of a rest is one of the most neglected. Failure to rest the rifle is a chief cause of missed and wounded deer. Sure, there are instances when time and circumstances make it impossible to use a rest. There are even situations, like a 30-yard broadside shot, when a rest is not needed. But in many cases, the few extra seconds spent steadying that rifle could be the most important time investment of the hunt. Resting my rifle is a priority on shots over 50 yards. I'll go to great lengths to prop up for shots over 100 yards. Offhand shooting beyond 100 yards is simply too risky. Any and everything in the field is a possible rest — rocks, the side of tree trunks, limbs, blowdowns, stumps, the siderails of stands, hay bales, farm equipment, to name a few. Even in the absence of apparent rests, kneeling to one knee, sitting or assuming a prone position are excellent options for steadying a rifle. Obviously, distance and target size dictate how steady the rifle must be and what type of rest is adequate. It doesn't take much to dampen the wiggles on a shot of 100 yards or less. From 100 to 200 yards, the rifle should be rested solidly. Beyond 200 yards, both the rifle and the hunter (particularly his elbows) should be rested against something to reduce body tremors. As a rule of

Failure to rest the rifle is a chief cause of missed and wounded deer. Any and everything is a possible rest, even your knee. Photo by Mike Biggs.

thumb, I always try to rest the rifle so that the crosshairs never leave the kill zone, although I admit that is not always possible.

Once the hunter has steadied his rifle, all that remains is the shooting mechanics. The scope should be adjusted suitably for the shot being taken. The shooter should take his deep breath, release half and relax. A smooth, controlled trigger squeeze should send the bullet on its way without a flinch or jerk. The sight picture at the instant of firing should be locked in his mind's eye as evidence of where the bullet struck. When all is done right, a trophy whitetail is the reward. If done wrong, the outcome is, as the saying goes, "not a pretty picture."

Chapter 24

Shot Placement
And Follow-Up

M Y PHILOSOPHY ON SHOT PLACEMENT is influenced by the fact that I am partially red color blind, meaning I can't see blood very well on the cluttered background of the deer woods. To overcome this handicap, my shot placement strategy is simple: I try to hit a buck in a spot that will anchor him instantly or within a very short distance. This is one of the reasons why I prefer powerful cartridges like the .270, .280 or 7mm Rem. Mag. While my problem with red color vision might have lead me to my particular stance, I believe that shot placement for instant or very quick kills is in the best interest of anyone aspiring to bring home a trophy whitetail. Let me explain.

As I've said before, trophy whitetails are bigger, more tenacious and just plain harder to put down than average deer. On a percentage basis, many more trophy bucks are hit and lost than are lesser bucks. The problem begins with the fact that trophy bucks react less to a hit, sometimes showing little reaction at all. And, big-bodied bucks don't tend to bleed as readily as other deer, partly because the bullet is less likely to exit. Far too many hunters take all this to mean a miss or a superficial hit and don't even look for the buck. Even if there is evidence

Although I usually don't attempt spine shots, I was forced to try one in December 1991 if I wanted this mid-160's 10-pointer. As he walked across a cutline about 200 yards away, the buck was just over a rise with only the upper one-third of his body visible. The rifle and both of my elbows were steadied against a tree, and I knew where the rifle would shoot at that distance. The bullet broke the buck's backbone about eight inches behind his withers. He went down instantly, although a finishing shot was required. Photo by Richard Jackson.

that the bullet made contact, the tenacity of a trophy buck can make recovery difficult even when he's fatally hit. This can be enough to discourage a hunter before the matter is brought to a happy conclusion. Considering all this, it is best to put a trophy buck down instantly or after traveling the least possible distance. Assuming the rifle can do its part, bullet placement is the answer.

All my life, I have read that the best place to shoot a whitetail is behind the shoulder. This is, of course, a lung shot, and there is no doubt that it is fatal. I believe this shot became the "standard" for whitetails because little edible meat is damaged when a buck is punched neatly through the lungs on a broadside shot. The average deer so hit typically runs 30 to 60 yards before falling. That's normally not much of a problem, especially in snow country or in open cover. But, trophy bucks aren't "average deer." While they, too, usually will go down within 60 yards when shot behind the shoulder, occasionally they will travel farther. In the wrong type habitat, such as thick clearcuts, swamps with water, tall grass or any kind of thick ground cover, finding a buck even a 100 yards away can be a daunting task, especially if the blood trail is meager or nonexistent. Wouldn't it be wise to choose a better option if one existed? And, I believe it does.

Before looking at the shot placement I prefer, let's consider a few things. About the only way to dependably drop a buck instantly is with a spine shot or a head shot, which is of little use in trophy hunting. The neck shot gets its reputation as a sudden killer from the fact that it is nothing more than an upper spine shot. Even a buck hit too far back in the spine, say mid-body and back, will be broken down and immobilized, although a finishing shot may be required. Despite all this, I do not depend on spine shots; not even neck shots. The margin of error is too small. A shot that just misses the spine may knock the animal down temporarily, but depending on where he's hit, the buck may recover in a few moments and decamp for parts unknown. This frequently happens with a neck shot, as my companion on a recent trip found out. Upon the shot, he saw the 150-class eight-pointer fall, prompting celebration. But when he reached the place the buck should have been, only a little blood and hair awaited him. A few hours later, a ranch hand saw the buck still on the move … with an ugly wound in his neck. Except in rare cases, spine shots, including neck shots, are just too risky.

Hunting the incredibly tough game in Africa taught me the value of hitting bone and breaking down an animal. When a bullet strikes bone, several things happen. One, the power of the bullet is transmitted through the bone to connecting bone and tissue. Two, the bone is shattered and the fragments themselves become destructive shrapnel. Three, because the bone is broken, the animal is disabled, even if not killed outright.

The largest single vital area is a buck's chest. At the bottom of the chest lies his heart and major arteries; in the center is the lungs, the largest of his vital organs; and across the top of the chest area is the spine. In a trophy buck, the size of this vital area (from a broadside view) would be something like 12 inches deep and 10 inches wide.

Given all this — the vulnerability of the spine, the benefits of hitting bone and the large vital area offered by the chest — I believe the best shot for trophy whitetails is a shoulder shot. True, this shot does result in the loss of some edible shoulder meat. However, I had rather lose a little venison than run even a slight risk of losing the whole animal.

I use a couple of variations of the shoulder shot, depending on how accurately I can place the bullet. At longer distances or when I can't steady the rifle well enough for exact bullet placement, I aim for the center of the shoulder straight above the front leg. Bucks hit there seldom run over 20 to 30 yards, and they normally show obvious signs of being hit. Also, a mid-shoulder shot is pretty much aimed at the center of the deer's largest vital area, providing the maximum margin of error. A hit lower than aimed will strike either the lungs or the heart and possibly will break the humerus bone. A hit farther back toward the body is the standard behind-the-shoulder lung shot. (By contrast, a hit too far back on the behind-the-shoulder shot will result in a gut shot.) A hit more forward than intended will almost surely break the shoulder and destroy the lungs. And if the bullet strays high of center, the resulting hit is the most devastating of all … and the shot I prefer for trophy bucks.

Anytime circumstances allow precise bullet placement, I opt for a high shoulder shot. A hit anywhere between two-thirds and three-quarters of the way up a buck's shoulder takes the worry out of tracking. He normally will drop where he stands. Typically, the buck's rear end collapses and his head rocks back. Such a shot shatters the shoulder blade, taking out the upper lungs with it, and/or breaks or severely damages the backbone, which lies lower in the buck's body at the withers (top of the shoulders) than elsewhere in the body proper. About the only way to get into trouble with a high shoulder shot is by shooting too high. For that reason, I seldom aim much higher than two-thirds of the way up the chest just to play it safe.

A picture is indeed worth a thousand words, so at this point, we'll let the accompanying pictures illustrate bullet placement for shoulder shots and for various other shots, some of which are dictated by off angles. The captions with the photos will discuss the virtues of and the deer's reaction to the different shots.

I believe the best shot for trophy whitetails is the shoulder shot. I use a couple of variations, depending on how accurately I can place the bullet. At longer distances or when I can't completely steady the rifle, I aim for the center of the shoulder (A). This is pretty much in the middle of the deer's largest vital area, thus providing the maximum margin of error. A buck hit there normally jumps and then runs 20 to 30 yards in a short-gaited, almost tiptoeing manner. When I can precisely place the bullet, I opt for a high shoulder shot (B). A hit anywhere between two-thirds and three-quarters of the way up a buck's shoulder takes the worry out of tracking. The buck drops where he stands. Typically, his rear end collapses and his head rocks back. Photo by Curt Helmick.

The behind-the-shoulder lung shot (A) is the "standard" for whitetails, but it is not my favorite. Normally, a buck punched neatly through the lungs will jump and run off like he is unharmed. Although the shot is fatal, deer hit there often run too far for my liking, sometimes 100 yards or more. In certain types of habitat, recovery can be difficult. The heart shot (B) is likewise lethal, but the margin of error is too slim. A buck shot through the heart will typically take off at full speed, running low to the ground in whatever direction he was pointed when the bullet struck. He will seldom run more than 75 yards, and the blood trail is easy to follow. The dread of all deer hunters is the gut shot (C). Even though this shot will eventually prove fatal, the buck can travel for very long distances, perhaps even miles, and may not leave much of a blood trail. A gut shot is often accompanied by a soggy "thud" when the bullet strikes. The deer usually kicks violently upon impact then humps up and goes off at a fairly slow, painful pace. Photo by Bill Kinney.

The straight-on shot is a bit tricky but quite lethal. Anywhere in the center of the buck's body from his throat patch down to a few inches above the bottom of his brisket will result in a fatal wound. But, my preferred placement is just above the base of his neck (A) so that the bullet will transverse the body about on the level with a high shoulder shot. A buck struck there usually falls instantly. A lower shot (B) will destroy the lungs and major arteries, but the buck will usually run a short distance. A very low hit (C) will take out the heart, but again, the margin of error is uncomfortably small. The biggest danger with a front-on shot is pulling off center since the exposed vital area is rather long and narrow. Photo by Mike Biggs.

This is a dicey shot. There are basically two options. One, a shot at the root of the tail (A) will immediately disable or outright kill the buck. Such a hit usually destroys the rear portion of the spine. Two, the buck is offering a good neck shot (B). The vertebrate is lower in a buck's neck than most people realize. Both of these shots call for accurate bullet placement. I would prefer to wait for a better angle, but since the buck is obviously alerted, I would probably opt for the root-of-the-tail shot. Photo by Mike Biggs.

On the front quartering shot, care must be taken not to shoot too far back. Imagine where the vital chest area is and be certain the bullet transverses it, regardless of the bullet's entry point. On this buck, I would go for a high shoulder shot (A) if conditions allowed accurate placement. If not, I would center his chest cavity (B). With either shot, bone is likely to be hit from this angle and the buck probably would fall instantly or travel only a short distance. Photo by Bill Kinney.

A rear quartering shot is lethal. Again, envision the vital chest cavity and aim so the bullet transverses it. The high shoulder shot (A) and the center chest shot (B) are depicted. Either shot will put the buck down in short order. The greatest danger on this shot is shooting too far forward, resulting in a nonfatal flesh wound or perhaps a broken shoulder. Hunters occasionally blow this shot because they are more concerned about the bullet's entry point than its path through the deer's body. If in doubt, aim for the off shoulder. Photo by Mike Biggs.

FOLLOW-UP

Follow-up to a shot should begin the instant the trigger is pulled. Immediately try to determine the buck's reaction to the shot, his departure direction and route (assuming he runs off) and the exact location of the last place you saw him. Look and listen. The sound of a departing buck can help establish the direction he is moving and can even let you know if he's down. Often, a buck will crash into brush as he falls or thrash about when he is down.

Before moving from where you shot, mark the exact spot the buck was standing when you fired. Find an identifiable landmark, such as a specific brush, tree, rock, etc. This is especially important on long shots or in places with low, relatively uniform cover. If the buck's initial location is not properly identified, even finding the whole animal can be surprisingly difficult in some situations, but it can be nearly impossible to blindly blunder upon a few specks of blood or a smattering of hair when that is the only thing left on the scene. Also, when you arrive at a spot you've viewed from a distance, the place can appear very different from what you had envisioned. More times than I care to remember, I've had to walk back to where I shot to reorient myself after a futile search for a downed buck, even ones I saw fall. To compound matters, the perspective of distance is different when walking through cover than when looking across country. On long shots, the tendency is to pull up short of where the buck was actually standing.

Now, the cardinal rule of follow-up: Never assume a miss! No matter what the deer's reaction or what the early evidence shows, treat each shot at a buck as though he is dead ... you just have to find out where. I can't tell you how many times on our Georgia plantation we have been told by guests that they missed a buck only to have a guide return to the scene and find the deer dead some distance away. Had those hunters been hunting alone, most would have returned home empty-handed while the animal lay dead in the woods.

After reaching the spot where the buck was at the time of the shot, look for blood, hair, scuff marks, running tracks, etc. Move slowly and deliberately. Don't walk all over the place. You may destroy sign. Stand or kneel in one spot and examine the immediate area carefully before moving on. Pay attention to the smallest details. Even on a good hit, sign can be scanty. It is not unusual for there to be little or no blood, especially for the first several yards of the buck's flight path.

If there is no evidence of a hit and/or no trail to follow, set your jaw and start the search anyway. Try to follow the buck's departure trail, hoping to either find him lying along it or to find sign of a hit. If a buck is seriously injured, he will usually follow the path of least resistance, which may mean an established trail or a downhill route. (Badly wounded bucks will sometimes run uphill, but that is not the norm.) Searching in the direction the buck ran, check out the most likely routes first, walking out trails and following the lay of the land. Comb the area. The initial search should extend 100 to 150 yards from where the buck was originally shot.

Should these efforts fail to turn up anything, the search area must be expanded. Obviously, the farther away you go, the harder it will be to thoroughly cover the entire area. If help is available, recruit as many eyes as possible to work for you. From here on, it is an odds game, assuming the buck is down somewhere. Check the thickets and any nearby water. Wounded bucks, especially those that are gut shot, will frequently seek out water. Stay with the search until all options are exhausted.

When a hit has been confirmed and a trail of some sort exists, I normally follow the trail carefully for 75 to 100 yards, scrutinizing the sign. If the shot was a good one, the buck will probably be recovered within that distance. If not, a decision has to be made whether to continue on the trail or to wait awhile. There are two trains of thought on this subject.

One favors waiting based on the theory that a wounded buck often will lie down within a certain distance, where he will die or at least stiffen up, limiting further mobility. The other position holds to the belief that a wounded buck should be pursued immediately. The idea is that the buck is still disoriented from shock and that by pushing the deer, bleeding will be increased because of movement and an elevated heart rate. While I tend to lean toward the latter theory, other factors must go into this decision, such as the prominence of the blood trail or the possibility of a pushed buck leaving the property being hunted or crossing a creek or river that might prevent further follow-up. Additional considerations include the prospects that rain or snow could erase the trail, the density of the cover, the time available, the presence of other hunters, the availability of help and, most importantly perhaps, where the buck

Thick cover like this five-year-old clearcut in the Northeast is why I like to put a trophy buck down in the shortest possible distance. This is a 300-pound whitetail! Photo by Gordon Whittington courtesy of **North American Whitetail.**

is believed to be hit. If possible, I will always wait a few hours if I have reason to believe the buck is gut shot. Although a gut shot is nearly always fatal, a buck so hit can run for miles if pushed. Left unmolested for a few hours, there is a good chance a gut shot buck will lie down and die within a reasonable distance of where he was shot. Other than on a gut shot, I normally will pursue the buck right away; however, each situation has to be evaluated based on the circumstances at hand.

Being partially red color blind, I cannot claim to be an expert in the art of blood trailing. Certainly, I know the basics of how it is done — proceed slowly and carefully; stay to the side of the trail to avoid destroying sign; mark or have a companion stand at the last sign for reference and to establish "a line"; be ready to get off a quick shot if you jump the buck; etc. And, the truth is that despite my color vision problem I can do a fair job of tracking by applying a basic principle taught me by a professional hunter in Africa.

The art of tracking is developed to perhaps its greatest degree in the African bush. I've seen native Africans perform tracking feats that were nothing short of miraculous. But, the most incredible tracking accomplishment I have ever been party to occurred after the native trackers had given up the trail of a big sable antelope I had shot. The meager blood trail had petered out soon after we took up the chase. Despite that, two native trackers had followed the sable's tracks for about three hours. Then, the trackers lost the trail among the myriad of other animal tracks. Along with losing the trail, they also lost interest. George Angeledes, the professional hunter, meticulously searched the area for several minutes and finally sorted out the trail and began to follow it. The only thing he said to me for the next 3½ hours was, "Stay just ahead of me and watch for that sable."

We inched our way across the African veldt. How George could tell that one sable's tracks from the countless other tracks I do not know. Even the natives were impressed and again joined in the pursuit. Finally, nearly seven hours after my original shot, I saw the sable standing under an acacia tree, a stream of dried blood high on his withers where the bullet, deflected by brush, had struck. The next bullet from my .300 Win. Mag. was unincumbered. The largest sable ever killed in Tanzania at that time fell to the ground, not because of my hunting skills but because of George's. After the congratulations were over, I asked George, "How in the world did you track that sable through all that mess?"

He replied matter-of-factly, "One track at a time."

Herein lies the key to tracking.

Section VII

Closing Thoughts

Chapter 25

A Look Toward Tomorrow

THE LAST 25 YEARS have seen whitetail deer expand into nearly all available habitat across North America. Populations are now at an all-time high, and an industry has emerged around the whitetail that involves millions of hunters and pours billions of dollars into the economy. As a group, whitetail hunters themselves have evolved. Once, hunters knew little about the animal they were after and their primary interest was just in killing one. Today, hunters are far more knowledgeable about whitetails and their interest extends well beyond the hunting season. More and more hunters have killed their share of "just any deer" and are looking for that something special, a trophy buck. Right now, interest in trophy hunting is on the rise, but what does the future hold? Let me polish up my crystal ball and take a stab at that.

The whitetail wave has not yet crested, at least as far as trophy hunting is concerned. I cannot say the total number of hunters will increase down the road, but I do believe the number of trophy hunters will grow, as will their enthusiasm. Whitetail hunters as a group will place greater emphasis on quality. They also will continue to elevate their knowledge of and involvement with the animal they hunt. Already, the momentum is moving in that direction. Whitetail shows, seminars, magazines, antler collecting, shed hunting, photography, hands-on management and all-season whitetail activities are evidence of the ever-heightening interest in this great game animal.

Dr. Jim Goodchild (front) and guide Phil Reddock passed up many lesser bucks en route to this record-class 13-pointer. The discipline required in trophy hunting teaches a hunter restraint and elevates his personal hunting ethics, which in the end is good for the sport of deer hunting in general.

Is the trend toward trophy hunting good for the sport of deer hunting in general? Absolutely! Trophy hunting calls for selectivity, and this brings with it a couple of pluses. One, since lesser bucks must be passed up en route to a trophy, the hunter is able to see and study more deer. This gives him a greater appreciation for and understanding of the animal and makes him a more skilled hunter. Two, the discipline required in trophy hunting teaches a hunter restraint and elevates his overall hunting ethics. His measure of "success" shifts from the focus of just killing a buck to the quality of the overall hunting experience, thus exemplifying the essence of true sportsmanship and perhaps helping to enhance the image of all deer hunters. Also, because trophy management calls for well-balanced deer herds (in terms of age structure, sex ratios and population levels), trophy hunting is beneficial to the long-term health of a herd. And, trophy hunters are willing to pay, not only to hunt big

One term that is sure to become increasingly familiar to hunters is "quality buck management." While true trophy management is geared toward growing the biggest bucks possible, the aim of quality management is to produce younger bucks representative of "quality" deer for that area. Georgia's Burnt Pine Plantation manages for quality 2½ and 3½-year-old bucks. These are some of the best of 80 or so bucks harvested during one hunting season. Obviously, a few real trophies are produced as a byproduct of quality buck management.

bucks but also to preserve and manage habitat for whitetails as well as for other game and non-game animals.

TROPHY MANAGEMENT PROSPECTS

Undoubtedly, the future will see the continued reduction of wildlife habitat; however, with the urbanization of America, it is possible that the rate of loss will be slowed. And, don't lose sight of the fact that this country is huge and whitetails number in the tens of millions. Whitetails, despite what some of the pseudo animal-righters might say, are here for the long haul and so are those who hunt them. Still, in the years ahead, greater emphasis must be placed on wise land use and sound game management in order to preserve quality deer hunting for large numbers of people. Progress is being made in that direction.

One term that is sure to become more familiar to hunters in the future is "quality buck management." Though similar to trophy buck management, quality buck management differs in the size buck it is geared to produce. In trophy management, the objective is to produce the largest bucks possible for that area. This requires growing out bucks until they reach the peak-size age classes, i.e., 5½, 6½ and 7½. Quality buck management, on the other hand, is designed to produce younger bucks, say, 2½, 3½ or perhaps 4½-year-olds, that are representative of "quality" deer for that area. Compared to trophy management, quality management allows more bucks to be taken by more hunters while still preserving a positive hunting experience. On most tracts of land where some type of management is possible, this is a much more achievable and feasible management practice. Although our following discussion will focus on trophy buck management, everything said about it will apply equally well to quality buck management.

The requirements of trophy buck management — a large land base, a limited buck harvest, a substantial doe harvest, hands-on management, etc. — are demanding. Because of landownership patterns and the demand to produce large numbers of deer, trophy buck management is not practical or even possible on most of the land within the whitetail's range. But in recent years, new information and techniques have surfaced that will make trophy management (and certainly quality management) more practical in many places in the future.

A promising new technique is called "core-area buck management," which was developed through a better understanding of the whitetail's social order. As we've discussed, it was long believed that dominant bucks forced yearling bucks out of their home range, thus dispersing young bucks over a large area and preventing the build up of a high buck population on a given tract of land. The fact that it is very difficult to "stockpile" bucks helped give rise to this theory. With the emergence of evidence suggesting that the matriarch or alpha does actually give young bucks the old heave-ho, core-area buck management was developed. It involves the elimination (or more realistically, the reduction) of matriarch does from a tract of land so that yearling bucks will remain and establish their core ranges on the tract. This allows for a buildup of bucks; stockpiling, if you will. This practice has been successfully employed on a number of tracts with some startling results.

A promising new management technique is called "core-area buck management." It revolves around the drastic reduction of matriarch does, which now appear to be responsible for dispersing yearling bucks. As a result of removing the dominant does from a tract of land, the yearling bucks will remain and establish their core ranges there, allowing for a high buildup of bucks. Photo by Mike Biggs.

One of the most encouraging aspects of core-area buck management is that it holds the promise of working on smaller tracts of land than required for traditional trophy management. Still, a sizeable tract is needed to maintain control of the bucks produced. How much land is necessary for an effective program? That depends on the nature of the property and the land surrounding it. Given the right set-up, I suspect core-area management would work to some degree on as little as 1,000 acres, certainly on 2,000 or 3,000 acres. One Georgia lease of 1,400 acres has experienced good success using this management technique for only three or four years. A plantation in South Carolina employs core-area buck management with remarkable results on 3,000 acres. I know of a large Texas ranch that manages under this concept on a grand scale, and it works for them.

While core-area buck management does offer promise, it also has one major drawback — the extreme difficulty of harvesting enough dominant does. Of course, the size of the property and its huntability are major considerations, but at best, this is no easy task. To start with, the game laws In most states are not adequate to allow the necessary harvest. Where the laws do make it theoretically possible, the amount of hunting pressure required to get the job done can be counterproductive to buck hunting success, the very reason for the program. Even the does can become practically unkillable in the face of the high pressure necessary. Also, it isn't always possible for the manager to come up with enough good hunters to harvest sufficient numbers of does. Even though the doe harvest is an ongoing headache, we will see more of core-area buck management in the years to come where landownership patterns and game laws allow.

Game-proof fences have long been popular management tools in Texas, and now they are spreading beyond the borders of the Lone Star State. I believe the use of high fences will increase significantly in the future; and for good reason — they work miracles in game management. A high fence allows the landowner to exercise almost total control over his deer herd. Deer ingress and egress is eliminated. Uncontrolled mortality (road kills, poaching, etc.) is greatly reduced. All this means that the number of deer, age structure, sex ratio, nutrition and even genetics can be managed with relative precision. In some states, property under a high fence is not subject to general game regulations, allowing the landowner absolute control of the harvest. Without question, high-fencing is the surest way to produce trophy whitetails.

Another big advantage of high-fencing is that it will work on any size tract of land. The lower limits of size for a high-fence operation are determined by aesthetic considerations and the number of bucks required to be produced. Actually, too much land under a high fence can be a problem. The larger the tract, the less control the landowner has over the herd. Depending on the management objectives and the habitat, many biologists feel that a high-fence operation of from 1,500 to 3,000 acres offers about the right balance between aesthetics, control and "mystery."

High-fencing may be the ultimate in trophy management, but it certainly comes with some heavy baggage. First, there is the cost. At somewhere between $15,000 and $25,000 a running mile — depending on the terrain, vegetation, clearing cost, type of fence, etc. — high-fencing is not for the faint of heart. For example, to fence 1,200 acres, the fencing cost alone probably would run better than $100,000!

Without question, high-fencing is the surest way to produce trophy whitetails, but it is expensive and raises questions about aesthetics and fair chase in the mind's of some hunters. Photo by Mike Biggs.

And then, there is the issue of fair chase. Is it really sporting to shoot a buck enclosed within a high fence? Certainly, the size of the property and the type habitat have great bearing on the answer to that question. I've only hunted whitetails once that were under a high fence. The place was an intensively managed, 2,700-acre ranch in South Texas. The cover was typical of that region — very thick. Four of us hunted there for five days. Only one trophy buck was killed. We may have had them hemmed up, but they were not easy! Whether or not hunting behind a high fence represents fair chase is a personal decision.

Aesthetic considerations can also be an issue with high fences. Some people just don't like the idea of hunting in an enclosure no matter what the size. They say it lacks the mystery and the romance found in hunting the wild and the unknown. Personally, I understand this concern.

My daddy never liked fishing small ponds for the same reason. Again, the size of the enclosure and the type of cover influence the aesthetic qualities of the hunt, but each person has to make his own judgement on that issue. Nevertheless, high fences are sure to become more commonplace across America in the coming years.

Feeding deer is nothing new, but until recently, it was done primarily to concentrate deer for harvest. Food plots of various clovers and winter grains, such as rye, wheat, oats, rye grass, etc., are planted extensively for deer. Where baiting deer is legal, hay, corn and various grains are frequently fed directly to facilitate harvest. Recently, however, deer feeding has begun to have a different purpose. It is emerging as a management tool to increase both deer numbers and deer size. This flies in the face of the biologists' official line of years past that feeding deer does no good. That simply ain't so. As one well-known biologist said, "Whitetails are basically little cows. Feed them enough and you could raise 'em in a feed lot."

In addition to the traditional deer feeds — hay, corn and the different grains — new high-nutrition feeds, mostly in pelleted form, are now available that can meet all the nutritional requirements of deer. Whether fed alone or in combination with other feeds, these potent feeds can have a dramatic impact on a deer herd. That impact is limited only by how much the landowner wants to spend. The benefits to the landowner depend on the control he has over the deer he is feeding. This, of course, is largely a function of land size. When feeding is used in combination with a high fence, a manager can almost "write his own check" as to how many deer he wants to carry. Some high-fence operations with intensive feeding programs are supporting a deer per acre. I've also seen feeding result in some very high populations on unfenced acreage. One 6,000-acre Southern plantation feeds heavily year-round and is harvesting about 300 bucks a year. However, I'm sure some of the bucks are the neighbors' deer that have come over for a free meal. Obviously, that level of harvest does not lend itself to trophy buck management, but it does dramatically illustrate what is possible with intensive feeding.

Every rose has its thorns, and feeding deer is no exception. The cost can be great, depending on how high the population is being maintained above the land's natural carrying capacity and on the total number of deer being fed. I know what the annual feed bill is on a large high-

In addition to the traditional deer feeds — hay, corn and the different grains — high-nutrition pellets are now available that can meet all the nutritional requirements of deer. Here, deer are being fed a corn and pellet mixture via an automatic feeder. Photo by Mike Biggs.

fence operation that intensively feeds, and it is enough to make a U.S. congressman blush. Another problem with pouring feed to deer is that a very dense herd will scour the habitat, practically denuding everything from the ground up to a tall man's eye level. Even when fed, population densities over about a deer per six acres will usually wear heavily on the habitat. Some biologists also express concern about the spread of diseases and parasites in high-density herds. While logic says this should be a problem, it seldom is if the deer are maintained in healthy condition. The question of fair chase is also raised with feeding either to concentrate deer or to artificially elevate a population. Again, this falls under the heading of personal conviction. Regardless of the issues surrounding feeding deer, I expect to see both feed plantings and direct feeding become even more widespread in the future.

Other management techniques will continue to emerge as we learn more about what makes the whitetail tick. Even though the whitetail is the most studied animal on the continent, there is much more to learn about such things as their senses, the role of scents, their social behavior, their movement patterns, their communication, their intelligence level, the aging process (and why it appears to differ from region to region), population dynamics and the impact of genetics and hormones on antler development. Speaking of hormones, I personally feel that the key to one of whitetail hunting's great enigmas — the so-called unkillable super buck — may lie in the area of hormones. This is a topic ripe for exploration.

THE UNKILLABLE SUPER BUCK

Stories of unkillable super bucks are circulated just about everywhere deer hunters gather. Undoubtedly, most of these bucks live only in the imaginations of the storytellers, but the myth of the unkillable super buck may have its roots in fact. Let's examine the evidence.

Consider the five largest known non-typicals. The world record Missouri buck; found dead. The No. 2 "Hole-In-The-Horn" buck from Ohio; found dead. The unofficial No. 3 scoring 288⁴/₈ from Ohio; found dead. The former world record 286-point buck from Texas, long believed to have been killed by Jeff Benson in 1892, may have, in fact, also been found dead based on new evidence. And finally, the 282-point Raveling buck from Iowa; killed on a deer drive. With three and possibly four of the top five non-typicals being pick-ups and the other having been shot as a result of forced movement on a deer drive, it is quite possible that none of these five giants were shot while moving around of their own accord! That seems much more than mere coincidence.

Evidence of secretive super bucks extends beyond just the top handful of non-typicals. Every once in a while, a buck will show up that is far beyond the size norms of a particular place. While these super

This is the unofficial No. 3 non-typical whitetail. He scores 288 ⁴/₈ and was found dead in Ohio. Amazingly, the three largest known non-typicals were all pick-ups! That lends credibility to the concept of unkillable super bucks. Photo by Dick Idol courtesy of **North American Whitetail.**

bucks can be either typical or non-typical, they are most often non-typical. Frequently, such bucks are unknown to area hunters, or at best known only through sign, shed antlers or perhaps a chance glimpse, most likely at night. On the rare occasion when one of these exceptional bucks is killed, it is usually through a fluke of some kind and often by a hunter who doesn't know a drop tine from a lost watch.

Given all this, two questions arise. One, why are these bucks so reclusive and hard to kill? Two, why do they reach such exceptional size? Taken individually, a number of things could explain either question, but when considered together, the picture changes. For example, a buck could appear reclusive and hard to kill because he just happens to live in a place that is difficult to hunt or where few hunters venture, but that would not account for exceptional size. Or, because of hunting pressure or sheer happenstance, a buck may have adopted movement patterns that limit his exposure to hunters. Again, that wouldn't necessarily result in large antlers.

As for why some bucks reach exceptional size, superior genetics certainly rank as a major factor, but I find it hard to believe that genetics for big racks would directly impact how killable a buck is. Age and experience, yes, but not genetics. Also, biologists now know that certain injuries to the rack during just the right time of the velvet period can cause antlers to grow wild, resulting in impressive non-typical headgear. But, I don't see why this would cause a buck to become more wary and more reclusive. No, it has to be something else, something that affects both killability and antler size. I believe that something is hormones; specifically, an imbalance of the male hormone testosterone.

We know that testosterone plays an important role in both buck behavior and antler development. We know that increased testosterone triggers the onset of rutting activity in bucks and changes their demeanor and movement patterns and even affects their wariness. We also know that hormonal imbalances can cause weird things to happen to antlers. For instance, the often strangely shaped, velvet-covered antlers of "stags" or "cactus-horned" bucks are products of hormonal imbalance caused by testicle injury or castration. And, it is a documented fact than an occasional buck, even an older buck that should have long ago demonstrated his genetic antler traits, will suddenly grow a non-typical rack that breaks his previous antler conformation pattern. Such a sudden and dramatic departure is unlikely to be due to genetics, but hormones are a likely explanation for this.

I discussed the theory that hormones might be at least part of the explanation for the secretive super buck with Dr. James Kroll, one of the foremost whitetail biologists in the country. He acknowledged the possibility and said that such a theory would explain a phenomenon he had seen while collecting semen for artificial insemination from truly exceptional bucks harvested by hunters. He explained that a disproportionate percentage of these great bucks had a low virile sperm count. In other words, they were infertile, or partially so! Low fertility in bucks certainly could be caused by, or at least a symptom of, an imbalance of male hormones. Dr. Kroll also said that from his experience the super bucks were "whimps." They were seldom dominate and often were not active, aggressive breeders.

Dr. Kroll went on to relate the story of a buck he had killed in East Texas that fit the theory perfectly. While conducting a vegetation study in a pine thicket in 1982, he had seen the buck as a yearling. Even then, the buck had "malformed antlers." Dr. Kroll's work continued to take him back to that thicket over the next few years, and he kept check on the buck, mainly through his rubs, which were abundant but never very large. Occasionally, he would even catch a glimpse of the buck. Although the club where the buck lived was hunted regularly, no other hunter ever saw the buck, which Dr. Kroll came to call "The Ghost." In 1986, the timber was cut next to the buck's core area and all evidence of the buck vanished. The following fall, Dr. Kroll was hunting another pine thicket several hundred yards from the buck's original stomping grounds when he found himself face to face with The Ghost. The bullet found its mark, but the fatally wounded buck still traveled a long distance … all the way back to his original core area! The heavy-racked buck scored 190⅜ as a non-typical! Oh, one other thing … he had only one testicle!

Assuming hormonal imbalances play into our secretive super buck theory, the greatest impact would be seen on bucks so afflicted for most or all of their lives, as may have been the case with Dr. Kroll's buck. Hormonal imbalances and related fertility problems may be more common in deer than we realize. Having been raised on a cattle farm, I know that low fertility can be an occasional problem with bulls and can inflict some of the best bulls, even at early ages. But, more common than life-long hormonal imbalances are probably the hormonal changes that accompany the aging process. In the animal kingdom, it is not unusual for older males to become less sexually active, even to the point of retiring to a sedate, solitary life. Often, these older males are said to be "on the mend" since they sometimes gain weight and become almost steerlike in appearance. It is quite possible that some old whitetail bucks follow this pattern and that a shift in testosterone levels accompanies this lifestyle change. I may well have shot such an animal on Texas' King Ranch in January 1989.

I was hunting a newly opened part of this famous ranch with my friend, Amos Dewitt. In three days of hunting, Amos and I had looked over more than 300 bucks! The great majority of the mature bucks we had seen would have scored between 120 and 135 points. We had come across a handful of 140-class bucks and a couple in the 150's. Then, on the fourth and last morning, we bumped into a buck eating contentedly that completely broke the size pattern we had previously observed. Needless to say, I shot him. The huge eight-pointer was massive and tall. He grossed 172 and netted 167⅜! Although the other bucks we had seen were gaunt and haggard from the rut, this buck was sleek and fat, practically steerlike. The buck, which was at least 7½ years old, showed no evidence of having participated in the rut.

Putting all this together, we can develop a theory around the possibility that at least some of the so-called "unkillable super bucks" can be attributed to hormonal imbalances. The theory begins with the

A hormonal imbalance may be the most logical explanation for the existence of secretive super bucks. Hormones can affect both the behavior and antler growth of a buck. Some giants like this 30-inch non-typical could be a product of an imbalance in the male hormone testosterone. Photo by Mike Biggs.

assumption that a hormonal imbalance would cause a buck to be less sexually active, if not totally inactive. By not actively participating in the rut, a couple of things could happen that factor into our theory. One, these bucks are not pulled down physically during the rut and therefore go into the winter and spring in much better condition than an active breeder, which may lose 25 to 30 percent of his body weight during the rut. By entering the spring in good condition, less of his nutritional intake has to go to body restoration and more is immediately available for antler growth, which, of course, would result in larger antlers next fall. Couple this with the possibility that a hormonal imbalance may also contribute directly to some form of exceptional antler development, i.e., non-typical conformation (as we see in stag bucks) or perhaps simply the growth of greater antler mass. All this could explain why a rare buck will show up that is far larger than the norm for that area.

The second way that sexual inactivity from a hormonal imbalance can contribute to our theory is in the killability of a buck. Without question, a buck's greatest vulnerability to hunters is during the rut. If it weren't for the rut, most mature bucks would be darn near unkillable, except for blind luck or forced movement. Imagine hunting trophy bucks only during the pre-rut or post-rut periods! If a buck is sexually inactive because of a hormonal imbalance, he has eliminated his window of greatest vulnerability and stands a very good chance of escaping a hunter's bullet. Because they are not drawn into compromising situations by the irresistible lure of the rut, such bucks may remain nocturnal, stay in a very small area and/or move only in thick cover, thereby avoiding encounters with hunters. This would certainly explain why some of these super bucks can live out their lives under the very noses of humans without anyone ever seeing them. It also explains why a surprising number of the real giants are killed by forced movement or flukes rather than by being shot while engaged in some sort of rutting activity, as would be expected. In fact, one of the most compelling arguments in favor of the hormone theory comes from the fact that so few super bucks are killed while chasing does, making scrapes or engaging in some type of rutting activity. Hormones may also figure into why exceptional bucks so rarely come to rattling.

I do not mean to imply that all super bucks or all "unkillable" bucks have hormonal imbalances. Most super bucks are simply genetically superior. And, most of the so-called unkillable bucks are that way because they happen to live in seldom-hunted or hard-to-hunt places or because they have adopted movement patterns that rarely put them in contact with hunters. But, the hormone theory does give some credence to the rumors and campfire tales that an incredible whitetail just may lurk somewhere beyond the next hill. We may eventually unravel the mystery surrounding the fabled unkillable super buck ... but in a way, I hope not.

THE "ANTI'S" AND YOU

The anti-hunting movement is not an easy subject to deal with because it is based on irrational emotions and misguided thought. The anti-hunting effort is simply an extension of the bigger animal-rights and preservationists movement that would elevate the importance of animals, trees and an untouched environment above that of human beings. Besides their views being blatantly contrary to historical precedent and to the Judeo-Christian principles upon which this nation was founded, the whole movement is inconsistent with the reality of nature, contradictory in its values and, worst of all, dehumanizing, even to the point of totally disregarding the sanctity of human life. Let's take a closer look.

According to the animal-rightists/preservationists, death is no longer an acceptable part of nature's cycle of life. All animals are to live together in harmony with no one animal or species having preference or rights over another. Even trees have rights ... and some extremists now go so far as to say that trees have feelings and a consciousness. All this, of course, leads to their position that humans have no right to exploit other species for their own benefit. No, man shouldn't trap animals for their fur. No, man shouldn't hunt for meat or sport. No, man shouldn't demean mice, cats or dogs by using them in medical research. No, man shouldn't kill cows, chickens or pigs to eat. It is no longer even acceptable to refer to your pet as a "pet." That is degrading to the animal and reflects a morally superior attitude in the pet owner ... no, not owner; man can't own another "free spirit" ... the pet's master ... no, that won't work either. You get the picture.

Unfortunately for the animal-righters, word has not yet gotten around to all the participants. Foxes still eat rats. Hawks still kill rabbits. Sharks still eat tuna. Wolves still kill moose. Coyotes still eat sheep. Lions still kill zebra. And yes, man still kills cattle so that even the anti-hunters can have their T-bone steaks for grilling out on the sly in the backyards of their suburban homes and their full-grain leather saddle oxfords for marching in their animal-rights demonstrations. Things are still getting killed and eaten all over the world ... just as they have from the beginning. Can it be that high-sounding words and catchy slogans are unable to change reality?

When the most enlightened animal-rights supporters finally come around to admitting that death is a necessary part of life in nature's

Ironically, many in the animal-rights/ preservationists movement are more interested in promoting themselves and their "cause" than they are in doing what's best for the animals they profess to be concerned about. It seems to matter little to them that a hunter's bullet is more humane than the alternatives of death by disease or starvation. This pitiful buck is starving, a fate that would await millions of deer without hunting. Photo by Mike Biggs.

scheme, they find themselves right in the middle of a contradiction. You see, on the one hand, they want to make man just another one of nature's creatures — no better, no worse — just a part of the cycle. On the other hand, however, they do not want man to carry out his role as the supreme predator, because as such, he has the power and authority to exercise dominion over all the animals of the earth. This contradiction poses a dilemma for the animal-righters. Is man just another animal, therefore entitled to carry out the natural functions of his lofty position at the top of the food chain? Or, is he morally superior to all animals, thus under a moral obligation to exercise restraint as the supreme predator? You would think that the animal-righters would acknowledge man's superiority if only for their own self-serving purposes. But, it is not that easy for the more faithful of the movement.

In a statement that clearly shows the incredible perversion underlying the animal-rights movement, Ingrid Newkirk, the co-director of the People for the Ethical Treatment of Animals (PETA), a leading animal-rights group, once said, "I don't believe human beings have the 'right to life'. That's a supremacist perversion. A rat is a pig is a dog is a boy." In another statement, that same person is said to have even related the slaughter of chickens to the suffering of the Jews under Nazi Germany! To attempt to equate the life of a rat to the life of a child or the death of chickens to that of humans is dehumanizing to an unimaginable degree. That type of attitude shows the twisted thinking at the root of much of the animal-rights/preservationists movement.

As radical as it is, this movement does pose a threat to hunting. How do we combat it? I don't think it is possible to reason with the anti's since they are not bound by facts, reason or morality. From my encounters with them, they are governed by mindless emotions and hatred. They don't even care about the animals they are supposedly trying to "protect." They are against everything and for nothing. While we hunters outnumber them right now, the great majority of Americans are in the undecided camp. They don't have enough information to side either way. We cannot stand by and let the anti's (or Hollywood or the liberal press, for that matter) be their main source of information. We must focus our battle on this undecided majority. Fortunately, we bring some powerful weapons to the battlefield.

The undecided majority must be educated to the facts, the real truth about the hunter's role. They must understand that hunting is the best of all conservation and management tools and that hunting is more humane than the alternatives of disease, starvation and habitat destruction. They must be told and shown through our ethical conduct that it is the hunter who really cares about the animal and who invests his time, effort and money into wildlife conservation. They must understand that the only real security for wildlife and wildlife habitat lies in its economic value. They must know that hunters have already footed an enormous bill for the incredibly successful restoration of deer, elk, pronghorns, turkey, wild sheep and many other species. In short, they must realize that it is the hunter, not the animal-rights activist, who will support sound conservation measures, protect wildlife habitat and safeguard the welfare of wildlife in the future with action and dollars, not with high-sounding slogans and empty words. This is a battle we can win, and win it we must, not only for the hunters of today but also for our children and their children to follow ... as well as for the deer themselves!

Chapter 26

In Conclusion

I MAY HAVE BEEN 12, PERHAPS 13, when I read that story in *Outdoor Life*, but I remember it as though it was yesterday. Warmed by the mid-morning sun, the hunter was dosing at the base of a white oak tree when the sound of rustling leaves awakened him. The sight of a big whitetail coming over the hill jarred him from his drowsiness. The man slowly lifted the rifle resting across his legs. He waited until the buck was 30 yards away then aimed and fired. The buck jumped and ran 20 yards down the hill, where he cut a tight circle ... and fell dead!

My mind could not grasp the scene. I stared at the painting that depicted the hunter sitting next to the tree as the huge buck topped the hill coming his way. Try as I may, I could not put myself there. Seeing a big whitetail ... moving in broad daylight ... only 30 yards away ... and then to actually kill him ... to be able to walk up and touch him ... it was more than I could fathom. But, it captured my imagination and kindled my dreams.

For some reason, the story of that big buck never left me. Perhaps it was because the hunt took place in Kentucky, so near to my home state of Alabama. Until that time, nearly everything I had read about whitetails took place in Pennsylvania, Wisconsin, Michigan, Maine, Texas or some other place that seemed as remote to a South

Alabama farm boy as Mars. But, that deer was shot in Kentucky, the South. We even had white oak trees on our farm. After reading that story, more than once I sat beside a white oak and tried to imagine what it would be like to have a big buck walk over a nearby hill. In those days, my immediate goal was just to see a whitetail buck in the wild and my distant dream was to someday actually shoot one for myself.

Now, some 30 years and well over 100 whitetail bucks later, the dream of shooting that first buck is far behind me, but the wonder of it all is not. I look back on my hunting career and marvel at the opportunities that have come my

When I first started deer hunting, a sight like this was more than I could imagine. Now, nearly 30 years and well over 100 whitetail bucks later, the wonder of it all remains. Photo by Curt Helmick.

way and the successes I've enjoyed. As a boy growing up in South Alabama, not in my wildest dreams could I possibly have imagined what the years to come would hold for me. To be able to see countless bucks … to shoot many trophies … to hunt fabulous places … to even make a living doing the things I love … only by the grace of God!

This book was born out of a sense of gratitude and a sincere desire to give something back to the sport that has been so good to me. It's my hope that something within these pages has given you a greater appreciation for the whitetail and perhaps has even hastened the day when you will stand over your next buck … but not just any buck, a trophy whitetail — one of the greatest game animals on earth!